CHINA
IN REVOLUTION

Originally published in the early 1970s, *The Yenan Way in Revolutionary China* has proved to be one of the most significant and enduring books published in the field. In this new critical edition of that seminal work, Mark Selden revisits the central themes therein and reconsiders them in light of major new theoretical and documentary understandings of the Chinese communist revolution.

From reviews of *The Yenan Way in Revolutionary China* . . .

"[A] strong presentation of the undeniably formidable achievements of the Chinese Communists during the anti-Japanese war years. . . . [E]ssential for understanding the dynamics of the greatest revolution of our time."

—*The New York Times*

"What makes this book persuasive is . . . the bold, original analysis based upon solid historical research."

—*American Historical Review*

". . . a well-documented, erudite, and readable study."

—*Library Journal*

"This is an extremely valuable piece of scholarship. [It offers] a series of significant insights into the development of Chinese Communism at a time when it was formulating or completing the formulation of most of the values, theories, and practices which have come to be regarded as Maoism."

—*The Journal of Asian Studies*

★ *Socialism and Social Movements* ★

CHINA IN REVOLUTION

The Yenan Way Revisited

MARK SELDEN

An East Gate Book

M.E. Sharpe
Armonk, New York
London, England

An East Gate Book

Photographs by Edgar Snow are used by courtesy of Lois Snow.

Library of Congress Cataloging-in-Publication Data

Selden, Mark.
China in revolution : the Yenan way revisited / Mark Selden.
p.   cm.
"East Gate book."
Includes bibliographical references and index.
ISBN 1-56324-554-X.   ISBN 1-56324-555-8 (pbk.)
1. Communism—China—San Kan Ning pien ch´ü.
2. Shan Kan Ning pien ch´ü. (China)—History.
3. China—History—1937–1945.
I. Title.
HX420.S48S44   1995
335.43´45´09514—dc20
CIP

Printed in the United States of America

BM (c)   10   9   8   7   6   5   4   3   2   1
BM (p)   10   9   8   7   6   5   4   3   2   1

For Kyoko

Contents

List of Tables and Maps

Tables

Maps

Preface

The original edition of this book was among the first products of a new scholarship on revolutionary China: in its use of party and intelligence archival and documentary sources in Taiwan, Japan, and the United States; in offering the first "microsocietal" study of a single base area; in attempting to locate revolutionary processes in the dual contexts of Chinese politics and society on the one hand and international forces on the other; and in turning away from dominant paradigms of totalitarian theory and international communist conspiracy to explore creative and populist wellsprings of revolutionary change.

This book was also a product of the tumultuous events of the 1960s, particularly those in the United States, China, and Indochina, and of the global realignments and new thinking of that era. The U.S.-China relationship had been one of unremitting strife dating back two decades to U.S. intervention in the Chinese Civil War and continuing from the battlefields of Korea and (by proxy) Vietnam and Southeast Asia to the global ideological, political, and armed conflicts over socialism, capitalism, colonialism, and North-South relations. Those clashes shaped American scholarship and perceptions of revolutionary China and global revolutionary processes.

In 1963, as I embarked on the archival research that eventually produced *The Yenan Way in Revolutionary China,* U.S.-China and global power relations were in flux. The United States was moving toward full-scale military involvement in the Vietnam War while fissiparous forces were at work that shortly erupted in the Great Proletarian Cultural Revolution in China and civil rights, antiwar, and new left movements in the United States. The sinews of the postwar international order everywhere appeared to be unraveling. The costly U.S. defeat in Vietnam, punctuating the decline of U.S. hegemonic power and the collapse of the Sino-Soviet alliance, paved the way for a breakthrough in U.S.-China relations and a rethinking of the Chinese revolution.

The times brought forth, even compelled us to address, new questions. I sought to understand how a poor and technologically backward agrarian nation could sustain a fifteen-year resistance in the face of the juggernaut of an invading colonizer that was sufficiently powerful to drive the United States, Britain, France, and the Netherlands from the region of their earlier colonial triumphs. I was particularly drawn to the possibility that resistance forces spearheading a broad popular movement in a poverty-stricken countryside had creatively addressed problems of poverty, inequality, and underdevelopment that confronted the contemporary postcolonial world.

In the preface to the original work, I posed this issue in terms evocative of that more hopeful epoch: "It is the central problem of our time. How can people break the shackles of oppression, poverty, and fear, how can they translate their hopes and dreams into dynamic action to expand human freedom and possibility? How can men stand up?" At that time revolutionary forces in another poor agrarian nation were delivering the coup de grace to an apparently invincible invader, precipitating a crisis in American and international political, cultural, and intellectual life.

By 1971, after two decades in which the United States blockaded, fought, and sought to isolate China as an international pariah, the two nations moved to reestablish diplomatic relations and then to redefine the map of global conflict and alliance. These processes were conducive to a rethinking of war and revolution in general and the long Chinese revolution in particular. *The Yenan Way* was published in 1971 just as the United States and China took large steps toward normalizing their relations and as the two countries' perceptions of one another entered a period of dramatic shift.

By the time that I set about preparing this expanded critical edition, U.S.-China relations had passed through two tumultuous decades. The Cultural Revolution had long since yielded to the market, the private sector, and the influx of foreign capital—although beneath the surface and in complex ways, Mao's legacy continues to shape China's course. Since the 1980s Teng Hsiao-p'ing's China has emerged at the center of the world's most dynamic economic and trading region. Equally important, the massacre of Tiananmen Square demonstrators and the crushing of democratic reform throughout China in 1989 and thereafter, as well as the death of communism in the former Soviet Union and throughout Eastern Europe and the end of the Cold War, have transformed the most basic equations of international politics and U.S.-China relations. The time is ripe to reconsider the questions that motivated this study.

This edition reaffirms propositions and perspectives at the heart of the original work. In particular, it locates the revolution and the resistance in the context of anticolonial national liberation movements; it finds in the Yenan Way several of China's seminal contributions to the theory and praxis of revolutionary change and social transformation; it affirms the importance of 1941–1942 as a watershed that produced a new synthesis in approaching issues of war and revolution; and it reiterates the proposition that important features of the Yenan Way took root in base areas behind Japanese lines.

Between 1937 and 1945, the Chinese Communist Party successfully united broad strata behind a mobilizational program of national resistance and socioeconomic and political reform. As the first edition concluded, "The ability of the Communist party to transform its program of agrarian revolution in accordance with united front wartime imperatives while leading a bold and creative attack on problems of rural oppression and disintegration is the hallmark of the Yenan period." This combination of nationalism and reform lay behind the party's ability to draw support from and transform relationships among diverse social classes, eventually making possible its rise to power through the successive defeats of Japan and the U.S.-backed Kuomintang.

The Chinese resistance was the pioneer, and in many ways the most influential, anticolonial struggle of this century, a harbinger of the movements that would sweep across Asia and Africa following World War II and ultimately change the face of global politics. While this study focuses on the communist resistance in a single base area, it frames a broader canvas of seven years of war and revolution that exacted a toll of fifteen to twenty million lives and irrevocably changed China and the world.[1] My research of the past two decades, and that of many other researchers, now permits more authoritative comparisons of the numerous base areas that constituted focal points of the wartime resistance, as well as extension of the discussion to international examples.

This edition reflects anew on issues posed in the first edition of *The Yenan Way* in light of several critical debates in the social sciences: the debate over the conceptualization of nationalism and colonialism and their relationship to revolution; the moral-economy–rational-peasant debate; the debate over party-centered versus peasant-centered perspectives on revolutionary change; and the debate between modernization and distributionist perspectives on the twentieth-century Chinese countryside. In a new concluding chapter, I assess these and other approaches to revolutionary change and rural development during the resistance epoch.

I use the metaphor "Yenan Way" in two discrete but integrally related ways. First, it refers specifically to the distinctive military and political style and institutional synthesis that emerged under communist rule in response to ecological and political conditions in the loess areas of Northwest China that were eventually incorporated as the Shensi-Kansu-Ninghsia Border Region, with its capital at Yenan. Core features of the wartime economic, political, and social program that I describe in detail here for Shen-Kan-Ning can be found, with significant local variations, in those rear base areas that had full-scale wartime governments, notably the Shansi-Chahar-Hopeh (Chin-Ch'a-Chi), Shansi-Hopeh-Shantung-Honan (Chin-Chi-Lu-Yu), and Shansi-Suiyuan (Chin-Sui) base areas. In short, Shen-Kan-Ning was both a microcosm and a critical node in the development of a body of theory and praxis that would shape the wartime resistance and profoundly affect the subsequent course of Chinese communism. For all the block-ade-driven self-reliance of the base areas and for all the differences among them, they had in common important features that coalesced in the course of building the resistance and addressing broadly shared problems of rural immiseration, economic blockade and attack, and the necessity to restructure the relationships among party, peasantry, and local elites. The New Democracy and the mass line provided theoretical direction for a geographically dispersed wartime movement.

In the course of the anti-Japanese resistance, the view from Yenan substan-tially shaped the characteristic vision of Mao Tse-tung and much of the top communist leadership. The lessons and legacies of the era, drawing on the expe-rience of more than a dozen base areas, would subsequently be played out in complex and contradictory ways in the People's Republic, a theme to which I return in the Epilogue.

The Yenan Way casts light not only on war and revolution in China but on the theory and praxis of twentieth-century revolutionary change and postcolonial development. In stressing innovative features of the Yenan Way as a response to the problems of socioeconomic and political disintegration and foreign domina-tion, and in suggesting the relevance of the wartime synthesis to the developmen-tal challenges that confronted China as well as numerous postcolonial agrarian nations, the original work challenged reigning paradigms in Western China scholarship and the understanding of revolution prevailing in the 1960s. In par-ticular it broke with perceptions of Chinese communism as a slavish imitator of Soviet communism, with dominant forms of modernization theory that saw the essential problems of the periphery in terms of incorporation and technological diffusion, and with conceptions of mass nationalism divorced from concrete social programs.

This new edition presents the original study with minor stylistic and factual additions and corrections in the conviction that the research and central elements of the analytical framework on which it was based stand up well to the test of time. In this new Preface and the Conclusion, and particularly in the extended Epilogue, however, I critically reassess the central issues posed in the original study and my own interpretation in light of alternative perspectives on revolu-tionary change in general and the Chinese revolution in particular. I also briefly examine earlier conclusions in light of the complex course of the Chinese revolu-tion and of world realignments over the past half-century, drawing on both my own subsequent research on the Chinese revolution and that of others to reassess *The Yenan Way* and the dynamics of rural revolution.[2]

In the Epilogue I reevaluate the resistance from the perspectives of human freedom, community, and rural development. Most important, in light of the repeated crushing of democratic aspirations from the antirightist movements of the 1950s to the Cultural Revolution in the 1960s and 1970s to the suppression of democratically inspired movements in the 1980s and 1990s, I inquire whether the roots of political and social tragedies such as the Great Leap famine and the political vigilantism of the Cultural Revolution can be traced to the Yenan era in general and the Yenan Way in particular. The Epilogue, then, provides an occasion to assess the relationship between the Yenan Way and China's subsequent twisting course.

The Yenan Way was the first of the wartime base area studies that shaped later research on the Chinese communist movement from the 1920s through the resistance and civil war periods and (in the form of local and regional studies) down to the present. This method permits the eye to range from the grass-roots level to regional, national, and global dimensions of social change, and from the international system down to the microcosm of base area, county, village, and household. It thus enables exploration of human dimensions of policies and programs, their emergence and modification, and their impact on economy and society in ways precluded by national or global studies. Although the method is particularly suited to the wartime era, when more than a dozen geographically isolated base areas constituted the loci of the communist-led resistance, it has been widely used for other historical periods as well, including that of the People's Republic. The study of a single locality, with appropriate attention to its ecological, demographic, class, cultural, and other specificities, is not predicated on the assumption that conditions in each base were identical, still less that the base areas were representative of national conditions. Rather, the bases, located for the most part in the rugged terrain on the borders of provinces and remote from major cities and rail communications, constituted interconnected yet highly autonomous nodes within a single national movement.

This study traces the origins of protracted socioeconomic disintegration as the prelude to three decades of revolutionary conflict in the Shen-Kan-Ning area whose wartime capital, Yenan, was the symbolic center of the communist movement in the years 1935–1947. In these years the movement was transformed from a twice-defeated force on the periphery of Chinese society to one poised to rule and transform China. My hope has been to convey a sense of the intensity and style of revolutionary change—as well as an understanding of the possibilities and limits of change—through examination of social, political, and class forces in this rural region over the first half of the twentieth century.

Let us begin with the social disintegration and quiet desperation that gave rise to the earliest rumblings of revolution in Shensi province, a cradle of Chinese civilization where the state of Ch'in once rose to create the first unified empire. Two thousand years later the region would spawn a new revolutionary China.

Notes

1. Lloyd Eastman, "Nationalist China during the Sino-Japanese War, 1937–1945," in John Fairbank and Albert Feuerwerker, eds., *Republican China 1912–1949*, vol. 13, pt. 2 of *The Cambridge History of China* (Cambridge, 1986), 547. Identical figures are given in William Kirby, "The Chinese War Economy," in James Hsiung and Steven Levine,

eds., *China's Bitter Victory: The War with Japan, 1937–1945* (Armonk, N.Y., 1992), 185. The war was not limited, however, to the years 1937–1945. It is better understood as a fifteen-year war that raged from 1931 to 1945 and from certain angles a fifty-year war extending from 1895 to 1945. The death toll in the fifteen-year war almost certainly exceeded twenty million; the vast majority of casualties were civilians.

2. Edward Friedman, Paul Pickowicz, and Mark Selden, *Chinese Village, Socialist State* (New Haven, 1991); Mark Selden, *The Political Economy of Chinese Development* (Armonk, N.Y., 1993).

Acknowledgments

In subtle but important ways, the ideas that inform this book were a product of the global intellectual and political ferment ignited by the Vietnam War. The reexamination of the United States and Asia initiated by the Committee of Concerned Asian Scholars and the courage and creativity of participants in the antiwar, GI resistance, and civil rights movements in the United States and Japan in the late 1960s and early 1970s contributed to shaping my understanding of war, revolution, and social change.

My heaviest debt in writing *The Yenan Way* is to Mary Wright, an extraordinary teacher and human being who vetoed the project when I initially proposed it as a dissertation. Once convinced of its promise as a historical study, however, she guided the work with her characteristic acumen and verve. Her counsel and that of Arthur Wright were valuable in the formative stages. Edward Friedman's friendship and his persistently scathing criticism of my ideas helped to cast this work in larger perspectives then and now. John Fairbank, Richard Kraus, Tetsuo Najita, James Peck, Benjamin Schwartz, and Arthur Wright provided perceptive readings of the original manuscript. Fairbank's intervention at a critical stage was instrumental in overcoming the reluctance of Harvard University Press to publish a controversial study.

This study would not have been possible without the generous assistance of the librarians and staff of the Hoover Institution, Yale University Library, Harvard-Yenching Library, Bureau of Investigation Library in Taiwan, Toyo Bunko in Japan, and Columbia University's East Asiatic Library.

In preparing this critical edition, I have benefited from the probing comments, suggestions, and insights of Marc Blecher, Linda Grove, Kenneth Straus, Sidney Tarrow, and especially Joseph Esherick, Ralph Thaxton, and Peter Zarrow.

Abbreviations Used in the Notes

BI　　Bureau of Investigation of the Nationalist Government.

"CCWT"　　Mao Tse-tung, "Ching-chi wen-t'i yü ts'ai-cheng wen-t'i" (Economic and financial problems).

CFJP　　*Chieh-fang jih-pao (Liberation daily).*

CFPK　　Shen-kan-ning pien-ch'ü cheng-fu wei-yüan-hui, *Shen-kan-ning pien-ch'ü cheng-fu kung-tso pao-kao* (Work report of the Shen-Kan-Ning border region government).

CTHP　　Shen-kan-ning pien-ch'ü cheng-fu, pan-kung-t'ing, ed., *Shen-kan-ning pien-ch'ü cheng-ts'e t'iao-li hui-chi hsü-p'ien* (Policies and statutes of the Shensi-Kansu-Ninghsia border region).

CTTL　　*K'ang-jih ken-chü-ti cheng-ts'e t'iao-li hui-chi* (Policies and statutes of the anti-Japanese bases).

HC　　*Mao Tse-tung hsüan-chi* (The selected works of Mao Tse-tung).

HCPP　　*Hung-ch'i p'iao-p'iao* (Red flag flutters).

HTHSL　　Shih Ching-t'ang et al., ed. *Chung-kuo nung-yeh ho-tso-hua yün-tung shih-liao* (Materials on the agricultural cooperativization movement in China).

LSWTCT　　Kao Kang, *Pien-ch'ü tang ti li-shih wen-t'i chien-t'ao* (Examination of questions concerning the history of the party in the border region).

MCTC　　Yenan nung-ts'un tiao-ch'a t'uan, *Mi-chih hsien yang-chia-k'ou tiao-ch'a* (Investigation of Yang chia-k'ou in Mi-chih district).

"SPCK"　　"Shen-pei kung-tang fa-chan ti kai-k'uang" (The situation in the development of the communist party in North Shensi).

SW　　Mao Tse-tung, *Selected Works.*

WHHC　　Chung-kuo k'o-hsüeh-yüan, li-shih yen-chiu so, ti san so, ed., *Shen-kan-ning pien-ch'ü ts'an-i hui wen-hsien hui-chi* (Collected documents of the assembly of the Shensi-Kansu-Ninghsia border region).

Weights and Measures

1 *mou*	= 1/6 acre
1 *hsiang*	= 3 *mou* = 1/2 acre
1 *chin*	= 1–1/3 pounds
1 *tou* or peck	= 40 pounds
1 *tan* or *picul*	= 400 pounds

Administrative Units

pien-ch'ü	Border region
fen-ch'ü	Subregion
hsien	District
ch'ü or pao	Subdistrict
hsiang	Township
hsing-cheng ts'un	Administrative village
ts'un	Village

1

Shensi Province: The Revolutionary Setting

"Of all the Provinces of China," observed O.J. Todd, "probably Shensi comes the nearest to being a liability. Certainly she is no great asset to any country as she lies there like a dying beggar in as distressful condition as she was just after the Mohammedan Rebellion [1862–1873] 50 years ago."[1]

Two millennia earlier the Kuan-chung region bisecting Shensi province and centered on the rich Wei River plain formed the cradle of a dynamic civilization. Well fortified against attack and strategically located as the natural corridor between North China and Central Asia, the area provided a nucleus from which the dynamic radiating power of early Chinese civilization would expand to create a unified empire.[2]

Three major dynasties eventually rose from power bases originating in this region. Ch'ang-an, in the area of modern Sian, repeatedly served as the imperial capital, center and symbol of the splendor of empire. But already more than a thousand years ago, even as T'ang dynasty (618–906) Ch'ang-an was the proud capital of the world's most cosmopolitan civilization, the Kuan-chung region was declining. As the balance of economic and political power shifted to the prosperous and populous rice-growing regions of South and Central China, a process of disintegration set in which would continue into the twentieth century.

The Kuan-chung area is the heart of the loess highlands which extend across more than 200,000 square miles in half a dozen provinces in North and Northwest China.[3] The almost surrealistic visual quality of the loess dominating this region is vividly described by the nineteenth-century German traveler Baron von Richtofen. Passing through the Wei River valley, he observed that "As far as the eye can see . . . all this is loess. We are here at the very center of the loess region. Everything is yellow. The hills, the roads, the fields, the water of the rivers and brooks are yellow, the houses are made of yellow earth, the vegetation is covered with yellow dust . . . even the atmosphere is seldom free from a yellow haze."[4] The fertile loess with its ability to hold moisture provided the setting for the initial development of Chinese agriculture. Dry crops such as wheat and millet were readily cultivated in the light loess soil of the plains, but the area's marginal and unpredictable rainfall placed severe strictures on its wealth-producing capacity.[5]

Journeying north from the Wei valley toward Yenan, the traveler enters sparsely populated, rugged, and inaccessible loess hills. Here in northern Shensi below the Great Wall other properties of the loess contribute to the plight of a region unsurpassed in its poverty and primitiveness in twentieth-century rural China. With its forest cover and the loess itself long eroded or destroyed by man, its steep hills provide marginal and unstable prospects for subsistence farming. In 1936 the American journalist Edgar Snow described the area this way:

> North Shensi was one of the poorest parts of China I had seen. . . . The farms of Shensi may be described as slanting and many of them also as slipping, for landslides are frequent. The fields are mostly patches laid on the serried land-scape between crevices and small streams. The land seems rich enough in many places, but the crops grown are strictly limited by the steep gradients, both in quantity and quality. There are few genuine mountains, only endless broken hills, hills as interminable as a sentence by James Joyce, and even more tiresome. Yet the effect is often strikingly like Picasso, the sharp-angled shad-owing and colouring changing miraculously with the sun's wheel, and towards dusk it becomes a magnificent sea of purpled hilltops with dark velvety folds running down, like the pleats on a mandarin skirt, to ravines that seem bottom-less.[6]

Above all, the remoteness and inaccessibility of the north Shensi area shaped conditions of life in the loess hills. George B. Cressey's description of communication difficulties in the loess areas applied with particular force to northern Shensi: "Many loess regions are impassable if one does not keep to the established roads. These roads form one of the distinctive features of the country. Each passing cart or pack animal stirs up the loess, which is so light that it easily rises in clouds. As a result of this continuous removal of material plus the wash of rains, some of the roads or trails come to be veritable canyons, of a width just sufficient to permit the passage of one vehicle and with almost perpendicular walls which rise overhead for as much as forty feet or more."[7] With few roads, many of them frequently washed out, commerce and communications among the small scattered settlements of the loess hills and between the region and other parts of China were at best primitive and sporadic. Almost without exception transportation was limited to pack animals traveling over precipitous mountain trails.

Remote from major provincial power centers, this rugged terrain long provided ideal sanctuary for roving armed bands. Here Li Tzu-ch'eng launched his campaign to overthrow the Ming dynasty (1368–1644), only to be thwarted by the Manchus after briefly taking Peking in 1644. Much of the region was devastated by Moslem rebels and their Manchu army adversaries in the mid-nineteenth century. The Yenan area in particular seems to have suffered heavily from a combination of military and natural disasters. One account recalls the toll on the area as follows:

> And then the spell of peace and prosperity was broken. In the third month of the sixth year of the Emperor Tung Chih [April 1866] a large Mohammedan army came. It had devastated all the towns on the route. . . . Happily Yenanfu was then well able to resist the rebels. . . .
>
> This was not done without the total depopulation and robbing of the whole countryside, and the crowding of this city with large numbers of people from other districts, involving a tremendous drain on local resources. . . .
>
> In the tenth Chinese month of the same year [November 1866] a branch of the Taiping rebel army reached Yenanfu. . . . It had completed the depopulation of the country, so thoroughly begun seven months earlier by the Mohammedans. . . .
>
> The city has never recovered from the devastating effects of the war and famine, far less has the surrounding country. Wild beasts have taken advantage of the absence of man. While the level country has been recultivated, and by gradual stages the wider mountain valleys are being won back, the narrower gullies are infested with leopards, wild boar, wolves, etc. . . . The whole Yenanfu area is therefore now one of the poorest in the whole of China.[8]

In the chaotic final years of the Ch'ing dynasty (1644–1911), from the ranks of the military, secret societies, and a population frequently on the brink of starvation, increasing numbers turned to banditry. In northern Shensi during the early decades of the twentieth century an uneasy balance of terror over the peasant population was maintained among "legitimate" warlord armies, landlord-sponsored local militia, and highly mobile armed rebels who swept down from the hills in swift plundering raids. As one twentieth-century British observer remarked, "In the mind of the average Chinese of the Eastern provinces . . . North Shensi is a nest of plunderers lost in a wilderness."[9] Chronic banditry in northern Shensi was a symptom, not the primary cause, of the misery of more than one million peasants striving to eke out a marginal existence in this area. Yet it in turn contributed to the further disintegration of the rural economy.

The Shensi Peasant and Rural Disintegration

Twentieth-century Shensi was the scene of profound rural crisis. Natural disaster and perpetual warlord-bandit strife compounded the burdens of rural poverty and oppression to exact a terrible toll in human lives. The overwhelming problems confronting the peasantry included famine, the destruction of war and banditry, chronic and worsening debt, accelerating tenancy, rising absentee landlordism, oppressive taxation, and desiccation of the soil. These conditions spelled the bankruptcy of a rural order incapable of meeting minimum needs of survival. Our concern here is the changing nature of socioeconomic relations in rural Shensi for the light it throws on subsequent patterns of revolution in the province. For this reason we focus on the areas of the Wei River valley and particularly the northern reaches of the province where revolutionary activity eventually achieved its most significant development.

Famine in the northwest was a periodic natural phenomenon, but it was a product too of a half a century of political collapse and incessant warfare which drained the resources and reserves of the countryside so that even minor natural calamities wrought immense suffering and loss of life. Successive warlord masters of the province engaged in perpetual fighting and relentlessly milked the peasant economy of the maximum revenues extortable. This meant taking much of the best land out of grain production and planting it in opium at a time when many peasants were already being forced to abandon their farms to take up the life of the bandit or soldier. Driving north from Sian toward Yenan in 1936, Edgar Snow observed:

> Opium poppies nodded their swollen heads, ready for harvest, along the newly completed motor road—a road already deeply wrinkled with washouts and ruts so that at times it was scarcely navigable even for our six-ton Dodge truck. Shensi has long been a noted opium province. During the great Northwest Famine which a few years ago took a toll of 3,000,000 lives, American Red Cross investigators attributed much of the tragedy to the cultivation of the poppy, forced upon the peasants by tax-greedy militarists. The best land being devoted to the poppy, in years of drought there was a serious shortage of millet, wheat and corn, the staple cereals of the North-west.[10]

Political instability of the warlord era also led to the seizure of grain reserves for immediate consumption by the military. This was of course in addition to the economic dislocation brought on by the direct ravages of fighting and plundering. Stretched to the breaking point by these military and political facts of warlord life, the economy collapsed completely when faced with prolonged drought.

During the years 1928 to 1933 literally millions in Shensi province alone died of sheer starvation in the Great Northwest Famine. By 1929, the China International Famine Relief Commission estimated that two consecutive years of famine had brought about the death of 2,500,000 persons, almost one-third of the entire Shensi population. Another half-million had migrated to other provinces and countless others were forced to sell their homes and land. Thousands of women and children were sold into servitude and three consecutive bitter years lay ahead. Emergency efforts to alleviate the famine by importation of relief grain from East China were almost totally thwarted by transportation bottlenecks.

There was neither a railroad nor a navigable river to carry grain across Shensi. Moreover, relief efforts frequently became enmeshed in squabbles among competing warlord factions. If the cost was hundreds of thousands of peasant lives, so much the worse in the calculus of the politics of the era.[11]

The fact was that such morally and religiously inspired efforts as famine relief, whether under Chinese or foreign auspices, could not stand aloof from politics. Dimes and dollars funneled from thousands of congregations in America (for it was principally American dollars that financed the famine relief in the northwest after 1928) to save starving Chinese contributed to the perpetuation of warlord rule. Charity which might in the short run ease famine suffering thus served to shore up the political-military system which loomed as a major obstacle to the eradication of the root causes of the problem. In any event, efforts to ameliorate the suffering caused by the Great Northwest Famine were minuscule in contrast to the magnitude of the problem. Among the most striking results of the famine was the acceleration of a process of economic decline and rising tenancy.

Tenancy in North and Northwest China was a problem of secondary importance compared to its pervasive character in South and Central China.[12] However, a rural survey of Shensi conducted by the National government in the years 1928 to 1933, coincident with the Great Northwest Famine, highlights two important points: first, in parts of Shensi tenancy constituted a serious problem; second, one effect of the famine was to generate a wave of land mortgages and sales, primarily to absentee landlords. A League of Nations investigation disclosed that "In the famine of 1930 twenty acres of land could be purchased for three days' food supply. Making use of this opportunity, the wealthy classes of the province [Shensi] built up large estates, and the number of owner-cultivators diminished."[13]

Southern Shensi, as the northernmost portion of the rice-growing paddy region of Central China, had long been plagued by severe problems of tenancy. By contrast, in the rich agricultural area of the Wei valley, tenancy had been a minor problem compared to recurrent famine, debt, and warlord exactions on the peasant freeholders who comprised the overwhelming majority in this area. However, the Great Northwest Famine forced thousands, including rich peasants and small landlords, to sell or mortgage land to stave off immediate starvation, while tens of thousands died and many more migrated.[14]

Recurrent natural disaster and rebellion had taken a heavy toll in Shensi ever since the ravages of the nineteenth-century Taiping and Moslem rebellions and the famines of the 1870s and 1901. Famine simultaneously reduced the population and turned large areas into wasteland. Thus fertile valley land was rare and concentrated increasingly in the hands of landlords. Moreover, one significant result of famine and rebellion was to drive the landlords off the land to the city. As Hsiao Kung-chuan observes: "Even before calamities struck their home communities the gentry tended to move from the countryside into towns and cities where they were likely to find a greater degree of comfort and safety or a wider sphere in which to exert their influences. In the event of disaster the rural elite were likely to forsake their ancestral homes and never return. The exodus of these elements must have aggravated the situation created by the decimation of the local population and in some instances contributed to the doom of many villages."[15] In short, absentee landlordism was on the rise, further accelerating the decline of village life. Increasingly, economic necessity forced the peasantry to choose tenancy, banditry, or starvation.

The Shensi rural survey intensively investigated Sui-te district (*hsien*) as representative of conditions in the loess hills which span this region. Sui-te was in fact the commercial center of northern Shensi with trade connections to Tientsin and Taiyuan. It was also among the most populous districts in this area, and absentee landlordism was unusually pervasive. Nevertheless many of the broad tendencies in the socioeconomic landscape of rural Sui-te are comparable to those in other parts of the region.[16] Study of four typical villages (*ts'un*) with 265 households (in 1928) revealed that tenancy was both pervasive and rapidly increasing. In 1928, of 197 poor peasant households, 89 were tenants. By 1933, tenant families numbered just under half the total, 133 out of 272 households. Official statistics indicate that within five years the tenancy rate had climbed by more than 40 percent. In the same period poor peasant landholding decreased from an average of .29 acres to a pitiful .21 acres per person. Yet the survey showed that the farms of middle and rich peasants also dwindled and local landlords increased their holdings only slightly from 4.46 to 4.88 acres per person. It was not the more prosperous families living in these villages who reaped the grim profits of famine and death. Rather the most striking change in land tenure was the rise of *absentee* landlordism. By 1933, 57 percent of the households in these villages owned no land, and the acreage farmed by tenants had increased from 40 to 53 percent of the total land under cultivation. In 1928, 481 of a total of 604 acres of land cultivated by tenants were the property of absentee landlords. By 1933, 808 acres had become tenant lands and 707 of these now belonged to absentee owners. Tenancy, coupled increasingly with absentee landlordism, was a critical and growing problem in Sui-te and throughout northern Shensi.[17]

There are indications that the quality of landlord-tenant relations in northern Shensi may have been unusually harsh. One vivid account of the physical and psychological burdens of tenancy in the area is that of Ching Chung-ying recollecting some of the painful ordeals of his youth:

> I am from Hengshan. My family has always lived there, but for several generations we have not had the land to make a living from. We had ten mu and Father worked as a day labourer for various landowners. Ours was not good land; it lay high up the hillside. We were five brothers. Life was hard for us and when I was twelve I had to go out and earn.
> It was in January 1920 that I began working for a landowner called Wang

Kou-ho. I was to get "two strings of cash" for the year; that is to say from January to October according to the moon calendar. The landowner woke me when the cock crowed. I had to carry the water and shit. I had to do everything. One summer day, when the melons had ripened, I dropped one on the ground and it split open. It was a sheer accident, but Wang Kou-ho was furious, and took his mattock and hit me on the head. You can still see the scar. I was unconscious, and it was late afternoon when I came round; I was soaked in blood and he had just left me lying where I fell. [Weeps.] No one knows how the poor people suffered. I was twelve and had no trousers. Everything was my fault. I often got five or six beatings a day. He was a big landowner. He had 600 mu. It was both valley land and hill land.

One day Wang Kou-ho took me with him when he went out to the sheep. That was in the summer and it was hot. We went eight li from the village. At dinner-time I was sent back to fetch his food. First he took off my cloth shoes and pissed in them, then he said: "You must be back with my food before my piss has dried." It was a hot summer and I had to run barefoot across sand and I could not stop and rest on the way. I ran as fast as I could, but when I got back the landowner's piss had already dried, because the sun was strong, and Wang Kou-ho beat me after he had eaten. [Weeps.] I was only twelve.[18]

Two qualities emerge forcefully in accounts of landlord cruelty in northern Shensi. First is the passivity or, better, the fatalism of the peasantry in the face of a life of degradation and exploitation. The second is the vividness with which such incidents of humiliation are etched into peasant consciousness. For many peasants such acts of mental and physical cruelty ranked among the formative experiences of youth. The repressed bitterness engendered by such accumulated incidents would eventually burst forth in radical peasant movements.[19]

The case of the Ma clan of Mi-chih district exemplifies how indebtedness, mercantile activity, and natural disaster contributed to the concentration of absentee landlord wealth, the impoverishment of growing numbers of tenants, and the disintegration of the rural political economy. The Ma landlords, with vast holdings throughout Mi-chih and adjacent Sui-te, were the most powerful in northern Shensi. They rivaled in wealth and power China's most prosperous families. Their case, the subject of an extensive rural survey, provides a detailed record of landlord exploitation.

The vitality of Ma organization was extraordinary for Northwest China where clans were a mere shadow of their powerful counterparts in the southeast.[20] Incomplete statistics for 1942 reveal that the clan's fifty-three families of landlords living in Yang-chia-k'ou village, the ancestral home, owned a total of 6,988.7 acres of land outright exclusive of large additional mortgage holdings. Several landlords possessed over 500 acres of land, vast holdings by the standards of Chinese agriculture. The clan consolidated its fortune prior to the mid-nineteenth century, and family records show that the largest accretions of property occurred during periodic famines.[21]

Ma clan account books revealing substantial increases in rent during the half century after 1884 point up the declining position of the tenant. Annual records of one prominent landlord family for those years show a steady increase in rent from an average of .33 piculs of hulled grain per acre of land in 1884 to .64 piculs per acre in 1932. In less than half a century the tenants' burden in real crop values had doubled while productivity remained stagnant.[22]

In 1917 the Ma clan founded the Tsung-te-hou or "Ancestral Virtue," patterned after and named in accordance with the traditions of clan ancestral and charitable organizations. However, as in several other parts of China which faced the decline of central authority and the drift toward anarchy, such organizations were motivated less by reverence for the departed than by the imperative to protect family fortunes. Ancestral Virtue coordinated activities ranging from land acquisition, mortgages, and loans to commercial transactions including grain purchase, speculation, and the opium trade. The organization facilitated the efficient concentration of economic power. It also maximized political and military pressures on recalcitrant tenants and debtors in an agrarian-commercial empire which dominated the economy of several districts. As its holdings expanded beyond the clan's initial base of operations in Yang-chia-k'ou, the political and military arm of Ancestral Virtue assumed added significance. However, directly controlling police functions, traditionally the preserve of the local magistrate, could prove a two-edged sword. In the short run it ensured the continued flow of revenue into the family coffers. But it meant too that peasant wrath, which frequently was vented against local officials, might now lash out against the landlords who increasingly assumed those functions.

In the early twentieth century throughout rural China, the role of the gentry class—composed predominantly of landlord families with semi-official status—as intermediary between the peasant and the state was being eroded. The demise of the examination system in 1905 was a key event in the loss of gentry legitimacy and the dissolution of a stable gentry-magistrate order at the local level. At the same time the gentry frequently was cut off from the village and transformed into an urban absentee-landlord class with strong commercial interests. Ancestral Virtue was one of the most successful (and ruthless) responses by landlord-commercial elements to the mounting threat of instability and social revolution. The Ma clan represents the most advanced example of transitional landlord institutions in the northwest. Similar activities designed to bolster landlord power in the face of rebellious peasants and competing warlord armies were occurring simultaneously in other parts of China.[23]

We possess one account of the Ma clan by a man whose family had suffered under its yoke. Twenty years after the power of the landlords had been destroyed and communism had begun to transform the face of rural China, sixty-five-year-old Ma Chen-hai in unembroidered fashion related his life story:

> I grew up in the village of Fengchiatsah in Suiteh hsien. It was a small village. My family had always been farmers. We owned fifteen mu and we rented

thirty mu from Ma, the landlord. We had to pay thirty-four jin per mu in rent. The landlord, Ma, had a money-lending concern called Tsunteh. We did not borrow money from him, but we were not able to pay our rent. He took interest on it and interest on the interest. It was a high rent. The years were not bad ones and the crops were middling good, but we were six mouths to feed in the family, and in the end our debt had increased to 1,200 jin of grain, so then he took our fifteen mu of land from us. I was twelve or thirteen years old then. There was no way we could get out of it. We could not get out of his clutches. The next year we rented the fields that before had been our own, and had to pay thirty jin per mu rental for them. Father said: "What can we do? The landowner is hard. He takes our land from us. We must bow to it." Father had no hope any longer. . . . Mother just wept. Having four children, it was hard for her to have lost those fifteen mu. She kept saying: "Life is much worse now." . . . The landlord Ma lived forty li away, so we did not see him often. But his agent, the manager of Tsunteh, his moneylending business . . . collected rents and ran the money lending.[24]

The history of Ma clan and its Ancestral Virtue reveals the pattern of indebtedness which had long plagued the peasant in northern Shensi. A combination of ruinous interest rates and periodic famine often permanently precluded repayment of loans which were of course passed on to one's heirs. Clan records show continued payment almost a century later of debts contracted to individual landlords as early as 1845! Typical interest rates were 15 to 20 percent *per month*. Loans amounting to 913 strings of cash in 1917 had by 1931, at the height of the famine, already increased sevenfold to 6,537 strings of cash. The step from debtor to tenant was a common one, particularly during famine years. Established with 177 acres of mortgaged land in 1917, over the next two decades Ancestral Virtue accumulated mortgages at an average rate of 150 acres per year. Small landowners forced to mortgage their property rarely recovered it in the face of ruinous interest rates.[25]

An examination of officialdom and taxation policies in Shensi suggests two interesting conclusions. First, a substantial majority of subdistrict (*ch'ü*) and township (*hsiang*) officials, that is those directly charged with tax responsibilities, engaged directly in mercantile activity. Second, these officials typically were landowners of at least comfortable means. The 1933 provincial rural survey concluded that "Generally speaking, political power in Shensi villages is presently held by comparatively old village gentry."[26] While there was striking continuity in local leadership in the chaotic years of the late Ch'ing and the Republic, change was underway in its economic and social functions as a result of absentee landlordism, growing commercial involvement, and the breakdown of civil authority. Shensi's landlords rarely rivaled the wealth of their southern counterparts, and northern Shensi remained among those parts of China least touched by commercial development. Yet as officials, moneylenders, grain speculators, and mortgage holders, Shensi's landlords secured an iron grip on the area's primitive political economy.

In 1933 a National government survey listed thirty-three kinds of taxes levied in Shensi beyond the basic grain tax. These included levies for repairing the Great Wall and quelling bandits, auto taxes (there were no cars but the tax was collected nevertheless), gatekeeping assessments, and so forth. Of particular importance were the heavy collections, as high as 300 dollars per acre, on opium lands, long a major source of warlord revenue. Moreover, taxes were often exacted three to five years in advance. Assessments continued unabated throughout the famine years of 1928 to 1933, and tax default was the major immediate cause of land mortgage and sale. But most burdensome of all were the periodic military levies characteristic of the warlord era.[27] Ironically, the rise of the peasant movement and eventually the guerrilla challenge to warlord authority contributed substantially to mounting warlord levies and a growing burden on the peasantry. A Kuomintang intelligence report noted that in Sui-te district, taxation spiraled from 20,000 dollars in 1930 to 170,000 dollars in 1934 in order to finance local troops engaged in counter-guerrilla operations.[28] In addition, locally based and supported public security forces were everywhere augmented throughout the province during the famine years in anticipation of increased peasant unrest. Most districts maintained a force of over 100 men.[29] Finally, "unofficial taxation" took its toll in the form of a succession of bandits and soldiers living in the hills and exacting tribute from both landlords and the peasantry. Indeed, the distinction between "official bandits" serving in local militias or warlord armies and ordinary bandits operating in the hills was of little moment to the beleaguered peasant.

Widespread banditry in northern Shensi not only increased peasant suffering, it impeded incipient tendencies toward the commercialization of the economy. At a time when much of rural China was experiencing increasing involvement in a marketing economy of regional and national proportions, control of the roads by local brigands brought trade in large areas of northern Shensi to a virtual standstill. Thus British Consul Eric Teichman reports of his 1916 expedition that "at no time during our tour of Northern Shensi, did we meet a single load of merchandise or a single traveler of the better class, so utterly has all trade and traffic in that region been destroyed by the brigands."[30]

Conditions of the peasantry, intolerable throughout China, were intensified in northern Shensi, where adverse natural conditions were compounded by the oppression of a social system in advanced decay. "There are districts," R.H. Tawney has observed, "in which the position of the rural population is that of a man standing permanently up to the neck in water, so that even a ripple is sufficient to drown him."[31] Throughout the entire northwest in the Republican era such ripples repeatedly turned into waves, sweeping millions to an agonizing death by starvation and relegating tens of millions of others to a marginal existence at the mercy of imponderable natural and political forces.

The Warlord Era

The socioeconomic plight of the Shensi peasantry was directly related to the political fragmentation among competing warlord interests. Whatever its economic liabilities, by virtue of location and geography Shensi was a strategic link in the defense of the capital at Peking and a base for military thrusts to the rich eastern provinces along the valleys of the Wei, Yellow, and Han rivers. It thus became deeply embroiled in the power struggles of the late Ch'ing and warlord periods. In its declining years the Manchu government dispatched troops from Anhwei province to secure Shensi for the Ch'ing. In initiating a hostile relationship between fiercely independent Shensi provincials and armies from Anhwei and elsewhere, the Ch'ing left a legacy of bitterness toward outside military forces which intensified during the subsequent warlord era.

The collapse of the dynasty in 1911 resulted in a contest for power between forces from Anhwei province, the recently formed provincial army, and troops loyal to the Elder Brother secret society (Ko-lao-hui). In the turmoil of the 1911 revolution, the Ko-lao-hui, best organized of the competing forces, quickly seized power in many parts of the province from revolutionary forces which had risen against the Manchus. Shortly the provincial capital at Sian, as well as Yenan and other key points, was in Ko-lao-hui hands. However, the situation remained fluid as Shensi militarists vied with outside forces and among themselves. Anhwei generals and their followers in the aftermath of the revolution repeatedly frustrated the hopes of Shensi provincials for autonomy. Thus in 1913 Lu Chien-chang, an Anhwei man, was appointed provincial governor.[32]

However, amidst the swirl of warlord politics, northern Shensi remained the preserve of the minor warlord Ching Yüeh-hsiu from 1911 until his death in 1935. Ching was a native of Shensi's P'u-ch'eng district on the northern periphery of the Wei valley. His twenty-five-year career as a petty warlord was notable only for an ability to move deftly from alliance with one armed camp to alliance with another in the treacherous currents of warlord politics. Thus Ching's power was successively recognized by forces from Anhwei and Shensi and eventually by the Kuomintang.[33]

In the northwest the real prize for ambitious warlords remained the strategic Wei valley area and the capital at Sian. Shensi was ravaged by factional wars following the death of Yuan Shih-k'ai in 1916 and was subject to chronic instability stemming from shifting alliances among Peiyang warlords, men predominantly from North China originally associated with Yuan's modernized forces. From 1916 to 1921 a series of bloody clashes erupted first within the Anhwei clique and between it and forces from Chihli province, and subsequently pitted Anhwei troops against Shensi forces. In 1916, in the first of these struggles, Ch'en Shu-fan, Shensi's military governor, enjoying the undisguised support of his uncle Tuan Ch'i-jui, the leader of the Anhwei clique, defeated the civil governor Lu Chien-chang. A series of clashes soon followed between Ch'en's

Anhwei army and the Shensi Nation Pacifying Army (Ching-kuo-chün). Ch'en retained control of the capital at Sian and the title of military governor until May 1921, when the decline nationally of the Anhwei-Fukien (Anfu) clique permitted the Peking government to name a Chihli general, Yen Hsiang-wen, to replace him.[34]

Following Yen's suicide in August, his ambitious subordinate, the "Christian General" Feng Yu-hsiang, was appointed military governor. A former member of the Anhwei group, Feng had shifted to the side of Chihli in 1920 after his uncle and mentor Lu Chien-chang was executed by Anhwei forces. Feng's post as military governor gave him control over Sian and the narrow but critical Wei valley in central Shensi while local warlords retained their grip on outlying areas. When Feng marched off to oppose Chang Tso-lin, "the Old Marshal of Manchuria," in the first Chihli-Mukden War in April 1922, his grandiose dreams of a sweeping reform program in Shensi died stillborn. Liu Chen-hua, a former subordinate of Ch'en Shu-fan, acceded to the post of military governor. Once again the struggle between Shensi and Anhwei forces was joined. In March 1925, Liu engaged in combat with the Nation Pacifying Army which succeeded temporarily in wresting control of substantial parts of Shensi.[35]

Shensi thus provides a classic example of the ravages and chaos of the warlord era. Although peripheral to the struggle for the rich and strategic preserve, the Wei valley and Sian, it was above all in the badlands of the north that the symptoms of chronic poverty and disintegration were most acute. In 1916 Eric Teichman made these prophetic observations: "The north of Shensi . . . was at the time of our visit in the hands of organized troops of brigands of a semi-political character, robbers one day, rebels the next, and perhaps successful revolutionaries the next . . . what with the ravages of brigands and the natural infertility of the soil, the few inhabitants were poor to the verge of starvation. Yenan seems to be the center of the most desolate area, by far the poorest region I have traversed in China outside the actual deserts."[36] The staggering human and material toll of warlord politics and landlord exploitation aggravated already intolerable conditions of rural disintegration and poverty in the countryside. The resulting massive discontent provided fuel for radical movements which developed in Shensi in the 1920s.

Notes

1. O.J. Todd, *Two Decades in China, Comprising Technical Papers, Magazine Articles, Newspaper Stories and Official Reports Connected with Work under His Own Observation* (Peking, 1938). Todd was chief engineer of the China International Famine Relief Commission. I am indebted to Jonathan Spence for supplying this quote.

2. On the importance of Kuan-chung in the development of Chinese civilization, see (Great Britain) Geographical Handbook Series, *China Proper* (n.p., 1944, 1945), I, 74.

3. George B. Cressey, *China's Geographic Foundations: A Survey of the Land and Its People* (New York, 1934), 183–84.

4. Baron Ferdinand von Richtofen, *Baron Richtofen's Letters, 1870–1872*, 96–97, quoted in George B. Cressey, *Land of the Five Hundred Millions* (New York, 1955), 255.

5. Cressey, *China's Geographic Foundations*, 189.

6. Edgar Snow, *Red Star Over China* (New York, 1961), 63–64.

7. Cressey, *China's Geographic Foundations*, 187; cf. *China Proper*, 197–98.

8. Ernest F. Borst-Smith, *Mandarin and Missionary in Cathay: The Story of Twelve Years' Strenuous Missionary Work During Stirring Times Mainly Spent in Yenanfu, a Prefectural City of Shensi, North China, with a Review of Its History from the Earliest Date* (London, 1917), 52–57, quoted in Hsiao Kung-chuan, *Rural China: Imperial Control in the Nineteenth Century* (Seattle, 1960), 406; cf. Ho Ping-ti, *Studies on the Population of China, 1368–1953* (Cambridge, 1959), 231–32.

9. J.C. Keyte, *The Passing of the Dragon: The Story of the Shensi Revolution and Relief Expedition* (London, 1913), 227.

10. Snow, *Red Star*, 29 (1961 ed.). One missionary report suggests that the opium problem was particularly intense in the area surrounding Yenan, where 90 percent of the inhabitants were said to have fallen prey to it. Borst-Smith, 72–73.

11. China International Famine Relief Commission, *Annual Reports, 1928–1933*, especially *1929*, 44; James Sheridan, *Chinese Warlord: The Career of Feng Yu-hsiang* (Stanford, 1966), 248, 251. By 1931 Yü Yu-jen, Chairman of the Control Yuan of the National government, reported the loss of life owing to famine at three million in Shensi alone. *Peking and Tientsin Times*, Jan. 21, 1931, cited in R.H. Tawney, *Land and Labour in China* (Boston, 1966), 76. On the sale of women and children, see Jan Myrdal, *Report from a Chinese Village* (New York, 1965), 204.

12. John Lossing Buck, *Land Utilization in China* (Shanghai, 1937), 9.

13. A. Stampar, "The Northwestern Provinces and Their Possibilities of Development," quoted in Snow, *Red Star*, 229 (1961 ed.); Hsing-cheng-yüan nung-ts'un fu-hsing wei-yüan-hui (Rural Rehabilitation Commission of the Executive Yuan), *Shen-hsi sheng nung-ts'un tiao-ch'a* (Shensi province rural investigation; Shanghai, 1934), passim.

14. Hsing-cheng-yüan nung ts'un fu-hsing wei-yüan-hui, *Shen-hsi sheng nung-ts'un tiao-ch'a*, 3–76, 136.

15. Hsiao Kung-chuan, 404–5.

16. *CFJP* (Dec. 30, 1941).

17. Hsing-cheng-yüan nung ts'un fu-hsing wei-yüan-hui, *Shen-hsi sheng nung-ts'un tiao-ch'a*, 79–112. The criteria used for classification of rural classes are not fully specified. Those classified as tenants may also have owned some land. For a contemporary communist assessment of growing land concentration and the opportunity thereby posed for rural revolution, see Chih T'ien, "Wo-men tse-yang ling-tao nung-min fen liang-shih ti tou-cheng" (How we lead the peasant struggle for grain distribution), *Hung-ch'i chou-pao* (Red flag weekly), 27: 53–54 (Dec. 17, 1931).

18. Myrdal, 125–26.

19. A number of reviewers have raised the issue of credibility concerning the accounts related by Myrdal. These stories were related following nationwide campaigns to "speak bitterness," to relate the evils of the old society. This does not, in my view, preclude their usefulness as an important and unique record of the period. Some of these accounts, like any personal recollections, have undoubtedly been exaggerated or conventionalized. As highly personal memoirs they should be read with this expectation. The abundance of verifiable contemporary evidence of comparable landlord exploitation in numerous other accounts of peasant life lends powerful substantiation to the general characteristics of the situation described by the peasants of northern Shensi. Roy Hofheinz' study of peasant movements in South and Central China documents many of the harshest features of landlord exploitation. "The Peasant Movement and Rural Revolution: Chinese Communists in the Countryside (1923–1927)" (Harvard University, Ph.D. dissertation, 1966), 93, 191. Compare the more graphic accounts of landlord brutality in another North China village in William Hinton's classic, *Fanshen: A Documentary of Revolution in a Chinese Village* (New York, 1966).

20. Hsiao Kung-chuan, 329. Hsiao notes that clans tended to be weakest in poverty

areas which could not support elaborate clan organization and activity.

21. *MCTC,* 2–14. Research for this study was completed in 1942. It was not published, however, until 1957. Although there are a number of Moslem communities in northern Shensi, the Ma clan of Mi-chih district are not Moslems.

22. *MCTC,* 71–74.

23. Evidence from other provinces suggests that new types of landlord organization with broad economic functions began to develop during the last half of the nineteenth century. In many cases military and political ends were also served. This appears related to the dual phenomena of rural commercialization and social disintegration characteristic of much of rural China from the nineteenth century. See Yuji Muramatsu's stimulating article, "A Documentary Study of Chinese Landlordism in the Late Ch'ing and Early Republican Kiangnan," *Bulletin of the School of Oriental and African Studies,* vol. 29, pt. 3 (1966). In addition, the description of the "carry-on society" (*chin-hsing-hui*) run by the Catholic Church in a Taihang Mountain village of Shansi after 1911 reveals similar features. Loans made by the "carry-on society" reportedly were at a rate of 30 percent interest per month. Hinton, 62–67, 121–23. Minglunt'ang (Enlightened Ethics Lodge), a lineage organization with immense landholdings in several districts of Kwangtung, performed similar functions. Compare also the activities of the "Congress for the Protection of Property" which arose in Kwangtung in 1924 in response to the threat of an increasingly militant peasant movement. Hofheinz. "The Peasant Movement and Rural Revolution: Chinese Communists in the Countryside (1923–1927), 130–31, 190.

24. Myrdal, 147–48. The "Tsunteh" referred to is of course the Tsung-te-hou, Ancestral Virtue, of the Ma clan.

25. *MCTC,* 52–56, 97.

26. *Shen-hsi sheng nung-ts'un tiao-ch'a,* 149.

27. Ibid., 151–56. The extensive cultivation of opium, particularly from the 1920s, contributed to the widespread starvation produced by the famine after 1928. Much fertile land which had been planted in grain was given over to opium.

28. Hatano Kanichi, *Chūgoku kyōsantō shi* (Tokyo, 1962), IV, 434–38, "Sen-kan ku to aka ni roku san go gun" (The Shen-Kan area and the 26th and 35th Red Armies), 435.

29. *Shen-hsi sheng nung-ts'un tiao-ch'a,* 150.

30. Eric Teichman, *Travels of a Consular Officer in North-west China* (Cambridge, England, 1921), 79.

31. Tawney, 77.

32. Jerome Ch'en, "Defining Chinese Warlords and Their Factions," *Bulletin of the School of Oriental and African Studies,* vol. 31, pt. 3 (1966), especially 566–67; Ralph Powell, *The Rise of Chinese Military Power, 1895–1912* (Princeton, 1955), passim; Teichman, 10–12; Keyte, 14–59; Borst-Smith, 107–13.

33. It is a pleasure to acknowledge the assistance of Jerome Ch'en in attempting to deal with the complex period of interregnum. Much of the data concerning Ching Yüeh-hsiu and warlord politics in Shensi are drawn from a personal communication of December 29, 1967.

34. Ch'en, "Defining Chinese Warlords," 574. The Nation Pacifying Army was led by the military men Hu Ching-i and Yü Yu-jen who later rose to the heights of Kuomintang leadership. Like Lu Chien-chang, they were natives of Shensi.

35. The fullest English accounts of Shensi warlord politics in the years 1916–1921 are given in Sheridan, 101–9, and Ch'en, "Defining Chinese Warlords," 574; cf. *The China Yearbook* (London, 1912–1939), *1925–1926,* 1130–32; Harley Farnsworth MacNair, *China in Revolution: An Analysis of Politics and Militarism under the Republic* (Chicago, 1931), 52. Teichman, 11–12, stresses the importance of feelings of provincial independence in Shensi as basic to the military upheavals of this period.

36. Teichman, 60, 63.

A 1926 view of the walled city of Yenan. *(Photograph by O.J. Todd)*

A fortified point used as a refuge against bandits in the eroded loess hills of Northern Shensi in the 1920s. *(Photograph by O.J. Todd)*

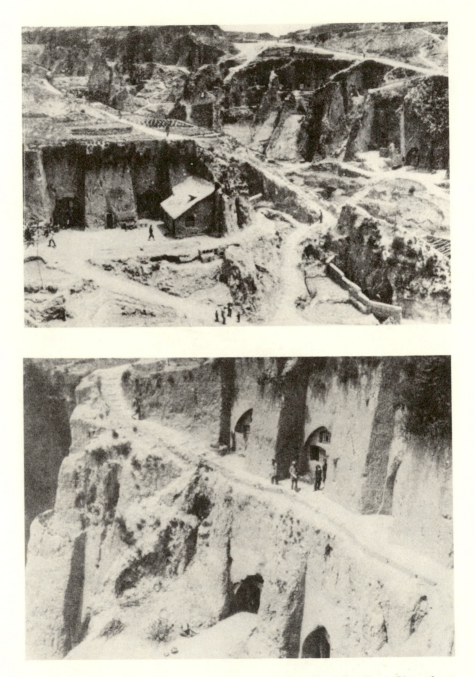

Cave dwellings like these cut from the loess soil of Northern Shensi are cool in summer, warm in winter and bombproof.

Donkey- and ox-drawn wooden wheeled carts in Yenan, 1917. *(Photograph by R. L . Wallace)*

2

Rebels and Revolutionaries in the Northwest

Shensi, like other provinces in Northwest China, was virtually isolated from the intellectual ferment which preceded the 1911 revolution and developed into a frontal attack on Chinese tradition during the New Culture movement in 1917. Geographically remote from foreign business and missionary and diplomatic activity, this area experienced little of the dislocation wrought in coastal and southern areas by direct Western impingement. In the absence of institutions of higher education, and with Western studies limited to a handful of missionary primary and middle schools, the radicalization of students and intellectuals through exposure to foreign ideas proceeded slowly. Provincial political and intellectual preoccupations centered neither on the issue of foreign domination nor on a moribund Confucian tradition but on the struggle for power against outside warlord forces and among competing Shensi military interests. Yet this insularity began to crumble during the warlord era.

The Origins of the Communist Movement in Shensi

Marxism along with other radical currents of thought was transplanted from the intellectual hotbeds of Peking and Shanghai in the aftermath of the May Fourth movement of 1919. During the May Fourth movement, student protest initiated a massive nationwide urban reaction that linked the bourgeoisie and the proletariat in protest against the incursions of imperialism symbolized by the sellout of Chinese interests at Versailles. The dominant intellectual issues of science and democracy which had challenged Confucian orthodoxy in the New Culture movement quickly receded into the background, replaced by a burning activism centering on nationalism and social revolution. In the populist spirit characteristic of the May Fourth era, Chao Tsung-jun and Wang Fo-tsung, like many young intellectuals seeking to carry the revolutionary message to the people, returned from Peking to their home district of San-yüan just north of Sian. There, probably in late 1919, they founded Shensi's first Marxist study group. In student circles, one reminiscence relates, *Das Kapital* and other Marxist and radical ideas of Western origin were often pitted in heated debate against the ideal of one world (*ta-t'ung*) as expounded by the late Ch'ing reformer K'ang Yu-wei—the most avant-garde position worked out within the Confucian framework.[1]

In Shensi during the years 1919 to 1927, revolutionary ideas including Marxism enjoyed their greatest vogue in the Wei valley, particularly in the vicinity of Sian. This was the intellectual and political center of Northwest China and the area most exposed by reasons of communications and geography to new currents of thought. However, in Sui-te and Yü-lin, the only districts in northern Shensi which could boast middle schools, revolutionary ideas also circulated and received a warm reception from students drawn from elite families in neighboring districts. In 1922 teachers Wei Yeh-ch'ou at Yü-lin Middle School and Li Tzu-chou at Sui-te Normal School were among the Peking University disciples of Li Ta-chao, the co-founder and leading intellectual of the Chinese Communist Party, who came to Shensi to recruit students and teachers. The student body at Yü-lin Middle School included not only Ching Wen-lung, son of north Shensi's leading warlord, Ching Yüeh-hsiu, but also a number of young men who were shortly to spearhead the communist guerrilla effort in this area: Liu Chih-tan, Kao Kang, Hsieh Tzu-ch'ang, and Wang Tzu-i among them. Indeed, virtually the entire leadership nucleus of the partisan movement in northern Shensi was drawn from student activists attending middle school in the exhilarating atmosphere which followed the May Fourth movement. These young men, in experience and outlook, and in the consciousness of their elite status, more closely resembled Western university rather than high school students. Typically they were in their late teens or early twenties. Liu Chih-tan, the central figure in the Shensi revolutionary movement, was nineteen years old (*sui*) on arrival at Yü-lin Middle School. On every hand these students saw their traditions and institutions in an advanced stage of collapse. Moreover, their education made them acutely aware of the challenge posed by a dynamic Western civilization. At a critical moment in the formation of their values, these students were exposed, to a degree unique among their contemporaries in the northwest, to the conflicting crosscurrents of traditional and Western conceptions challenging the very basis of the social order. Teaching in Yü-lin, remote from foreign influence and the fierce currents of the May Fourth movement, Wei Yeh-ch'ou introduced his students to *The Communist Manifesto,* Lenin's *State and Revolution,* and of course such radical Chinese student journals as *Hsin Ch'ing-nien* (New youth).[2]

In 1922 when Wei helped initiate a student union at Yü-lin Middle School, perhaps the first in Northwest China, Liu Chih-tan became chairman and the following year led two student boycotts directed against warlord interests. These issues were dramatized in a campaign against the special privileges accorded Ching Wen-lung. The campaign reportedly ended successfully with young Ching's transfer to a school in Sian, after troops had been called out in an abortive attempt to intimidate the student demonstrators. The incident is suggestive of the leverage which middle school students could bring to bear on local officials and even warlords. If warlord armies could ride roughshod over the peasantry, laying waste the land and leaving misery in their wake, in northern Shensi they could not afford to ignore the pressures of prominent landlord families or their scions. In an area of approximately 98 percent illiteracy, these educated youths could muster substantial local power in support of their demands. Nevertheless, the issue of political control remained explosive during the next decade, and the students were by no means always victorious. Thus, one year after the boycott Wei Yeh-ch'ou was forced to leave Yü-lin Middle School as a result of reaction to the student activity he had pioneered.[3]

In 1923 agreements reached between Sun Yat-sen and representatives of the Communist International led to the First United Front between the Kuomintang and the fledgling communist party, which was formed just two years earlier in Shanghai. Following the First Kuomintang Congress in January 1924, communists entered the Kuomintang and even secured some leadership positions. The domestic policies of the two parties were brought into line, initiating a period of cooperation with and assistance from the Soviet Union.[4]

Marxism had been introduced into Shensi in the spirit of heated inquiry which characterized the May Fourth era. It was not, however, until the Kuomintang-communist alliance that communism as an organizational force appeared in the northwest. In the spring of 1924 the communist party and its youth arm, the Socialist Youth Corps, established branches in northern Shensi at Sui-te and the following year at Yü-lin. Party and Youth Corps branches, reflecting the work of Wei Yeh-ch'ou and Li Tzu-chou, were probably semiofficial at this time, as there is no evidence of a provincial party organization. They did, however, serve as a nucleus for organizing radical student youth. Liu Chih-tan, for instance, joined the Youth Corps before graduation from middle school in 1924 and the communist party early in 1925. That autumn he was among the communist youths enrolled in the second class at the Kuomintang's Whampoa Military Academy in Canton.[5]

The communist movement in Shensi at this time was centered in a small coterie of students and intellectuals, isolated from the workers and peasants.[6] Although large-scale peasant movements spread across several provinces in South and Central China prior to 1926, little such activity can be discerned among the rural poor in the northwest despite sporadic uprisings in a number of rural districts. As for the labor movement, which had been expanding rapidly in China's coastal cities and other areas of rapid commercialization and industrialization since 1919, even the powerful impetus of the May 30th movement of 1925, involving nationwide strikes and boycotts in response to the massacre of Chinese demonstrators by foreign policy, created scarcely a ripple in Shensi. Despite communist efforts, Shensi's minuscule proletariat remained weak and disorganized. We need not look far to discover the reasons for this. The entire northwest lay outside the area of China's industrial concentration and railroad network. With the exception of a single small oil field in the far north, Shensi province was bereft of foreign industry. Such "proletarian elements" as we can discover barely numbered in the thousands. They were predominantly concentrated in Sian where various small-scale industries—"handicrafts" might be more appropriate—had developed. These consisted for the most part of textile shops employing a maximum of a few dozen workers. Shensi remained virtually untouched by the industrial revolution. Efforts to mobilize the weak and disorganized "proletariat" in Sian were abortive.[7] Nevertheless, circumstances would shortly provide the communist party with access both to the workers and to the peasants.

Revolutionary activity, long quiescent while Shensi remained a battleground for competing warlord factions, developed dramatically after the summer of 1926 when the Northern Expedition, the culmination of the Kuomintang military drive to unify the country, unleashed a variety of latent forces. The return of Feng Yu-hsiang as the dominant figure in Shensi politics at this time augured the beginning of a new era. Feng, accompanied by Yü Yu-jen, the leading figure in the Shensi Kuomintang, had just returned from a study trip to the Soviet Union. If Feng was once again the warlord master of the province, he reigned this time under the banner of alliance with an activated Kuomintang and the communist party. Feng's Kuominchün army quickly routed the forces of Liu Chen-hua, this time permanently eliminating the Anhwei armies whose presence had plagued the province since the waning years of the Ch'ing dynasty. Throughout 1926 the Kuominchün consolidated control over central Shensi, including the rich and strategic Wei River valley and Sian. Feng's army was the most formidable in the northwest, and his government in Sian was legitimized and aided by the National government whose confidence and power increased with each victory in the Northern Expedition. If Feng's case illustrates the way in which the Northern Expedition legitimized select warlords by incorporating them in the Kuomintang rather than breaking their power, the situation in Shensi also reveals that significant changes might occur with shifts in warlord hegemony. Under Feng's leadership, Kuomintang and communist cadres shortly provided an impetus to radical peasant, worker, and student movements.[8]

While Ching Yüeh-hsiu held unquestioned sway in northern Shensi, in the Wei valley communist influence developed rapidly within the framework of collaboration with Feng Yu-hsiang and the Kuomintang. In May 1926 a provincial party organization headed by Keng Ping-kuang was established to coordinate the activities of existing party branches. Communists were shortly to be found not only leading the fledgling labor and peasant movements, but in influential positions in the Kuominchün and the provincial government. Feng hoped to use both communist and Kuomintang cadres, many of them talented organizers, to strengthen his army and administration. The head of the political department of the Kuominchün at this time was a communist, Chang Mu-t'ao, while Liu Chih-tan, who had graduated from Whampoa in time to participate in the Northern Expedition, served as a political commissar of the Kuomintang's Fourth Route Army. Political cadres penetrating to the platoon level of the Kuominchün were predominantly Kuomintang and communist party members. Teng Hsiao-p'ing, later the party's top leader, was among those communists who attained important positions in the political department. In addition, communists held key educational positions. Wei Yeh-ch'ou, for instance, headed the provincial education department, responsible for supervising all Shensi schools. Perhaps more significant, admission to the newly founded Chung-shan Military and Political Academy in Sian was largely restricted to communist party and Youth Corps members. The academy, the major training center in the northwest for military, labor, and peasant movement cadres, was headed by the communist Shih K'o-hsüan. Liu Chih-tan and Teng Hsiao-p'ing were among its instructors, and the student body included Kao Kang, Hsieh Tzu-ch'ang, Hsi Chung-hsün, and Huang Tzu-wen, all of whom subsequently achieved prominence in the Shensi partisan movement. By late 1926 the nucleus of leadership which was to form about Liu Chih-tan had begun to develop among radical youths at Yü-lin and Sui-te middle schools and the Chung-shan Academy.[9]

Among the graduates of the sixth session of the Kuomintang Peasant Movement Training Institute in Kwangtung were sixteen Shensi youths who had been exposed to the passionate teaching of their principal, Mao Tse-tung, and other peasant movement leaders. They had, moreover, spent two weeks in Hai-Lu-Feng observing the radical peasant revolution led by P'eng P'ai. Many of these young cadres returned to Shensi in late 1926 and helped develop the peasant movement, particularly in the area north of the Wei River (Wei-pei), in San-yüan and Fu-p'ing districts where the Kuominchün held undisputed power.[10]

Student organizers going into the countryside in 1926 discovered a tense situation which had already begun to explode in peasant riots and such traditional expressions of peasant protest as the Red Spear societies. Thus in Wei-nan district, peasant uprisings were repeatedly ignited by "harsh taxation and exploitation by local bullies [landlords]" in the years 1923 to 1927. Peasant wrath descended on both local officials and landlords, sometimes reportedly involving several thousand peasants in pitched battles against local military forces. If student activists were increasingly involved in the peasant movement developing in the Wei valley, Red Spear organizations in southern Shensi and Honan developed without reference to student youth of the May Fourth generation.[11]

Here was an extraordinary opportunity for the communist party. The Red

Spears represented the most militant, highly organized and armed peasant force in large areas of the countryside. Like the peasant movement itself, these and other secret society organizations had developed in response to rural misery and social disintegration. They thus represented a spontaneous explosive force totally independent of the party. The communists, however, were unable to grasp and develop the revolutionary potential implicit in Red Spear organization. From the perspective of revolutionaries committed to the total destruction of "feudal" values and practices en route to the creation of a new society, the Red Spears represented many of the worst elements of the old order. The Central Committee's July 1926 "Resolution on the Peasant Movement" summarized the party's position this way: "In view of [the Red Spear movement's] loose organization and addiction to superstition, it cannot stand the test of battle. Furthermore it is full of destructive tendencies and lacks constructive tendencies. . . . The directing power of the Red Spear Association falls easily into the hands of the local bullies."[12] There were of course other reasons for the wariness of communist leadership toward the Red Spears. Most important was its commitment to maintain the alliance with the Kuomintang, a task which would have been jeopardized by sponsorship of a radical and uncontrollable peasant movement. In Shensi, therefore, communist organizers for the most part ignored the Red Spear movement flourishing in the south. They concentrated rather on organizing the peasant movement in the Wei valley where they enjoyed the protection of the Kuominchün and where secret society organization was much weaker.

Nevertheless, despite Central Committee strictures, peasant movement leaders at the local level began to develop a strategy to integrate secret society, bandit, and other "floating elements" (p'i-tzu) into the movement. These groups, with abundant experience in fighting state power, traditionally played pivotal roles in Chinese rebel movements. Not only did they offer a tempting counterforce to entrenched warlord and militia power, but they were alienated from a society which defined them as outlaws and parasites. While party leadership rejected alliance with such heterodox elements, Liu Chih-tan in Shensi, P'eng P'ai in Kwangtung, and Mao Tse-tung in Hunan were among the most successful peasant movement leaders who recognized the revolutionary potential of these groups. The relationship of the communist-led rural movement to other armed forces would provide one of the continuing challenges to party leadership and local activists.[13]

Meanwhile, from 1926 under the auspices of a revolutionary government, the labor and student movements centered in Sian developed rapidly. For example, by 1926 the student organization in San-yüan, center of virulent peasant disturbances, boasted more than 200 members, placing it among the largest groups in Shensi.[14]

Feng Yu-hsiang, to a degree unparalleled among warlords, for many years provided solid support for the labor movement. In the northwest from 1926, Feng's administration acted to improve working conditions through enactment of progressive legislation. In Sian the work day was officially restricted to nine hours and child labor regulated. Additional labor legislation established a minimum wage and legalized collective bargaining. There is little evidence that these measures were ever implemented beyond a few model factories, but the climate for labor organizing undoubtedly improved.[15] Nevertheless, despite the efforts of communist organizers, the labor movement remained peripheral to the more politically explosive peasant and student movements which developed rapidly in 1926. In each of these communists played a leading role, and the party's own organization expanded accordingly.

At the 1927 Shensi Communist Party Congress, a Shensi-Kansu Area Committee was established to coordinate growing activity along the border between the two provinces and to publish a party organ, *Hsi-pei jen-min* (People of the northwest). If students and intellectuals continued to dominate the party, there was growing worker and peasant participation. However, the very success of the rapidly expanding peasant movement may have contributed to the communists' demise in Shensi. Although officially organized in the name of the Kuomintang, communist cadres were closely associated with the peasant associations which soon revealed radical tendencies. This nascent peasant radicalism alarmed and alienated not only Feng Yu-hsiang but even members of the Wuhan ("Left") wing of the Kuomintang, leaving the communists and their peasant and worker allies isolated and without independent military support.[16]

By the spring of 1927 the communist party was searching frantically for alternatives to its crumbling United Front with the Kuomintang. Among the most interesting and prophetic of the strategies considered, though ultimately rejected, was the "Northwestern Theory" advanced by the Comintern adviser, Michael Borodin. Borodin advocated a temporary communist withdrawal from all major cities, where powerful and increasingly antagonistic Kuomintang forces threatened to crush the movement, to the remote northwest. There, Borodin insisted, the party would be safe from its most dangerous Kuomintang and warlord enemies, and could, moreover, rely on the support of the loyal revolutionary general Feng Yu-hsiang whom it had assiduously courted for years. Less than a decade later, the communists would withdraw to precisely this area at the completion of the Long March, not under the patronage of a warlord but at the head of their own revolutionary army. In 1927, however, the absence of independent military power limited their options to reliance on uncertain military allies and such leverage as could be provided by organized mass movements.[17]

The communist party's organization was dealt a series of crushing blows in the latter half of 1927. Following the Chengchow and Hsü-chow conferences between Feng Yu-hsiang, Chiang Kai-shek, and various Wuhan and Nanking leaders of the Kuomintang, Feng suddenly demanded in June the dismissal of Russian advisers and expulsion of all communists from the Kuomintang. He then swiftly eliminated known communists, among them Liu Chih-tan, from his own staff. The Shensi communist party, as well as the labor, peasant, and student

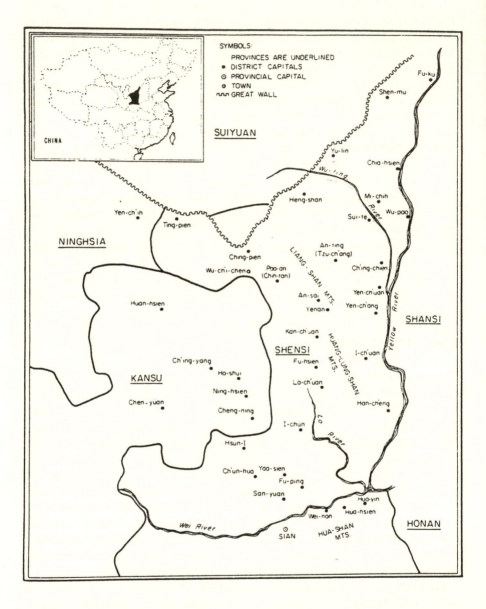

Partisan Activity in Northwest China

movements it had fostered, was shattered. The speed with which it was rooted out of all areas of activity in Shensi suggests the fragility of the party's hold over its membership and the mass movements it championed, a fragility which was the result of its weak position vis-à-vis the armed might of the Kuominchün. The Shensi purge appears to have been relatively mild by comparison with the bloody slaughter of communists and their supporters initiated elsewhere at this time by Chiang Kai-shek. Apparently none were killed in Feng's initial counterrevolutionary sweep in the summer of 1927, although harsh measures were taken to crush continued resistance later in the year and in 1928. Shensi communists, along with their comrades in other provinces, learned the bitter lesson that without military forces of their own, wooing of the elite, creation of a party organization, and leadership in the peasant and labor movement came to naught in the treacherous currents of warlord China where military force proved politically decisive.[18]

In the summer of 1927, surviving communist leaders began to start a new course of armed uprising linked to peasant revolution. On August 1, approximately 10,000 Kuomintang troops under the command of communist generals Ho Lung and Yeh T'ing staged the abortive Nanch'ang uprising. In accordance with plans of the August Seventh Emergency Conference, while Mao Tse-tung directed the Autumn Harvest uprising in Hunan and communist-led rebellions sprouted elsewhere, similar movements were initiated in Shensi.[19]

Initial Partisan Efforts

During late 1927 and 1928, three Communist-led armed uprisings were staged in central and northern Shensi, none involving more than a few hundred rebels, and all rapidly quelled by government troops. The first of these was at Ch'ing-chien in north Shensi in September 1927, under the leadership of T'ang Shu and Hsieh Tzu-ch'ang with the support of a brigade of defecting warlord troops. It was smashed after spreading briefly to three surrounding districts. In April 1928 Liu Chih-tan returned to Shensi from the Anhwei–Hupeh border where he had participated in several abortive attempts to incite peasant uprisings. Beginning with the defection of warlord troops, a "worker and peasant revolutionary army" led by Liu, T'ang Shu, and Hsieh Tzu-ch'ang was organized in the two central Shensi districts of Wei-nan and Hua-yin, an area in which peasant movement activity had earlier attained peak development. Five hundred armed men including many former cadets at the Chung-shan Academy participated, peasant and youth associations were organized, and property of "local bully" landlords was confiscated in what became known as the Wei-hua uprising. But within a month and a half, Feng Yu-hsiang's crack troops overwhelmed the poorly armed partisans and pacified the area. Finally, at Hsün-i on the Shensi-Kansu border in the summer of 1928, a peasant rebellion led by Hsü Ts'ai-sheng hastily proclaimed a "soviet" government, only to be crushed by the combined forces of Feng Yu-hsiang and the militia (min-t'uan) of Shensi and Kansu.[20]

In the Wei-hua uprising, by far the most ambitious of this period, we may observe a number of patterns representative of the early stages of partisan uprisings in Shensi. It was initiated when government forces defected and joined rebels already operative in the hills surrounding the Wei valley. The reasons for these and subsequent defections involve three factors which are crucial to an understanding both of warlord politics and of rural revolution: personal ties, ideological appeals, and objective military and economic conditions.[21]

In the prevailing military system, troops owed allegiance and their livelihood to their immediate superiors, who were in turn bound to a warlord general or, in the case of a militia unit, to prosperous landlords. This meant that a defecting brigade or regimental commander often retained command of his men. In situations where loyalties were fluid and generals often unable to provide adequately for their entire army, or where military setbacks rendered old relationships untenable, defections were legion. In addition, other important ties cut across military lines. Notable among these were secret society membership and bonds arising from kinship, common birthplace, or school.

All Shensi troops who even nominally came under Kuomintang or Kuominchün control prior to 1927 were imbued with militant nationalist and sometimes revolutionary teachings. Antiforeign themes, Sun Yat-sen's Three People's Principles, and ideals of service to the common people were stressed initially by Feng Yu-hsiang and subsequently by communist and Kuomintang political cadres. After 1927 Shensi communists reiterated all of these in wooing dissident commanders. While other armies sometimes promulgated similar teachings, their rapacious actions belied their words. Over the next decade communist partisans in Shensi could point to a unique record of dedicated efforts to implement some of these principles and to serve the interests of the poor.

In the half century or more during which Shensi was ravaged by successive bandit and official military forces, defection became, as we have seen, a routine occurrence. The common euphemism "returned from the northern hills" (*kuei-hui pei-shan*) was used to refer to former bandits presently serving a regular army. As Eric Teichman observed in his travels through the northwest in 1917, "The brigands of northern Shensi are mostly ex-soldiers and Ko-Lao-Hui men, and are composed of the same material as the provincial troops with whom they exchange roles from time to time. It is therefore not possible to use the latter against them. Further they constitute in a way the reserves of the provincial army which are thus maintained without cost to the provincial Government. The Shensi soldier . . . serves either as a soldier or a brigand according to his own tastes and the military requirements of the local Government. In either character he is about equally obnoxious to the people."[22] Two prime causes of defection were defeat in battle and inability of warlord armies to provide necessary supplies for their men. Military units frequently turned to outright banditry, but in several notable instances defecting troops joined partisan forces to attack landlord and warlord hegemony. Defections in all directions occurred regularly among the forces of the Kuominchün and National government, minor warlords, Ko-lao-hui, and other armed bandits as well as communist-led partisans. The problem of fidelity, of winning and maintaining the permanent loyalty of diverse military and heterodox elements, provided a continuing challenge to party and partisan leaders.

The choice of the Wei-hua area for a major uprising had a number of significant dimensions. Interestingly, the first episodes related in the perennially popular novel of bandit exploits, *Shui-hu chuan* (Water margin), were set in precisely this area. In the novel, Hua-yin district and the nearby Shao-hua mountains served as the target and hideout respectively of a formidable Sung dynasty (960–1279) rebel band numbering over 700 men. The initial pattern of partisan uprising in Shensi was in fact deeply rooted in a living tradition of hero banditry combined, to be sure, with nationalist and social revolutionary impulses derived from outside the tradition. Particularly in its early phases, the partisan movement bore striking similarities to other armed bands operating in the Shensi hills, even as the stories relating Liu Chih-tan's legendary exploits are reminiscent of numerous popular tales of officials who turned to banditry in times of dynastic interregnum.[23]

Wei-hua was at the center of the developing peasant movement during the period of the First United Front. This was a rich and densely populated agricultural region located within the orbit of Kuominchün hegemony in the Wei valley just eighty miles east of Sian. Interestingly, it was in this area that foreign impact, reflected in the concentration of missionary activity, was greatest. San-yüan and Wei-nan districts, the scene of active student movements and peasant unrest, were among the most Christianized districts in the province, and the entire Kuan-chung area ranked high in this regard. In San-yüan for instance, students in missionary schools constituted 20 percent of government primary school enrollment, compared to a provincial average of 2 percent. The heavy concentration of missionary work in conjunction with the unsettling effects of other new currents of thought provided a challenge to the hegemony of traditional ideas and elites.[24]

When Feng Yu-hsiang turned against the revolutionary movements which had flourished under his auspices, it was natural that partisan forces continued their attempts to build on the Wei valley peasant base which had earlier shown such promise. Moreover, although this area was relatively accessible to attack by government forces stationed near Sian, nearby mountains provided the rebels a safe haven whenever the retreat sounded.

Nevertheless, despite these favorable conditions, repeated partisan efforts to secure a foothold in this area after 1927 came to naught. With monotonous regularity, partisan forces attempted to return to the areas of earlier peasant movement strength. Inevitably they failed, leading eventually to the development of a new rural strategy. The central reason for these failures may be put succinctly: areas of revolutionary strength under the United Front subsequently became impregnable fortresses of counterrevolutionary power. Prior to 1927 the peasant and labor movements achieved peak development in areas like the Wei valley, which were controlled by and accessible to Kuominchün forces. It was these same areas in which the forces of repression including the Kuomintang were strongest after 1927. Areas of developed transportation and communications in populous and productive agricultural regions were not only prized assets but also the very terrain in which the large standing armies of the Kuomintang and warlords enjoyed maximum advantage against rebel bands. Moreover, it was precisely these areas in which a prosperous landlord class could readily support powerful militia corps to repress unruly peasants.

The Shensi experience, confirming evidence from peasant movements in other parts of China and elsewhere, leads us to reject out of hand two compelling but ultimately unsatisfactory hypotheses concerning rural revolution. The first is that agrarian revolution emerges as a direct function of peasant discontent, and in particular that there is a high correlation between high tenancy rates and the rise of peasant movements. Peasant discontent *did* provide the major impetus for rural revolution in China, as it continues to do throughout much of the Third World. But, as we have observed, that discontent cannot be measured exclusively or even principally in terms of tenancy rates. The Wei valley region had one of the lowest tenancy rates of any part of Shensi and for that matter of all China, yet it was here that the Shensi peasant movement attained its peak activity in the years 1924–1927. In any event, it was in northern Shensi, a region virtually untouched by the early peasant movement and of a markedly different socioeconomic character, that the revolution ultimately took hold. There tenancy rates were somewhat higher (although far lower than in southern Shensi and most of South China). Yet tenancy was only one and not *the* dominant source of disaffection. In Republican China rural misery was a complex amalgam of tenancy, debt, taxation, famine, and the dislocation created by the rapid development of a marketing economy, whose specific character differed from district to district and region to region. Any effort to link peasant discontent with rural revolution requires a comprehensive analysis of the quality of life in the area, an understanding of the specific content of landlord and warlord domination, and the nature of the foreign economic and political impact.[25]

If peasant discontent provides the major impetus to revolution, discontent alone cannot define the revolutionary situation. The transformation of discontent into revolution faced the intense opposition of the warlord and landlord masters of Shensi and all China. In tracing the rise of the Shensi revolutionary movement, we must focus not only on the peasant and revolutionary side of the equation but on two other critical factors. One is the shifting balance of forces within the warlord camp. The other is the terrain and other communication factors which profoundly affected the struggle between competing armed forces. We have observed that the arrival of Feng Yu-hsiang's Kuominchün in the Wei valley in 1926 created the basis for an upsurge in the revolutionary movement.

Yet that movement was simultaneously circumscribed by dependence on a war-lord army, a fact made brutally clear by the total annihilation of the movement when Feng's forces turned against it. The strength of organized landlord power, local militia forces, secret society organization, and coordination among warlord armies are all critical factors affecting the prospects for peasant revolution.

This brings us to the second hypothesis, which suggests a high correlation between revolution and rural "modernization," the latter usually defined in terms either of advanced commercialization and transportation or of intensity of foreign impact. Examination of the period of the First United Front from 1924 to 1927 lends qualified support to this view. The peasant movement flourished primarily in Kwangtung and Hunan, areas with relatively high modernization coefficients and long revolutionary traditions. Moreover, in Shensi it achieved its peak development in the Wei valley, the area which best exhibits these qualities in the entire northwest. Yet it must be noted that in Kwangtung the peasant movement failed utterly in the Canton delta, the area of maximum commercial development and Western impact, and despite prevailing high tenancy rates.

The modernization-revolution hypothesis, however suggestive concerning development in rural China up to 1927, fails utterly to illuminate the dynamics of revolution which eventually brought the Chinese Communist Party to power. The Kuomintang's Northern Expedition of 1926 marked the apogee of a revolutionary thrust from south to north, the victory of the Westernized and urban coastal south over the backward northern hinterland. The Kuomintang's counterrevolutionary coup of 1927 shifted the focus of revolution from the city to the countryside and, in rural China, to remote and inaccessible backwaters. Driven underground, the peasant movement could develop subsequently only as a movement of armed partisans. In the process, a new geography of revolution was defined. Many of the areas in which revolution flared most fiercely prior to 1927 subsequently became bastions of the counterrevolutionary power of the Kuomintang and warlords and, later, of invading Japanese armies. The combination of wealth, strategic location, and efficient communications made these areas vital and enabled regular armies to defend them readily against peasant and partisan forces. The peasant movement would eventually take root and prosper not in South and Central China where it had earlier centered, but in the north. In Shensi, the Wei valley, center of the earlier peasant movement, gave way to the northern hills as the locus of partisan activity. In short, from 1927, the movement's development tended toward the most backward regions of rural China, mountainous areas with primitive economic, commercial, and communications systems and minimal exposure to both Western influences and earlier currents of revolution. Rugged mountain terrain, remote from the power of regular Kuomintang and warlord armies, provided a secure base for armed peasant partisans during the initial stages of growth.[26]

Following the anticommunist upsurge and the failure of initial efforts to mount a successful partisan movement, the Shensi communist party was weak and deeply divided. In the spring of 1928, the first overt struggle occurred between communist advocates of immediate armed uprising in the countryside and those who emphasized preparatory work organizing labor unions and educating workers and students in the cities. At this time Tu Heng was secretary-general of the Shensi party, whose membership stood at about 800.[27] As the intraparty conflict developed during the next seven years, Liu Chih-tan remained the leader of advocates of partisan and peasant uprising who eventually improvised a viable guerrilla strategy in northern Shensi. During much of this period, Liu and his group consistently opposed the main thrust of party leadership, not only at the provincial level but also at the regional level in the Northern Bureau and at the national level in the Central Committee.[28]

Returning to his home district of Pao-an after the abortive Wei-hua uprising in 1928, Liu was appointed secretary of the Military Committee, subordinate to Yang Kuo-tung, who was then secretary of the North Shensi Special Committee of the communist party. With the support of Kao Kang and other rural insurrectionists, Yang was reportedly overthrown, and Liu assumed the post of secretary of the Special Committee.[29]

Turning to the problem of military support, Liu, with the aid of Wang Tzu-i and Ts'ao Li-ju, sought control of the militia in their native district. Liu's local connections enabled him to speak directly to the district magistrate. After elaborate negotiations, the support of leading landlord families, gained through the lobbying of local students, proved decisive. Liu became commander and Ts'ao deputy commander of the militia, the locally supported military force to preserve order, that is landlord hegemony. The story as told in an amusing and revealing reminiscence thirty years later highlights the importance of privilege and connections which enabled Liu and other young scions of prominent families to maneuver boldly and effectively within and outside the local establishment.[30]

Liu of course proved to be no ordinary militia commander. Edgar Snow describes Liu's brief militia career as follows: "He used his office to arrest and execute several landlords and moneylenders. Strange caprice, for a min-t'uan leader! The magistrate of Pao An was dismissed, and Liu fled, with but three followers, to a neighboring hsien. There one of General Feng Yu-hsiang's officers invited them to a banquet, in the midst of which Liu and his friends disarmed their hosts, seized twenty guns, and made off to the hills, where he soon collected a following of about 300 men."[31]

By the end of 1930, the Shensi communist party nevertheless found its efforts thwarted at virtually every turn. Initial attempts to launch rural revolution proved abortive despite some short-lived victories. Party organization and membership had never recovered from the effects of the 1927 coup. Efforts to develop and lead the labor movement were uniformly frustrated by a repressive administration. In Sian party membership reportedly totaled a mere twenty-three. Meanwhile, the political-military situation remained fluid. In February 1930, Chiang Kai-shek's clash with his warlord allies, Feng Yu-hsiang and Yen Hsi-shan, had serious repercussions in Shensi. In the course of a bloody and costly six-month campaign, Feng's forces were destroyed and he ceased to be a factor in the subsequent struggle for power in the northwest. His subordinate, Sung Che-yüan, was replaced as governor of Shensi by Yang Hu-ch'eng in December 1930. Ching Yüeh-hsiu, weathering each successive shift in the political climate, remained in control of northern Shensi. He hastily strengthened ties with the Kuomintang, and his troops were reorganized as the National government's eighty-sixth division. Ching was required in return to demobilize several units. Many of these soldiers immediately turned to banditry just as the province was ravaged by the Great Northwest Famine of 1928 to 1933.[32] The communists were unable, however, to capitalize on the unstable situation that was compounded by dissension among warring military factions and prolonged and debilitating natural disasters.

The 1931 Party Crisis

From 1928, with the successful formation of a Kiangsi Soviet base area under the leadership of Mao Tse-tung and Chu Te, a growing divergence occurred between the Central Committee in Shanghai, preoccupied with the urban labor movement, and leadership striving to build a revolutionary movement in the countryside. In a desperate effort to secure an urban base, on July 28, 1930, P'eng Teh-huai, following orders of the Li Li-san Central Committee, led the Third Red Army in an attack on Changsha, the capital of Hunan. Two weeks later the communists were driven from the city with heavy losses. The defeat at Changsha brought about Li's resignation from the Politburo, and the Li Li-san line was denounced at the Central Committee's Fourth Plenum in January 1931.

The new leadership of the party, which became known as the "Russian Returned Students," was comprised of graduates of the Sun Yat-sen University in Moscow who returned to China in 1930 with the Comintern representative and loyal follower of Joseph Stalin, Pavel Mif. The Fourth Plenum soon provided Mif the opportunity to install his protégés in positions of dominance in the party in place of the discredited Li Li-san and others. However, resistance to the Fourth Plenum quickly jelled. Labor leaders, acutely aware of the steady erosion of communist influence in organized labor, criticized the party's rigid insistence on political strikes. They advocated a nationwide strike campaign to improve wages. Another clique, led in Shensi by Chang Mu-t'ao, former political commissar of Feng Yu-hsiang and a man who subsequently figured prominently in the intra-party struggle, also opposed the Fourth Plenum but for a different reason. He advocated a broad alliance of all patriotic classes and armies to resist Japanese inroads into Manchuria and North China. For Chang the issue of nationalism took precedence over the imperatives of social revolution.

Wang Ming, the most prominent leader of the Russian Returned Students, challenged both these formulations as well as those of partisan leaders in the countryside. In *Liang-t'iao lu-hsien* (The two lines), Wang focused the brunt of his slashing attack on "rightist deviations," particularly the failure to recognize that in China capitalism in any guise is counterrevolutionary. In practice this meant the unequivocal rejection of an alliance with the bourgeoisie or with other parties and armies whether to resist Japan or the Kuomintang or for other purposes. Wang sought the creation of a revolutionary movement based squarely on the proletariat. Consequently he was critical both of the view that the peasantry might play an independent or predominant role in the revolution, and of a rural policy which sought alliance with rich peasants or landlords. Wang's views thus led him on a collision course with partisan leadership throughout China as well as with advocates of a nationwide alliance to resist Japan.[33]

Following a brief but bitter struggle for control of the Shensi party, supporters of the Fourth Plenum triumphed and installed new provincial leadership. Li Chieh-fu, a supporter of the new Central Committee line, criticized the former provincial leadership for its pessimistic (rightist) assessment of the revolutionary situation and for its total reliance on legal activities to the exclusion of armed struggle. It had, he charged, blindly insisted that North China's backwardness precluded armed revolution, overlooking the upsurge in the revolutionary movement.[34]

The concept of "northern backwardness" was central to the intra-party debate in Shensi. Two issues were involved. First, should the party concentrate its slender national resources of men, money, and armed power exclusively in areas where the revolution was already most developed, or should it attempt to foment revolution throughout the entire country? Nationalist and revolutionary activity since 1911 had secured its firmest foothold in South and Central China, particularly in areas exposed extensively to foreign economic, political, and intellectual penetration. And yet, if the north remained the bastion of conservatism, its division among competing warlords and the weakness of Kuomintang power there presented an opening wedge for a revolutionary movement. Second, was revolutionary activity in a backwater such as Shensi to focus on political education and organizational work to build toward a *future* victory, or had the time arrived for armed revolution and the creation of one or more northern soviets? The new leadership of the Russian Returned Students, focusing its intra-party attack on rightism, insisted that the party move boldly in all areas to take advantage of the revolutionary upsurge sweeping the country, emphasizing the pivotal position of the proletariat.[35]

Examination of conditions in Shensi, however, reveals no revolutionary high tide at this time. Party membership in 1931 not only lagged far behind pre-1927 levels, but it remained stagnant. Exclusive of armed partisans, many of whom had only tenuous party connections, there were no more than twenty full-time cadres at work in the entire province, and finances presented critical problems. Moreover, overtures to the working class had proven futile, as had efforts to lead the peasant struggle. Minor warlords continued to guard their independence, but power of the Kuomintang throughout much of the province had expanded and stabilized under the governorship of Yang Hu-ch'eng.[36] Li Chieh-fu's analysis, which parroted the current Central Committee insistence upon a revolutionary upsurge, suggests little awareness of conditions in Shensi province.

The Partisan Movement on the Shensi-Kansu Border

The socioeconomic crisis in Shensi, heightened by years of famine, presented the communist party with an abundant harvest of discontent. Yet, the striking fact about the 1931 intra-party debate was its remoteness from questions of rural disintegration and revolution in the countryside. Taking its cue from the national leadership, the provincial party kept its attention riveted on the small and unresponsive urban proletariat. There was passing mention of the peasant struggle as a sign of revolutionary upsurge, but no indication that the party was actively preparing to capitalize on it. The recent experience of Liu Chih-tan and the partisans on the Shensi-Kansu border was nowhere touched upon, and it appears that Liu himself took no part in these polemics at provincial or higher levels of the party. However, within a year partisan victories turned the attention of party leadership to the countryside.

E.J. Hobsbawm's description of the conditions in which social banditry becomes endemic is strikingly suggestive of the early rebel movement in northern Shensi and a number of other parts of China:

> The fundamental pattern of banditry . . . is almost universally found in certain conditions. It is rural, not urban. The peasant societies in which it occurs know rich and poor, powerful and weak, rulers and ruled, but remain profoundly and tenaciously traditional, and precapitalist in structure . . . even in backward and traditional bandit societies, the social brigand appears only before the poor have reached political consciousness or acquired more effective methods of social agitation. . . .
>
> In such societies banditry is endemic. But it seems that Robin-Hoodism is most likely to become a major phenomenon when their traditional equilibrium is upset, during and after periods of abnormal hardship, such as famines and wars, or at the moments when the jaws of the dynamic modern world seize the static communities in order to destroy and transform them . . . social banditry, though a protest, is a modest and unrevolutionary protest. It protests not against the fact that the peasants are poor and oppressed, but against the fact that they are sometimes excessively poor and oppressed. Bandit heroes are not expected to make a world of equality. They can only right wrongs and prove that sometimes oppression can be turned upside down.[37]

A bandit subculture had flourished for decades in northern Shensi when Liu Chih-tan and other young communist leaders first took to the hills. The Shensi partisan movement developed after 1927 in a context of rural disintegration and warlord politics. These conditions were characteristic of earlier periods of dynastic decline, but there were also new elements which contributed to a pattern of

Robin Hood–style banditry. Unlike Shanghai or Canton where the foreign presence had become familiar during nearly a century of trade and missionary activity, the impact of the foreigner was just beginning to make itself felt in areas like northern Shensi where traditional values and institutions were being undermined and destroyed by famine and war. It was among elite youth exposed to diverse ideological currents in the area's middle schools that the tensions between two worlds and the insecurity bred by the bankruptcy of traditional values and institutions were sharply focused. These young men frequently assumed leadership of partisan movements.

Communist-led rural partisans shared more than disaffection with prevailing warlord and landlord authority with the numerous rebel and secret society bands who roamed the hills of northern Shensi. Particularly in the early years, they frequently engaged in Robin Hood banditry—taking from the rich to give to the poor. Their raiding tactics and their retreat to the hills closely paralleled those of other rebel bands. Moreover, passage from one rebel camp to another, as well as into and out of the ranks of regular military forces serving the state and the status quo, occurred frequently and easily. Our concern here is to delineate the milieu in which the partisans emerged and to perceive how slowly, painfully slowly, their movement was transformed into full-scale peasant revolution.

In northern Shensi the key figure in the transformation from social banditry to revolution was Liu Chih-tan. His career reflects the sharp crosscurrents of the era and the problems of generating peasant revolution. As we have observed, while a middle school student leader, Liu was swept into the mainstream of the intellectual revolution generated by the May Fourth movement. Having joined the communist party and received a Whampoa education, Liu returned to Shensi in 1926 with the Northern Expedition. Between 1926 and 1930, he was prominent in Kuominchün, Kuomintang, and communist politics and military affairs; between guerrilla efforts on the Anhwei-Hupeh border, in Wei-hua, and on the Shensi-Kansu border, he moved smoothly to a position of leadership in the militia and later served as chief of staff with Ch'en Kuei-chang's Kuomintang forces stationed in western Shensi. Throughout he maintained close relations with and active membership in the Ko-lao-hui. Jailed briefly when his communist record was discovered while serving with Kuomintang forces in Kansu, Liu's influential friends and teachers secured his release. From this time on his career was inseparable from the partisan movement.[38]

Following the defeat of Ch'en Kuei-chang in 1931 by warlord troops mobilized to resist the expansion of Kuomintang power, Liu, with the remaining men under his command, launched guerrilla operations in the Huang-lung mountains of northern Shensi. In the autumn they were joined by approximately 200 Shensi natives who had deserted Kao Kuei-tzu's eighty-fourth regiment, formed the Twenty-Fourth Red Army, and crossed the Yellow River into Shensi. After the Mukden Incident leading to Japanese takeover in Manchuria in September 1931, these forces were reorganized as the Northwest Anti-Imperialist Allied Army

(Hsi-pei fan-ti t'ung-meng chün) with 600 men and 300 weapons. Liu served as deputy commander and chief of staff in the new army. A contemporary communist source notes that the preponderance of bandit elements among the troops precluded raising the banner of the Red Army, although it may be surmised that the name Anti-Imperialist Allied Army was selected with a watchful eye to winning support, particularly from the middle and upper classes among whom the Northern Expedition had most successfully sowed the seeds of nationalism.[39]

The Shensi partisan movement developed rapidly from late 1931. In the spring of 1932 its modest success prompted a Central Committee directive calling for reorganization of the guerrillas into a regular Red Army and the formation of a soviet on the Shensi-Kansu border. At this time the partisan Twenty-Sixth Red Army grew to approximately 1,000 men, armed for the most part with weapons seized from Ching Yüeh-hsiu's warlord forces.[40]

The Central Committee hailed the partisans as peasant forces whose "spontaneous uprisings" were smashing once and for all the myth of "northern backwardness." This analysis neglected the important role of professional military forces which had already defected to the side of the rebels (although it called on the Shensi party to strive vigorously to provoke defections). The Central Committee once again demanded the dispatch of proletarian elements from the cities to purify and strengthen the partisan armies—an impossibility in view of the overwhelming weakness of the labor movement in Shensi. It also urged strengthening party control over the partisans and raising political consciousness through a rigorous system of political commissars. Having at last awakened to the revolutionary potential of peasant uprising in the northwest, higher echelons of the party began to pay increasing attention to its direction and control.

The sights of the Shensi party were now riveted on the partisan movement. On orders of the Northern Bureau, it dispatched the reliable Li Chieh-fu to the Shensi-Kansu border as political commissar with a mandate to overcome the opportunism said to have plagued partisan activity from its inception. A report of April 30, 1932, noted that partisans in Hsün-i had arrested landlords, redistributed their grain, and eliminated oppressive taxes. As a result, the peasants rose to support the partisans. Shortcomings, however, were evident inasmuch as many peasants still believed the partisans were warlord troops. The principal error lay in hesitation to carry out land redistribution and develop a broad soviet movement.[41]

Before long party representative Li Chieh-fu himself was charged with propagating an opportunist line. Among his most flagrant errors were his contention that the backward northwest peasant was not ready for land redistribution, his failure to establish a revolutionary committee preliminary to the creation of a soviet, his retreat to the mountains instead of consolidating a rural base area, and his abandonment of political work and the mass movement. The analysis of Li's errors is of interest because the subsequent recurrence of similar charges suggests chronic problems impeding the creation of an effective peasant movement by party leadership remote from rural problems. The charge of rightism was to be reiterated, as it had been for some years, in virtually every discussion of partisan activity by the Shensi party leadership, the Northern Conference, and the Central Committee. The fullest and most devastating critique of Li Chieh-fu's policy was delivered by Li Chün as he was about to replace him as political commissar.[42] But errors patently obvious in Shanghai or Sian proved difficult to eradicate when party leaders carried the Central Committee's mandate into partisan territory. Others were to follow by the summer of 1932, but Chi Hen and Yü Ch'ih, like Li Chieh-fu and Li Chün before them, soon fell victim to similar criticisms and dismissal by their superiors in the party.[43]

We must consider why the partisans persisted in their "errors" despite a cacophony of party charges of rightism and the parade of political commissars sent to reform them. The partisans operated in a milieu reminiscent of traditional Chinese bandit heroes. While *some* of their leaders were trained revolutionaries, their own roots and the network of local ties upon which their survival depended were grounded in the hills of northern Shensi. This meant that they possessed a strong sense of local power realities. In contrast to their party superiors in Shanghai and Tientsin, their perspective on the revolutionary situation was informed by a detailed understanding of local conditions. In the years after 1927 these partisans groped toward their own distinctive guerrilla strategy. In the process hero banditry eventually gave way to full-blown agrarian revolution.[44] Moreover, they had formed their own hardened cadre nucleus whose primary allegiance was to its commanders and fellow partisans rather than to a remote party hierarchy or an imperfectly understood ideology which remained alien to its needs and experience. Party representatives armed with military and political principles framed in accordance with the current Central Committee line, frequently without military experience, clashed repeatedly with partisan leadership on four points: military tactics, socioeconomic policy, leadership, and class composition. On each of these issues partisan leaders held a less sanguine ("rightist") view of current revolutionary potential and the prerequisites for survival than their party superiors. Hence they were castigated for "flightism" (retreat and abandonment of the masses rather than standing and fighting), a rich peasant line (failure to carry out land redistribution), insubordination (resistance to the leadership of party emissaries and directives), and class impurity (amalgamation of local bandits, Ko-lao-hui, and defecting soldiers and the failure to develop a proletarian base).[45]

The partisans, several hundred men facing overwhelming forces on the rugged Shensi-Kansu border, were not prepared at this time to stake everything on land redistribution as demanded by the party, particularly since famine, exorbitant taxes, and debt were the predominant problems in many of the mountainous areas where they were based. Most important, unless they possessed the power to withstand returning government troops, land redistribution merely exposed friends and allies to harsh retaliation. It is not difficult to understand the reluctance of tenants and poor peasants to carry out or even accept land redistribution in areas where warlord or Kuomintang reconquest was imminent.[46] In the famine years after 1928 the partisans initially attempted to win support by resolving the single most critical and immediate problem of the rural population—drought-induced starvation. This end was served by the seizure of grain and stores from landlords for distribution to the poor without subjecting the people to the dangers of retribution inherent in land redistribution. At the same time the guerrillas replenished their own supplies. The major drawback of this policy, as higher party representatives were quick to perceive, was that the peasant might remain aloof from the revolutionary struggle even as he covertly stored his share of confiscated grain. And in fact this commonly occurred. There is little in the record of these initial endeavors to suggest the raw power of an awakened peasantry which had characterized peasant movements of the 1920s in Hai-Lu-Feng or as described by Mao in his 1927 Hunan Report.[47] However, the guerrillas on the Shensi-Kansu border continued to add to their strength and experience while making modest advances in building peasant support. The very factors of remoteness, desperate poverty, primitive communications, and partisan tactics of raiding and grain distribution which mitigated against development of a dynamic mass movement at this time were essential for survival and modest growth.

The Wei-pei Peasant Movement and the Creation of a Soviet Area

While partisan strength developed on the Shensi-Kansu border in 1932, San-yüan district again became the center of the peasant movement in the central Shensi Wei-pei area. Developments seemed sufficiently promising for the Shensi party to call for creation of a new soviet and to project the eventual merger of the Wei-pei and Shensi-Kansu soviets to encompass the entire northern half of Shensi province.[48]

The movement was not, to be sure, without shortcomings, as the same resolution was quick to point out. Most serious was the fact that land redistribution was limited to the single Wu-ch'ing-yüan-tzu subdistrict in San-yüan. The provincial party committee demanded confiscation of all landlord and rich peasant lands for redistribution to hired peasant laborers, poor and middle peasants, and soldiers. While stressing opposition to a "rich peasant line," it was nevertheless prepared to allot small amounts of the poorest land to rich peasants who were not counterrevolutionaries. To launch the land revolution and guide the partisans in eliminating landlords, rich peasants, local bandits, and criminals from their ranks, it dispatched Chih Fu and I Ch'eng to the area.

The party's cautiously optimistic appraisal of the Wei-pei peasant movement in June gave way by autumn to a series of diatribes directed at right opportunists and rich peasant leadership. The attacks provide the only available contemporary analysis of the concrete practice of agrarian revolution in Shensi. During the summer of 1932, the partisans attempted to mobilize the poor and middle peasantry of San-yüan primarily through an extensive program of grain and seed confiscation and distribution.

Interestingly, the partisans were not alone in attempting to aid the San-yüan peasantry through grain distribution. For some years the American-financed China International Famine Relief Commission had concentrated its efforts in the Wei-pei area and, above all, in San-yüan district. The commission's work proceeded with the support of Governor Yang Hu-ch'eng, who recognized not only its humane potential but, perhaps more crucial in the calculations of warlord politics, its possibilities for reinforcing his hegemony by reducing discontent. In 1930, in addition to grain relief, it undertook to provide seed for planting the next crop. Subsequently a large-scale irrigation project, involving 5,000 workmen, was carried out jointly with the provincial government. San-yüan was a famine area located within the narrow orbit of Yang Hu-ch'eng's power in central Shensi, conveniently accessible from Sian. With partisan activity growing, we may conjecture that it was selected for relief aid in part to counter the threat of rebellion.[49]

By the summer of 1932, nature and warlordism had prevailed over the well-intentioned acts of the China International Famine Relief Commission. The situation was again critical. Tens of thousands in the district had starved to death or been forced to migrate. Owing to drought, large numbers of the remaining peasantry were confronted with imminent disaster. Moreover, thousands lacked seeds to plant the next crop. Wu-ch'ing-yüan-tzu was the center of the communist drive in the Wei-pei area. The provincial party representative, Chih Fu, reported that the peasantry participated in the arrest and killing of a number of landlords and the redistribution of their grain. This marked the first involvement of the peasantry in this area in armed struggle. Concurrently, mass organizations expanded rapidly, with peasant association membership reportedly exceeding 1,000. Chih Fu pointed to growing peasant strength and determination, widespread demand for land redistribution, and the fact that in a number of places the poor peasants had actually begun tilling confiscated lands.

However, rich peasant leadership in San-yüan had retarded and diverted the surging revolutionary movement. Chih Fu's enumeration of errors serves as a corrective for his preliminary description of a dynamic peasant movement. Rich peasants not only received a share of confiscated grain, they actually led the movement; grain distribution was not used as a vehicle to mobilize and organize the peasants, in fact it frequently occurred at night to avoid implicating local activists; instead of an equal distribution of grain, members of the peasant association received additional shares. The local leadership was charged with failure to arm the masses, organize local peasant militia forces, and expand the guerrilla movement. But the most serious error, Chih Fu charged, lay in the persistent opposition to the redistribution of land.[50]

Chih Fu's report scrupulously mirrors the contemporary Central Committee line. On the one hand, a broad revolutionary tide was declared to be sweeping the country. The peasants were aroused, prepared to support armed struggle, and demanding land. On the other, rich peasant leadership was restraining the revolutionary forces, perverting the party's program, and acting as a check on the masses.

What is clear is that despite rampant famine-induced discontent the explosive dynamism of full-scale peasant rebellion was lacking. The evidence suggests that often the peasantry accepted a handout from the Red Army, becoming only marginally involved in the struggle. Far from providing the impetus for a radical peasant movement, the grain distribution strategy, like the work of the China International Famine Relief Commission, may have sapped discontent, thus increasing the difficulty of building a sustained revolutionary movement.

In one subdistrict at least, Wu-ch'ing-yüan-tzu, land redistribution was attempted, but there too a rich peasant line was said to have prevailed: "Following a rich peasant line, an average distribution of the land of the entire village (ts'un) was made according to the total population (except excessively corrupt landlords and counterrevolutionary rich peasants). Rich and poor families were treated alike, purely on the basis of the number of persons." From this perspective, the most important error lay in "not completely confiscating the land of counterrevolutionary rich peasants, but in confiscating only surplus land; this rich peasant line completely preserves the interests of the rich peasants."[51]

Two principles were apparently involved in the land redistribution in Wu-ch'ing-yüan-tzu. First, as we have seen, the partisans confiscated and redistributed only surplus land rather than all land in the village. After a quota was determined for each family on the basis of the family size, excess land was confiscated from rich peasant and landlord families. Second, equal distribution meant no discrimination between poor and rich, exploiter and exploited. Everyone, regardless of class, and apparently regardless of age, sex, or ability to work the land, was entitled to an equal share. These principles, designed to minimize dislocation and divisiveness, ensure continuity in production, and equalize landholdings, were attacked by higher party authorities as reflections of a rich peasant mentality. Most important, land was reportedly distributed to the peasants by the Red Army, rather than seized by an aroused peasantry. Peasant fears and insecurities, bred of harsh experience, died slowly. There was, as yet, no mass peasant struggle committed to the destruction of the landlord system and the political order upon which it rested.[52]

In rural Shensi, the Wei-pei area had received maximum exposure to revolutionary currents and was at the center of the peasant movement prior to 1927. Nonetheless, subsequent efforts at land redistribution there met a cold response. In part this may have been owing to the fact that the rural population included large numbers of owner-cultivators, although, as we have seen, successive famine years after 1928 sharply reduced peasant landholdings, and landlords frequently monopolized the most fertile lands. One basic reason for the failure of land redistribution, however, concerns military realities. Located up the valley from Sian, Wei-pei was particularly vulnerable to government attack. Recipients of land, in that event, offered the most obvious target for retaliation.

The Shensi guerrilla movement continued to spread despite periodic forced retreats to the northern hills and numerous defections. A number of minor military successes during 1932 brought partisan strength to over 1,000 men, while at other times it ebbed to as low as 200. By the spring of 1933, Kuomintang intelligence sources estimated party membership in Shensi at over 3,000.[53]

A more important indicator of growing strength was the creation in 1932 of the Northwest Revolutionary Committee, responsible for paving the way for a unified northwest soviet area. Its first chairman, Li Miao-chai, was succeeded by Huang Tzu-wen. The plan was to expand the Shensi-Kansu Border Soviet formally created in 1932 to include substantial areas north of the Wei River and in northern Shensi where active movements were developing. A rudimentary soviet political structure was elaborated, extending, at least on paper, to the township and village levels. It seems doubtful, however, that a functioning soviet government existed at this time. Meng Po-ch'ien, himself active in the new soviet, later described partisan success at this time as follows: "Because the communists and guerrillas are for the most part their close relatives, friends, and villagers, the *lao-pai-hsing* [people] in the northwest soviet area cannot but protect them. Since the Communist party and the guerrillas, in this year of famine, supply their livelihood, they cannot but protect them."[54] Meng's account is suggestive in stressing the importance of family and other local ties, as well as famine conditions, in partisan efforts to create institutions to assume the functions normally performed by governments. He relates that in the area of the soviet, all taxes were remitted and the Northwest Revolutionary Committee issued grain, clothing, draught animals, and tools to a people still suffering under famine conditions. The Shensi-Kansu Soviet signals the preliminary stages of transition from mobile raids to establishment of a stable base. At the same time, the flavor of traditional hero bandits lingers on in the dominant role of armed partisans *giving* grain to and remitting taxes for a passive but grateful peasantry, in the failure to destroy the landlord order, and in the quality of personal and family bonds underlying the movement.[55]

The Destruction and the Resurgence of the Guerrilla Movement

Development of the partisan and peasant movements in Shensi was abruptly halted in July 1933 by the extermination of the second regiment of the Twenty-Sixth Red Army's forty-second division, precipitating the provincial party's gravest crisis since 1927. The second regiment, a hardened corps of over 400 men, with 200 rifles and 30 horses, was the crack partisan force in Shensi. Commanded by Wang Shih-t'ai, with Liu Chih-tan chief of staff and Tu Heng political commissar, the second regiment engaged a superior Kuomintang force in what was apparently a set-piece battle in the Wei-hua area. The communists were routed, and the peasant movement in the entire region of the Wei valley was completely crushed.

In its post-mortem, the Central Committee charged once again that failure was caused by right opportunist leadership and singled out Tu Heng for the major share of blame. However, Kao Kang's subsequent analysis seems closer to the mark. Abandoning the guerrilla practice of retreat before an overwhelming enemy force (or perhaps out-maneuvered), the second regiment stood and fought superior government forces, and paid heavily for it.[56]

One final factor which contributed to the destruction of the Wei-pei peasant movement illustrates a fascinating side effect of Western incursions on the internal Chinese balance of forces. This was the major improvement in communications linking Sian and other parts of the Wei valley. As we have observed, the activities of the China International Famine Relief Commission in Shensi for several years were concentrated in the Wei River region. From 1930 to 1933, in a manner which anticipated practices shortly after in the United States during the New Deal, the commission experimented with public works as alternatives to the dole for coping with starvation. It initiated major building and improvement projects on the three roads which emanated from Sian. One of these ran east to Tung-kuan passing through the Wei-hua area, another ran north to San-yüan district, and the third ran west to Lanchow in Kansu. Once the road between Sian and San-yüan became passable for motor vehicles in 1930, the thirty-mile trip, including the crossing of two rivers, was reduced from one day's hard travel to two hours. The eighty-mile trip from Sian to the Wei-hua area, which formerly required three days, was also substantially reduced. These advances did facilitate the speeding of relief grants to the needy. But for our purposes other consequences are more significant. Improved communications expanded the area of effective control of the government garrison near Sian and reduced the relative mobility of guerrilla and bandit forces just as their buildup was beginning to pose a serious threat to landlord and warlord authority in the San-yüan area.[57]

In the summer of 1933 the Kuomintang destroyed the communist party organization in Shensi. Over 160 party and Youth Corps members, including key leaders, were imprisoned or defected, and the peasant movement was decisively eliminated from the Wei-pei region.[58] Although remnants of the second regiment were reorganized into a fourth regiment, the seventy-odd remaining soldiers were soon forced to scatter in the wake of a suppression campaign in which 400 peasants were reportedly killed and 700 others arrested. In the classic pattern of suppression, the unarmed peasants, not the guerrillas, suffered the greatest hardship. As a result of the rout of the second regiment and the flight of the fourth regiment in the summer of 1933, the provincial party committee ordered the Twenty-Sixth Red Army disbanded and reactivated a number of separate guerrilla units.[59] The communist movement in Shensi stood at a low ebb.

In late 1933, the first, third, fifth, seventh, ninth, and eleventh guerrilla branches formed on the Shensi-Kansu border. Their strength was bolstered by the return from the Wei-pei area of Liu Chih-tan and Wang-Shih-t'ai at the head of troops who had survived the disastrous defeat of the previous summer. These units dispersed in the loess hills on the provincial border and attempted to develop the peasant movement. Meanwhile, the long-brewing rift between the guerrillas and the Shensi party hierarchy came to a head. Huang Tzu-wen arrived in the guerrilla areas from Sian to discuss formation of a new Shensi party committee only to be arrested by guerrilla leader Kao Kang. The charge against Huang, as later related by Kao, was plotting to establish rightist leadership. Although Kao was to have been nominated to the new committee, he apparently felt that it was weighted against the partisan leadership group and in favor of "defeatist" elements who viewed the armed struggle as fruitless and favored nonmilitary activity. In Kao's retrospective version of these events, Huang is said to have denounced Kao and Liu Chih-tan as "Hitlers."[60] The conflict between partisan leadership and high-level party representation, each seeking to control and direct the course of the guerrilla movement, had reached the stage of open resistance. This overt power struggle intensified after January 1934 with the arrival in the border area of Kuo Hung-t'ao, representing the Northern Bureau.

By early 1934 the strength of independent units had grown sufficiently to reconstitute the forty-second division. The partisans enjoyed a resurgence on the Shensi-Kansu border and took firm root for the first time in north Shensi.[61] This was not the earliest attempt to develop the movement in the far north. The first communist uprising of September 1927 had briefly flared here. In December 1930 the young, impetuous Kao Lang-t'ing, recently expelled from the Shensi Youth Corps for violations of party discipline, "borrowed" 100 dollars from his family to purchase weapons and entered the hills as leader of a small rebel band. Kao's wrath, in the manner of righteous Chinese rebels of all times, is said to have been directed against "local bullies" and corrupt officials. After several defeats in early 1932, the rebels, ninety men strong, proclaimed themselves the Northwest Vanguard Corps of the Chinese Anti-Imperialist Volunteer Army (Chung-hua fan-ti i-yung chün hsi-pei hsien-feng tui). Despite Kao's earlier expulsion from the Youth Corps, he proceeded independently to establish communist party and Youth Corps branches in north Shensi. However, it was not long before the Ko-lao-hui infiltrated the partisan ranks and seized control so that their activity became indistinguishable from that of roving bandits. Following a military defeat that precipitated the flight of many of the Ko-lao-hui, the determined remnants of Kao's band finally reestablished relations with the party's North Shensi Special Committee. Although censured for insubordination, Kao was reinstated in the party. In September his troops were reorganized into the ninth guerrilla branch, one of six units operating in north Shensi. Despite the party's severe reverses during the summer of 1933, by early 1934 Kao's band had been joined by the first, second, and third guerrilla branches in the north

Shensi area. The above account suggests the party's difficulty in forging small bands of roving partisans, many of them hardened soldiers, bandits, and secret society members, into a disciplined organization committed to peasant revolution and responsive to a distant party hierarchy. In its early activity there was little to distinguish Kao Lang-t'ing's ragged corps from the Ko-lao-hui and other local bandits preying on the landlords in this area.[62]

In early 1934 partisan activity expanded rapidly and its character noticeably shifted. In February in Ch'ing-yang district, the Shensi-Kansu Border Region Revolutionary Committee was established as a provisional soviet government. The new guerrilla base area was centered in heavily forested and mountainous Ch'ing-yang, Pao-an, and Ho-shui districts on the Shensi-Kansu border, a sparsely populated area notorious as a bandit lair. The development of the guerrilla movement continued throughout the spring of 1934 with minor victories against Ching Yüeh-hsiu's eighty-sixth division in north Shensi, and bolstered by the defection of over 200 warlord troops.[63]

Two significant developments lay at the heart of these successes after nearly a decade of largely futile struggle to lead armed insurrection in the countryside. First, prolonged efforts in the Wei valley area were abandoned, and partisan activity was centered on north Shensi and the Shensi-Kansu border area where logistical, political, and economic factors proved more favorable. Not only was this rugged mountain terrain, it was also far from major centers of government power and lines of supply and communications. Local warlord troops in this destitute area were notoriously ill-paid and maltreated. They were particularly susceptible to appeals for defection. The peasantry of northern Shensi, beyond the pale of Kuomintang and Kuominchün power in the 1920s, was untouched by the peasant movement and revolutionary currents developed prior to 1927 in the Wei valley. Yet the northern peasant was, if anything, more oppressed by landlord power and accustomed to operating in an outlaw or antigovernment milieu in his native hills whenever conditions on the land became intolerable. Plagued by a higher rate of tenancy than peasants in central Shensi, he may have been more responsive to the land redistribution program, although it must be stressed that this was but one of many potent socioeconomic programs which included distributing grain, abolishing debts, and eliminating oppressive taxation. Increasingly, as a nucleus of revolutionary cadres strengthened its position within the partisan forces, they alone spoke directly and dynamically to the most pressing problems in the Shensi countryside.

Second, I believe we can detect the evolution of an effective guerrilla style linked to the transition from a Robin Hood type of roving banditry to broadly based agrarian revolution centered in stable base areas. Early military endeavors were strongly influenced by the ready model of Shensi's numerous roving bands such as Ko-lao-hui and local bandits, despite the continued efforts of party and some partisan leaders to consolidate soviet areas. Eventually, however, partisan forces succeeded in creating a base area in northern Shensi.

The concept of base areas is central to the Chinese approach to rural revolution and guerrilla warfare. Examination of conditions in northern Shensi, a classical base area by virtue of geography and location, illuminates many characteristic features of the movement that eventually brought the communist party to power. In important respects, the outbreak of the Sino-Japanese War in 1937 marks the major divide in the strategy and fortunes of the Chinese communist movement. However, one crucial continuity that cuts across that divide is the base area concept developed in numerous parts of China after 1927 and expanded subsequently throughout the resistance war against Japan.

Base areas required rerouting traditional political and economic channels away from major commercial and administrative centers to regions beyond their borders in order to create self-sufficient territorial units resistant to enemy attack. The survival and growth of a base area depended on active peasant participation in destroying landlord hegemony and creating new broadly based political and military institutions. Consolidation of a base area set the stage for expanding into adjacent regions which frequently were richer and more populous but less readily defensible by a guerrilla force.

In the guerrilla strategy developed independently by Mao Tse-tung in Kiangsi and Liu Chih-tan in northern Shensi, base areas were essential for building a mass movement in the countryside.[64] Indeed, their continued preoccupation with rural bases at a time when Central Committee leadership urged attack against strategic cities led to repeated intra-party strife.[65]

Below a minimum threshold of security, it was not possible to destroy local land-based power interests or create effective political-military institutions rooted in broad popular support. In northern Shensi, that threshold appears to have been crossed by early 1934. Growing partisan strength at that time overcame peasant fears, and land redistribution was widely effected. Land redistribution marked the key stage in the creation of symbiosis between partisans and peasants. The armed strength of a guerrilla force embracing substantial numbers of local peasants was the bulwark of a new egalitarian social order. Active peasant support secured for the partisans an increasingly effective intelligence monopoly, and enabled them to tap the local population for economic and tactical aid as well as increase their numbers of recruits.[66]

A June 26 report of the Shensi-Kansu Border Region Revolutionary Committee notes that thirty-five branches of the peasant association, averaging fifty members, and eight branches of hired farm laborers had been organized in addition to over 1,000 men in ten units of red guards. The report goes on to offer the inevitable lament about the rudimentary state of political organization and inadequate party control. However, against the background of nearly a decade of frustration, I believe it must be read as heralding a new level of revolutionary development in northern Shensi.[67]

Partisan strength increased rapidly at this time in conjunction with the spread of land revolution. The contemporary Kuomintang intelligence analysis of this development is instructive. It observes that in 1934 Yen Hsi-shan launched an anti-opium campaign; it is not clear whether he did this to eliminate the drug or reap the lucrative profits for his own administration. In any event, the report notes that many who were engaged in the illegal opium traffic between Shensi and Shansi turned to banditry and were eventually assimilated into the guerrilla forces. It was one of the bitter ironies of warlord politics that a "progressive" action in the satrapy of a single warlord—in this case cracking down on opium— often increased the outlaw component in adjacent areas rather than eliminating that activity. This development notwithstanding, guerrilla success was primarily the product of a movement increasingly attuned to the socioeconomic plight of the peasantry. For the first time guerrilla tactics were effectively integrated with agrarian revolution. In this case (and invariably), Kuomintang intelligence sources tell only a part of the story. Nowhere does one find reference to the causes of peasant misery or to rebel attempts to redress the grievances of the poor. Here partisan successes were invariably ascribed either to troop defections or to violations of military discipline, particularly looting, on the part of troops engaged in counterinsurgency.[68]

In late June, the third regiment of the forty-second division, which had been operating on the Shensi-Kansu border, moved north to establish the North Shensi Revolutionary Area with its center at An-ting.[69] Kuo Hung-t'ao was chosen general political commissar and Ho Chin-nien commander in chief of Red Army forces in the new base area. The third regiment routed two companies of the eighty-sixth division and added to its arsenal. Two days later a meeting of political and military cadres created the first regiment of the North Shensi Independent Division. With the return of the Twenty-Sixth Red Army to the Shensi-Kansu base area, and with increasing activity in two new regions, there were now four major guerrilla concentrations, and plans were formulated to link them. Kuomintang intelligence at this time estimated that the guerrillas numbered over 3,000 men with 1,000 weapons, a formidable force in the sparsely populated reaches of northern Shensi.[70]

The First and Second Encirclement and Annihilation Campaigns

The rapid expansion of the guerrilla movement triggered the first encirclement and annihilation campaign in northern Shensi. Three regiments of the Nationalist eighty-sixth division converged on the north Shensi area. Despite the fact that at least one guerrilla unit was surrounded and annihilated in early September, the movement continued to grow. During 1934 land redistribution was carried out on an increasing scale.

From October, local suppression forces were bolstered by the National government's forty-second and eighty-fourth divisions. The growing strength of the revolutionary movement is suggested by the fact that for the first time troops were brought in from outside Shensi to cope with the insurgents. However, operating in the difficult and unfamiliar terrain of north Shensi, the government troops, although superior in numbers and weapons, proved unable to cope with the guerrillas' mobility, experience, and growing local support. Government forces were outmaneuvered and defeated as the insurgents' strength developed further. The first suppression campaign ended in failure in the winter of 1934.[71]

Partisan victories set the stage for the First North Shensi Soviet Congress held in January 1935 in An-ting. The congress established a Shensi-Kansu Provisional Soviet Government as well as the Northwest Work Committee and the Revolutionary Military Committee to coordinate the four major guerrilla regions. The composition of these organs concentrated power in the hands of local partisan leaders long associated with Liu Chih-tan, including Kao Kang and Ma Ming-fang, although Kuo Hung-t'ao and Hsieh Hao-ju, representatives of the Northern Bureau, also retained important posts. At this time the eighty-fourth division of the Twenty-Seventh Red Army was organized, prompting the opposition commander, Kao Kuei-tzu, to complain of communist duplicity in choosing identical numbers for their three divisions. Thus, the Red forty-second, eighty-fourth, and eighty-sixth divisions faced the National government's forty-second, eighty-fourth, and eighty-sixth divisions, a classical example of parallel hierarchies that presumably compounded confusion among soldiers and peasants alike.[72]

In May 1935 conflict between local partisans and higher party authorities came to a head at the Wang-chia-wan-tzu Conference, subsequently described by Kao Kang as a struggle meeting directed against the "leftism, theoretical immaturity and unorthodoxy" of Kuo Hung-t'ao's leadership. What is clear is that Kuo, the highest-ranking party official among the guerrillas, clashed with local partisan leaders then and again in August at the Chou-chia-chien Conference over plans to repel the Kuomintang's second campaign. Kuo's "adventurist" plan to attack in areas of tight Kuomintang control and his successive proposals to move against cities were rejected. Instead, Kao Kang asserts, the partisans adopted the classical guerrilla line advocated by himself and Liu Chih-tan and concentrated in the vicinity of Pao-an on favorable terrain. At this time Kuo reportedly charged the local leadership with right opportunism and sought to eject Kao from the party.[73]

The second campaign, mounted with twenty battalions of government troops directed by the Kuomintang General Ho Ying-ch'in, culminated once again in partisan victories. The rebels added to their arsenal and expanded both regular Red Army forces and guerrilla units. Kuomintang intelligence reported that following an attempt by the Central government's sixty-first division to disarm certain units participating in the suppression campaign—they were alleged to have oppressed the people—over 1,000 armed men defected to the guerrilla camp. The record of the warlord era repeatedly indicates that frictions between Shensi troops and outside armies sent in to pacify the province were easily aggravated. The defectors seem to have been Shensi troops, while those who attempted to disarm them were outsiders. The move of Shensi troops to the partisan side was facilitated by their provincial antagonism to outside control, a feeling they shared with the guerrillas. It is a noteworthy indication of the partisans' increasing strength and boldness in an escalating war that for the first time they occupied and held six district capitals: Yen-ch'ang, Yen-ch'uan, An-sai, Pao-an, An-ting, and Ching-pien.[74] At this time partisan victories forced official cancellation of grain taxes throughout northern Shensi. This was a striking demonstration of rebel domination in much of this area, particularly when we recall that not even five years of famine after 1928 had forced suspension of taxes. It represented a desperate if belated bid to win the disaffected peasantry to the side of the government.[75]

In a report on partisan expansion from 1934, Edgar Snow writes: "By the middle of 1935 the Soviets controlled twenty-two counties in Shensi and Kansu. The 26th and 27th Red Armies, with a total of over 5,000 men, were now under Liu Tzu-tan's command, and could establish contact by radio with the main forces of the Red Army in the south and in the west."[76] Moreover, he cites other examples of increased maturity at this time: land redistribution, establishment of the Shensi Soviet Government, a cadre training school, a soviet bank and post office, and the beginnings of a soviet economy. Out of the turmoil of prolonged war and rural disintegration we may detect the emergence of a subgovernment moving to restore order, an order based on the egalitarian vision of land revolution.

During 1934 and 1935 the program of land redistribution was widely implemented for the first time. As the movement spread rapidly to new areas, guerrilla forces provided the impetus, the initial leadership, and the power to lead peasants in seizing the land in the face of official repression. Contemporary accounts and official directives concerning the guidelines followed in the land revolution of 1934–1935 are lacking. By 1942, however, Mao Tse-tung and Kao Kang were in agreement that leftist excesses had been committed, and that followers of the Wang Ming Central Committee, notably Kuo Hung-t'ao, were responsible for them. Kao reports that a policy of distributing only surplus lands and animals, allowing rich peasants an equal share of land, and postponing redistribution in unstable areas was originally followed by the partisans in northern Shensi. Kuo Hung-t'ao, however, condemned these policies as rightist, insisted on redistributing land everywhere regardless of the danger of returning government forces, called for a harsher policy toward rich peasants, and even allegedly advocated immediate collectivization of land.[77] Written seven years later as a weapon in the ongoing struggle in the party and as a passionate defense of the strategy developed by local leadership, Kao's analysis must be treated cautiously. Nevertheless, its basic thrust is consistent with the long-developing pattern of conflict between partisan forces and party representatives over the issues of land redistribution and the "rich peasant" line.[78]

The land revolution of 1934–1935 was instrumental in generating peasant support for the guerrillas in northern Shensi. The violent release of long repressed peasant fury provided the basis for active peasant commitment and the vehicle for expanding and strengthening military and political organization.[79] What had once primarily been a military movement centered in small guerrilla bands of a Robin Hood type, by 1935 had developed into full-scale agrarian revolution.

In the early autumn of 1935, Central Committee representative Chu Li-Chih arrived in northern Shensi. On the eve of the third and most ambitious Nationalist extermination program, Kao Kang later charged, Chu allied with Kuo Hung-t'ao in support of an adventurist line. Chu is said to have formulated ambitious plans for the consolidation and expansion of the north Shensi and Shen-Kan bases in conjunction with the Red Army in southern Shensi, creation of a soviet in western Shensi, and coordination with a Szechuan soviet, as well as advocating a direct assault against the Japanese. In the face of a formidable enemy offensive he allegedly proclaimed the slogan, "Attack everywhere and do not allow the enemy to enter a single foot of Soviet territory."[80]

Kao's defense of local partisans is framed after the fact in terms of orthodox Maoist canons of guerrilla warfare. And his criticism of Chu and Kuo parallels Mao's critique of the military deviations of the "Third Left Line." However, as we have seen, hero banditry had eventually given way to viable guerrilla tactics and agrarian revolution in the face of constant opposition from higher party authority. In the course of eight years of setbacks, local partisans had independently developed a set of military and political postulates appropriate to survival and revolutionary growth in the northern Shensi base area. When Kuo and Chu arrived bearing the party's mandate and instructions to overcome guerrilla rightism, they may well have been appalled by tactics of retreat before overwhelming forces, by the relatively moderate land policy, and above all by the heterodox character of this movement which included Ko-lao-hui, former bandits and warlord soldiers, some local peasant recruits but no proletariat. But the movement had already developed an agrarian revolutionary style adapted to the special conditions and problems of northern Shensi.

Merger of the Twenty-Fifth, Twenty-Sixth, and Twenty-Seventh Red Armies

In September 1934, complying with a Central Committee directive, Hsü Hai-tung led the Twenty-Fifth Army of the Fourth Front Red Army from the Oyüwan (Hupeh-Honan-Anhwei) Soviet to the Hupeh-Honan-Shensi border where a new soviet base was established. Under pressure of attack from Yang Hu-ch'eng, the Twenty-Fifth Army began the trek which eventually linked it with the guerrillas in northern Shensi. This activity during early 1935 was not part of a coordinated plan to join all communist forces in the northwest. Hsü had lost contact with the Central Committee and the main Red Army forces which had embarked on the epic Long March that would eventually take them more than 5,000 miles from their starting point in Kiangsi across China's most difficult terrain to Shensi. Hsü learned that the Red Army was moving north from Szechuan from a bulletin in a captured copy of the independent newspaper *Ta Kung Pao* and surmised that its destination was the north Shensi base area. Nor was there prior communication between the Twenty-Fifth Army and the guerrillas in northern Shensi. Arriving in the Shensi-Kansu Soviet area in September 1935, Hsü encountered partisan forces under Liu Ching-fan (younger brother of Chih-tan) and Hsi Chung-hsün, who led him to the main force of the Red Army. In late September Hsü joined the Twenty-Sixth and Twenty-Seventh Armies, bringing combined guerrilla strength to 7,000 or 8,000 men.[81]

At the junction of the three armies, Chu Li-chih, the highest-ranking party official, convened the Yung-p'ing Conference, resulting in extensive reorganization of military and political organs. A newly created Central Committee organ (*tai-piao-t'uan*), wielding the highest party authority in the area, was composed of Chu, Ch'eng Tzu-hua, and Nieh Hung-chün, all of them outsiders recently arrived in the base area.[82] The Northwest Work Committee and Military Committee were reshuffled, and a Shensi-Kansu-Shansi Provincial Committee was established under the direction of Chu and Kuo Hung-t'ao. The Twenty-Fifth, Twenty-Sixth, and Twenty-Seventh Red Armies were consolidated into the Fifteenth Army Corps commanded by Hsü Hai-tung with Liu Chih-tan deputy commander and Kao Kang heading the political department.[83] Examining these multiple changes, it is clear that local partisan leaders were excluded from the highest party councils, eliminated from the Work Committee, and reduced substantially in the command of forces. Liu and Kao retained influential positions in the Fifteenth Army Corps, but their superior was now Hsü Hai-tung. With the arrival of the Twenty-Fifth Army, a new element was introduced into the internal power balance. The party hierarchy, supported for the time by an outside force, Hsü's army, attained military supremacy. The era of independence for Liu Chih-tan's partisan forces, based on military hegemony within their own area of operation, was permanently ended by the arrival of higher-ranking party and military forces.

Under Hsü's command, the Fifteenth Army Corps sallied forth to resist the third encirclement campaign, but not before Hsü and Liu Chih-tan clashed over strategy. Hsü's memoir, written more than twenty years later, relates that Liu advocated attacking the forces of Ching Yüeh-hsiu and Kao Kuei-tzu as a first step in expanding the soviet area. However, he was overruled by his commanding officer, who directed the subsequent campaign against the more powerful Manchurian army. Liu failed, Hsü relates, to perceive that the time was not ripe for expansion of the soviet in the face of a strong enemy. We may surmise, however, that Liu was advocating the tested guerrilla tactic of striking first at the most vulnerable enemy, in this case Ching Yüeh-hsiu's eighty-sixth division, rather than attempting to attack formidable Manchurian forces.

In any event, Hsü's strategy of successive attacks on the Manchurian 110th division at Lao-shan and the 107th division at Yü-lin-ch'iao produced victories despite a Kuomintang strategy of building blockhouses and progressively reducing guerrilla territory, a method which had proven decisive in destroying the Central Soviet base in Kiangsi.[84]

The Purge of Local Guerrilla Leaders and Their Reinstatement

The Red Army victory at Lao-shan was followed by the famous purge of the entire top echelon of local partisan leadership, numbering over 100 men, including Liu and Kao. Events surrounding their detention remain shrouded in obscurity in emotional and conflicting reports. As described by Kao Kang, the arrests were ordered by Nieh Hung-chün and Tai Chi-ying, both of whom had arrived in northern Shensi with Hsü Hai-tung's Twenty-Fifth Army. However, they were merely front men. It was, Kao charged, Chu Li-chih and Kuo Hung-t'ao, the leading representatives in the soviet area of the "Third Left Line," who were really behind the purge, although they subsequently denied all responsibility for the arrests.[85]

On October 25, 1935, remnants of the First Army Corps, the advance wave of battered troops from the Long March, arrived to join the Fifteenth Army Corps at Wu-ch'i-chen, bringing total Red Army strength in the soviet area to 15,000. With them came Mao Tse-tung, Chou En-lai, Lin Piao, P'eng Teh-huai, and other ranking party and military leaders. The arrested partisans were quickly rehabilitated, and Nieh and Tai were reportedly punished for ordering their arrest. Chu and Kuo, however, were officially vindicated. They retained positions of high trust in the party and, Kao reports, continued to slander and obstruct the work of local cadres.[86]

Meng Po-ch'ien offers an intriguing variation on Kao Kang's interpretation. Nieh Hung-chün, described as the central figure in the arrests, acted out of fear of powerful anti-Mao forces among the local partisans. Meng relates this fear to the independent line taken by the Shensi party as early as 1931 in opposing the Central Committee's Fourth Plenum, and to the important role in Shensi revolutionary politics once played by Chang Mu-t'ao, who was subsequently branded a Trotskyite.[87] This interpretation implies (but cites no supporting evidence) that the arrests were carried out at Mao's behest rather than under orders of his predecessors who controlled the party prior to the Tsunyi Conference and who had long criticized the guerrilla strategy of the partisans in northern Shensi. Meng does not elaborate on these suggestions. He offers no proof of local opposition specifically to Mao or to the strategy formulated by the party at Tsunyi under Mao's leadership in January 1935. Nor does he suggest that Chang Mu-t'ao was actually involved in the 1935 leadership struggle in the base area. Nonetheless, Meng's analysis is suggestive of continuing feelings of localism and hostility to outside control characteristic of Shensi politics in general and of the partisan movement in particular. Moreover, the reference to Trotskyism raises the question of local resistance to abandoning the land revolution in favor of the new united front policy which was implemented following the arrival of Mao and the First Army Corps in northern Shensi. The Trotskyites, even after war with Japan erupted in 1937, remained bitter opponents of united front collaboration with the Kuomintang, which they regarded as a sellout of worker and peasant interests.

Edgar Snow presents yet another cast of characters in the arrest of Kao and Liu:

> In August there came to North Shensi a delegate of the Central Committee of the Communist Party, a stout young gentleman named Chang Ching-fu . . . this Mr. Chang (nicknamed Chang the Corpulent) was empowered to "reorganize" the Party and the Army. He was a kind of super-inspector.
>
> Chang the Corpulent proceeded to collect evidence to prove that Liu Tzu-tan had not followed the "Party Line." He "tried" Liu, and demanded his resignation from all posts. Now it is either ridiculous or miraculous, or perhaps both, but in any case it is a striking example of "Party discipline" that Liu Tzu-tan did not put Mr. Chang against a wall as an interloper for presuming to criticize him, but he quietly accepted his sentence, retired from all active command, and went, Achilles-like, to sulk in his cave in Pao An! Mr. Chang also ordered the arrest and imprisonment of more than 100 other "reactionaries" in the Party and the Army.[88]

While the evidence is sometimes contradictory, the main features of the incident, centering on the issue of the independence of local guerrilla forces and conflict over strategy, are clear. If we substitute Chu Li-chih, the villain in Kao Kang's account, for Snow's Chang the Corpulent, the two accounts mesh and all agree that the conflict hinged on the injection of outside leadership into the soviet area.[89] Snow's account, however, makes no mention of military realities. Local partisans, after nearly a decade of fiercely independent activity, did not passively stand aside at the request of a party emissary. The arrival of Hsü Hai-tung's forces gave the party hierarchy military superiority for the first time. Liu, Kao, and their comrades submitted to incontestable military might.

The arrival of the First Army Corps on the heels of the Twenty-Fifth Red Army ended an era of rural insurrection led by radical Shensi youths who consistently opposed policies emanating from higher party authority while groping toward a viable guerrilla strategy in the barren hills of northern Shensi. However, these intra-party frictions were by no means eliminated with the arrival of the Central Committee and armies from the south. During the next decade conflicts between regional and national interests and varying perspectives on social revolution would require mediation. Independent local leadership preoccupied with development of the border region as a revolutionary base was frequently at odds with a party hierarchy dominated by southerners whose concerns were primarily national. However, reinstated by the party in November 1935, most local leaders were absorbed smoothly in the expanding movement. Liu Chih-tan himself served as vice-chairman of the Northwest Military Committee and commander of the Northern Route and Twenty-Eighth Red Armies until he was killed in action in the spring of 1936. He was subsequently honored by the party as a martyr. As early as the summer of 1936 the capital of Pao-an, where Liu was born, and later the district itself were renamed Chih-tan. Campaigns in the Shensi-Kansu-Ninghsia border region during the war of resistance lauded Liu as a model for youth, as did the nation after 1949, and his exploits are recorded in numerous reminiscences and tales. After Liu's death, his protégé Kao Kang rose to the position of the leading party and military figure in the border region and eventually in Northwest China. Not only did many local partisans serve prominently in the wartime party, its government, and its military hierarchy, but after 1949 they served in the People's Republic of China as well. Nonetheless, after the autumn of 1935 all were directly subordinate to the authority of the Central Committee, whose headquarters was established in the base area, and to the evolving united front line which shortly became the focus of party policy. The era of partisan independence had ended.[90]

Agrarian Revolution and Guerrilla War

In the warlord-bandit-secret society environment of its base area and in its fierce resistance against outside controls, the partisan experience in Shensi offers striking parallels with Mao Tse-tung's formative guerrilla experiments in 1927 and 1928 in the Chingkang mountains. Mao's report of November 25, 1928, frankly recorded the heterodox nature of his army, composed of:

> (1) troops formerly under Yeh [T'ing] and Ho [Lung] in Chao-chow and Swatow; (2) the former Guards Regiment of Wuchang; (3) peasant militiamen from Liuyang and P'ing-kiang; (4) peasant militiamen from southern Hunan and workers from Shuikou-shan; (5) men captured from the forces under Hsü K'e-hsiang, T'ang Sheng-chih, Pai Ch'ung-hsi, Chu P'ei-te, Wu Shang, and Hsiung Shih-hsi; and (6) workers and peasants from the various *hsien* in the border area . . . the first four groups . . . are far outnumbered by the last two. In the last two groups, the prisoners are more numerous; without reinforcements from this group, manpower would have become a serious problem . . . *(a few soldiers desert every time we are defeated). Few of the peasants in the border areas are willing to serve as soldiers. Since the land has been divided up, they have all gone to till it. Now the soldiers of peasant or working class origin . . . constitute an extreme minority. . . . One part consists of workers, the other of éléments déclassés. . . . The contingent of éléments déclassés should be replaced by peasants and workers, but these are not available* now.[91]

Fighting for survival in a remote mountain area, Mao initially found the peasants unresponsive. Like the Shensi partisans, the communists in Chingkangshan turned to *éléments déclassés* to man their armies, which were composed primarily of captured soldiers or deserters from warlord and Kuomintang armies, former bandits, and so forth. These men were skilled fighters and many were disaffected peasants forced to leave their land, but the problem of transforming them into committed revolutionaries proved formidable. As Mao has written, defections were common, particularly in the face of military defeat. Moreover, the report suggests one of the classical problems of building a dynamic agrarian revolutionary movement. Far from automatically providing the key to military mobilization of the peasantry, land revolution might sap its vigor by resolving the most critical problem of the disaffected. Both peasant and soldier recipients of land, rather than continuing to resist enemy forces or striving for victory on a national scale, might drift away from the movement to devote all their energies to tilling their newly acquired land.[92]

The same report is shot through with tensions between the Chingkangshan guerrillas on the one hand and the Hunan Provincial Party Committee and the Central Committee on the other:

> As regards the plan for our action here [the Chingkang Mountains], the Hunan Provincial Party Committee changed its mind three times within a few weeks in June and July. At first Yuan Te-sheng came and approved of the plan for establishing our political power in the middle section of the Losiao mountain range. Then Tu Hsiu-ching and Yang K'ai-ming arrived, and proposed that the Red Army should drive ahead to Southern Hunan "without the least hesitation," leaving only a force of two hundred rifles to defend the border area together with the red guards; they said that this was an "absolutely correct" policy. The third time, barely ten days later, Yuan Te-sheng came again bringing us a letter which contained, besides much admonition, a proposal that the Red Army should set out for eastern Hunan; this was again said to be an "absolutely correct" policy . . . [it was] considered dangerous to go to southern Hunan and [we] decided not to carry out the proposals of the Provincial Committee.[93]

Mao also recorded dissatisfaction with the provincial party's inadequate financial support and ultra-leftist policies, and the Central Committee's land policy and criticism of guerrilla activity.[94] Operating at a distance from the party hierarchy, with independent power based on control of a guerrilla force, Mao frequently ignored or defied outside directives which conflicted with his own developing pragmatic and flexible guerrilla strategy, closely attuned to local conditions in his base area. Yet friction between the guerrillas and the party hierarchy continued to grow. The problem of achieving a unified perspective was eventually resolved only by the transfer of party headquarters to the base area in Kiangsi, as it would subsequently be resolved in Shensi.

In essential respects the guerrilla forces of Mao and Chu Te in the Chingkang mountains faced problems similar to those of the partisans in northern Shensi. In each case, communist-led troops moved into rugged mountainous territory and attempted to mobilize the local peasantry through a revolutionary program calculated to win broad-based support. Unlike P'eng P'ai's earlier Hai-Lu-Feng Soviet in Kwangtung, they could not rely on a highly organized peasantry long engaged in anti-landlord struggle.[95] In Chingkangshan and Shensi, Mao and Liu Chih-tan respectively led armed rebels in mountain areas where the peasantry had not been awakened to the revolutionary cause and was inured to the suffering of successive armed forces (both government troops and bandits) living off its toil. There were of course differences. Liu and his men in northern Shensi, unlike many of the soldiers in the Chingkang mountains, were natives of their guerrilla base area and profited from an intimate knowledge of local conditions and personalities. Mao's Chingkang area, while a backwater from the perspective of South and Central China, nevertheless had been much more exposed to the winds of economic and political change than had the peasantry in the north Shensi hills. However, situated in regions with primitive economies and communications, both areas were relatively untouched by the revolution during the years 1919 to 1927, and both were remote from the military and administrative power of the Central government. In each case the guerrillas initially found the peasants cold to the message of agrarian revolution, although they were apparently more frigid in Shensi.

The contemporary land policies in the Central Soviet, like those of the Shensi partisans, were subjected to sharp criticisms from the Central Committee dominated by Russian Returned Students, just as they had been since the earliest experiments with agrarian revolution in the Chingkang mountains. The two principles central to the Chu-Mao agrarian policy, as articulated in early 1930, *equal* distribution of land to all persons regardless of class, and distribution only of *surplus* land rather than all land, were identical with those applied by Shensi partisans in 1932 and subsequently in San-yüan. These principles were summed up in two slogans of Mao's land resolution ratified on February 7, 1930, at the Ku-t'ien Conference: "Take from those who have much to help those who have little," and "Take from those who have fertile land to help those who have poor land."[96] The egalitarian principles of the Chu-Mao land policy were designed to broaden the base of guerrilla support by allying with the poor peasants (the great majority), preserving middle peasant interests, and curbing the power of rich peasants rather than annihilating them as a class. There was also recognition of the fact that redistribution of *surplus* land would minimize the disruption of production, thereby ensuring needed supplies for the guerrilla forces and benefiting all classes except the big landlords.

The Chu-Mao land policy, like that of the partisans in Shensi, was subjected to a consistent volley of criticism over the issue of the rich peasants from the Central Committee under the leadership of Wang Ming. Ever since the publication of *Liang-t'iao lu-hsien* (The two lines) in 1931, Wang hewed consistently to a policy of bitter and uncompromising struggle against landlords and rich peasants as well as the urban bourgeoisie. Mao's more flexible policy was keyed to the problems of survival under extremely arduous conditions in the base areas. This enabled his forces to concentrate on the major enemy at any given time by uniting with a variety of classes and factions, including dissident military and secret society elements and even at times rich peasants.[97] Central Committee objections to equal distribution of land in Kiangsi and Shensi were undoubtedly correct in noting that this practice obscured the sharp lines of class struggle by not clearly distinguishing between rich peasants and poor in redistributing land. But in both cases local leaders were preoccupied with problems of wooing a broad stratum of the rural population, including the middle and even some of the upper ranks of the peasantry, to enhance prospects for staving off defeat by powerful enemy armies.

The basic guerrilla problem lay in coordinating agrarian revolution with military victory. In the absence of extended military success, the prerequisite for creating and preserving a stable base area, it was impossible to energize the peasantry to play an active role in land revolution and soviet military and political affairs. To attempt land redistribution prematurely merely invited severe reprisal. Yet concrete benefits were essential if the peasants were to support the military struggle, or even distinguish the partisans from local bandits and warlord armies. Facing forces overwhelmingly superior in arms and numbers, both Mao and Liu initially adopted raiding tactics similar to those of roving bandits in the quest for survival while learning to utilize mountain retreats, remote from the centers of official power. Eventually they began to construct stable base areas whose populations were committed in the course of land revolution to active military and political participation in a wide range of organizations which embodied the new order of rural equality and deepened the revolutionary movement.

From 1934, the partisans' military power in northern Shensi reached the point where permanent base areas could be secured and land redistribution attempted on an increasing scale. One senses a shift from preoccupation with the predominantly military concerns of survival to the initial stages of a mass movement. By the fall of 1935 with the arrival of the Central Committee and Red Armies from the south, land revolution was spreading rapidly. Political consolidation, the construction of a new revolutionary order, had, however, scarcely begun.

The Long March had not brought the surviving faithful to a promised land. Indeed, many were to cast longing glances back to more promising days in Kiangsi. As Hsü T'e-li told Edgar Snow, "this is culturally one of the darkest places on earth. . . . Such a population compared with Kiangsi is very backward indeed. . . . Here the work is much slower. We have to start everything from the beginning. Our material resources are very limited."[98] But the wilderness of northern Shensi was to provide a haven and home for the party's high command, and the springboard from which revolution would spread throughout the land. The arrival of the party leadership and the veteran soldiers from the Long March launched a new era in the history of the Chinese communist movement.

Notes

1. Meng Po-ch'ien, *Hui hsiang jen-tao* (Return to humanity; Hong Kong, 1953), 2–8. Meng was a founding member of the Marxist study group in Shensi and active in communist and Kuominchün military work until his defection from the communist party in 1938. The most extensive treatment of the May Fourth movement in English is Chow Tse-tsung, *The May Fourth Movement: Intellectual Revolution in Modern China* (Cambridge, 1960).

2. *LSWTCT,* 2–3. This is the basic source for the study of the guerrilla movement in Shensi. Kang's passionate account reflects his own deep involvement in the revolutionary and intra-party struggles described. This report was originally presented to the Senior Cadres Conference in Yenan on November 17 and 18, 1942, at the height of the first great rectification (*cheng-feng*) campaign. *CFJP* (Feb. 7, 1944). Li Tzu-chou, a native of Sui-te district in northern Shensi, studied philosophy under Li Ta-chao at Peking University. An activist in the May Fourth student movement, he was posthumously honored as the founder and guiding spirit of the Shensi communist party. Maurice Meisner, *Li Ta-chao and the Origins of Chinese Marxism* (Cambridge, 1967), 71–104. Li Li-kuo, "Wan-pei su-wei-ai ti ch'uan-shih-jen chih i—Wei Yeh-ch'ou" (Wei Yeh-ch'ou: A founder of the north Anhui soviet), *HCPP,* V, 20–27.

3. "Hsi-pei ti yi-k'o hung hsing: Liu Chih-tan ku-shih p'ien-t'uan" (A red star in the northwest: sketches of Liu Chih-tan), *HCPP,* V, 108–10. "Liu Chih-tan t'ung-chih ko-ming shih-lüeh" (A revolutionary biographical sketch of comrade Liu Chih-tan), in Hua Ying-shen, ed., *Chung-kuo kung-ch'an-tang lieh-shih chuan* (Biographies of Chinese communist martyrs; Peking, 1951), 149. Li Li-kuo, 7.

4. Benjamin Schwartz, *Chinese Communism and the Rise of Mao* (Cambridge, 1951), 37–39; O. Edmund Clubb, *Twentieth Century China* (New York, 1965), 118–35.

5. "Hsi-pei ti yi-k'o hung hsing," *HCPP,* V, 108–10; Li Li-kuo, 20–23.

6. Ch'en Yen, *Shen-kan tiao-ch'a chi* (Record of an investigation of Shensi and Kansu; Peiping, 1936), I, 80.

7. Jean Chesneaux, *The Chinese Labor Movement, 1919–1927* (Stanford, 1968), 24–47, 288.

8. Sheridan, 206–9; *The China Yearbook, 1928,* 164; *LSWTCT,* 3–4; Li Chien-nung, *The Political History of China, 1840–1928* (Princeton, 1956), 467–502.

9. Chesneaux, 288; Sheridan, 199, 210–11; *HCPP,* V, 111; *CFJP* (Nov. 19, 1941); Meng Po-ch'ien, 19.

10. *LSWTCT,* 4–6; Hofheinz, "The Peasant Movement and Rural Revolution: Chinese Communists in the Countryside (1923–1927)," 32–56; Meng Po-ch'ien, 17; Eto Shinkichi, "Hai-Lu-Feng—The First Chinese Soviet Government," *The China Quarterly,* 8 and 9 (October–December 1961, January–March 1962), pt. 1, 182. Stuart R. Schram, *Mao Tse-tung* (Harmondsworth, 1966), 91–92; Jerome Ch'en, *Mao and the Chinese Revolution* (London, 1965), 100–101.

11. Yen Sheng, "Wei-nan ti nung-min ho ch'ing-nien i-nien lai tou-cheng ti ch'eng-chi" (Accomplishments of the past year's struggle of peasants and students in Wei-nan), *Chung-kuo ch'ing-nien* (Chinese youth), 52:45–46 (Jan. 29, 1927). I am indebted to Roy Hofheinz for calling this article to my attention.

12. "Resolutions on the Peasant Movement," Second Enlarged Plenum of the Central Committee, quoted in C. Martin Wilbur and Julie Lien-ying How, eds., *Documents on Communism, Nationalism and Soviet Advisors in China, 1918–1927* (New York, 1956), 298–300. In sharp contrast to the position taken by the party, Li Ta-chao responded enthusiastically to the Red Spear movement, emphasizing its populist and revolutionary impulses. Cf. Meisner, 246–56, and Sheridan, 91.

13. Hofheinz, "The Peasant Movement and Rural Revolution: Chinese Communists in the Countryside (1923–1927)," 158–63, 175, 253. On the contribution of "floating classes" to traditional rebel movements, see Yuji Muramatsu, "Some Themes in Chinese Rebel Ideologies," in Arthur F. Wright, ed., *The Confucian Persuasion* (Stanford, 1960), 241–67.

14. T'ing Chieh, "Shan-hsi ch'ing-nien yün-tung chih chi-kuang chi tsui chin lien-ho yün-tung" (The situation in the Shensi youth movement and the most recent united movement), *Chung-kuo ch'ing-nien* (Chinese youth), 123:653–56 (June 13, 1926).

15. Chesneaux, 288.

16. *LSWTCT,* 4–6; Sheridan, 215, 226.

17. Schram, *Mao Tse-tung,* 108.

18. Sheridan, 230–31; *LSWTCT,* 4–8; MacNair, 119.

19. John Rue, *Mao Tse-tung in Opposition, 1927–1935* (Stanford, 1966), 40–81; Hofheinz, "The Peasant Movement and Rural Revolution: Chinese Communists in the Countryside (1923–1927)," 265 ff.

20. *LSWTCT,* 9–11; Meng Po-ch'ien, 37–44; *HCPP,* V, 112; Wang Chien-min, *Chung-kuo kung-ch'an-tang shih-kao* (Draft history of the Chinese Communist Party; Taipei, 1965), II, 263.

21. In the following discussion I have relied heavily on James Sheridan's excellent analysis of loyalty and defection in warlord China, 16–21, 210–15.

22. Teichman, 74–75.

23. I have found no evidence that Liu or his compatriots were directly inspired by these stories as was, for example, Mao Tse-tung. But the exploits of traditional bandit heroes were common knowledge and provided a ready model for action. Shih Nai-an, *Water Margin,* tr. J.H. Jackson (Hong Kong, 1963). Cf. Schram, *Mao Tse-tung,* 21, 43–44, 128, 159.

24. Milton T. Stauffer, ed., *The Christian Occupation of China: A General Survey of the Numerical Strength and Geographical Distribution of the Christian Forces in China* (Shanghai, 1922), 217.

25. Roy Hofheinz' study of peasant movements in Kwangtung and Hunan points up the inadequacy of tenancy rates as the exclusive index of revolutionary potential and demonstrates the necessity for analysis of the complex socioeconomic and political factors, that constitute the local environment. See particularly "The Peasant Movement and Rural Revolution: Chinese Communists in the Countryside (1923–1927)," 191, 219–20, 246–54.

26. The clearest statement of the revolution-modernization hypothesis is that of John W. Lewis, "The Study of Chinese Political Culture," *World Politics,* 18.3:507–12 (April 1966). Lewis bases his argument in part on the mistaken notion that the Yenan area ranked higher on the modernization scale than Mao's initial base in western Kiangsi (512). Robert McColl has also attempted to find an underlying ecological pattern for peasant revolution in China. See his articles, "A Political Geography of Revolution: China, Vietnam, and Thailand," *Journal of Conflict Resolution,* 11.2:153–67 (June 1967), and "The Oyüwan Soviet Area, 1927–1932," *Journal of Asian Studies,* 27.1:41–60 (November 1967). Both McColl and Lewis emphasize the geographical continuity of peasant revolution. In the face of massive evidence to the contrary, they assert that the same areas in which the peasant movement initially flourished prior to 1927 (modernized areas integrated with urban networks) continued as revolutionary centers or base areas during the subsequent rise of the communist movement. My emphasis on the geographical discontinuity of the revolution, the shift from relatively advanced to remote and primitive regions, is further developed below with reference to the establishment of base areas. Cf. Hofheinz, "The Peasant Movement and Rural Revolution: Chinese Communists in the Countryside (1923–1927)," particularly 250 ff.

27. Ch'en Yen, 80.

28. It should be noted that nowhere in the voluminous contemporary intra-party debates available for the period do we find reference to the analyses and strategies adopted by Liu and his followers. We must rely for information about them on the critiques of their activity by provincial and higher leaders and on the writings of later analysts more sympathetic to their guerrilla strategy.

29. *HCPP*, V, 112; *LSWTCT*, 8.

30. *HCPP*, V, 112–14; *CFJP* (May 15, 1943). In Wang Tzu-i's recollection of the incident, published in *CFJP*, Liu is said to have organized the poor, who provided the decisive margin of support. But Wang also notes how Liu wooed the district magistrate through connections with the local gentry. We may infer that the latter proved conclusive. Roy Hofheinz relates a similar incident that suggests the importance of access by elite youth to a district magistrate and the immense gulf which had developed between a generation of officials reared in the traditional system and young revolutionaries. In that case peasant movement cadres in Kwangtung were unsuccessful in their bid to enlist official support for the movement, 102–3.

31. Snow, *Red Star*, 220.

32. *LSWTCT*, 11; *The China Yearbook, 1931–1932*, 523; BI (Bureau of Investigation), *Shen-kan-ning pien-ch'ü shih-k'uang* (The true situation in the Shen-Kan-Ning border region), 2; China International Famine Relief Commission, *Annual Reports, 1928–1933*.

33. Rue, 243–44; Schwartz, 254–57; Meng Po-ch'ien, 88–94; *LSWTCT*, 10–11; Hsiao Tso-liang, *Power Relations within the Chinese Communist Movement, 1927–1934* (Seattle, 1961), 114–24.

34. Liao Hsing-hsü, "Shen-hsi kung-ch'an-tang chih chiu-fen" (Confusion in the Shensi communist party), passim, *Chen-li* (Truth), 1 (April 12, 1931); this newspaper was an organ of the Shensi communist party. *LSWTCT*, 12.

35. Rue, 242–57. By contrast, Mao Tse-tung, writing in 1928, implied the necessity of concentrating base areas in South and Central China rather than in areas "unaffected by the democratic revolution, like Szechwan, Kweichow, Yunnan or the northern provinces." "Why Can China's Red Political Power Exist?" *SW*, I, 65.

36. *Chen-li*, 1; Chung-kung shen-hsi sheng-wei (The Shensi Communist Party Committee), "Cheng-chih i-chien shu" (Political manifesto), manuscript, Feb. 25, 1931 (BI).

37. E.J. Hobsbawm, *Primitive Rebels: Studies in Archaic Forms of Social Movement in the 19th and 20th Centuries* (New York, 1965), 23–24.

38. Snow, *Red Star*, 220–21. Edgar Snow's account, based on interviews with one of Liu's staff officers in 1936, highlights the Robin Hood features of Liu's early activities and is strongly evocative of the legendary qualities which had already begun to surround his career. BI, *Shen-kan-ning pien-chü shih-k'uang*, 1–2; BI, *Shen-kan-ning pien-ch'ü tiao-ch'a chuan-pao* (Special investigation report on the Shen-Kan-Ning border region), 1–2.

39. Kuan Feng, "Hung erh-shih-liu chün ti erh-t'uan shih-pai ti ching-yen yü chiao-hsün" (The experience and lessons of the defeat of the second regiment of the Twenty-Sixth Red Army), *Tou-cheng* (Struggle), 61:41 (Jan. 12, 1934). *Tou-cheng* was a Shanghai organ of the Central Committee. *LSWTCT*, 12–14; Hua Ying-shen, 149.

40. *LSWTCT*, 14; *HCPP*, V, 115; "Ch'ing-chu chung-kuo kung-nung hung-chün shen-kan-ning yu-chi-tui ch'ung-p'o pai chün ti ying-yung sheng-li" (Celebrate the courageous victory of the Chinese workers' and peasants' Red Army guerrilla forces of Shen-Kan-Ning in smashing the White Army), *Tou-cheng*, 11:8 (Apr. 30, 1932). "Chung-kung chung-yang kuan-yü kan-shen pien-ch'ü yu-chi-tui ti kung-tso chi ch'uang-tsao kan-shen pien hsin ch'ü ti chüeh-i" (Resolution of the Central Committee of the communist party on the work of guerrilla forces on the Kansu-Shensi border and establishment of a new Kansu-Shensi area), *Pei-fang hung-ch'i* (Northern red flag), 4:44–46 (June 12, 1932). *Pei-fang hung-ch'i*

was the organ of the Northern Bureau. Kuan Feng, 41, estimates the size of the guerrilla force at 1,000 men. "Shen-kan hung-chün erh-shih-liu hung-chün ti hsin sheng-li" (New victories of the Shensi-Kansu Twenty-Sixth Red Army), *Pei-fang hung-ch'i*, 4:59–60 (June 12, 1932). The latter's claim that partisans on the Shensi-Kansu border numbered 3,000 men with 2,000 weapons probably exaggerates the strength of the movement.

41. "Ch'ing-chu sheng-li," 8–9.

42. Li Chün, "Chung-kuo kung-nung hung chün shen-kan yu-chi-tui ti ch'e-ti kai-tsao yü liang t'iao chan-hsien" (Thoroughly reform the Shensi-Kansu guerrilla forces of the Chinese workers' and peasants' Red Army and struggle on two fronts), *Tou-cheng*, 15:10–11 (June 9, 1932).

43. Kuan Feng, 40–42; Shensi Provincial (Communist Party) Resolution, "Kuan-yü ti-kuo-chu-i kuo-min-tang ssu-tz'u wei-chiao ch'uang-tsao shen-kan pien-ch'ü hsin su-wei-ai ch'ü chi hung erh-shih-liu chün chüeh-i" (Resolution on the imperialist Kuomintang's fourth encirclement campaign, the creation of a new soviet on the Shensi-Kansu border, and the Twenty-Sixth Red Army), August 25, 1932 (BI).

44. The Chinese term *yu-chi-tui*, translated as "guerrilla," obscures essential differences between roving armed bands and guerrillas as defined in the writings of Mao Tse-tung and other theoreticians of guerrilla warfare. Liu and his men were *yu-chi-tui* in their initial ventures to incite insurrection after the 1927 split. So too were the bands of robbers and brigands who, through the centuries, were based in the hills of northern Shensi. From 1932, and particularly after 1934, the behavior of Liu's partisans appears increasingly consonant with classic guerrilla principles linked with agrarian revolution and the creation of base areas.

45. Kuan Feng, 41–44. Cf. John Rue's account of similar Central Committee criticisms of Mao Tse-tung's policies in the Kiangsi Soviet, 238–65.

46. This hesitation concerning the staying power of the partisans, one of many armies to pass through their villages, was emphasized repeatedly by Jan Myrdal's peasant informants reflecting on the revolutionary past in northern Shensi. Myrdal, 67, 79, 136.

47. Eto Shinkichi, passim; Mao Tse-tung, "Report on an Investigation into the Peasant Movement in Hunan," *SW*, I, 21–59.

48. Shensi sheng wei (Shensi Provincial Committee), "K'ai-chan yu-chi yün-tung ch'uang-tsao wei-pei hsin su-ch'ü chüeh-i (Resolution on the development of the guerrilla movement and the creation of a new Wei-pei soviet area), manuscript, June 6, 1932 (BI). The Shensi-Kansu Soviet which was established soon afterward is discussed below.

49. China International Famine Relief Commission, *Annual Reports, 1929*, 43; *1930*, 40, 65; *1931*, 8, 30; *1932*, 5–8, 61; *1933*, 9. Lucien Bianco cites a fascinating example of the incendiary effect which such "good works" often had in the rural environment. In Hopeh, peasants attacked 2,800 workers who were sent from Shantung by the International Famine Relief Commission to build a road which would permit relief work in time of famine to proceed more effectively. "Les paysans et la révolution: Chine, 1919–1949," *Politique étrangère*, 13.2–3:127 (1968).

50. Chih Fu, "San-yüan mu-ch'ien hsing-shih yü tang ling-tao ti chien-ch'a" (An investigation of the present situation and party leadership in San-yüan), *Tou-cheng yü hsüeh-hsi* (Struggle and study; Oct. 1, 1932), 6–13. This was an organ of the Northern Bureau. Yü Ch'ih, "Wo tui-yü fen-liang tou-cheng chung ts'e-lüeh shang ti ts'o-wu" (My strategic errors in the grain redistribution struggle), *Tou-cheng yü hsüeh-hsi* (Sept. 10, 1932), 28–31.

51. "Wu-ch'ing-yüan-tzu fen t'u-ti i-i yü ts'o-wu" (The significance and the errors in land redistribution in Wu-ch'ing-yüan-tzu), *Tou-cheng yü hsüeh-hsi* (Oct. 1, 1932), 15. Meng Po-ch'ien describes a highly developed and radical peasant movement, which included land redistribution, in the Wu-tzu subdistrict of San-yüan as early as 1926. It was led by a local landlord and communist Huang Tzu-wen. Meng Po-ch'ien, 40, 41.

52. "Wu-ch'ing-yüan-tzu fen t'u-ti ti i-i yü ts'o-wu," 14–17; Kuan Feng, 41. A number of specific instances are recorded in which rich peasant interests were allegedly protected at the expense of middle peasants. A rich peasant family of fourteen people, with twenty-two acres of land, cultivated seventeen acres with no hired labor. It had, however, accumulated heavy debts and claimed to be short of draught animals so that it was necessary to rent out rather than cultivate the remaining land. In this case, the partisans accepted the villagers' opinion that even 1.7 acres per person was insufficient to maintain the family's livelihood, despite the fact that soviet laws declared one acre per person ample. No action was taken to confiscate the lands or property of this family, including the land cultivated by tenants. As a result, the partisans were accused of protecting rich peasant interests.

Other examples of the rich peasant line were cited in San-yüan. It was reported that a middle peasant family with a modest amount of valley land was forced to exchange part of its holdings for slope land. The slope land required greater labor to produce only half the crops. In this case, the decision was criticized for being unjustifiably detrimental to a middle peasant family. Still another family of six with five acres, claiming to be unable to earn a living, leased the land and moved to the city. Although this land was confiscated and redistributed, the local "soviet" continued to pay the former owners half their rent. In all these instances the rich peasant mentality was said to have prevailed. These examples suggest the enormous complexity of meting out revolutionary justice under conditions of extreme deprivation as partisan forces sought to secure broad-based peasant support.

53. Kuan Feng, 41; BI, *Liang-nien lai chih chung-kuo kung-ch'an-tang* (Two years of the Chinese Communist Party), mimeograph, 1933, 100.

54. Meng Po-ch'ien, 66.

55. Meng Po-ch'ien, 63–69; *LSWTCT,* 14–16; "Chung-kung chung-yang kuan-yü kan-shen pien-ch'ü yu-chi-tui ti kung-tso chi ch'uang-tsao kan-shen pien hsin ch'ü ti chüeh-i."

56. BI, *Liang-nien lai chih chung-kuo kung-ch'an-tang,* 100; Kuan Feng, 42–45; *LSWTCT,* 15–16; Hatano, V, 667–701, "Sen-kan kosaku ni kansuru bunken" (Documents concerning Shensi-Kansu work), 677–79.

57. China International Famine Relief Commission, *Annual Reports, 1930,* 24, 28; *1931,* 30; *1932,* 5, 8; *1933,* 10, 15. Teichman, 6, 84. The completion of the Sian–Tung-kuan road is not reported; work was finished on the section between Sian and Wei-nan by November 1930.

58. BI, *Liang-nien lai chih chung-kuo kung-ch'an-tang,* 98–101; BI, *Chung-kuo kung-ch'an-tang chih t'ou-shih* (Penetration of the Chinese Communist Party), mimeograph, Apr. 1, 1935. Among the defectors were the secretary general of the provincial committee, the leading party official in the Wei-pei area, the Sian party secretary, and Tu Heng, who was concurrently political commissar of the Twenty-Sixth Red Army and head of the organization department of the Shensi party. Meng Po-ch'ien, 120. Meng points out that in 1933 the Kuomintang adopted its much vaunted "seven parts political, three parts military" policy, intensifying efforts to get communists to defect with promises of safety and jobs.

59. Hatano, V, 680–81; *LSWTCT,* 17.

60. *LSWTCT,* 18. Kao Kang's 1942 account is the only available one concerning this incident. Huang Tzu-wen reportedly proposed that the new committee be composed of Li Chieh-fu, Chang Wen-hua, Wang Lin, P'u Chien-sheng, Kao Kang, and Huang Tzu-wen. Only Kao had fought with the partisans.

61. The term "north Shensi" refers to An-ting, Ch'ing-chien, and adjacent districts which came to be known as the north Shensi base or soviet area as distinguished from the Shensi-Kansu border area. Both of these guerrilla regions are located in loess hills of the northern part of Shensi.

62. "SPCK," 1–21. I think it may be said with assurance that the unsigned report on which this account is based was written by Kuo Hung-t'ao, who joined the guerrillas as a representative of the Northern Bureau in 1934. In his polemic on party history, Kao Kang charges that in *Shen-pei tang-shih* (North Shensi party history) Kuo Hung-t'ao deliberately distorted the facts of the guerrilla movement in that area. While Kuo may in fact have taken pains to emphasize the characteristics it had in common with traditional banditry, in order to emphasize his personal contribution to its subsequent disciplined development, the account is a plausible one in terms of what we know of the early phases of the partisan movement in northern Shensi.

63. Hatano, V, 682–86. Hsi Chung-hsün was elected chairman of the Revolutionary Committee and Liu Chih-tan chairman of the Military Committee.

64. It was of course Mao alone who developed in his military writings a fully formulated and explicit guerrilla strategy. For a perceptive analysis of the strategies of roving insurgents and the necessity to develop stable base areas as the focus of guerrilla activity, see Mao's "Strategic Problems in the Anti-Japanese Guerrilla War," *SW*, II, 132–45.

65. Robert McColl has analyzed the characteristics of base areas in "A Political Geography of Revolution: China, Vietnam, and Thailand." McColl is incorrect in his insistence that a major factor in the location of base areas was their strategic location with respect to major cities (155). This was certainly not the case in northern Shensi or in the most important base areas established during the anti-Japanese war. I have seen no evidence (least of all in his data) that it was a critical determinant even in the Kiangsi period when Central Committee leadership envisioned a speedy return to the cities. Mao Tse-tung's analysis of factors which led to his choice of a site for the first base area in Chingkangshan explicitly rejects such conditions as paramount. See "The Struggle in the Ching-kang Mountains," *SW*, I, 71–104, particularly 101.

66. "SPCK," 20–26.

67. Hatano, V, 682–87.

68. *Shen-kan-ning chuan-pao*, 2.

69. "SPCK," 21–22.

70. "SPCK," 23–24. The two new regions were in the vicinity of Heng-shan, Ching-pien, and An-sai districts and in the Wu-pao, Chia-hsien region. *Shen-kan-ning chuan-pao*, 2.

71. *LSWTCT*, 22; "SPCK," 23–24. Kuomintang reports note that undesirable elements among government forces, under the pretext of destroying the guerrillas, engaged in plundering and looting. The only recourse for many poor peasants was to join the rebels for protection. This analysis conveniently ignores the positive appeals of the rebel movement but implies the development of a more broadly based peasant struggle. *Shen-kan-ning chuan-pao*, 2.

72. "SPCK," 25–26; *LSWTCT*, 22–23; Hatano, V, 485. Ma Ming-fang was chairman, and Wang Ta-ch'eng and Ts'ui T'ien-ming were vice-chairmen of the Shensi-Kansu Provisional Soviet Government. In the Northwest Work Committee, Ts'ui T'ien-fu served as secretary, Kuo Hung-t'ao as head of the organization department, and Ma Ming-fang as head of the propaganda department. Hsieh Hao-ju was the chairman of the Military Committee with Kao Kang and Liu Chih-tan vice-chairmen.

73. *LSWTCT*, 23–24. Kao Kang's is the only available account of these meetings. It is of course highly critical of Kuo Hung-t'ao and complimentary to the local partisans.

74. *LSWTCT*, 25; *Shen-kan-ning chuan-pao*, 2. The latter does not include Yen-ch'ang among the district capitals listed by Kao Kang as captured by the guerrillas. Kuo-fang pu shih-cheng-chü (Historical Office of the Department of Defense), ed., *Chiao-fei chan-shih* (History of bandit suppression wars; Taipei, 1962), XI, 990.

75. *Shen-kan-ning chuan-pao*, 2.

76. Snow, *Red Star*, 222. The guerrillas did not yet control the capitals and larger

towns in many of these twenty-two districts. Cf. Kuo-fang pu shih-cheng-chü, *Chiao-fei chan-shih,* XI, 990. The latter estimates 20,000 troops under Liu Chih-tan's command by July 1935. Snow's information seems much more plausible on this point.

77. *LSWTCT,* 28–29.

78. Cf. Mao, *SW,* IV, 171–218, "Resolution on Some Questions in the History of Our Party." The resolution was passed by the Seventh Congress in 1945 but not published until 1953 when it was included in the *Selected Works.* The accord between central and local leaders, principally Mao and Kao, leading to official agreement on the early history of the border region, is discussed further in Chapter 5. The policies attributed to Kuo, the representative of the Northern Bureau, are consistent with the Central Committee line and its critique of partisan land policies throughout the period 1931–1935, except for the issue of collectivization. I am familiar with no calls for immediate collectivization subsequent to that by Li Li-san on May 30, 1930. Li was subsequently criticized by the Comintern for advocating collectivization prematurely.

79. One deleterious side effect was later criticized by Mao as a "leftist excess." This was the sharp drop in agricultural production as a result of the dislocation of the land upheaval.

80. *LSWTCT,* 28–29. Cf. Mao's charge that the Kiangsi Soviet went down to defeat following the adventurist slogan of the Central Committee: "Do not yield a single inch of territory in the bases." "Resolution on Some Questions in the History of Our Party," *SW,* IV, 196, 201–4.

81. Hsü Hai-tung, "Shen-pei hui-shih" (Junction in north Shensi), *HCPP,* III, 181–82. The meeting date of July 25 given in Snow, *Red Star,* 223, is incorrect. Cf. Kuo-fang pu shih-cheng-chü, *Chiao-fei chan-shih,* XI, 990.

82. Hsü Hai-tung, 174–81; Meng Po-ch'ien, 136. Ch'eng and Nieh came to north Shensi with Hsü Hai-tung's army. Ch'eng, the leading party functionary with the Twenty-Fifth Army, became political commissar in the new Fifteenth Army Corps.

83. *LSWTCT,* 29; Snow, *Red Star,* 223; Hua Ying-shen, 150. Kao states that Nieh Hung-chün became head of the Northwest Military Committee at this time. Snow and Hua indicate that Liu continued to head the committee at this time.

84. *LSWTCT,* 33; Hsü Hai-tung, 182–84. The use of the blockhouse strategy is outlined in the official Kuomintang military history of the northwest campaigns. Kuo-fang pu shih-cheng-chü, *Chiao-fei chan-shih,* XI, 991.

85. *LSWTCT,* 32–33; Mao, *SW,* IV, 341, presents an identical interpretation, listing Central Committee representative Chu Li-chih as collaborating with Kuo Hung-t'ao to stage the purge. No mention is made of Nieh or Tai. Chu and Kuo are described as carrying out "the line of 'left' opportunism in political, military and organizational work."

86. BI, *Pan-nien-lai shen-kan-ning chi ch'uan-k'ang pien-ching ch'ih-fei ts'uan-jao kai-k'uang* (Red bandit disturbances during the past half year on the Shen-Kan-Ning and Szechuan-Sikang borders), 9. This dispatch, dated March 1937, lists Tai Chi-ying as head of the political department in the Northwest Soviet Government. See also *CFJP* (Dec. 10, 1941); Kasumigaseki-kai, *Gendai Chugoku jimmei jiten* (Modern Chinese biographical dictionary; Tokyo, 1962), 96, 256. Chu Li-chih in late 1941 was director of the board of trade and president of the Border Region Bank in the Shen-Kan-Ning border government. Kuo Hung-t'ao served as secretary of the Shen-Kan-Ning Party Committee, the highest party post in the area, until 1938, when he was transferred to the Shansi-Chahar-Hopeh area, where he likewise became secretary of the Party Committee. After Kuo's transfer, Kao Kang replaced his rival in the top party post in Shen-Kan-Ning and thereafter steadily increased his power within the border region as the leading figure among Shensi communists.

87. Chang Mu-t'ao's figure looms large in the first two decades of Shensi communist politics. Unfortunately, reliable information about him remains elusive. He served in 1926

as head of the political department of the Kuominchün with which he maintained a long association; he is said to have been linked closely with Li Li-san and in 1931 to have advocated a broad alliance to resist Japan. Meng Po-ch'ien also points out that Chang Kuo-t'ao, after his arrival in the Shensi base area in 1936, was rumored to be Chang Mu-t'ao's younger brother. Meng Po-ch'ien, 19, 88, 94, 136–37, 164. See *Chieh-fang* (Liberation), 29–30 (Jan. 2, 1938), for charges of Trotskyism leveled against Chang Mu-t'ao.

88. Snow, *Red Star,* 223–24; cf. Jerome Ch'en, *Mao and the Chinese Revolution,* 201.

89. The mystery concerning the identity of Mr. Chang, far from being resolved, was subsequently further complicated. In the 1968 revised and enlarged edition of *Red Star over China,* 212, Snow suggests that Chang Ching-fu may have been Chang Mu-t'ao. This interpretation seems to me unlikely in view of the fact that Meng Po-ch'ien's account, which repeatedly analyzes the role of Chang Mu-t'ao in other contexts, makes no mention of him here. It should also be noted that, according to Kao Kang, one Chang Ch'ing-fu was appointed by Chu Li-chih to the Central Committee in 1935 only to be arrested by him shortly thereafter. My tentative conclusion is that Kao Kang has correctly identified Chu Li-chih as the man responsible for the arrests. Chu remained an important official in the border region at least until 1941, when Kao Kang's power had grown to a point where he may have been able to force his transfer from the base area.

90. Meng Po-ch'ien, 151–63. Meng describes the frustration of some local leaders whose power was reduced after Mao's arrival in northern Shensi. *Shen-kan-ning shih-k'uang,* 5, also notes continued friction and the defection of local communist forces after the arrival of the Long March troops. Tensions between local guerrilla leaders and cadres arriving from the south were a source of concern throughout the subsequent decade. Although Kao Kang eventually clashed with the Mao Tse-tung leadership after 1949, Mao apparently was the central figure both in the rehabilitation of local leaders in November 1935 and in Kao's subsequent rise to national power. None of the individuals purged with Kao in 1954 was involved in the early partisan movement, although several worked closely with him during the resistance war.

91. Mao Tse-tung, "The Composition and Training of the Red Army in Earliest Days," from a report to the Central Committee of November 25, 1928. Quoted in Stuart R. Schram, *The Political Thought of Mao Tse-tung* (New York, 1963), 195–96 (italics in original).

92. James Petras describes precisely this situation in the case of the "Red Republic" of Colombia. "Surrounded by jungles and virtually inaccessible to government forays, they had their own administration. 'Red Viota' could not be defeated from outside, but the hardworking peasants and Communists became so successful in their farming that they virtually lost all interest in extending their 'good thing' to other areas, thus defeating, in a sense, their own original goals seeking agrarian reform." "Revolution and Guerrilla Movements in Latin American: Venezuela, Colombia, Guatemala and Peru," in James Petras and Maurice Zeitlin, eds., *Latin America, Reform or Revolution: A Reader* (New York, 1968), 335.

93. *SW,* I, 102. This is the report of November 25, 1928, revised for inclusion in the *Selected Works.* In the *Selected Works* it is entitled "The Struggle in the Chingkang Mountains." Cf. Jerome Ch'en's sensitive portrayal of this incident in *Mao and the Chinese Revolution,* 142–43. Since Mao's writings were in many cases extensively revised for inclusion in the *Selected Works,* the original text will be cited wherever possible. In those instances where I have been unable to obtain the original, including several items first published in *Selected Works,* this fact is noted.

94. *SW,* I, 90–100.

95. Eto Shinkichi, passim.

96. The February 7, 1930, land law is translated in Rue, 300–4. Rue (196) notes that in the face of Central Committee opposition, these slogans never again appeared in a land law of the soviet period. As we will discuss below, their spirit emerged repeatedly in the programs carried out after 1937, and particularly following the rectification movement of 1942.

97. The theoretical and practical differences between Wang and Mao have been exhaustively analyzed by John Rue, passim, particularly 254–57.

98. Snow, *Red Star,* 253–54; cf. Snow, *Random Notes on Red China* (Cambridge, 1957), 49, 60–61.

3

From Land Revolution to United Front: The Shen-Kan-Ning Soviet, 1935–1936

With the arrival of advanced units from the south in October 1935, the small and isolated guerrilla base in northern Shensi achieved national prominence as the lone remaining soviet stronghold, the new home of the top party leadership, and the focus of the Kuomintang annihilation campaign. In the next two years the communist movement not only ensured its own survival but laid the groundwork for its subsequent spectacular expansion by adopting a position as the leading advocate of a national united front to resist Japan. Under the new leadership of Mao Tse-tung, the party emerged as the most effective spokesman for patriotic sentiment at a time of mounting concern about Japanese incursions in China.

The transition to a united front policy was a complex and challenging task. Throughout 1936, conflicting policy lines coexisted within the soviet area. Eventually, it was the party's nationalistic united front stance which led to a military détente with warlord and Kuomintang armies directly threatening the soviet and prompted significant support among middle school and college students, thousands of whom shortly flocked to Yenan. Communist appeals provided a focus for nationwide pressure to end the civil war, and paved the way for the Sian Incident and the Second United Front. But in the Shensi base it was not nationalistic rhetoric but agrarian revolution, implemented widely in 1935 and developed along more moderate lines during 1936, that initially won widespread support and paved the way for the increasingly effective military and political participation of the rural population. In this chapter we will consider the role of the Shensi peasant in land revolution, the socioeconomic effects of land redistribution, and the significance of the transition to a united front policy for the formation of a viable base area.

Land Revolution: The Socioeconomic Impact

Land revolution radically altered the pattern of village life in much of the soviet area, creating the preconditions for an egalitarian social order. In the absence of adequate contemporary records of economic and political transformation in a village undergoing land revolution, we are fortunate to possess a 1939 field investigation of a township in Yen-ch'uan district. Its comprehensive data contrasting the economic life of all pre- and postrevolutionary classes provide a valuable index of the effects of the land revolution on rural life and enable us to sketch a tentative economic profile of the border region.[1]

Third Township, located directly on the road to Yenan, was the most prosperous market town in Yen-ch'uan, one of the more developed districts in northern Shensi. It was among the first areas to become engulfed in the revolution during the winter of 1934. In January 1935 a party branch was formed, followed shortly by a township government and land redistribution. Although subjected to blockade during 1936, a municipal market and four new elementary schools were established, and Third Township became the seat of party and government in Yü-chü subdistrict.

The major economic consequence of the land revolution in Third Township was to destroy large concentrations of wealth and substantially enlarge the middle peasantry by distributing the land and property of rich peasants and landlords to the poor. All hired laborers and poor peasants, comprising three-fourths of the entire township population of 321 families, were the immediate direct beneficiaries of the revolution as recipients of land. The position of the fifty former middle peasant families was more equivocal. The majority declined slightly in wealth. However, of twenty-two families classified as rich peasants in 1939, ten had risen from the middle peasantry and eight were former poor peasants.

Table 3.1 contrasts the class structure of the township prior to land revolution with its composition four years later in 1939. Over one-third of all poor peasant and hired laborer families had become middle peasants, and the landlord class was entirely eliminated. The size of the middle peasantry increased two and one-half times, while the number of poor peasants and hired laborers decreased by one-third and one-half respectively. Poor peasants and the few remaining hired laborers still constituted nearly half the population, but their economic lot was substantially improved.

Table 3.1

Class Composition of the 321 Families in Third Township

Class	Prerevolution (January 1935)		Postrevolution (December 1939)	
	Number	Percent	Number	Percent
Hired laborer	31	9.6	15	4.9
Poor peasant[a]	204	63.7	136	42.6
Middle peasant	50	15.6	123	38.2
Rich peasant	16	4.9	22	7.0
Landlord	12	3.8	0	0
Worker	3	0.9	7	2.0
Small merchant	1	0.3	7	2.0
Vagrant	4	1.2	3	0.9
Spirit medium	0	0	3	0.9
Intellectual[b]	0	0	5	1.5

Source: Yang Ying-chieh, "Yen-ch'uan hsien yü-chü ch'ü san-hsiang ti chieh-chi kuan-hsi chi jen-min sheng-huo" (Class relations and the people's livelihood in the Third Township of Yü-chü subdistrict in Yen-ch'uan district), *Kung-ch'an-tang jen* (The communist), 3:51–95 (December 1939).

Notes:

[a]The category "poor peasant" includes tenants but not hired laborers, the "rural proletariat."

[b]"Intellectuals" were elementary school teachers.

Accounts from a poorer and less populated area not far from Yenan reinforce these impressions of the economic impact of land revolution. The ten families living in the hamlet of Liu Ling divided the land, allotting shares to each family, including the landlord, on the basis of family size. One family of nine reportedly received seventeen acres; another had four acres of fertile valley land and seventeen acres of hill land; and a third received three acres of the best land in the valley.[2] It was the tendency for most families to reach or approach middle peasant status—still a life of severe poverty but free from tenancy, debt, and imminent starvation—which constituted the central economic achievement of the land revolution. The entire class balance shifted toward the center with the elimination of extremes of wealth and poverty as well as gross forms of exploitation. Four years afterward, the pattern of economic equality established during the revolution had been modified only in minor respects and few changes in landownership had occurred.

Detailed data on the prerevolutionary status of twelve landlord and rich peasant families comprising the elite of one administrative village (*hsing-cheng ts'un*) in Third Township reveal both their dominance over the primitive village economy and the fact that none approached the affluence of the leading landlord families in northern Shensi.[3] The landholdings of these twelve families ranged from 60 to 135 acres. The data on landownership indirectly suggest the importance of political factors and personal relationships in determining class at the height of the land revolution. Classification as a landlord could bring death and resulted at the very least in confiscation of land and property. The two families which were classified as landlords for whom statistics are available were actually among the smallest landowners of the twelve, with sixty-three and sixty-five acres of land respectively. Nor is there indication of their greater wealth or exploitation in comparison to others classified as rich peasants. In addition, four of the families classified as rich peasants in 1939 were landlords or rich peasants prior to land revolution. They were able to retain some but not all of their wealth during the land upheaval.

The majority of these landlord and rich peasant families prior to the revolution possessed an ox, a donkey, and a horse, but the wealthiest owned no more than three of any of these animals. In Third Township sheep were a major index of prosperity, and nearly all these families owned upwards of 100, with the largest flock numbering 220. One full-time hired laborer was employed in each instance with the exception of two rich peasants who hired two and three persons respectively. They had made fairly substantial loans locally, ranging in amount from 400 to 1,100 dollars. The prerevolutionary elite in Third Township, in addition to its substantial land interests, was engaged in sheep raising, commerce, and money lending.

A few landlords were killed for counterrevolutionary activity during the revolution, although most fled. Rich peasants frequently remained and came to terms with the revolutionaries, while some left temporarily to return in 1937 after the groundwork of united front had been firmly laid and assurances of their safety granted. Some sense of the process in which the peasantry rose against entrenched landlord interests is provided in an account of the confiscation of the property of a powerful family near Yenan in 1935:

> When we turned our attention to a certain Chang Pei-yi, six hundred of the people on his estates came to the meeting and told us how he had oppressed them. It was a long meeting. We found that he had 300,000 jin of grain, 400 goats, 6 donkeys and 21 oxen. He told us that he only owned 10,000 mu, but he really owned more. He had more than 20 villages under him and received 60,000 jin a year in rents. Well, we parcelled up his land and distributed his corn and his animals and his tools and implements. We kept back part as public property to cover the expenses of the Red Army, but the rest we divided up. Chang Pei-yi himself had fled to Yenan, for he knew what his tenants would do with him if they got hold of him. But when we liberated Yenan in 1936, there was the united front against Japan, so he was able to go on living there.[4]

In a single dynamic sweep the land revolution ended domination of the economy by a small landlord-commercial elite. Rather than eliminating class distinctions entirely, it eliminated the most glaring inequalities and exploitative aspects of the old order and improved conditions for the majority of poor residents. If the most important former class distinction had differentiated the economic elite from the poor, after land revolution in 1939 the most important distinction was between poor and middle peasants, both striving to secure a meager livelihood.

Table 3.2 provides data clarifying the equalizing tendencies wrought by the redistribution of land and property in Third Township. In 1939 47 percent of the inhabitants were still classified as hired laborers or poor peasants, but many of their most oppressive economic burdens had been eliminated—perennial debt, ruinous taxation, and scarcity of good land. Although they remained locked in a cycle of poverty and economic stagnation, the major obstacles to resolving these problems were a harsh natural environment and primitive methods of production rather than exploitation by landlords, the military, or the state.

Prior to the revolution eleven of the richest families owned one-quarter of all cultivated land in Third Township. Although statistics for the seventeen remaining rich peasant and landlord families in the township are not cited, there was clearly a high concentration of landed property in the hands of these classes, probably in the neighborhood of 50 percent, including of course the most productive land.

In 1939, however, with the landlords eliminated, poor peasants had only slightly smaller per capita landholdings (2.1 acres) than middle peasants (2.4) or rich peasants (2.8). Moreover, when lands were classified as being of top, medium, or low grade, no significant differences were discerned in the quality of land owned by the various classes. The striking fact is that the remaining poor peasants, as a result of the land revolution, were scarcely deficient in land. Indeed, in the absence of additional productive power provided by draught animals or hired labor, it is doubtful whether poor peasant livelihood would have been substantially improved by an increase in landholding.

If landownership had for the most part been equalized and debt largely eliminated, the possession of draught animals and livestock provided the major index of wealth and class differentiation (see Table 3.3 on page 71). Animals had also been redistributed during the revolution, but because they remained in short supply, and because joint or cooperative ownership was not practiced, in 1939 they remained the prized exclusive assets of a minority of families. Indeed, many and probably most poor peasants, but for want of an ox, would be classified as middle peasants. Middle and rich peasants averaged just under one ox per family, compared with less than one ox for every three poor peasant families and none for hired laborers. Ownership of an ox, which was used in ploughing and opening new land, meant doubling or even tripling the area a peasant could cultivate. A man alone could cultivate seven to ten acres, but with the use of an ox he was able to farm from eighteen to forty-three acres. Rich peasants with average holdings of twenty-one acres per family usually owned an ox and thus were able to handle the bulk of the farming without hired labor. Poor and middle peasant families,

Table 3.2

Landownership, Productive Power, and Class in Third Township, December 1939[a]

Class	Number of families	Total labor power	Labor power per family	Total land in acres	Percent of land	Land per person	Land per family	Total oxen	Oxen per family
Hired laborer	15	17	1.1	58	1.5	0.97	3.6	0	0
Poor peasant	136	138.5	1.0	1,488	37.7	2.14	10.9	44	0.32
Middle peasant	123	156	1.3	1,813	46.8	2.44	14.8	119	.97
Rich peasant	22	38	1.7	465	12.0	2.77	21.2	18	.82
Other[b]	25	1.5	0	78	2.0	1.79	3.0	3	.12
Total or average	321	351	1.1	3,871	100.0	2.22	12.1	184	.60

Source: Yang Ying-chieh, "Yen-ch'uan hsien yü-chü ch'ü san-hsiang ti chieh-chi kuan-hsi chi jen-min sheng-huo" (Class relations and the people's livelihood in the Third Township of Yü-chü subdistrict in Yen-ch'uan district), *Kung-ch'an-tang jen* (The communist), 3:51–95 (December 1939).

Notes:

[a]A number of discrepancies, perhaps the result of typographical errors, are incorporated in these statistics directly from the original. For instance, the individual figures on landownership add up to 3,801 acres rather than 3,871 as given in the original and reproduced here. Percentages of landownership likewise vary slightly in a few instances.

[b]"Other" includes workers, small merchants, intellectuals (elementary school teachers), vagrants or gangsters, and spirit mediums.

Table 3.3

Livestock and Class in Third Township, December 1939

Class	Donkeys	Donkeys per family	Pigs	Pigs per family	Sheep	Sheep per family	Horses	Horses per family
Hired laborer	—	—	2	0.1	—	—	—	—
Poor peasant	54.7	.40	141	1.0	140	1.0	—	—
Middle peasant	101	.8	199	1.6	774	6.3	2	0
Rich peasant	31	1.4	52	2.4	581	26.4	—	—
Other	1.5	0.1	—	—	—	—	—	—

Source: Yang Ying-chieh, "Yen-ch'uan hsien yü-chü ch'ü san-hsiang ti chieh-chi kuan-hsi chi jen-min sheng-huo" (Class relations and the people's livelihood in the Third Township of Yü-chü subdistrict in Yen-ch'uan district), *Kung-ch'an-tang jen* (The communist), 3:51–95 (December 1939).

with an average of eleven and fifteen acres respectively, owned lands amounting to approximately their capacity for cultivation in terms of available labor and animal power. The major poor peasant hope for improving his livelihood rested no longer on the dream of owning his own land or freeing himself from the burden of debt and taxation but on saving enough to purchase an ox.

Inequalities in productive power were accentuated by the ability of rich and middle peasants to hire additional labor. Rich peasant families in Third Township hired an average of one laborer for 5.5 months in the year, and middle peasants hired an average of one laborer for 1.6 months. While these amounts seem modest, hired labor was extremely important in the planting and harvest seasons.

By 1939, although middle and rich peasants were better endowed with donkeys and sheep than their poorer neighbors, the revolution had eliminated great inequalities in the possession of these types of livestock. Among poor peasant families, 40 percent possessed a donkey compared to 82 percent of middle peasant families, and rich peasants averaged 1.4 per household. The size of sheep flocks represented one of the major differences in wealth between middle and rich peasants. With 27 sheep per family, rich peasants possessed an important supplementary source of income, although these flocks were quite small compared to the flocks of several hundred owned by prerevolutionary landlords and rich peasants. Middle and poor peasants had only six and one sheep per family respectively, but even this probably represented a substantial improvement on their prerevolutionary situation. The revolution had redistributed wealth in the form of livestock by eliminating large concentrations and aiding the poor. However, a shortage of oxen and donkeys and modest concentrations of sheep herds in middle and rich peasant hands meant that livestock rather than land provided the most clear-cut measure of differences in wealth.

The rich peasants were the most prosperous class in the postrevolutionary elite. In 1939 rich peasants owned 21 acres of land per family or 2.8 acres per person, .8 oxen, 1.4 donkeys, 2.4 pigs, and 26.4 sheep, and they hired an average of .45 laborers per year to supplement their own labor of 1.7 persons per family. Even by Chinese standards this standard of living could scarcely be considered affluent and certainly did not permit them a life of leisure. In Third Township and other areas exposed to land revolution, income and property inequality had been sharply reduced but not eliminated. The new rich peasants were the most prosperous and economically secure elements in the new order, but along with their fellow villagers they too now toiled on the land. Most significant, the new rich peasants, unlike former landlords and rich peasants, no longer constituted a dominant socioeconomic elite controlling the destinies of the poor and monopolizing military and political power.

In eliminating large concentrations of wealth, in sharply reducing the distinctions between classes, and particularly in materially aiding the hired worker and poor peasant, the experience of Third Township was typical of the broad socioeconomic leveling effects of the land revolution of 1934 to 1936 in northern Shensi. In other parts of the soviet area where there was no land shortage, the egalitarian thrust of the revolution was principally manifested in the confiscation of property and animals and the cancellation of outstanding debts. The success of land revolution swept large numbers of peasants into the revolutionary camp, yet it left unresolved basic problems which long afterward plagued the backward rural economy and challenged the ingenuity of local cadres and peasant activists. In particular, no systematic attempt was made to restructure individual family farming to rationalize and raise productivity or to prevent the recurrence of elite domination. Yet the impact of land revolution far exceeded the changes in the distribution of wealth. It transformed the sociopolitical dimensions of rural society.

Land Revolution and Mass Mobilization

The political consequences of rural revolution in Shen-Kan-Ning were immense. The domination of an elite comprised predominantly of landlords and rich peasants was destroyed. Everywhere land revolution broke the political monopoly of the rich by striking at its economic roots and creating new leadership and institutions. Not only was the land revolution critical for winning peasant confidence and active support, but in the course of struggle a new village leadership was forged and assumed authority. As the communist theoretician Po Ku told Edgar Snow in 1936, "Once land redistribution has actually occurred they begin to believe we are serious. . . . But before that they believe nothing."[5]

The communists moved swiftly to channel energies unleashed in the upheaval by coordinating it closely with drives for party membership and military recruitment and the establishment of local organs of government. In 1935 and 1936 violent revolution that combined a millennial vision of equality and prosperity with concrete measures to destroy the old order quickly served to swell the ranks of the party and army. Poor peasant youth, the most explosive element in the land revolution, not only supplied the manpower for local guerrilla and paramilitary units but began to assume leadership positions in communist-sponsored mass organizations, party branches, and local government. In Shen-Kan-Ning land upheaval held the key to peasant support. Only after substantial numbers of peasants had been activated during land revolution and the subsequent organizational drive did more abstract concepts such as a united front to oppose a remote Japanese enemy assume a place among the newly absorbed ideas.

Edgar Snow's vivid account of his talk with a group of peasants in the summer of 1936 captures much of the excitement and sense of liberation created by the revolution. After some good-natured grumbling about the shortage of goods available for purchase in the blockaded soviet area ("What can we buy with Soviet money? We can't even buy opium!"), conversation turned to the Red Army and its foes. A ragged old man with a queue who had been the most vociferous complainer then asked heatedly:

> "What happens when the Whites come? . . . They demand such and such amounts of food, and never a word about payment. If we refuse, we are arrested as Communists. If we give it to them we cannot pay the taxes. *In any case,* we cannot pay the taxes! What happens then? They take our animals to sell. Last year, when the Red Army was not here and the Whites returned, they took my two mules and my four pigs. These mules were worth $30 each, and the pigs were full grown, worth $2 each. What did they give me?
>
> "Ai-ya, ai-ya! They said I owed $80 in taxes and rent, and they allowed me $40 for my stock. They demanded $40 more. Could I get it? I had nothing else for them to steal. They wanted me to sell my daughter; it's a fact! Some of us here had to do that. Those who had no cattle and no daughters went to jail in Pao An, and plenty died from the cold. . . . "
>
> I asked this old man how much land he had.
>
> "Land?" he croaked. "There is my land," and he pointed to a hilltop patched with corn and millet and vegetables. . . .
>
> "Land here isn't worth anything unless it's valley land," he said. "We can buy a mountain like that for $25. What costs money are mules, goats, pigs, chickens, houses and tools."
>
> "Well, how much is your farm worth, for example?"
>
> He still refused to count his land worth anything at all. "You can have the house, my animals and tools for $100—with the mountain thrown in," he finally estimated.

Land, a measure of prosperity and stability, and freedom from the harsh and arbitrary exactions of the military and the tax collector were the primary gains which revolution offered to adult and elderly peasants. But the revolution carried another dynamic message, particularly to the young and spirited not yet beaten down by a life of hopelessness and grinding poverty:

But now a barefooted youth in his teens stepped up, engrossed in the discussion, and forgetful of the foreign devil. "You call these things crimes, grandfather? [Joining the Poor People's League, voting for the district Soviets, having children in the Red Army or Red schools, etc.] These are patriotic acts! Did we have a free school in Chou Chia before? Did we ever get news of the world before the Reds brought us wireless electricity? Who told us what the world is like? You say the cooperative has no cloth, but did we ever even have a cooperative before? And how about your farm, wasn't there a big mortgage on it to landlord Wang? My sister starved to death three years ago, but haven't we had plenty to eat since the Reds came? You say it's bitter, but it isn't bitter for us young people if we can learn to read! It isn't bitter for us Young Vanguards when we learn to use a rifle and fight the traitors and Japan!"[6]

Chou-chia village was located in Pao-an, the home district of Liu Chih-tan. Among the poorest sections of northern Shensi, it had been extensively exposed to revolutionary currents during years of partisan activity dating back to 1928. In 1934 land revolution swept the district, which became one of the first to be incorporated in the soviet area. To be sure, the White armies of the Kuomintang returned briefly after the land redistribution, but their rapacity apparently increased the devotion of aroused peasants to the revolution. Moreover, after the destruction of the traditional elite during land revolution, Kuomintang and warlord forces encountered increasing difficulty in creating a loyal organized nucleus in villages such as Chou-chia.

The contrasting views of the old man and the excited youth seem to me illuminating. The former, who was in fact the chairman of Chou-chia's poor people's league (p'in-min hui), had deep grievances against the old order and was among the beneficiaries of land revolution. With his meager landholdings mortgaged prior to the revolution, his economic prospects were certainly grim. By the time White armies passed through his village after the land revolution, the old man owned at least two mules and four pigs which could be confiscated— some or all of which had most likely been obtained in the recent distribution of land and property. In the summer of 1936 he again possessed livestock and tools. From his brief description, he might have been classified as a new middle peasant and possibly even a rich peasant by the minimal postrevolutionary standards which, as we have seen, were established in Third Township of Yen-ch'uan. And Pao-an was a much poorer district. The old man's account is interesting too in that it dwells on the horrors of the old regime, particularly plundering armies, rather than the accomplishments or hopes of the new. He represents an uncommon example of an elderly peasant rising to a leadership position in the course of the land revolution. In the main, it was the young who responded most vigorously and enthusiastically to the call for agrarian revolution and to the dream of building a new world.

Like the old man, the barefoot teenager dwells on concrete aspects of village economic life, but he is bursting as well with a new and unfamiliar vision of education, discovering a world that extends far beyond his village, and fighting for a cause so manifestly just and inspiring as to merit deep personal sacrifice. These were exceedingly compelling themes to peasant youth growing up in the north Shensi hills. For young men and women who responded to the call at this time much more was involved than the immediate material benefits of land revolution. Suddenly they were exposed to visions beyond the narrow confines of their isolated villages and the network of family and landlord ties which circumscribed their future. The young man in Chou-chia had three years earlier seen his sister starve to death, along with many others in the Great Northwest Famine, and we may assume that his pre-revolutionary prospects at best consisted of eking out a living and holding off his creditors, or perhaps turning to brigandage. Now education and the revolutionary movement opened extraordinary vistas to the young and vigorous.

The northern Shensi backwater initially presented formidable problems to revolutionaries seeking to rouse the peasants, among them the scattered and isolated nature of village life and a certain stoic quality of peasants who had been untouched by new ideas and aspirations, who were virtually without a glimmer of hope for their own future. But these same conditions might also cut the other way. Once the peasantry, particularly the youthful poor, could be aroused and moved to action—and in Shensi in 1935 and 1936 this occurred in the course of land revolution—commitment to the movement which had liberated them might be all the greater.

In analyzing communist efforts to mobilize the peasantry prior to the outbreak of the Sino-Japanese War, Chalmers Johnson has argued that "at the beginning of the war the Communists had virtually no interests in common with the peasants of North China. The Communists at this time were predominantly a corps of veteran military adventurers who had engaged in warfare against the National Government for a decade."[7] However, the preceding analysis of conditions in northern Shensi, as well as the work of Donald Gillin on Shansi, has shown conclusively that the communists as agrarian revolutionaries did speak directly and forcefully to the needs and desires of the peasantry prior to the war of resistance against Japan.[8]

This view receives powerful support in the writings of Japanese authorities seeking to crush guerrillas in Manchuria from 1931 and throughout North China after 1937. One vivid testimonial to the appeal of the communists' rural program is provided by Itagaki Teiji, a prefectural vice-governor in Manchuria who was extensively involved in the Japanese pacification program. Itagaki noted:

> The farmers are ignorant, but they are not so ignorant as to be unaware of the destitute condition they have fallen into. The Communists have been appealing to the masses by stressing this fact. The farmers will never follow [the communists] blindly on the basis of emotional appeals that are detached from actual life, but when the appeals are focused on actual problems concerning their livelihood, unremitting collective revolt may occur. . . .

> Even though the farmers are not moved by theoretical propaganda advocating the construction of a Communist society or the defense of the fatherland of farmers and workers—i.e., the Soviet Union—one cannot guarantee that they will not be moved when the realities of life are pointed out to them. We are not afraid of Communist propaganda; but we are worried because the material for propaganda can be found in the farmers' lives. We are not afraid of the ignition of fire; rather we are afraid of the seeping oil.[9]

The failure of the revolutionary movement to sweep to national victory during the Kiangsi period must be ascribed less to the inherent lack of appeal of agrarian revolution than to the strength of the forces of counterrevolution, including the landlords, warlords, and Kuomintang, to internal conflicts within the movement, and an inability to consolidate the gains of land redistribution.

Virtually every observer of the communist movement during the Kiangsi and Yenan periods has remarked on the predominance of youth from the lowest ranks up to the leadership. Shensi partisans from 1927 were led by young men, most of them in their early twenties and who at the time of the arrival of soldiers completing the Long March were barely thirty years of age. The party's highest-ranking leadership was dominated by men who had been students at the time of the May Fourth movement of 1919. On the eve of the outbreak of war with Japan, after more than a decade of leadership, they were still only in their mid-thirties or early forties. Edgar Snow reported that the average age of the rank and file of the Red Army in 1936 was nineteen, while that of its officers was twenty-four.[10]

Erik Erikson's insights into youth and youth movements seem to me helpful for understanding at least in part the communist appeal and success in the northwest: "Fidelity, when fully matured, is the strength of disciplined devotion. It is gained in the involvement of youth in such experiences as reveal the essence of the era they are to join—as the beneficiaries of its tradition, as the practitioners and innovators of its technology, as renewers of its ethical strength, as rebels bent on the destruction of the outlived, and as deviants with deviant commitments. This, at least, is the potential of youth in psychosocial evolution."[11] Erikson stresses the immense capacity of youth, striving to forge its own identity, for commitment either to an ongoing tradition or, if the prevailing order appears decadent or outmoded, to a radically new vision. To the extent that youth has not yet become fully enmeshed in well-defined social patterns and roles, it enjoys the freedom to contemplate other possibilities and, if presented with alternative courses, to cast caution to the winds and act decisively. In the revolutionary situation in northern Shensi many initially turned to the Robin Hood style banditry of Liu Chih-tan and eventually to peasant risings against the landlord order. For a generation of revolutionary youth in northern Shensi participation in land revolution was the decisive act in breaking the bonds that tied them to a decadent and oppressive order and in defining their involvement and leadership in the new society.

Veneration of the elderly as well as a predilection for stability contributed to the traditionally low status of youth in China. Among leaders, both in the bureaucracy and the local elite, age was an important determinant of prestige and power. However, in one area at least, positions of some responsibility (if not high esteem) were traditionally accessible to the young and vigorous; these were in the military, particularly in local defense and policy groups. Consequently, in periods of dynastic interregnum, when the importance of the military as a regulating mechanism of a society in disintegration increases, opportunities for youth to assume leadership roles in military and paramilitary organizations multiply. Rebel movements in particular, which have flourished in such periods of Chinese history, present youth with dramatic possibilities for action, power, and mobility. In times like these, including the warlord era, opportunities for rejecting the status quo and becoming rebels, or for committing oneself to its defense through participation in landlord-sponsored militia organizations, open new martial options for youth. Finally, it is precisely in times of chaos and strife that youthful strength and capacity for bold action are at a premium. In contrast, traditional leadership skills, which have slowly matured among the cultivated manipulators of the Confucian system with its emphasis on harmony, are coveted in times of stability or in the wake of chaos to restore order and maintain continuity. In 1935 and 1936 it was predominantly poor peasant youth who spearheaded agrarian revolution in thousands of villages in the soviet area and formed the backbone of peasant militia and regular Red Army forces which defended the new order.[12] Yet even as a new soviet base was created in the northwest, leadership was undergoing an agonizing reappraisal of the full range of party policies.

United Front and the Moderation of Agrarian Revolution

During the Long March, chastened by the crushing defeat of the Kiangsi Soviet and the loss of base areas throughout Central and South China, in the midst of full-scale retreat, and increasingly sensitive to the threat of Japanese domination and a powerful nationalistic reaction centered in students and soldiers, Mao Tse-tung emerged as a leading exponent of a united front with the Kuomintang. From the Tsunyi Conference which installed Mao as the party's highest leader, and with the support of Russian Returned Students who retained considerable power in party councils, he charted a course which eventually culminated in the Second United Front with the Kuomintang and abandonment of a rural strategy predicated on agrarian revolution.

The August 1, 1935, Mao-erh-kai joint declaration of the Chinese Soviet Government and the Central Committee marked the initial significant if halting steps toward united front. While sharply attacking Chiang Kai-shek and the Kuomintang, it appealed to all classes to join the communists in the fight against Japan under a "united national defense government" of all patriotic forces. The declaration expressed a willingness to collaborate with all armies, including those of the Kuomintang, which were prepared to resist Japan and which ceased to attack soviet territory.[13] The party thus held out an olive branch to those within the Kuomintang and warlord camp who were increasingly restive with Chiang's policy of "crushing the communists first and then resisting Japan."

The debate over the Second United Front had profound implications for the movement in Shensi. From 1934, at the very time that communist bases in South China were being annihilated, local partisans in northern Shensi enjoyed their greatest military victories and successfully launched agrarian revolution. The arrival of the first units from the Long March, depleted by battle, desertion, and disease, and the very fact that their base area was chosen as the new Central Soviet, must have contributed to a high sense of accomplishment among the partisans in Shensi and to the conviction that *their* course was sound. We have no direct evidence of the role Shensi partisans played in framing a united front line after the arrival of the party leadership in the northwest. Initial decisions to move toward united front had already been implemented. Moreover, there were no ranking party leaders among local partisans. Theirs was at best a subordinate role in the policy deliberations which firmly established a united front course. Indeed, the release of partisan leaders from jail and their reincorporation in the movement may have been partially contingent on their acceptance of the new line.

The debate over the Second United Front, among the most heated in the party's history, came to a head in late December 1935 during the Politburo meeting at Wa-yao-pao. After a decade of being locked in mortal combat with the Kuomintang, some party members, despite the party's grave weakness and their own strong nationalist sentiment, were understandably opposed or at least reluctant to join in embracing former enemies. This opposition was quelled. With the December 25 "Resolution on the Present Political Situation and the Party's Tasks," united front with the Kuomintang may be said to have replaced agrarian revolution as the fundamental tactical line of the communist party. Lyman Van Slyke has assessed the significance of the new line as follows: "This meant, among other things, the subordination of class struggle to fight against Japan; the determination to ally with the bourgeoisie provided it opposed Japan and did not attack the CCP; the affirmation of the CCP's hegemony and ultimate goals, coupled with a candid recognition of its present weakness; insistence upon maintaining the Red Army and territorial base as guarantees of independence; and tactical flexibility, with the strategic goal of enlisting maximum forces against an isolated enemy."[14]

Ten days prior to the Wa-yao-pao manifesto, the communists took the first concrete steps to make internal soviet policy more consonant with their united front stance. On December 15, Mao Tse-tung, as chairman of the Central Soviet Government, now reestablished in the northwest, issued guidelines for moderating the agrarian revolution. The communists thus bid directly for broader support among rich and middle peasants in the soviet area, but above all they showed in *deed* to all Chinese a willingness to compromise as a basis for united front agreement. "The rich peasants," Mao hopefully concluded, "have already modified their hostility toward the soviet revolution and begun to sympathize with anti-imperialism and land revolutionary struggle."[15] Although Mao's order affirmed both land revolution and united front, it emphasized steps to mollify the rich peasants as a concrete indication of the party's patriotic course.

The Politburo statement of December 25, incorporating both the sentiment and much of the rhetoric of Mao's earlier directive on land, represented a national commitment for unilateral steps to de-escalate the internal conflict in the interest of achieving a broad united front. The first step lay in moderating the land revolution: "The Soviet People's Republic will change its policy toward rich peasants; rich peasant property will not be confiscated, rich peasant land, except for that portion of it in feudal exploitation, regardless of whether it is under self-cultivation or whether tilled by hired labor, will not be confiscated. When land is being equally distributed in a village, rich peasants will have the right to receive the same share of land as poor and middle peasants."[16] The statement thus emphasized that the enemy in land revolution was feudal exploitation, not rich peasants as individuals or a class, for they could and must be allied with against the primary enemy, Japan. Moreover, the party matched rhetoric with prompt action in moderating the peasant revolution.

Throughout 1936 land revolution continued to spread throughout the Shen-Kan-Ning area. But as the leadership demanded increased restraint appropriate to the evolving Second United Front, local cadres were incessantly criticized for leftist excesses. These criticisms suggest the tensions between united front concerns and those of activists striving to unleash forces of peasant revolution, and the tensions between the preoccupation of central leadership with issues of national scope and the local orientation of Shensi partisan leaders. Throughout 1936 official reference was repeatedly made to resolutions of December 1935; this was designed to curb the excesses of local cadres in policy implementation.

The "Directive to All Levels of the Communist Party and Soviets on Execution of the Revised Rich Peasant Policy," issued jointly by the Central Committee and Central Soviet Government on April 4, 1936, clarifies the transitional agrarian policy and provides the fullest elaboration of alleged errors in its implementation. The party called for a review of earlier judgments, emphasizing in particular greater leniency in the classification of middle and rich peasants, and even went so far as to insist on restitution of property where injustices had occurred. In no case was redistributed land to be reclaimed from its new proprietor by the original owner. But in the event of error, provision was made for due compensation after an elaborate review by a party branch meeting, the village presidium, a mass meeting of the entire village, and finally the subdistrict land department.[17]

The April directive charged that land revolution in the Shensi-Kansu border area had dealt too harshly with rich peasants, and that even after the December resolutions "leftist" deviations continued. At the same time a warning was issued against rightists who clandestinely sought to overturn the accomplishments of the land revolution by permitting landlords or rich peasants to recover confiscated lands. The view that "in the past everything was wrong" or that "once the Central [leadership] arrives everything is changed" was sternly rejected. But after nearly a decade of constant high-level attacks on local partisans for dragging their feet in the land revolution, criticism now centered on excessive radicalism in connection with land policy.[18] The primary reason for this change was, of course, the increasing united front preoccupation of party leadership. Criticism of "leftism" represented in part the leadership's way of signaling its own shift toward a more moderate class line. But it suggests, too, continued resistance to party leadership committed to united front collaboration and the abandonment of agrarian revolution. It is in this context that the bitter attack on the Trotskyites during the years 1936 to 1938 must be understood, for the Chinese Trotskyites continued to view united front as an abandonment of the revolution through unprincipled compromise.[19]

Finally, it should be recalled that Mao Tse-tung, who stood at the pinnacle of party leadership from 1935, had long favored a relatively moderate land policy stressing preservation of the interests of middle and (at times) even rich peasants and was himself criticized for rightism throughout the Kiangsi period. With the memory of the defeat in Kiangsi still fresh, Mao sought a land policy which would elicit broad peasant support with a minimum of dislocation in the primitive rural economy upon which the Red Army depended for supplies and the peasantry for its livelihood. United front imperatives reinforced the lessons of defeat of the soviet movement in Kiangsi to produce a more moderate agrarian policy.

Throughout 1936, successive resolutions further restricted the land revolution. On July 22, the Central Committee stated unequivocally that "lands of all anti-Japanese soldiers and those involved in anti-Japanese enterprises must not be confiscated," thereby permitting even large landlords to come to terms by the simple device of enlisting a son in the Red Army. It specifically prohibited seizure of lands belonging to skilled artisans, teachers, and small merchants whose livelihood did not stem principally from tilling the soil. Small landlords and others of modest income renting out land might be permitted to retain it. Landlord-merchants, while still subject to land confiscation, could freely engage in trade. Although it stopped short of terminating land revolution entirely, the party had softened its impact considerably and spread wide its arms to embrace a broad anti-Japanese stratum within the base area.[20]

Moreover, party directives now clearly recognized for the first time that in certain areas land was not the most pressing need even of poor peasants. An internal party report in the summer of 1936, for instance, stated that in the districts of Ting-pien, Yen-ch'ih, and Huan-hsien tenancy was a secondary problem. The peasant demand for grain and animals ranked first.[21] In sections depopulated by famine or war there was even surplus (though usually marginal) land. Edgar Snow told that in areas where land was plentiful and population particularly sparse, no attempt had been made to confiscate lands of resident landlords and rich peasants, although the redivision of wasteland or land belonging to absentee landlords was common and in some cases the most fertile land was redistributed.[22]

In Shensi land revolution had been the crux of the communist program, since 1934. When terminated in January 1937, it had been carried to completion in ten to twelve districts and in significant parts of a dozen or more others comprising most of the area of northern Shensi and the Shensi-Kansu-Ninghsia border.[23] In a few districts which came under soviet control late in the civil war, and in others which were contested even after the formation of the Second United Front, the economic and political problems of landlordism remained unresolved. However, throughout most of the twenty-three districts which eventually comprised the border region, land revolution was the crucial first step in the creation of a new egalitarian order which featured large-scale peasant participation in a growing network of political and military organizations.

United Front and the New Political Order in the Northwest Soviet

The moderation of land revolution in the soviet area was the most significant of a series of measures instituted from December 1935 to bolster communist claims to national leadership. Auguring the approach implemented shortly in the proliferating anti-Japanese base areas throughout North China, the Workers and Peasants Soviet Government was changed to a Soviet People's Republic with broadened representation: "The Soviet People's Republic proclaims: It is willing to have the broad petit-bourgeois class unite with the masses in its territory. All petit-bourgeois revolutionary class elements will be given the right to vote and be elected in the Soviet."[24] Although it was almost two years before the political rights of rich peasants and landlords were formally restored, following the consolidation of the Second United Front in late 1937, the communists began to move decisively in this direction.

As the year 1936 dawned, the military situation was grave. Chiang Kai-shek's forces in combination with an assortment of warlord armies had substantially reduced the size of the base area and, with the end of winter approaching, supplies in the soviet camp were critically short. On February 20, 1936, in an effort to break out of the tightening encirclement, but above all to dramatize, make credible, and rally nationwide support for its united front appeals, 34,000 Red Army soldiers marched east across the frozen Yellow River into Shansi. They immediately appealed to the local warlord, Yen Hsi-shan, to join in fighting Japanese forces in North China and Manchuria, while simultaneously rousing the Shansi peasantry primarily through a program of agrarian revolution.

Finding his hegemony suddenly threatened by the overwhelming response of poor peasants to radical socioeconomic appeals, Yen called for full-scale mobilization to drive out the invaders. Nonetheless, communist influence continued to spread rapidly until the arrival of powerful Kuomintang reinforcements turned the tide. In April the Red Army withdrew to the soviet base in northern Shensi, bearing the fatally wounded partisan leader Liu Chih-tan with them. There had of course been no attack on the Japanese by the small force in Shansi. But the communists accomplished their united front goals, dramatizing to the nation their commitment to anti-Japanese resistance. Moreover, the Eastern Expedition enabled the Red Army to recruit 8,000 fresh troops in the Shansi countryside and to break the back of the encirclement campaign.[25]

From the summer of 1936, pressures to end the civil war and resist Japan mounted among the Kuomintang's warlord allies. In June the rebellion of Kwangtung and Kwangsi warlords demanding a united front against Japan further weakened Kuomintang capacity to pursue its anticommunist crusade at a time when warlord armies involved in the campaign in the northwest were becoming increasingly restive about Japanese encroachments.[26]

In July Mao Tse-tung, on behalf of the Central Soviet Government, issued his famous appeals to the Ko-lao-hui and the Moslems to join in a patriotic alliance against Japan. Both were major forces in the northwest and were frequently at odds with Kuomintang and warlord authorities. In his ringing praise of the Ko-lao-hui as righteous rebels, Mao recalls the heroic tradition out of which the partisan movement in northern Shensi and his own guerrilla movement in the south had developed. Here Mao is at his eloquent best as a nationalist leader, appealing to the glory of the Hans and rallying all patriots to the cause of Chinese salvation:

> Formerly, following its principles—"Restore the Han and exterminate the Ch'ing," "Strike at the rich and aid the poor"—the Ko-lao-hui participated actively in the anti-Manchu revolutionary movement in 1911. The revolution in northern Shensi has also benefited from the considerable aid, support and active participation of comrades from the Ko-lao-hui. Comrades such as Hsieh Tzu-ch'ang and Liu Chih-tan are not only leaders of the Red Army; they are also exemplary members of the Ko-lao-hui. This revolutionary spirit, these glorious feats, must be manifested even more widely in today's heroic struggle to save the country and save ourselves....
>
> The Ko-lao-hui has always been representative of the organizations of the resolute men of our nation, and of the broad masses of peasants and toilers. It has constantly been the victim of the oppression of the militarists and the bureaucrats.... In the past, you supported the restoration of the Han and the extermination of the Manchus; today we support resistance to Japan and saving the country. You support striking at the rich and helping the poor; we support striking at the local bullies and dividing up the land. You despise wealth and defend justice, and you gather together all the heroes and brave fellows in the world; we do not spare ourselves to save China and the world,

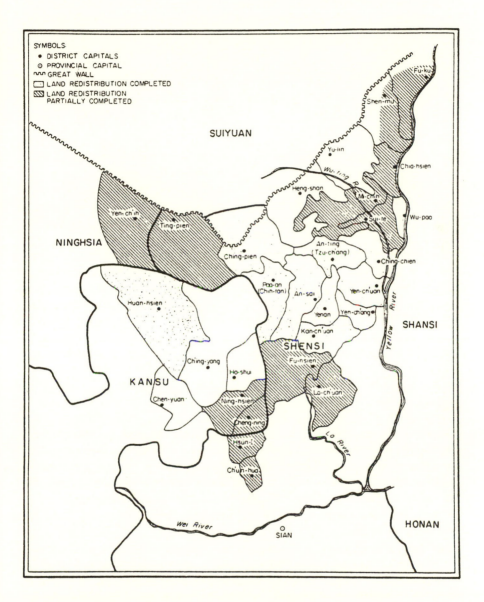

Land Revolution in the Shen-Kan-Ning Border Area

we unite the oppressed and exploited peoples and social strata of the whole world. . . . Let us constitute a close and intimate alliance of brothers, let us together defend righteousness and come to the aid of our country in its need. This is your sacred duty, and the sacred duty of the whole Chinese people![27]

During the years of struggle in Chingkangshan and afterward, Mao had recognized a common bond between revolutionaries and secret society and other armed outlaw organizations. He had consistently solicited the support of such groups despite criticisms from the party hierarchy. This reflected in part his identification with the ancient tradition of hero banditry, in part his populist sense of their revolutionary potential. Perhaps most important, Mao had an abiding faith in the voluntarist principle that all could be fundamentally reshaped in the course of struggle to become dedicated and committed revolutionaries. Peasants, soldiers, and even the bourgeoisie could transcend their class background through education and revolutionary process. His appeals for support to Moslems and secret society members in 1936 were more than the stroke of a master propagandist. They represented deep nationalist and voluntarist strains, which, as we have seen, were shared by partisan leaders in the north Shensi movement. These not only would prove decisive in constructing a communist-led nationwide resistance in the coming decade, but would continue to reverberate long after 1949 in the struggle to build a new China.

All evidence points to the fact that by the summer of 1936, the campaign to suppress the communists had reached an impasse. The Eastern Expedition into Shansi in February marked the turning point. Shortly after the communists returned to the soviet area in April, fighting between them and warlord armies was terminated although no formal agreement was announced. By the spring of 1936 Chang Hsüeh-liang, whose troops were eager to return to their Japanese-occupied Manchurian homeland, had secretly come to terms with the communists on the basis of joint support for resistance to Japanese encroachments. Edgar Snow, who was in the soviet area from June to October and spent much time at the front, reported no fighting. Rather, he noted a general spirit of camaraderie between the Red Army and its major warlord "adversaries." Finally, Red Army forces were strengthened in October 1936 by the arrival of the Second and Fourth Front Armies, which reunited all major communist units in the northwest. The armies commanded by Chang Kuo-t'ao, Ho Lung, and Chu Te had separated following the August 1935 decision at Mao-erh-kai to make north Shensi the new Central Soviet. After a year on the Szechuan-Sikang border, they now joined earlier arrivals from the Long March. Thus, long before the communists concluded a satisfactory agreement with the Kuomintang, indeed before the Sian Incident forced the Kuomintang leadership to reevaluate its position, the suppression campaign had been thwarted. There is no basis whatsoever for Kuomintang and other claims that the communists were on the verge of annihilation when they were fortuitously saved by national pressures for a Second United Front following the Sian Incident.[28]

Soviet Organization in the Northwest

The cease-fire in effect from the spring of 1936 made it possible for the communist leadership to pay increasing attention to the tasks of establishing the soviet party and government apparatus. Shortly after arriving in the northwest, the party transplanted in skeletal form the full panoply of central organs and departments from Kiangsi. At this time Shen-Kan-Ning was the only functioning soviet in China. Consequently, the Northwest Office of the Central Soviet Government, as the highest executive organ for the soviet area, incorporated the entire administrative structure of the former Central Government.

The personnel in the Soviet Government reflects substantial continuity with the Kiangsi Soviet, whose top officials, sometimes in absentia, were officially installed in identical posts in the Northwest Office established at Wa-yao-pao in late 1935. Whatever changes in real power at the highest levels of the party had taken place during the Long March or after the arrival of the troops in Shensi, there were no visible changes in the top echelons of the Soviet Government, whose personnel was as follows:

The Central Soviet Government and the Northwest Office
(December 1935 to September 1937)[29]

1. Mao Tse-tung, Chairman, Central Soviet Government.
2. Hsiang Ying and Chang Kuo-t'ao, Vice-Chairmen, Central Soviet Government.
3. Hsieh Chüeh-tsai, Secretary, Central Soviet Government.
4. Po Ku, Chairman, Northwest Office (December 1935 to summer 1937), Foreign Minister.
5. Wang Kuan-lan, Land Commissioner, Northwest Office.
6. Hsü T'e-li, Education Commissioner, Northwest Office.
7. Mao Tse-min, National Economic Commissioner, Northwest Office.
8. Lin Po-ch'ü, Finance Commissioner and, from the summer of 1937, concurrently Chairman, Northwest Office.
9. Ts'ai Shu-fan, Interior Commissioner, Northwest Office.
10. Liu Shao-ch'i, Labor Commissioner, Northwest Office.

The official Soviet Government roster in the border area was based on positions secured at the Second All-China Congress of 1934. It contains the names of three men who played no significant role in the Shen-Kan-Ning Soviet after the Long March: Hsiang Ying (who remained in South China in command of troops), Chang Kuo-t'ao (who arrived only in 1936 after earlier rejecting Mao's plan for regroupment in Shensi, and who never regained his former influence), and Liu Shao-ch'i (who did not make the Long March to the Northwest and was organizing in the White areas at this time). Available party writings, official orders, and directives of the Northwest Office and the reporting of Edgar Snow and Nym Wales in 1936 and 1937, indicate that the other top officials listed filled their respective posts. The Northwest Office was responsible for administration in the border region, but it was the Politburo, as the highest organ of the party, which held the initiative in formulating major national policy guidelines. It consisted of the following members:

Politburo Leadership, 1935 to 1937

Mao Tse-tung (Chairman)	Chou En-lai	Po Ku
Wang Chia-hsiang	Chu Te Chang	Kuo-t'ao
Lo Fu (Secretary-General of the Central Committee)		

The Politburo was elected during the Long March at Tsunyi in January 1935, and the composition of that organ reflects a balance between longtime guerrilla associates of Mao Tse-tung (Chu Te) and prominent Russian Returned Students (Po Ku, Wang Chia-hsiang, Lo Fu).[30] Chou En-lai and Chang Kuo-t'ao were not closely identified with either group. A similar balance is observable in the Soviet Government. Mao Tse-min, Liu Shao-ch'i, Hsü T'e-li, Lin Po-ch'ü, and Hsieh Chüeh-tsai were old associates of Mao, with the relationship in many instances dating back to the peasant movement period or earlier. Po Ku, who held the top post in the Northwest Office, and Wang Kuan-lan and Ts'ai Shu-fan were Russian Returned Students.

The fragmentary information which has thus far come to light on the make-up of the Soviet Government, the party, and the Red Army suggests that Mao, in the course of the Long March, emerged from the intense criticisms, policy debates, and power struggles within the party as the single most influential figure in the Chinese communist movement. At Tsunyi, he assumed the newly created posts of chairman of the Politburo and head of the party's Military Committee. From these positions and as chairman of the Central Soviet Government, a post he had held earlier in Kiangsi, Mao's voice became the most important one in the party, army, and government. Both his authority and the party's united front orientation stemmed from the internal dynamics of the communist movement in China rather than from decisions in Moscow.[31] But if Mao had recently become the party's foremost leader, his power rested on his ability to influence the consensus at the highest levels, where powerful rivals retained prominent posts. Above all it depended on his ability to produce results. With the departure of Wang Ming for Moscow prior to the Long March, Po Ku was the most prominent leader among the Russian Returned Students. At Tsunyi he was removed as secretary-general of the Central Committee. However, Po's successor was Lo Fu (Chang Wen-t'ien), another influential member of the same group. The secretary-general was the party's highest official, but after Tsunyi that officer was eclipsed in importance by the chairman of the Politburo. All available evidence suggests that, despite changes in the party alignment during the Long March, Russian Returned Students retained key positions and substantial power. The available record offers no hint that Mao and his supporters clashed with them during 1935 and 1936 over the evolving united front policy or internal soviet affairs. Rather, the evidence suggests a smooth working relationship at this time between the two groups, that they were closing ranks in the face of the challenges from "Trotskyites" opposed to the Second United Front and Chang Kuo-t'ao, who had rejected the choice of Shensi as the new base of operations.

The Northwest Office of the Soviet Government served as the border region's highest level of political authority, superseding organs formerly under the full control of local partisans. Particularly in late 1935 and early 1936, while fighting continued to rage, it proved virtually impossible to create a soviet-wide network of government offices responsive to directives from the temporary capital established at Pao-an. The Northwest Office had to depend heavily for policy implementation on exhortation and the willingness and capacity of local military units which held sway in many areas to carry out its directives. Under these circumstances a number of ambitious programs, some of them transplanted directly from Kiangsi, had to be abandoned. For instance, by January 1936, within weeks of the establishment of the Northwest Office, Wang Kuan-lan, the energetic twenty-nine-year-old Russian Returned Student who was land commissioner of the Soviet Government, issued orders to initiate a program of mutual aid (*lao-tung hu-chu-she*) in the spring planting in an effort to increase productivity. However, this earliest effort to organize cooperative labor was abortive. Under wartime conditions and without a developed cadre nucleus in the border area's isolated village communities, the effort to stimulate cooperative endeavor was quickly and quietly abandoned. Seven years would pass before the communists attempted seriously to launch the "second agrarian revolution" in the border region, whose goal was a far more ambitious restructuring of the rural economy along cooperative lines.[32]

Mao Tse-min, the younger brother of Mao Tse-tung, as head of the department of the economy, attempted to restore and develop the war-shattered economy, and to place critical sectors such as salt fields and coal mines under government administration. His detailed report of April 1936 indicates the primitiveness and the degree of disintegration of the economy. It suggests too the strenuous efforts by the new government to stimulate the economy despite the immediate priorities of war and land revolution. The vigor of these early measures underlines the fact that the party and army arrivals from Kiangsi represented a technically advanced and experienced nucleus of cadres and administrators who eventually proved most valuable in reconstructing the economy of the border area. Moreover, as Edgar Snow reports, "They brought with them (6,000 miles, over some of the world's most difficult routes) many lathes, turning machines, stampers, dies, etc. They brought dozens of Singer sewing machines, which now equip their clothing factories; they brought silver and gold from the Red mines in Szechuan; and they brought lithographing blocks and light printing machines."[33] Within a few months of their arrival, in the face of continued fighting and a tightening blockade, scarce financial resources were invested in expanding the small oil-drilling operation at Yen-ch'ang, in opening the first paper factory in the border area and a small textile mill, and in producing primitive armaments. In addition, attempts were made to revive commerce and stimulate agricultural production. While these efforts were crude and on a minuscule scale, they undoubtedly contributed to survival in the face of encirclement and blockade, and they formed the nucleus for subsequent development of the public sector of the economy.[34]

Throughout 1936, as politics at the highest levels of party and government remained focused on the transition to a united front and the creation of stable institutions, parallel developments occurred at the village level. Third Township in Yen-ch'uan again provides unique local data illustrating the relationship between land revolution and political participation. Party recruitment in Third Township occurred on a large scale in the wake of the land upheaval and throughout 1936. The majority of the 134 who had become party members in Third Township by 1939 reportedly joined because they believed in the communists' commitment to redistribute land, improve standards of living, and abolish oppression. It was found that many peasants placed faith in the party only after "bad elements" were killed, that is following the destruction of the local power structure. In participating in the land upheaval, and still more in physically attacking landlords, peasants committed themselves by their deeds (as well as in the eyes of Kuomintang and warlord authorities) to the revolution, and in some cases violence liberated them from immobilizing fears of a return to oppressive landlord rule. On one point the report is unequivocal. As late as 1939, after three years in which united front was reiterated as a fundamental principle, only one person out of the total of 134 had joined the party primarily to resist Japan, and that was in 1937 long after communist control and land revolution had been consolidated. In Shen-Kan-Ning land revolution and other socioeconomic programs, not united front, provided the focus of the mobilization of the peasantry.[35]

Prior to land redistribution in May 1935, party work and membership in Third Township were secret and involved great personal risk. The dedicated few who joined at this time did so only after successfully executing an assigned and sometimes dangerous revolutionary task, and in later years they were regarded as the most reliable party members. But after April 1935, with land revolution under way and the communists in full military control of the area, the party surfaced and recruited openly and widely. The rapid increase in membership from April 1935 to the end of 1936, the ease in joining, and the exceptionally high ratio of party members to total population, make plain the party's desire to incorporate and involve large numbers of supporters in consolidating the revolution. The emphasis at this time was on rapidly recruiting a mass party rather than developing an elite party and on an immediate willingness to participate in radical action rather than on exceptional leadership, class, or ideological qualifications.

By 1937 when membership requirements became stiffer, there were 126 party members out of a population of only 321 families, better than one in every three families.[36] One-fourth (thirty-four) were women, who in certain respects, even more than youth and the poor, formed the most oppressed and backward stratum of the society. It is probable that these figures represent an unusually high ratio of party members, reflecting the fact that Third Township was a center of revolutionary activity. A party membership figure of 8 percent exceeded the norm of approximately 2 to 3 percent, and party membership among women in many parts of the border region was rare.[37]

Of a total of 134 persons who had joined the party by 1939, 72 percent were hired laborers, poor peasants, or "workers" prior to the revolution, and almost one-fourth were middle peasants. By December 1939, as a result of the land revolution, slightly over half of the party's membership was classified as middle peasants, 10 percent were rich peasants, and only one-third were poor peasants. There were no hired laborers. Party members, drawn predominantly from the ranks of the disadvantaged in prerevolutionary Third Township, had been major beneficiaries of the land revolution. In 1939 their numbers included a disproportionately large number of new middle and rich peasants and significantly fewer poor peasants and hired laborers. If party members formed a new political elite, in Third Township they had also prospered, although they did not dominate the local economy and society in a manner comparable to that of the former elite.

Party membership in the soviet area was composed largely of former poor peasants, and hired laborers, many of whom had prospered under revolutionary auspices to the extent of becoming middle peasants. They had a powerful stake in preserving the gains of land redistribution and communist rule. Yet precisely because the egalitarian ideals of the revolution were so widely embraced, the relative prosperity enjoyed by leadership elements in some areas posed a threat to the new order. The frictions which might arise during land distribution and smolder long afterward are suggested by Jan Myrdal's account of village attitudes toward a revolutionary martyr:

> People say of Tung Yang-chen: Theirs is the biggest and finest cave in Liu Ling. It belonged to Li Hsiu-t'ang's father, Li Yu-tse. Tung Yang-chen's family was given it, because Tung Chi-hwei, Tung Yang-chen's father, was a hero and a martyr. Everybody loved Tung Chi-hwei. He did so much. He was one of the poor people's leaders and because he was beheaded, when the Red Army came back and was victorious, the biggest cave in the village was allotted to his family . . . .
>
> The Tung Yang-chens aren't so well liked. They had the best land in the valley after it was divided up. They had the biggest caves, three big caves.[38]

In the case of Tung Chi-hwei, his revolutionary comrades looked after their slain leader by providing generous economic benefits to his family, making it among the most prosperous (and most resented) families in the village.

Despite conflicts over the equitable distribution of the fruits of the revolution, the strength of the "new middle class," which included many former poor peasant activists, was an asset in consolidating the revolution and in creating a stable, functioning base area. However, its vested interests offered a potential barrier should the party attempt to carry the revolution further. The question that the party would eventually have to face was this: Could the new leadership, the young and poor activists who had joined the partisan ranks and had led and benefited from agrarian revolution, provide leadership and support changing party policies within the isolated hamlets which made up the border area? Or rather, would they succumb to the conservative tendencies inherent in their new economic status or bow to the challenge from traditional leadership elements who were routed during revolutionary upheaval but might prove more resourceful and tenacious once order was restored?

Party membership in Third Township included two people originally classified as rich peasants, four landlords, and one "vagrant" (liu-mang) who was expelled in 1939. A few of these former landlords and rich peasants may have been compelled to join during the land revolution, although most probably joined after 1937 when the Second United Front took effect. In 1939 one former landlord served as a member of the nine-man executive committee in charge of the party branch. The communists were extremely wary of traditional elite elements, but as the party's attention turned from land revolution to stabilizing the economy and the social order, it valued their literacy and leadership skills and sought to incorporate them into new organizational activities.

One final aspect of the influx of party members during and after the land revolution merits attention. While there was considerable danger of reprisal against party members if White armies returned, so long as the Red Army held sway, military and political pressures as well as the hope for personal reward figured in decisions to support or join the party. This was an inevitable consequence of the transition of party activists from partisan rebels to rulers in the soviet area, and of the destruction of the old order and the creation of the new. In time of crisis, when the party was struggling to survive and attempting to secure a popular base, membership was open to all willing to share the dangers of partisan activity. While wartime conditions prevailed, there was a premium on the energies and capacity for bravery and commitment of poor peasant youth, most of whom were stimulated to action by agrarian revolution. Party membership for these local activists meant continued exposure to revolutionary ideals and practice. The movement in action would provide the major educational and ideological training of peasant activists.

The new local leadership of peasant revolutionaries was committed to the goals of the land upheaval, which had recently provided its political baptism. In spearheading the peasant movement in their own villages and in service with local partisan forces, many had demonstrated impressive courage and leadership ability. However, from the perspective of the creation of stable political institutions to perpetuate the new social order, their deficiencies were glaring. These included a high rate of illiteracy, a total absence of administrative training or experience, and inadequate exposure to revolutionary theory. These problems were particularly serious in light of the importance which the party placed on linking isolated and remote village units in an expanding military-political network responsive to policy directives from above.

Throughout 1936 in relatively secure areas there appears to have been substantial progress in constructing a network of interrelated government and mass organizations rooted in but linked beyond the village. Yet everywhere this network remained extremely primitive, and fragmentary evidence suggests that in large regions virtual anarchy prevailed despite efforts to develop administrative institutions to supplant the authority of the army. The clearest picture of this ongoing struggle to organize and stabilize at the village level emerges from the pages of the little-known intra-party journal, *Tang ti kung-tso* (Party work), mimeographed issues of which Edgar Snow brought back from the soviet area in the fall of 1936.

Writing in the September 14 number, Che Fu made clear that although village soviets on the Kiangsi model were theoretically the governing bodies at the local level, even in the most politically advanced areas power still remained concentrated in the hands of revolutionary committees (*ko-ming wei-yüan hui*). Revolutionary committees were viewed as transitional forms of government, lying between the purely ad hoc rule by military units stationed in an area on the one hand, and the formation of soviets or elected local self-governing units representing all workers, peasants, and soldiers on the other. Military instability, the constant threat of the return of counterrevolutionary forces, prevented the holding of soviet elections in Shensi. Consequently, revolutionary committees, comprised typically of local activists as well as a few outside military personnel or cadres, constituted the interim local organization.

Local activists emerged as leaders in the course of violent land revolution and then were organized as the nucleus of the revolutionary committees. Che Fu stressed the importance of this temporal sequence and the dangers of carrying out land revolution from above (by the army alone) or of attempting to organize revolutionary committees prior to involving the masses in struggle, the process by which local leadership was to emerge. In the very act of lashing out at local landlords, men cut the ties binding them to the traditional power structure and its values of subservience to entrenched landlord power, and committed themselves to the new order. Here was the key to communist insistence, sometimes honored in the breach, that the people seize power with their own hands, that the unleashed fury of oppressed peasants rather than the organized might of the Red

Army provide the impetus for land revolution. The army provided security against resurgent landlord power and played an important role in carrying the message of land revolution to the village, but in the land upheaval its role ideally was simply to support and cooperate with the aroused local masses.[39]

Revolutionary committees provided leadership and minimal order at the village level, preserving the gains of the land revolution and ensuring against a resurgence of power by the former elite or counterrevolutionaries. This work was performed in coordination with locally based military forces, and, as it progressed, party and mass military and political organizations were simultaneously created within the village. The most important and widespread of the new mass organizations was the peasant association (*nung-min hui,* sometimes *nung-min hsieh-hui*). Instructions from the party's organization department in September 1936 stressed that not only the "rural proletariat" and poor peasants but also middle peasants should organize under the banner of the peasant association. Peasant associations, uniting the poor and middle peasant majority, were closely integrated with the revolutionary committees, which they served as a readily mobilizable base. Within the peasant association itself, a nucleus comprised of members of the "workers' organization"—probably a euphemism for the communist party—provided active leadership.[40]

Efforts were made to develop other mass organizations at this time, notably the women's association and a new united front organization known as the Anti-Japanese National Salvation Association (K'ang-jih chiu-kuo lien-ho hui). But the same report makes clear that little had as yet been accomplished in the women's movement. Caution was urged in developing a movement for women's rights at this time in view of its potentially divisive effects. The liberation of women was temporarily suspended. High priority was given instead to the creation of the National Salvation Association to spearhead the mass movement for a Second United Front; its aim was both to coordinate the campaign in the soviet area for the unification of former class enemies and to allay peasant fears of a return to the *status quo ante.* However, the single most important function of the National Salvation Association was to provide the impetus for a united front in Kuomintang-controlled areas, particularly those bordering the soviet.

As the focus of the communist drive shifted from land revolution to united front, in the autumn of 1936 orders were issued to abandon use of the name communist party at the subdistrict level and replace it with that of the Anti-Japanese National Salvation Association. Armed red guard units, organized locally and consisting of workers, peasants, and other soviet citizens (but excluding rich peasants and landlords), were styled Anti-Japanese Red Guards (K'ang-jih ch'ih-wei chün). Indeed, from late 1936, the rhetoric of class struggle gave way to that of united front, and mention of the communist party in published sources became increasingly rare, although its organization continued to develop.[41]

By late 1936, the communists had consolidated the land revolution in approximately a dozen districts, held sway in portions of ten more, and were in the process of giving institutional and administrative expression to a new political order. A growing network of party, government, and mass organizations had begun in the most secure and politically advanced areas to replace institutions that had been shaped by decades of anarchy under warlord hegemony. These developments were suddenly cast in a new perspective by a series of startling events at Sian in the final weeks of 1936.

The Sian Incident and the Second United Front

Pressures for cessation of the anticommunist military campaign and creation of a nationwide alliance against Japan mounted steadily from the latter half of 1935, particularly among the military, students, and the bourgeoisie. The National Salvation movement launched in the spring of 1936, following massive student demonstrations in December 1935 demanding internal peace and resistance against Japanese encroachments, provided a focal point for united front activity. The arrest of seven of its most prominent leaders (the "Seven Gentlemen") in a crackdown by Chiang Kai-shek's Nanking government provided the movement with a new cause célèbre in the autumn. As popular demand for united front continued to grow, it became abundantly clear that no possibility existed for rapid suppression of the communist movement.

Despite mounting Japanese pressures and disaffection within his own military and political camp, through the autumn of 1936 Chiang Kai-shek remained adamant about crushing the communists. But as Chiang prepared to announce the launching of a new suppression campaign on December 12, 1936, he was suddenly detained in Sian by his subordinate generals Chang Hsüeh-liang and Yang Hu-ch'eng. The Sian Incident has been viewed by many as the critical turning point in modern Chinese history, marking the apogee of Kuomintang power prior to its demise in the war against Japan as well as creating extraordinary opportunities for a communist movement to spearhead a mass nationalist movement. While this view tends to exaggerate communist weakness in the autumn of 1936 and to disregard the powerful trends already set in motion for the formation of a united front, the Sian Incident clearly was decisive in halting the civil war which had raged for almost a decade after the demise of the First United Front.

In the next two weeks, while Chiang was detained in Sian, secret negotiations between his captors and representatives of the Kuomintang and the communist party centered on the cessation of civil war and the formation of a united front against Japan, the primary aims of the dissident generals. This was also the time of the first prolonged discussions between a communist delegation led by Chou En-lai and Kuomintang representatives, who included T.V. Soong and W.H. Donald. On Christmas Day 1936 agreement was reached allowing Chiang to return to Nanking.[42]

Chiang Kai-shek emerged from captivity not only with his prestige untarnished but with the aura of a national hero. He shortly found himself at the head of a national movement to resist Japanese encroachment and not, as previously, the leader of a crusade to rid China permanently of communism. Whatever assurances he had given in private, Chiang publicly made no written or oral commitment to terminate the civil war and support a united front. However, immediately upon his release, in January 1937, a major stride was taken toward rapprochement with a verbal agreement to halt fighting and maintain existing positions in the Shen-Kan-Ning Soviet area. Thereafter both sides, in word and act, edged cautiously toward implementation of the Second Kuomintang–Communist United Front. More than half a year of tortuous negotiations lay ahead before acceptable terms were finally hammered out in late summer. Even then it required the atmosphere of crisis following the Marco Polo Bridge Incident of July 7, subsequently regarded as the outbreak of the Sino-Japanese War, and the dire military threat to the Kuomintang position in North China to produce a final accord. However, in the end the agreement virtually mirrored the proposal advanced in the communists' February 10 telegram to the Third Plenary Session of the Kuomintang's Central Executive Committee:

> (1) All over the country the policy of armed insurrection for overthrowing the National Government will be discontinued;
> (2) The workers' and peasants' democratic government will be renamed as the government of the special region of the Republic of China, and the Red Army will be designated as a unit of the National Revolutionary Army, and will accept guidance directly from the Central government in Nanking and its Military Council respectively;
> (3) In the areas under the government of the special region, a thoroughly democratic system based on universal suffrage will be put into effect;
> (4) The policy of confiscating the land of the landlords will be discontinued and the common programme of the Anti-Japanese National United Front resolutely carried out.[43]

In return for these concessions, the communists set forth their own conditions: cessation of the civil war; guarantees of democratic rights; summoning a conference of representatives of all parties and armies to unite for national salvation; immediate preparations to resist Japan; and improvement of the people's livelihood. Without pausing for acceptance or even acknowledgment, the communists in early 1937 unilaterally implemented their united front proposals. Although land redistribution may in fact have been halted by late 1936, in March 1937 formal assurance was given that it would not be resumed. Moreover, the communists set in motion machinery for replacing the soviet with a Shensi-Kansu-Ninghsia Special Region of the National Government, which was proclaimed as a model united front government based on universal elections by all "patriotic elements" regardless of class.[44]

In the years 1935 and 1936 a small and peripheral partisan struggle in the remote northwest became the focus of national efforts to generate revolution.

With the development of the Second United Front in 1937, and particularly with the subsequent creation of a network of resistance base areas throughout North China, the communists appealed to all classes on the basis of anti-Japanese nationalist fervor.

Chalmers Johnson has argued that communist success in the countryside was predicated on peasant nationalism that sprang directly from the dislocation and suffering inflicted by Japanese attacks. In this view, the communists merely filled a leadership vacuum created by the flight of Kuomintang and warlord forces and the landlord interests they supported. The political windfall produced by the Japanese invasion enabled the communists to march at the head of a mass nationalist movement based on the unification of all anti-Japanese classes.[45]

This interpretation correctly focuses on the relationship between the communist movement and the peasant as the critical factor in people's war. In attempting to define that bond exclusively in terms of nationalism, however, it ignores central features of the wartime resistance movement. The Second United Front was crucial in winning the support, or at least the tolerance, of the urban bourgeoisie and substantial segments of the landlord-commercial elite in the countryside. But such appeals were effective in securing active peasant support only when linked to a program focused on rural problems. The ability of the communist party to transform its program of agrarian revolution in accordance with united front wartime imperatives while leading a bold and creative attack on problems of rural oppression and disintegration is the hallmark of the Yenan period. In the resistance war a peasant revolution was transformed into a national revolution, and a people's war was directed simultaneously against Japanese imperialism and the root problems of rural society.

Notes

1. Yang Ying-chieh, "Yen-ch'uan hsien yü-chü ch'ü san hsiang ti chieh-chi kuan-hsi chi jen-min sheng-huo" (Class relations and the people's livelihood in the Third Township of Yü-chü subdistrict in Yen-ch'uan district), *Kung-ch'an-tang jen* (The communist), 3:51–75 (December 1939). *Kung-ch'an-tang jen* was circulated internally among ranking party cadres. The criteria used in defining class, unfortunately, are not strictly specified; nevertheless the economic data presented produce a relatively clear picture of the class structure.

2. Myrdal, 80, 87–88, 130.

3. Cf. the discussion in Chapter 1 of the powerful Ma clan landlords living in Mi-chih.

4. Myrdal, 50–51.

5. Snow, *Random Notes,* 19.

6. Snow, *Red Star,* 261–64.

7. Chalmers A. Johnson, *Peasant Nationalism and Communist Power: The Emergence of Revolutionary China, 1937–1945* (Stanford, 1962), 72.

8. Cf. Donald Gillin's analysis of the communist movement in Shansi in early 1936. "'Peasant Nationalism' in the History of Chinese Communism," *Journal of Asian Studies,* 23. 2:271–77 (February 1964).

9. Itagaki Teiji, "Personal Reflections," in Office of Information, Department of General Affairs, Council of State (Manchukuo), *Senbu Geppo* (Pacification monthly report), 4.4

(April 1939). Quoted in Chong-sik Lee, *Counterinsurgency in Manchuria: The Japanese Experience, 1931–1940,* Rand Corporation Memorandum RM–5012-ARPA (1967), 34.

10. Snow, *Red Star,* 279–80, 362–70; cf. Nym Wales, *Inside Red China* (New York, 1939), 33–43, 97–109; Claire and William Band, *Two Years with the Chinese Communists* (New Haven, 1948), 321–22.

11. Erik H. Erikson, "Youth: Fidelity and Diversity," in Erikson, ed., *The Challenge of Youth* (New York, 1965), 22–23.

12. Robert M. Marsh, *The Mandarins: The Circulation of Elites in China, 1600–1900* (Glencoe, 1961), 164–74; Franz Schurmann, *Ideology and Organization in Communist China* (Berkeley, 1966), 409.

13. Lyman P. Van Slyke, *Enemies and Friends: The United Front in Chinese Communist History* (Stanford, 1967), 55–59.

14. Van Slyke, *Enemies and Friends,* 59. BI, Chung-kung chung-yang cheng-chih chu (Politburo of the Chinese Communist Party), "Mu-ch'ien cheng-chih hsing-shih yü tang ti jen-wu" (The present political situation and the party's tasks), manuscript, Dec. 25, 1936. The resolution is translated with significant alterations in *SW,* I, 328–30. Cf. Mao's report of Dec. 27, 1935, "On the Tactics of Fighting Japanese Imperialism," *SW,* I, 153–74.

15. "Chung-hua su-wei-ai kung-ho-kuo chung-yang cheng-fu chih-hsing wei-yüan hui ming-ling (Order of the Executive Committee of the Chinese Soviet Republic), manuscript, signed by Mao Tse-tung, Dec. 15, 1935 (Harvard-Yenching Library).

16. BI, Chung-kung chung-yang cheng-chih chu, "Mu-ch'ien hsing-shih."

17. Chung-hua su-wei-ai jen-min kung-ho-kuo chung-yang cheng-fu hsi-pei pan-shih-ch'u (Northwest Office of the Central Government of the Chinese People's Soviet Republic), "Kuan-yü chih-hsing kai-pien fu nung ts'e-lueh chi ko-chi kung-ch'an-tang yü su-wei-ai ti chih-shih" (Instructions to all communist party branches and soviets on the execution of the revised policy concerning rich peasants), manuscript, April 4, 1936 (Hoover Institution).

18. Cf. the following brief recollection of a local military commander on the strategic shift in this period: "Chairman Mao came to us and spoke of the necessity for forming a united front. The Central Committee now stopped our activities against the landowners. They insisted that we have been guilty of departing from the correct revolutionary way, so we re-investigated the true class circumstances of every family. We had been far too strict, we were told. We were now to fight shoulder-to-shoulder even with landlords." Myrdal, 56.

19. Nym Wales, *My Yenan Notebooks* (Madison, Conn., privately distributed, 1961), 97. This account reflects the strong tensions between the united front wing and its "Trotskyite" detractors within and outside the communist party during 1936 and 1937. These tensions were alleviated but by no means eliminated by the outbreak of full-scale hostilities with Japan in the summer of 1937.

20. "Kuan-yü t'u-ti cheng-ts'e ti chih-shih" (Directive on land policy), in Yü Ch'i, comp., *Shih-lun hsüan-chi* (Collection of current documents; Shang-hai, 1937).

21. Che Fu, "Kuan-yü hsin-ch'ü kung-tso chung ti chi-ko wen-t'i" (Some problems concerning work in the new areas), *Tang ti kung-tso* (Party work), 12:24–40 (Sept. 14, 1936). The article is dated August 20.

22. Snow, *Red Star,* 239.

23. An article in *CFJP* (Nov. 15, 1941) listed the following fifteen districts as having completed land redistribution: Yenan, Kan-ch'uan, An-sai, Pao-an, Yen-ch'ang, Yen-ch'uan, Huan-hsien, An-ting, Ching-pien, Ch'ing-chien, Ch'ü-tzu, Ku-lin, Shen-fu, Wu-pao, and Hua-ch'ih. Ten others were identified as having completed partial redistribution: Fu-hsien, Sui-te, Mi-chih, Chia-hsien, Ting-pien, Yen-ch'ih, Hsin-cheng, Hsin-ning, Ch'ih-shui, and Ch'un-hua. However, of these twenty-five districts, seven were newly created by dividing and amalgamating existing districts. Of the fifteen districts in

which land redistribution was reportedly completed, eleven were in existence in 1936 and four were subsequently created. A Kuomintang intelligence report, BI, *Chung-kung ti ching-chi cheng-ts'e* (Chinese communist economic policy), 20, states that land redistribution was completed in seven of those districts claimed by the soviet. It lists twelve others in which partial redistribution occurred, including six which were not included in the communist list. The Nationalist report differs in part because it includes districts which were not eventually incorporated in the border region and because it was based on the old boundaries rather than those subsequently adopted by the new administration.

24. BI, Chung-kung chung-yang cheng-chih chu, "Mu-ch'ien hsing-shih."

25. Donald Gillin, *Warlord: Yen Hsi-shan in Shansi Province, 1911–1949* (Princeton, 1967), 218–28.

26. Kuo-fang pu shih-cheng-chü, *Chiao-fei chan-shih*, 995–96; Van Slyke, *Enemies and Friends*, 64; Clubb, *Twentieth Century China*, 204–5.

27. "Appeal of the Central Soviet Government to the Ko-lao-hui," signed by Mao Tse-tung as Chairman of the Central Government of the Chinese People's Soviet Republic, July 15, 1936. The translation is Stuart Schram's in his article, "Mao Tse-tung and Secret Societies," *The China Quarterly*, 27:12 (July–September 1966).

28. Snow, *Red Star*, 370–78. The military stalemate in the soviet area is clearly reflected in a contemporary Kuomintang intelligence report concerning the period July to December 1936, *Shen-kan-ning chi ch'uan-k'ang kai-kuang*, 5–10. Cf. the subsequent official Kuomintang interpretation of this period in Kuo-fang pu shih-cheng-chü, *Chiao-fei chan-shih*, 995–1002.

29. Wales, *Inside Red China*, 342–43.

30. Mao, *SW*, I, 153. The official claim is that at Tsunyi "a new leadership of the Central Committee headed by Comrade Mao Tse-tung had been established in place of the former leadership of the 'Left' opportunists."

31. Van Slyke, *Enemies and Friends*, 49–74; Rue, *Mao Tse-tung in Opposition*, 266–73; Ho Kan-chih, *A History of the Modern Chinese Revolution* (Peking, 1960), 268–70.

32. "Chung-hua su-wei-ai jen-min kung-ho-kuo chung-yang cheng-fu chu hsi-pei pan-shih-ch'u t'u-ti pu hsün-ling: Wei ch'un keng yün-tung" (An order of the land department, Northwest Office of the Central Government in the Chinese Soviet People's Republic: on the spring planting movement), manuscript, Jan. 28, 1936 (Hoover Institution). The cooperative movement in agriculture is discussed in Chapter 6.

33. Snow, *Red Star*, 267–68.

34. Mao Tse-min, "Shen-kan su-wei-ai ch'ü-yü ti ching-chi chien-she" (Economic reconstruction in the Shen-Kan Soviet area), *Tou-cheng*, 96 (Apr. 24, 1936). The development of the economy is discussed in Chapter 6.

35. Yang Ying-chieh et al., "Yen-ch'uan hsien yü-chü ch'ü san-hsiang chih-pu ti t'e-tien, tang yüan ho kan-pu" (Characteristics of party members and cadres in the party branch of Third Township, Yü-chü subdistrict in Yen-ch'uan district), *Kung-ch'an-tang jen*, 4:50–68 (January[?] 1940). The accounts of Jan Myrdal's informants confirm the importance of land revolution in generating enthusiasm for party membership, 48–49, 67–68, 80.

36. New communist party membership in Third Township, 1927 to 1939:

1927 to 1934	3
January to March 1935	11
April to December 1935	47
1936	41
1937	24
1938	7
1939	1
Total	134

37. The figure of 2 to 3 percent is extrapolated from Franz Schurmann's nationwide calculations for the 1950s. *Ideology and Organization in Communist China,* 135–36.

38. Myrdal, 95.

39. Che Fu.

40. "Chung-yang tsu-chih pu kuan-yü su-ch'ü ch'ün-chung tsu-chih ti chi-ko chüeh-ting" (Some resolutions of the Central Organization Department concerning soviet area mass organization), *Tang ti kung-tso,* 12 (Sept. 14, 1936).

41. Ibid.

42. For a detailed assessment of the Sian Incident and a guide to its voluminous journalistic and historic literature, see Van Slyke, *Enemies and Friends,* 85–106. Cf. Snow, *Random Notes,* 1–14; Charles B. McLane, *Soviet Policy and the Chinese Communists, 1931–1946* (New York, 1958), 79–90; Chiang Kai-shek, *Soviet Russia in China: A Summing-up at Seventy* (New York, 1957), 72–79; Clubb, 202–10.

43. The full text of the telegram is given in Mao, *SW,* I, 332–33, and Chiang Kai-shek, 79–80. Compare the final agreement as published by the Kuomintang Central News Agency on September 22, 1937, and translated in Brandt, *Documentary History,* 245–47.

44. The term "special region" (*t'e-ch'ü*) was replaced by early 1939 by the more widely known designation "border region" (*pien-ch'ü*).

45. Johnson, *Peasant Nationalism and Communist Power,* passim.

A Red Army sentry at an outpost in North Shensi, 1936.
(Photograph by Edgar Snow)

Mao Tse-tung addresses Red Army troops in Pao An, 1936.
(Photograph by Edgar Snow)

A 1936 photo of Mao and his second wife, Ho Tzu-chen, a former teacher who was among those who made the Long March. Mao's decision to divorce Ho and marry Chiang Ch'ing precipitated acrimonious debate in the highest levels of the Party. *(Photograph by Edgar Snow)*

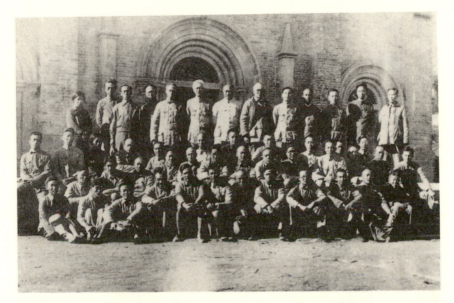

The Sixth Plenum of the Sixth Central Committee met in Yenan's large Catholic Church in October–November, 1938. Mao, reportedly armed with Stalin's ratification of his leadership of the party, clashed sharply with Wang Ming over the United Front. The participants included front row from the left: Kao Kang (2), Chu Teh (4) Liu Shao-ch'i (8) Po Ku (9), Hsiao K'o (10), Hsiang Ying (11), Hsieh Chüeh-tsai (12). Second row: P'eng Teh-hui (3), Hsü T'e-li (4), Hsü Hai-tung (7), Yang Shang-k'un (8), Lo Jui-ch'ing (10), Li Wei-han (11), Chu Li-chih (12). Third row: Li Fu-ch'un (1), Teng Hsiao-p'ing (5), P'eng Chen (6), Wang Ming (7), Wang Chia-hsiang (8), Chou En-lai (9). Top row; K'ang Sheng (3), Lin Po-ch'ü (6), Ho Lung (7), Po Ku (8), Ch'en Yun (9), Lin Piao (11), Mao Tse-tung (13). Party historians state that Wang Chia-hsiang transmitted Comintern approval of Mao's ascension as the top leader at this Congress during which Mao and Wang Ming repeatedly clashed.

The Politburo members who convened in Yenan on December 9 to 14, 1937, following the formation of the Shen-Kan-Ning Border Region and Wang Ming's return from the Soviet Union. Front row from the left, Hsiang Ying, Ho K'ai-feng, Wang Ming, Ch'en Yun, Liu Shao-ch'i. Rear: K'ang Sheng, P'eng Teh-huai, Lo Fu, Chang Kuo-t'ao, Lin Po-ch'ü, Po Ku, Chou En-lai, Mao Tse-tung.

Left to right: Chou En-lai, Chu Teh, John Service, Mao Tse-tung, Yeh Chien-ying in Yenan, September 1944. Diplomat John Service was in Yenan with American observers in the Dixie Mission to assess the Communist movement as a potential partner against Japan and to consider the implications of growing Communist strength for the post-war situation.

Wu Man-yu (left), the Border Region's top labor hero, and Wang Chen, commander of the 359th Brigade, famed for military production symbolic of the drive to achieve self-reliance. Wu defected to the Kuomintang occupying forces who briefly regained control over the Shen-Kan-Ning Border Region in 1947.

The writer Ting Ling and the painter Hu Man (right) and writer-poet Emi Siao (left) in Yenan. *(Photograph by Edgar Snow)*

Local partisans transport wounded fighters.

Women graduates of the Resistance Military Academy (K'ang Ta) in Northern Shensi.

A militia company carrying home-made wooden cannons. Made of elm with a three-inch bore, they were loaded with stones and scrap metal and fired by a match-lock mechanism tripped by a long string.

4

The New Democracy in the Shen-Kan-Ning Border Region, 1937–1941

Following the Sian Incident and the cessation of civil war, the border region experimented with new approaches to mass participation, local leadership, and administration. These approaches constituted New Democratic politics, which sought initially to stabilize and then gradually to transform the institutional fabric of the border region as a Second United Front model area. Building on a legacy of administrative experience in Kiangsi and other soviet areas, but conscious of the shortcomings of earlier experiments and the present imperatives of war, the new programs rapidly took shape. Moreover, in proclaiming Shen-Kan-Ning a model area, the party asserted the larger relevance of its political conception for all China. Within a year it attempted to substantiate this claim in the establishment of a growing network of bases throughout North China. But it is with the development of their prototype, and particularly the administrative and socioeconomic experiments carried out in Shen-Kan-Ning, that we are presently concerned.

Shen-Kan-Ning was not a microcosm of rural China, not even of communist-led base areas created during the war of resistance against Japan. In many respects the area was almost a caricature of twentieth-century rural China, of the growing gulf between a dynamic and dominant metropolitan culture and remote rural areas mired in oppressive tradition and hopelessness. Yet precisely for these reasons it is important for what it reveals about the possibilities for the transformation and development of the most hard-core depressed areas. Its isolated villages had long remained resistant to change engendered elsewhere through contact with the economic and ideological vanguard of the West. The vicissitudes of poverty and despair, endemic features of peasant life in late Ch'ing and Republican China, were magnified in the barren loess plateau of the border region, which was plagued by periodic famine and dominated by a succession of marauding bandits and petty warlords.

The experience of Shen-Kan-Ning was unique among wartime base areas in another important respect. It alone enjoyed relatively stable communist rule in contrast to conditions of heavy fighting which prevailed in guerrilla areas behind Japanese lines. From 1937, the communist administration in Shen-Kan-Ning was tacitly recognized by Chiang Kai-shek's National government and unchallenged by the Japanese except for repeated bombing and sporadic border skirmishes. Unlike the front-line guerrilla areas, Shen-Kan-Ning did not live under the constant hail of overwhelming enemy fire power. Here it was possible to develop a variety of political and economic programs free from the dislocation of perpetual combat.

The New Democracy, as Mao Tse-tung labeled the party's wartime program in the base areas, was shaped at its inception by preoccupation with united front. As fighting and land revolution subsided in the border region during the spring and summer of 1936, the primary concern of party leadership became the political consolidation of the soviet area. This meant principally the formation of stable institutions to combat the disintegration and arbitrary oppression characteristic of prolonged warlord rule. Stabilization substantiated communist claims to governing the border area, increased control over resources essential to the war effort, provided effective channels through which new leadership could consolidate the gains of the land revolution, and initiated the shift from land revolution to united front.

The problem of stabilization was a perennial one for successful rebels. As in earlier Chinese movements in the phase of consolidation, the party also sought to construct an elaborate administrative bureaucracy. In the wake of fighting and agrarian revolution within the border area, the abilities of the administrator and technical expert were at a premium, in contrast to the activism and revolutionary ardor which had characterized leadership during the land revolution. However, in contrast to earlier Chinese rebel movements, egalitarian and participatory features were modified, not abandoned.

During the Kiangsi period, mass participation was predicated on class struggle manifested in the land revolution. Political mobilization during the Sino-Japanese War continued to be closely related to concrete problems of rural life, including those posed by Japanese "pacification" efforts designed to crush resistance in the base areas. Consequently, wartime mobilization frequently emphasized patriotism and self-sacrifice in national rather than class terms. Its spirit of selfless dedication and the party's open willingness to cooperate with supporters of the resistance regardless of class were summed up in a slogan advanced by Mao and reiterated thereafter in many other forms: "Let those who have money give money, those who have guns give guns and those who have knowledge give knowledge."[1] From 1937 both mobilization and administrative approaches to government and other organizations developed under conditions of war nationally but vigilant peace within the Shen-Kan-Ning base area and in forms appropriate to the change from a soviet area to a special region of the National government.

After a decade of frustration and defeat nationally, the fortunes of the movement changed dramatically in the next three years. In the early years of anti-Japanese resistance, communist forces grew in strength and numbers as the base areas rapidly expanded.

Patterns of leadership and administration developed in Shen-Kan-Ning after 1937 were in significant respects characteristic of those in other base areas. However, since Shen-Kan-Ning alone enjoyed virtual sanctuary from Japanese attack throughout the war, in contrast to the fierce fighting that went on in areas behind Japanese lines, mobilization played a less central role in the political process. Moreover, Shen-Kan-Ning was the communist capital, the area of maximum party control and the home of much of its top leadership. In other base areas United Front leadership included many important noncommunist figures who wielded substantial power. Under conditions of guerrilla war and with only primitive communications linking them with Yenan, resistance bases enjoyed a high degree of autonomy. Nevertheless, despite these significant variations, a characteristic leadership style and common approaches to problems of war and rural life lent a certain unity to all the base areas. Throughout the war Yenan served as a focal point for communications as well as the party's model area, providing general direction to other base areas. Particularly after the party rectification movement of 1942, the Yenan model, which was derived in significant measure from the party's analysis of its experience in Shen-Kan-Ning, was advanced with increasing persistence and clarity for implementation elsewhere.

In the spring of 1937, when the transition from a soviet area to a special area in the Republic of China began, the communists were active in approximately twenty-five districts in north Shensi and on the Shensi-Kansu border, although the control of several districts remained disputed. Land revolution was completed in a central area of fifteen districts and partially effected in ten more. There had been no opportunity to revolutionize substantial portions of the base area which had only recently come under Red Army hegemony. At the local level military rule prevailed. Ad hoc revolutionary committees shared administrative and political power with army units in most areas.

The Northwest Office was an elaborate administrative structure transplanted from the Kiangsi Soviet to oversee the administration of the border region. By the fall of 1937 when it was replaced by the Border Region Government, it had yet to develop an effective network of offices penetrating to the district level or below. A number of schools were opened and some rudimentary government-sponsored factories and cooperative efforts were initiated, but such developments were few and tentative.

The land revolution marked the early stages of awakening and the assimilation of revolutionary ideas among the peasantry, as well as the emergence of new leadership. But the critical test of the revolution, the ability to permanently supersede the traditional elite and create a viable political economy, remained ahead. The local elite, as it had in the wake of Chinese rebellions for millennia, returned to the villages, and, in areas where land redistribution had not occurred, it retained a powerful voice in local affairs.

If Mao Tse-tung was the foremost architect of the National Anti-Japanese United Front, it was left to his fellow Hunanese Lin Po-ch'ü to direct the early phases of transforming the Shen-Kan-Ning Soviet into the embodiment of the new spirit—a model anti-Japanese area. Lin was eminently suited to the task. His revolutionary credentials, dating back to his 1905 membership in Sun Yat-sen's T'ung-meng Hui (Alliance Society) and his long association with the Kuomintang, symbolized the communists' united front posture and made him an effective link with the National government. In these tasks his authority was enhanced by his standing as a party elder (he was fifty-two years of age in 1937), a broad classical education prior to study in Japan and the Soviet Union, and his experience as an administrator. Finally he enjoyed a high standing within the party as a ranking Central Committee member, chairman of the Northwest Office of the Soviet Government, and a close associate of Mao Tse-tung since 1926 when he was Mao's superior in the Kuomintang Peasant Department.[2]

In the May 24, 1937, issue of the party journal *Chieh-fang* (Liberation), Lin set forth the basic principles which were to guide the new special area government in Shen-Kan-Ning.[3] Echoing Mao's recent pronouncements at the Congress of National Representatives of the Communist Party in early May, Lin stressed that the primary conflict confronting the Chinese people was that between China and Japan. Consequently, the struggle to overcome contradictions within Chinese society became secondary; this was expressed in a new slogan, "Everything subordinate to the war." This necessitated a fundamental shift from soviet principles of class struggle centered in the land revolution to an Anti-Japanese National United Front predicated on interclass unity and a republican government based on universal elections. Not only was this necessary but it had now become possible because elements hostile to the communists were similarly threatened by Japan and were prepared to unite against a common enemy. The new rhetoric was heavily laced with phrases from Sun Yat-sen's Three People's Principles as articulated in 1924 at the height of the First Kuomintang–Communist United Front. Nationalism, democracy, and the people's livelihood were central themes in the communist wartime appeal.[4] In numerous statements intended for internal use, party representatives made clear that they had not abandoned the class struggle entirely. For instance, in discussing the 1937 elections, an official source stated, "The class struggle continues to exist but its weapons now are the pen and the sword, not the gun; before the area of struggle was confined to the Soviet area, now it is all China."[5] Nonetheless, particularly during 1937 and 1938—the heyday of the Second United Front—national unity and resistance provided the basic thrust of communist policy. The communists emphasized a spirit of harmony and self-sacrifice in attempting to outbid the Kuomintang for nationalist support as the true republicans and direct heirs of Sun Yat-sen.

In May 1937 the party set in motion the process for creating a "new democratic system" (*hsin min-chu chih-tu*) of government.[6] Universal elections at all governing levels of the special region were to provide the core of the new government's effort to ensure broad participation. Simultaneously the bureaucracy, with primary responsibility for social and economic reform in the border area, was remodeled on the pattern of provincial administrations of the National government. In making much of Sun Yat-sen's rhetoric their own and above all in implementing reform programs on a scale unprecedented in Kuomintang China, the communists implicitly and later explicitly challenged the legitimacy of Chiang Kai-shek's claim to Sun's mantle as China's preeminent nationalist leader.

The Election of 1937 and the Second United Front

The elections and administrative reorganization carried out in Shen-Kan-Ning in the spring of 1937 were significant not only for the internal politics of the base area; they had national and international implications. Universal elections appealed to Chinese proponents of republican government within and without the Kuomintang. Even prior to the 1911 revolution, modern-minded Chinese had begun to associate great power status with democratic government, and the Kuomintang subsequently maintained its verbal commitment to democracy while ignoring its substance. Consequently elections in Shen-Kan-Ning in 1937 increased pressure on the National government to permit elections and liberalize restrictions on political activity in areas under its control.[7] By returning full political and economic rights to their former class enemies, the landlords and rich peasants, the communists simultaneously moved to utilize the administrative and leadership skills of these groups and manifested to the nation a spirit of compromise and unity. Foreigners, particularly British and American, whose governments subsequently fought and provided aid against Japan, were also impressed by democratic developments in the border area. As Edgar Snow whimsically noted, "Even missionaries who formerly saw nothing but evil in the Reds now returned from brief visits to the ex-Soviets singing the praises of the 'liberals' of Yenan, who had overnight 'abandoned Communism in favor of democracy.'"[8]

In Shen-Kan-Ning the second major mobilization, a peaceful one following on the heels of violent agrarian upheaval, was the election campaign of 1937. If the land revolution had destroyed significant elements of the old order, th⌄ election movement was a step toward the integration of a new polity and a new community. In it the communists sought both to harmonize broad elements of the population, including the former elite, and to establish new channels of legitimate power to ensure the economic and political gains of the revolution. Although the conception of elections would develop and be enriched in the next decade, its basic features emerged at this time. Earlier elections in the Kiangsi Soviet and in other parts of China had been restricted by class or other criteria. Now, perhaps for the first time anywhere in China, a government was to be elected on the basis of universal suffrage. The campaign became the prototype for hundreds of subsequent wartime elections.

The election law of May 12, 1937, is the earliest legislation in the language and spirit of the New Democracy. Like subsequent laws drafted during the Second United Front period, its flavor is that of Western liberal democracy with no hint of class struggle or other Marxist categories. The law established democratic principles that might apply throughout the entire nation with Shen-Kan-Ning serving as a model area for their immediate implementation. Such legislation typically was framed in the precise language of model laws drafted but never implemented by Kuomintang policy makers since the time of Sun Yat-sen.

The highest powers in the new government were officially vested in four levels of directly elected councils; these were the major legislative organs, which would in turn choose their own executive officers, ranging from the township head (hsiang-chang) up to the chairman of the Border Region Government. Four successive elections would choose representatives at the township, subdistrict, district, and regional levels.

An "electoral system of universal direct equal suffrage by secret ballot" extended voting and office-holding privileges to everyone who was at least "16 years of age, regardless of sex, religion, race, financial situation or culture."[9] The law stipulated that all political parties as well as mass organizations were entitled to nominate and campaign for their candidates. Special provisions enabled military units to select their own representatives for higher-level councils. Councils were to meet and elect officers on the following basis:

	Council Meetings	Term of Office of Council Presidents and Highest Executive
Township	every 2 months	six months
Subdisdrict	every 2 months	nine months
District	every 6 months	one year
Regional	every 12 months	two years

This first election law took effect in May 1937 even before the change from the soviet had been accomplished. The elections conducted by the department of the interior of the Soviet Government played an important role in that transformation.[10]

As Lin Po-ch'ü later observed, "The election movement is a great lesson in voting and being elected."[11] Not only was election propaganda intended to familiarize the people with a strange political phenomenon, it also reiterated the necessity for national resistance and a united front. Moreover, elections reinforced such diverse government projects as mobilizing peasants to form local self-defense units and cooperatives. In short, one of the major party goals in the election movement was to spur interest and participation in a variety of new social, political, and military institutions. The campaign provided an effective vehicle for spreading information and securing support for official policy, which many were prone to question at the time the land revolution was terminated.

In many areas which had recently come under soviet control, and particularly in those where land revolution had not occurred, elections marked the first large-scale effort to break ingrained patterns of subservience to a landlord elite. Where land redistribution had succeeded, the peasantry was called upon to abandon techniques of violent struggle in favor of a politics of class accommodation, stabilization, and civil rule, but one which would also institutionalize peasant participation and safeguard the gains of the revolution. The leadership made a concerted effort to ensure election of new "positive elements" who had risen during the land struggle, to provide a core of revolutionary cadres, and prevent renewed domination by the previously routed elite. Nevertheless, as long as the Second United Front remained in effect, the party's preoccupation with constructing a broad-based national movement of anti-Japanese resistance led it to encourage landlord and rich peasant participation in border region politics.

Before united front could become a reality throughout the border area, it was necessary to overcome opposition in local communities and even in many party branches. Fear of and hostility to the Second United Front tended to be strongest where land revolution was most successful, that is where the return of the former elite threatened the new economic and political order, and where peasants had already embraced a revolutionary political vision. The party called on those whom it had led in the land upheaval, primarily poor peasants and hired laborers, to accept concessions in the soviet area in the interests of anti-Japanese national unity and for the quid pro quo of enabling workers and peasants in other parts of China to win freedoms, including the right to vote. These were rather abstract propositions to convey to a peasant population that had not itself experienced the hardship of Japanese attack but had known landlord and warlord oppression prior to the exhilaration of land revolution.[12]

In calming peasant fears that the land revolution would be subverted, the communists insisted there would be no return of confiscated landlord property and that the old elite would never again dominate rural life. Subsequent experience, however, would reveal the extraordinary difficulty of preventing landlord domination in the isolated rural communities of the base area. The 1937 election movement illustrates a central dilemma facing communist leadership not only in Yenan but in the other wartime base areas and after 1949 as well. This was the tension between the desire to utilize the skills and influence of privileged elements, notably landlords and rich peasants, and the desire to curb their power in order to bar the threat that such groups might subvert popular interests and party power.

The massive education programs launched under the auspices of election committees during the spring and summer of 1937 were designed to stir the peasantry to political action. The ultimate goal was participation of the entire population in a political program penetrating to every township and including party, government, mass organizations, and local military units. The elections, by permitting the peasants to participate in and select a responsible government, helped overcome their fears of the political process. For most peasants this was their first election; indeed, many had probably never before heard of elections.[13]

Township elections in Pao-an, long a communist stronghold, involved elaborate preparations and coordination to sustain popular interest over the six-month period during which four different councils (one for each level of government) were to be elected. Election work began with a leadership meeting which included village heads and peasant association chairmen. After reports from the county election committee, the significance and methods of the elections were discussed, and a five-man committee was chosen to conduct the campaign. In each village the population was summoned to a meeting to learn about the elections and the Second United Front program, and discussions followed in gatherings in individual homes. Finally, with much fanfare the first election day arrived and eligible voters assembled to choose from the roster of candidates nominated by local communist party organs and peasant associations.

With their own village as the electoral unit, all candidates were well known to the voters. For this reason township elections were far more meaningful than district or regional elections; in the latter cases, the candidates were neither personal acquaintances nor, in many instances, familiar by name or reputation. Discussions concerning individual candidates, local issues, proposals for the new government, and evaluation of the old were frequently heated. Such groups as the peasant or merchant association submitted proposals ratified by their respective constituents for voter approval. In this district more than 80 percent of the eligible voters participated in township elections. This figure compared favorably with claims of a minimum of 50 percent everywhere in the border area, but was below the 90 percent reported in a few outstanding districts.

Two-thirds of the newly elected representatives attended the first council meeting to elect the township head and offer criticisms of and suggestions for the local administration. The incumbent township head was frequently subjected to bitter criticism, and in the elections which followed, thirteen out of thirty-four were defeated in bids for reelection. Most but not all of the new heads were communist nominees.[14]

Table 4.1

Class Breakdown of Councillors Elected in Yen-ch'ang, An-ting, Ku-lin, and Ch'ü-tzu Districts (in percent)

Class	District council	Subdistrict council	Township council
Worker	4	4	6
Poor peasant	65	67	71
Middle peasant	25	22	17
Rich peasant	1	2	2
Merchant	1	1	2
Intellectual	2	2	1
Landlord	2	2	1

Source: Lin Po-ch'ü, "Report on the Work of the Border Region Government to the First Regional Council," *WHHC,* 17.

Note: The category "worker" probably refers to hired farm laborers.

The single available account of a 1937 district election is from Yen-ch'ang, whose experience in the land revolution was examined in the preceding chapter. The report reflects the pageantry, reminiscent of a country festival, which was skillfully utilized to spur popular participation. Balloting climaxed a four-day election meeting in the district seat. After opening-day ceremonies which featured colorful performances by children's groups and mass organizations, the second and third days were devoted to reports and discussion as well as criticism of the government and individual officials. On the final day elections were held. The enthusiasm of the peasants was reportedly manifested in the numerous gifts of rice, meat, and melons which many brought to the election meeting.[15]

One report provides a class breakdown of the councillors elected in Yen-ch'ang, An-ting, Ku-lin, and Ch'ü-tzu districts, all of which had experienced land revolution (see Table 4.1). The percentages set forth in this breakdown suggest the party's effort to ensure leadership by poor and middle peasants in the political process. At all levels well over 90 percent of the seats were held by individuals defined as poor and middle peasants or workers. Rich peasants, landlords, merchants, and intellectuals, who comprised the traditional elite, were permitted and encouraged to hold office but efforts were made to circumscribe their power.

In elections for district magistrate, a position of considerable power, scattered reports attest to the success of "worker-peasant elements," which is suggestive of continuity with the revolutionary leadership of the soviet period. Many of these magistrates were illiterate and without administrative experience, but in their bold and committed leadership of the land upheaval they had demonstrated ability and loyalty to the revolution. They now assumed positions of local authority in civil government.[16]

The available writings concerning local elections suggest the scope and ambition of the movement. Elections were a vehicle to activate an overwhelmingly prepolitical population dispersed throughout a mountainous area in which rudimentary administration remained vested in local military forces pending the establishment of government organs. In practice many provisions of the election laws were ignored or modified. The penchant of communist leadership for drafting model legislation was coupled with a high degree of flexibility and a pragmatic approach to government. For instance, although secret ballot was stipulated, well over 90 percent of the electorate was illiterate, and thus balloting frequently was conducted openly by the raising of hands.[17] Subsequently, other voting methods, such as dropping beans into jars placed behind the candidates were improvised to circumvent the problem of illiteracy and retain a secret ballot.

The 1937 election campaign was carried out widely in approximately ten districts. However, the elaborate four-stage election process was never completed. As Japanese offensives from the summer of 1937 began to threaten all North China, official preoccupation quickly shifted from local elections to military mobilization. Elections for the border region council, which were to have climaxed the election movement, were discontinued so that it was not until 1939 that the first regional council was convened.[18] Both the enormous organizational energies devoted to the election movement and its abandonment in mid-course are characteristic of the mass-movement style of politics, which shunts aside routine procedure and legal niceties to focus on the most pressing problem of the day.

This first election campaign inaugurated New Democratic politics in the border region and served as a model for other base areas. Elective government emerged as one important dimension of a political program designed to encourage peasant participation. Election campaigns also served to legitimize a government which lacked the sanction of time and the traditional symbols of gentry and imperial rule. They provided an opportunity for a broad education in party goals, and for periodic assessment, criticism, and renewal of government. The elected councils, particularly at the township level where their members were widely known, served as constant reminders that the arbitrary power of the landlord elite had been curbed. Councils were a public forum outside the private confines of the teahouses where local landlords once congregated to air and act on local problems. Thus they were prominent symbols of a new order whose ability to resolve the pressing problems of rural life was being tested within each isolated community. These first elections began the restoration of civil order, in areas where military and informal party rule had provided only a temporary and improvised stay against the confusion of war-induced anarchy.

It should be abundantly clear that this conception of elections differs in striking aspects from both the ideal and the reality of politics in Western democracies. The election campaign emphasized popular education and participation rather than contention between independent parties and political programs. There was and could be no assumption of an enlightened or even literate electorate, still less of a broad political consensus or a stable system of government. A major function of electoral politics was to begin to create an informed and politically active population. Elections in the border region were also marked by the absence of corruption, vote buying, and manipulation by economic and political interests to further private ends.

Although the laws stipulated that all anti-Japanese parties were entitled to campaign, there was at this time but one party, the communist. Elections were predicated on the assumption of sustained communist rule, even after 1941 when electoral procedures had been considerably refined and noncommunists were more actively encouraged to hold office. This did not eliminate debate, discussion, or criticism, nor did it assure that all candidates elected were party members. Indeed, party branches had not yet been established in large areas of the border region. But it defined the grounds for discussion; these focused more often on policy *implementation* than on formulation of policy guidelines, and on the performance of individual officials and local issues where there was considerable latitude for maneuvering within established policies. Finally, elected government was never the highest authority; rather, it was but one facet of New Democratic politics in which power was shared by the party, the bureaucracy, the army, and mass organizations.

The party remained the ultimate arbiter in policy matters. If the rhetoric of the New Democracy frequently resembled that of liberal democracy, the actuality was different. But the relevant yardstick here is the Chinese political system, not that of the West. From the perspective of transitional Chinese politics, the New Democracy represented a significant stride—unmatched elsewhere in the Chinese polity or, at that time, in the entire Third World—toward creating responsible, corruption-free, and broadly based governments.[19]

Mobilization for War and the Second United Front

In the weeks following the military incident at the Marco Polo Bridge on July 7, 1937, the Sino-Japanese War began in earnest. As hopes for an acceptable peace with Japan faded and nationalist fervor rose, the prolonged negotiations between the communists and the Kuomintang at last produced an accord.

The earliest concrete achievements of the Anti-Japanese United Front reveal fundamental differences between it and the alliance of 1924–1927, the most important of which is the greater independence of the communists stemming from control of their own military force. On August 22, following Japan's advance on Shanghai, the National government officially designated the Red Army in the northwest as the Eighth Route Army and limited its size to 45,000 men.[20] The Eighth Route Army nominally came under the control of the Central government, but in fact, in the manner of the Kuomintang's warlord allies, it operated independently.

Just eighteen months earlier the advance of communist forces in the Eastern Expedition into Shansi had met the concerted opposition of Yen Hsi-shan and Kuomintang forces. However, by early September 1937, Yen faced the loss of his satrapy to advancing Japanese forces, while the Kuomintang confronted the imminent prospect of the destruction of its entire power base in coastal China. Under these circumstances, communist forces in the Shen-Kan-Ning base again crossed the Yellow River into Shansi to harass and fight the Japanese invaders— this time at the urgent request of Yen Hsi-shan and with Central government approval. The action was the first and one of the most solid achievements of the United Front. It also marked the beginning of communist expansion behind Japanese lines throughout North China, a development which became a source of increasing friction.[21]

The departure of Eighth Route Army forces for the front was followed immediately by a drive to recruit local military forces for defense of the border region. Quotas set for each district suggest that the goal was military service in his home village for every able-bodied man between the ages of eighteen and forty, and some women were reportedly organized in separate units as well. Approximately 120,000 persons were enrolled in the self-defense army throughout the entire border region, and 50,000 received special training for entry into the crack corps.[22] Mobilization combined patriotic appeals to youth with concrete benefits including tax exemption, assistance in cultivation, free schooling for dependents, and additional relief measures for dependent families.

Perhaps the most ambitious dependent aid program was substitute cultivation (*tai-keng*) of land. By 1938 there were reportedly 46,358 brigades organized throughout the border region, and in 1939 the number increased to 63,797. In 1942 in the district of Yen-ch'uan more than 8,000 acres were farmed on behalf of 2,742 military families eligible for assistance.[23]

Simultaneously, the collection of "Public Grain for National Salvation" (Chiu-kuo kung-liang) marked the first large-scale attempt to collect taxes. Particularly in the early years of the war, when administration was still rudimentary, it was collected at mass meetings through appeals for voluntary patriotic donations. The initial levies were relatively mild, and large numbers of peasants, approximately 60 percent, were exempted entirely. Under 15,000 piculs of grain, or slightly less than 3,000 tons, valued at 420,000 Chinese dollars, were reportedly collected in 1937. This was less than 2 percent of the border region's total crop. The only other levies at this time were on salt and exports, amounting to 591,000 dollars. In 1937 total government income from all internal sources was 1,191,000 dollars.[24] A critical factor in securing and sustaining popular support at this time was the extraordinarily light tax burden made possible by supplementary funds received from outside the border region, including a Central government subsidy.

The United Front on the battlefield was paralleled by Kuomintang de facto recognition of the special area status of the Shen-Kan-Ning base. Although never granted formal recognition, the transition from a soviet area to a special area or border region may be dated September 22 when official Kuomintang sources published without comment the communists' united front proposals of July 15.[25]

Basic United Front provisions for Shen-Kan-Ning were negotiated in secret in July at Lu-shan and confirmed at a December meeting in Hankow. The boundaries of the border region were defined to include twenty-three districts, several of which were not yet under complete communist control in the summer of 1937.[26] In particular the relatively rich and populous districts of the Sui-te subregion in northeast Shensi and parts of the Lung-tung area on the Shensi-Kansu border remained disputed. In 1937 parallel administrations were established in these contested districts. Central government and communist appointees served simultaneously as magistrates, each presiding over a separate local administration. The Kuomintang's *pao-chia* system of mutual surveillance and control remained in effect side by side with communist-sponsored governments at the district and township levels. Later as strains increased, periodic eruptions of fighting would occur.[27]

As part of the process of integrating the border region, its administration was patterned closely after that of a province of the Central government. It included an executive who presided over an executive committee and departments of civil affairs, finance, education, and reconstruction as well as a public security headquarters. This structure was identical with Kuomintang administration in Shensi province.[28]

A face-saving device enabled both sides to agree on the top-level personnel in the new government. The key provision installed Ting Wei-fen, a Kuomintang official, as head of the government. However, Lin Po-ch'ü, who was named his assistant, assumed the top position when "pressing obligations" prevented Ting from fulfilling his duties. In this way Lin headed the border government as he had headed the soviet and provisional border governments earlier. Appointments to the seven-man executive committee, the highest organ of government, included the other key officials already serving in the interim government: Hsü T'e-li, Kao Tzu-li, Kao Kang, Ch'eng Fang-wu, and Liu Ching-fan. As in the designation of Red Army forces as the Eighth Route Army, the communists retained a free hand in ordering their internal affairs. But other provisions of the agreement had more concrete results.

The Central government agreed to furnish 100,000 dollars per month for regional education and reconstruction, in addition to the 500,000 dollars per month it provided to maintain the Eighth Route Army. These amounts were significant in relation to the slim resources available to the communists at this time. Having pared the border region's administrative budget to 150,000 dollars annually, of which two-thirds was raised internally, much of the National government subsidy could be diverted from administration to military purposes, particularly to expanding and supplying the Eighth Route Army.[29] In the early years of the Sino-Japanese War, funds provided by the Central government enabled the communists to mobilize rapidly and keep taxation light as they attempted to consolidate and institutionalize power in the border region.

Interlocking Power: Party, Government, Army, and Mass Organizations in the Border Region

With the cessation of Kuomintang-communist fighting, the political and administrative tasks in Shen-Kan-Ning were divided among four types of organizations. These were the government, the communist party, the army, and the mass organizations. Each established independent channels of communication and command that extended from the township upward to the border region and beyond to the national level. Their functions were coordinated through formal and informal exchanges that included joint meetings, mutual campaigns, and interlocking leadership. After 1937 as the independent role of the military was curbed, the scope of party and government activity expanded rapidly, and these organizations wielded increasing power in the politics of the border area. With the most highly trained and educated staff of professional cadres, the government assumed responsibility for all state services and administration. Such functions as education, tax collection, and economic reconstruction were vested in government. Government was composed on the one hand of popularly elected councils, which in turn elected the major executives at each level of administration, and on the other of an elaborate bureaucracy or centrally appointed civil service.

The party set broad policy guidelines and ensured their implementation by government, mass organizations, and the army primarily by securing key positions in these organizations and by informally utilizing its prestige and power. The party, like the mass organizations, was responsible for mobilizing popular support for programs administered by government. It was also expected to provide leadership for government and mass organizations while eschewing dictatorial methods and monopolization of power.[30]

The border region's highest party organization was the Shen-Kan-Ning Party Committee. From 1938 when he assumed the post of secretary of the party committee, Kao Kang became the leading official responsible for the base area. When the party's Northwest Bureau was created sometime prior to 1942, Kao became its secretary, increasing his stature at the national level.[31]

A system of departments was created under the direction of the party committee at each level of administration down to the township. As of 1940, the major departments at the regional level were the secretariat, organization, propaganda, military, united front, traitor prevention, youth, and women. Most were structured for the efficient mobilization of different sectors of the population in support of party programs; they stood in contrast to functional departments of government that were charged with specific tasks such as tax collection or education. Lower levels frequently had fewer departments. For instance, the district party organization in Kuan-chung subregion had only three departments: organization, propaganda, and united front. But the trend in party as in government affairs was toward increased division of labor.[32]

Party membership reflected the heterodox social composition of the earlier revolutionary movement and the border region itself. The leadership continued to grapple with the complex and often exasperating problems of building a unified party, responsive to higher-level directives and committed to the social and economic transformation of the border region, from a predominantly peasant membership with little education or training. Many party members maintained Ko-lao-hui and Buddhist ties, as well as a deep-seated suspicion of government or other outside forms of authority.[33] After 1937, the increasing number of students, former officials, and landlords, whose primary commitment was based on adherence to the United Front, posed other problems in the party. These included conflicts between recent recruits, many of them better educated newcomers to the border region, and the predominantly peasant local cadres who had joined the party during the land revolution. Overcoming these problems, which hindered the work of all organizations functioning within the border region, continued to be a major preoccupation of party and government.[34]

Routine administration, the responsibility of government and particularly its bureaucracy, was constantly punctuated by campaigns to cope with urgent problems or to stimulate mass action and support. At such times regular bureaucratic channels were suspended or reorganized and the party and mass organizations assumed enlarged powers.

Unlike the party, which consisted of a small elite group of committed activists, mass organizations provided a framework for incorporating the entire population in the political process. At the beginning of 1938 the leading mass organizations in the border region claimed the following memberships: Workers Organization, 45,000; Youth National Salvation Association, 168,000; Women's Association, 173,000; Peasant Association, 421,000.[35] From early 1938, more than twenty mass organizations including the peasant, youth, and women's associations were consolidated into the Rear Area Enemy Resistance Association (K'ang-ti hou-yüan hui). Mass organization work focused on united front and military mobilization tasks.[36] However, information concerning the work of mass organizations after 1938 is notably sparse. One suspects that these organizations for the most part lapsed into inactivity and that their functions were taken over principally by government and party. During the land revolution and once again in the rent-reduction campaign that began in 1942, mass organizations did play important roles in popular mobilization. In between such periods of intense activity their membership and organization existed largely on paper.

The army was made up of the following local, regional, and national components: the self-defense army (tzu-wei chün), the public security forces (pao-an tui), and the Eighth Route Army units defending the base area. The self-defense army or local militia was the successor of the red guards (ch'ih-wei tui) of the soviet period. These forces, composed primarily of peasants drilling in their villages in spare time, could be mobilized in emergencies for local defense and police work or to support regular armies. By 1941, 224,355 persons reportedly participated regularly in the work of self-defense forces. Public security forces were formed initially by amalgamating partisan armies under the leadership of Liu Chih-tan with other guerrilla units which had fought earlier on behalf of land revolution. These regional forces comprised of inhabitants of the border area eventually became regular armies that constituted the backbone of border region defense and security. There was a major concentration of public security forces in each subregion. In addition, each district had a public security complement of 150 to 200 men. By 1941 80,000 men trained initially in self-defense forces or with the Youth Vanguards had been mobilized into the regular army. Many of these went to the front to fight the Japanese in North China. Finally, Eighth Route Army units were stationed on a rotating basis in the border area en route to and from the guerrilla areas. For instance, Ho Lung's 3,000-man 120th division crossed the Yellow River from Shansi in the fall of 1940 both to reinforce communist forces in Shen-Kan-Ning and to allow its men to provide a respite from combat in the war zone.[37]

Kuomintang intelligence sources estimated communist troop strength in the border region in late 1939 and early 1940 as follows: regular Eighth Route Army forces, 18,000, and public security forces, 15,000, for a total of 33,000. The report deemed the self-defense army incapable of fighting owing to a lack of weapons and training.[38] However, for defensive purposes, the militia was an important supplement to the regular armies, allowing dispatch of a larger force to North China; it also permitted a tax burden considerably smaller than that which a large standing army would entail. Public security and self-defense forces were integrated with government at every level through the public security departments and by means of officials concurrently holding military and government posts. The magistrate commanded district self-defense forces, and the head of public security forces at the subregional level often served simultaneously as party secretary.[39]

In the years after 1937 the communists erected a complex interlocking network of military and political organizations to administer the border area. At the top of the pyramid stood the imposing figure of Kao Kang. As party secretary, chief of public security, and president of the regional council, Kao united the top party, military, and government posts in his person. There is, unfortunately, a paucity of information concerning the actual workings of the party and army. On the other hand the regional government, as the showpiece of United Front politics, was extensively analyzed in the contemporary literature. Because of this abundance of data, but more importantly because of the significance of the construction of a bureaucratic administration in the development and transformation of the border region, we will consider the work of government in some detail.

Government in the Border Region, 1937 to 1941

In the period 1937 to 1941 the major aims of government included strengthening the united front image nationally by conspicuous public cooperation with all individuals regardless of class; military and political mobilization of the population and resources of the border region to ensure a flow of revenue, maintain security, and advance the war effort; stabilizing administration and initiating reform programs in such areas as education and economic reconstruction.

The election campaign and military mobilization in the latter half of 1937 provided the focus of efforts to achieve the first two goals. Simultaneously, with none of the fanfare which marked the elections, the construction of an extensive bureaucratic network to carry forward party and government programs was quietly but deliberately proceeding.

Let us consider the problems facing communist leadership in shaping an administrative and political structure appropriate to its goals and the limitations of manpower and resources in the base area. The party was firmly committed to a United Front course with Shen-Kan-Ning serving as a national model. Toward this end, it invited the traditional elite to support the resistance and help administer the area. In addition, the communists also looked to cadres who had made the Long March, to local cadres, many of whom had fought in the land revolution, and to students who flocked to Yenan from all parts of China to support the war effort. Among the cadres from the south were men of considerable administrative experience and tested party loyalty. However, in the course of the war most of these administrators were dispatched to guerrilla base areas and did not figure significantly in the administration of Shen-Kan-Ning.

The original leadership core among the local partisans enjoyed middle school or higher education, extensive revolutionary and military experience, and an intimate knowledge of local conditions. They were not, however, versed in Marxist-Leninist theory, and because the movement in Shensi had developed far from the center of communist activity prior to 1935, they were without national standing in the party hierarchy. Nevertheless, the upper echelons of partisan leadership moved relatively smoothly into positions at the highest levels of party and government in the border region, sharing power with a number of nationally prominent party leaders. On the other hand, the overwhelming majority of local activists who emerged in the course of the land revolution were illiterate peasants or soldiers whose courage and commitment had been tested under fire but who were innocent both of revolutionary ideology and of the workings of stable administration. They had acted boldly and effectively in destroying the power of the landlord elite, but were they capable of leading the way to the construction of a New Democratic and stable framework for the future transformation and reconstruction of rural life?

Finally there were the students from throughout China, drawn to the patriotic Mecca, Yenan, to contribute their talents and their lives to the struggle against

Japan. As early as February 1936, the communists called on patriotic youth from throughout the nation to enroll in the Northwest Anti-Japanese Red Army University, later known as K'ang Ta or Resistance University, to train as cadres in the resistance struggle.[40] These high school and college youths were typically from elite backgrounds. Thousands who eventually made the arduous trip to Yenan had rarely experienced hardship, knew little of the previous land revolution, and were totally unfamiliar with the problems of the border area; moreover, only a few were communist party members. Nevertheless, their education and dedication proved valuable assets. The pool of potential leaders and administrators thus consisted of people of radically different backgrounds, including class, education, geographical origin, and revolutionary experience. After 1937, all were incorporated in the machinery of government, although not, as we will observe, without friction.

Two types of cadres, distinct elites, began to form within government at this time. The bureaucracy, centered at the regional level of Yenan, maintained regular channels to the district as in Ch'ing and Nationalist China. It was staffed by educated officials capable of handling the heavy flow of paper work and reports. On the other hand, popularly elected governments and local officials, including party and military cadres at the district level and below, were overwhelmingly comprised of local activists who rose in the course of the land revolution or in subsequent mobilization campaigns. A 1943 government resolution analyzed the composition of the administration as follows:

> Ninety percent of the subdistrict and township cadres are products of the revolutionary peasant struggle and are positive elements closely linked to the masses. But generally they are deficient in cultural and intellectual development, thus limiting their ability for independent work. Moreover, their progress is greatly limited by concepts of village and family.
>
> District-level cadres likewise are of worker and peasant background (especially peasant) in a majority of cases. Forty percent received primary and middle school education, 80 percent had extensive experience in the revolutionary struggle through which they became cadres of the border region government; but their theoretical level is low and culture insufficient. They cannot avoid being narrow-minded, and are often unable to cope with the new and complex circumstances [i.e., the United Front].
>
> At the regional level more than 70 percent of the cadres have participated since the war in the program for youthful intellectuals. They have spirit and the desire to learn but are deficient in actual learning, work, and practical experience.[41]

Bureaucratic channels functioned at the regional and district levels. It was of course difficult to regularize administrations at lower levels, remote from the district capital, staffed predominantly by peasant revolutionaries, and lacking a tradition of formal government.

If the regional and the township levels exemplified respectively an administrative approach and a mobilization approach to government, the two intersected at the district level. As policy accentuated one or the other of these political styles, the shifts were most apparent and the contradictions were sharpest there. A central political issue was the control and coordination of administrative organs at the district level, the basic working level. The magistrate, the highest elected district official, and superiors in the regional government each claimed the prerogative to direct district sections. The struggle which ensued pitted national and regional concerns against local concerns; the prerogatives of specialized expertise centered in administrative officials against the power of elected officials who were frequently revolutionary activists; administrative centralization and rationalization against decentralized mobilization. The balance of power was of course continually redefined, but in the years 1937 to 1941, when the emphasis was on unity and stability, basic authority and responsibility were vested in a bureaucracy primarily responsive to directives from Yenan at the expense of elected local officials and of mobilization politics.[42] A significant corollary of this approach was the declining position of local revolutionaries vis-à-vis more experienced administrators whose skills were at a premium in a burgeoning bureaucracy.

These trends contrast sharply with the land revolution and military rule prior to 1937 and the mobilization politics which enjoyed a resurgence after 1942. To be sure, the degree of administrative formalization in the primitive conditions of the border area ought not to be exaggerated. From 1937 to 1941 government developed so rapidly that flexibility was at a premium even within the bureaucracy; mobilization continued to play a part in campaigns for production, elections, taxation, and so forth; a shortage of skills, primitive channels of communication, a lack of time-sanctioned procedures, and a dearth of supplies hampered administrative regularization; finally, a tradition of direct action and local autonomy militated against absolute bureaucratic control. Nevertheless, the major development in government from 1937 to 1941 was the growing strength and independence of the bureaucracy and the concentration of administrative functions in its hands.

Elected Councils

According to the laws of the border region, elected councils at the regional, district, and township levels wielded the highest authority of government. However, in practice, the councils were overshadowed by the smaller and more efficient governing committees and the bureaucracy both in drafting and in implementing legislation. Councils, particularly those at higher levels, met infrequently. In addition to providing symbolic support for United Front and communist rule, councils primarily served the purpose of endorsing and, particularly at lower levels, criticizing the administration, explaining new policies to their constituents, and offering suggestions. The regional council, for instance, did not meet initially until January 1939, more than a year after the regional government was officially constituted. Thereafter, contrary to constitutional requirements, which stipulated two meetings per year, it did not convene again until November 1941, almost three years later. Although councils met in all or most districts after the region-wide elections of 1941, it appears that most lower-level councils had met rarely during the preceding four years.[43]

In 1938 Kao Tzu-li, a prominent regional official, complained that despite some progress the councils failed to exercise their full powers. The problem was not "a too low cultural level on the part of the people" or "lack of interest in democracy." Rather, "certain workers have substituted the administrative conference (*hsing-cheng hui-i*) and the joint conference (*lien-hsi hui-i*) for the democracy of the council system."[44] Kao's brief remarks suggest the genuine difficulties that stemmed from trying to invest councils with substantial powers under conditions prevailing in the border region. Administrative or joint conferences, particularly at the district level, served certain purposes for which the councils had been conceived and were unencumbered by complex and unwieldy procedures. In particular, by bringing together a small leadership core from party, government, and army, they facilitated coordination of the diverse functions of individual departments of the government bureaucracy with the work of party and army, and permitted a broad review of the problems of the district. The failure to hold frequent council meetings was recognition also that they were expensive affairs requiring considerable organizational and mobilization work including the transportation of and provisions for many people. Moreover, small group meetings of high-level cadres free from the glare of publicity and the cumbrous procedure which characterized council meetings represented a continuity in political style for a leadership which had grown to maturity under guerrilla conditions. For these reasons, vital decisions tended to be made at joint conferences or within departments rather than at full-dress council sessions.[45]

Regional Government and Bureaucratic Proliferation

The regional administration, designed as a carbon copy of that of a province of the Central government, initially consisted of the following departments under the direction of the chairman of the regional government:

1. Secretariat
2. Civil Affairs Department
3. Finance Department
4. Education Department
5. Reconstruction Department (Economic Development)
6. Public Security Headquarters (Army)
7. Public Security Commission (Police and Intelligence)
8. Audit Commission[46]

In addition, the regional government administered various auxiliary agencies whose number eventually grew to thirty-five. These were primarily concerned with taxation, health, and education, and included the regional bank, the hospital and medical school, and the salt bureau. In short, a complex bureaucracy centered at the regional and district levels, and strikingly similar in structure and administrative practice to its counterparts in Kuomintang areas, dominated the administration of the border region.[47]

Examination of top regional personnel suggests scrupulous attention to maintaining a balance between local cadres and outsiders in the government. For the entire period 1937 to 1945 the two most prestigious positions in the government were held by Lin Po-ch'ü (government chairman) and Kao Kang (council president). Lin, a southerner, had served prominently in the Kiangsi Soviet Government, and after 1937 he was the highest-ranking party official in the regional government. As chairman, a position he held continuously until after 1945, he was the most influential figure in the administration of the border region during the early Yenan period. Kao, a Shensi partisan leader, quickly ascended to the position of the leading representative of local revolutionaries after Liu Chih-tan's death in 1936. Although Lin's voice seems to have been dominant in government affairs prior to 1941, and although he was projected nationally as the central figure in the politics of the border region, Kao eventually emerged as the key figure in coordinating the work of the party, government, and army. From 1942 his power increased dramatically to overshadow that of Lin and all others in the politics of the base area. Only one other high-level government post was consistently held by a single individual. Chou Hsing, a southerner, remained throughout the war period as head of the public security commission, a sensitive position from which he controlled police and security functions. Chou had specialized in security work since the early 1930s in the Kiangsi Soviet. Thus, at the top levels of party and government and in the military and security branches there was striking continuity in personnel and clear-cut division of responsibility among local partisan leaders and outsiders. By contrast, there was a high rate of turnover among heads of major departments of the regional government, as the following lists for 1938 to 1941 indicate (an asterisk denotes a Shensi local partisan; italics denote known membership on the Border Region Party Committee, 1939 to 1940):

Secretariat	*Ts'ao Li-ju**	Hsieh Chüeh-tsai	Wang Tzu-i*	Chou Wen*(?)
Civil Affairs	Ma Ming-fang*	*Kao Tzu-li*	Huo Wei-te*	*Liu Ching-fan**
Finance	*Ts'ao Li-ju**	*Chang Mu-yao*(?)*	Nan Han-ch'en	
Education	*Hsü T'e-li*	*Chou Yang*		
Reconstruction	*Liu Ching-fan**	*Kao Tzu-li* [48]		

A number of these men, Kao Tzu-li, Liu Ching-fan, and Ts'ao Li-ju in particular, served as heads of several key organs successively. They thus gained broad familiarity with the workings of the bureaucracy without permanently dominating any single sphere of activity. One goal of this rotation was to increase coordination between departments at the highest levels and prevent excessive independence within the bureaucracy.

The basic governmental organs in which bureaucratic practice flourished were the secretariat, and the departments of civil affairs, finance, education, and reconstruction. Each maintained branch (*pu-men*) or vertical organizations linking the region, subregion, and district offices. Lower echelons were directly responsible to their superiors within these departments. Administrative appointments were made at the regional level by the civil affairs department in conjunction with personnel officials in the individual departments.[49] The result was a centralized and autonomous bureaucratic system penetrating to the district level. It was relatively immune from control by the party or elected government officials such as the district magistrates.[50]

By December 1941 the bureaucracy had attained peak development. Communist-controlled portions of the region then encompassed twenty-nine districts with a population of approximately 1,400,000.[51] At this time there were an estimated 7,900 full-time salaried government officials of whom "over 1,000" served at the regional level, 4,021 served at the subregional, district, and subdistrict levels, and the remainder served in township governments. These figures included administrative appointees in all departments as well as elected officials such as district magistrates and township heads, but they excluded persons serving in a part-time capacity such as those elected to councils or lower-level governing committees.[52]

One index of bureaucratic administrative practice is salary differentiation on the basis of rank or office. In May 1937, Lin Po-ch'ü noted that the government was unable to provide a salary for cadres beyond a subsistence allowance in grain. Moreover, he established the firm egalitarian principle that in the future cadre and military salaries would never exceed those of ordinary workers in the border region.[53]

Although all salaries were closely pegged to subsistence needs in the wartime spirit of economy and sacrifice, the party's guiding principle was not total uniformity. By late 1937 basic differences in salary and allowances emerged for various classifications of party, army, and government cadres. The major component of cadre income was a food allotment usually provided directly in grain. The daily grain allowance for all government cadres, regardless of rank, as well as for students on government subsidy, was one and two-thirds pounds of millet or the equivalent. All soldiers regardless of rank received one and three-quarters pounds of grain, and men in combat were allotted two pounds. Clothing and a small cash allowance for vegetables and oil completed the subsistence income for all cadres. The government assumed the additional burden of feeding and clothing cadre and soldier families.[54]

Cadres, as well as workers in government factories, received small differentiated salaries. In 1937 and 1938, in addition to meeting subsistence needs, the government paid a top salary of five dollars per month to heads of regional departments and two and one-half dollars to district magistrates.[55] At 1937 Yenan prices, the top supplemental salary of five dollars per month had a purchasing power of ninety pounds of millet.[56] Since most salaries were paid in kind rather than in dollars, they were less affected by the wartime inflation which so drastically cut into the purchasing power and destroyed the morale of officials in Kuomintang China.

Principles of "absolute egalitarianism," which rejected all differences in the nature of the task or the rank of the individual, were not adopted. Rather a system was devised to provide a subsistence income for everyone on the government payroll with increments for cadres performing arduous or dangerous tasks and modest supplemental salaries differentiated on the basis of rank. Official salaries, even at higher echelons, remained pegged at levels comparable to those of factory workers, and corruption, traditionally a major source of official income, seems to have been effectively curbed.

The contrast between the austerity in the communist-led base areas and the splendor of Kuomintang official establishments highlights significant differences between the two rivals. As the American reporter Jack Belden recorded, "I was ashamed to go from one Kuomintang general to another, eating special delicacies from their well-laid tables, while peasants were scraping the fields outside the yamens for roots and wild grass to stuff into their griping stomachs. But I was more than ashamed—I was overcome with a feeling of loathing when I learned that these same generals and the Kuomintang officials were buying up land from starving farmers for arrears in taxes and were holding it to wait tenants and rainy days."[57] The horror of peasant life in wartime Kuomintang China was graphically detailed by a generation of American reporters sensitive both to the tragedy of the Chinese peasantry and to the hopeful contrast provided by the communist-led base areas. Theodore White recorded these observations following a 1944 tour of famine-stricken Honan:

> The peasants, as we saw them, were dying. They were dying on the roads, in the mountains, by the railway station, in their mud huts, in the fields. And as they died, the government continued to wring from them the last possible ounce of tax. . . . The government in county after county was demanding of the peasant more actual poundage of grain than he had raised on his acres. No excuses were allowed; peasants who were eating elm bark and dried leaves had to haul their last sack of seed grain to the tax collector's office. Peasants who were so weak they could barely walk had to collect fodder for the army's horses, fodder that was more nourishing than the filth they were cramming into their own mouths. Peasants who could not pay were forced to the wall; they sold their cattle, their furniture, and even their land to raise money to buy grain to meet the tax quotas. One of the most macabre touches of all was the flurry of land speculation. Merchants from Sian and Chengchow, small government officials, army officials and rich landlords who still had food were engaged in

purchasing the peasants' ancestral areas at criminally low figures. Concentration and dispossession were proceeding hand in hand, in direct proportion to the intensity of hunger. . . . Bitter of heart, we returned to Chungking. The bland equanimity of the capital was unruffled. . . . The dead bodies were lies; the dogs digging cadavers from the loess were figments of our imagination.[58]

The contrast between Kuomintang and communist rural programs highlights the failure of the former to reap the potential nationalist benefits which accrued from foreign invasion. The Kuomintang, as the wielder of Central government power, did reap substantial *elite* nationalist support in the early war years. The same Kuomintang appeals to rally against the Japanese, however, fell on deaf ears when directed to the peasantry. The Kuomintang failure in the countryside should be seen in the perspective of a pervasive Third World problem, exemplifying a major barrier to transformation of peasant societies by "military modernizers" or other elite groups cut off by training, experience, and world view from their people. This failure stemmed from a fundamental *structural* barrier implicit in its social composition and political power base. Firmly committed to landlord hegemony from which its own power principally derived, the Kuomintang proved incapable of leading a popular movement which alone could withstand the onslaught of Japanese attack and provide a base for resistance. In the final analysis the Kuomintang had little to offer the peasantry.

In striking contrast to Kuomintang officials, no communist cadre lived in a style even remotely approaching comfort, much less affluence; the hardships of war and poverty fell on cadre and soldier as well as on the peasant. The continuing criticism of the small perquisites accorded ranking communist officials in fact highlighted one of the movement's most compelling appeals to the Chinese people, the spartan and egalitarian spirit of the Yenan era.[59]

Subregional, District, and Township Government

By 1941 the border region was divided administratively into the four subregions of Sui-te, Kuan-chung, Lung-tung, and San-pien, each comprised of two to six districts with the remaining eleven districts administered directly from Yenan. Each subregion maintained a core staff of twenty-six to thirty-one cadres to coordinate the administration of its subordinate districts.[60] However, in contrast to the regional and district levels, the subregion never became a significant bureaucratic echelon requiring extensive staffing and division of labor. A major unit of the Eighth Route Army or public security forces was based in each subregion, and the practice of leading cadres holding multiple offices was particularly pronounced at this level.[61]

In 1941 district government, the basic level of administration included a secretariat, civil affairs, financial, educational, and public security sections, a public security corps, and a judge (ts'ai-p'an yüan).[62] Each district was staffed by twenty-five to thirty-five cadres, which meant that there were more than 900 district-level officials in the border region.[63] In the years 1937 to 1941, in line with the policy of administrative stabilization, the regional and district bureaucracies handled the major tasks of government.

In an effort to develop formal administration below the district level, the subdistrict was originally conceived as a basic level of administration. However, subdistrict councils elected in 1937 were abolished shortly thereafter and the functions of the subdistrict were subsequently restricted. The subdistrict operated as a liaison and in a coordinating capacity between the district and township governments in much the same way as the subregional administration mediated between regional and district government. Each district was divided into four to eight subdistricts, with approximately 150 subdistricts in the entire border region. Typically there were only a small number of subdistrict government cadres; all of them, including the subdistrict head (ch'ü-chang), were appointed by the district magistrate.[64]

The township was the border region's lowest level of formal administration. Governmental powers were vested in elected township councils and, in an important departure from traditional administrative practices, the township head (hsiang-chang) was a full-time salaried official. In 1941, 1,549 townships reportedly elected some 30,000 councillors to the local councils.[65]

The key figure in local government was the township head, who was elected by and from among members of the people's council. In practice, with the work of party and government frequently indistinguishable, the local party leader might assume major burdens of leadership.[66] At the township level, government depended almost exclusively on face-to-face relations, on skills of persuasion and mediation. The critical problem for party and government was effectively breaking the isolation of the township and village so that policies formulated at higher levels could be effectively implemented and grass-roots leadership committed to overcoming local problems might come to the fore. The difficulty was that many township heads were illiterate peasant activists whose world view, experience, and personal relationships were firmly grounded in their local communities and whose revolutionary perspective was limited to the land upheaval of an earlier era. A 1940 report on township government cites the example of Huan-hsien, where twenty-one of thirty-seven township heads were illiterate, fourteen could read a little (but were presumably incapable of regular reporting), and only two were "comparatively literate" and thus able to maintain continuous communications with higher levels. A report on Yenan district of September 1941 observed bluntly that virtually all township heads were illiterate.[67] Crash literacy programs designed particularly for lower-level officials made some headway, but given the press of official duties and the shortage of teachers, the task was formidable.

Efforts to bridge the literacy gap by convening district-wide meetings of township heads to discuss and transmit policy were productive, but their frequency was limited by the difficulty and expense of journeys to and from the district seat which often required several days. In the years 1937 to 1941 when the major governmental preoccupation was the creation of stable administration, the township remained relatively insulated against outside influences. With professional administrators and literate cadres concentrated in the regional and district bureaucracy, there was minimal effort to introduce leadership from outside the township. Moreover, prior to 1942 little attention was focused on transforming economic and social life within the townships. When this task, as well as a renewed challenge to elite domination assumed priority, radical changes in local administration would be required.

Probably the most important, and certainly the most sensitive, function performed by township government in the years 1937 to 1941 was the collection of taxes. Analysis of taxation policies in these years suggests the changing relationship between mobilization and administrative approaches, particularly the tendency for the former to yield to standardized administrative procedures. In 1937 with the first region-wide efforts to collect grain in support of the war effort, village-level mass meetings solicited "voluntary" contributions. Party activists played a key role in spurring enthusiasm and ensuring that local quotas were filled. With a goal of only 10,000 piculs of grain, this first levy exempted the majority of peasant families entirely and placed the extremely light burden of 1 to 5 percent of their harvest on families whose annual grain output exceeded 400 pounds of millet per person.[68]

These initial quotas, like so much legislation of the border region, were often honored in the breach or served only as general guidelines. Taxes were frequently collected less with reference to legal requirements than on the basis of cadre obligations to fulfill quotas handed down from their superiors. Once the regional government established a quota, it was divided into district subquotas, and these were further divided down to the village level. Several kinds of abuses were criticized in party journals. In some villages, the tax quota was divided equally among all families in violation of the principle that "those who have more give more." More often, in a striking reversal of practices of the Ch'ing and warlord periods, the entire burden was borne by a few relatively prosperous families. In 1939 in Yen-ch'ih district, one internal report noted that the entire tax was paid by only 16 percent of the families, and in Kan-ch'uan only 12.8 percent paid taxes. Moreover, because of the failure to apply uniform standards throughout the border region, a family with 2,000 pounds of grain was assessed 7.5 percent in one district and 20 percent elsewhere.[69]

In matters such as tax collection, local party and government cadres continued to manifest their commitment to poor peasant welfare long after the land revolution had subsided. The swing of the revolutionary pendulum meant that the poor who had been squeezed dry by the tax collector in the old days now were largely exempt. But this primitive revolutionary justice sometimes imposed heavy unin-

tended costs. Internal party reports observed that in some areas excessive burdens placed on rich peasants resulted in production sabotage, adversely affecting
overall output.[70]

In the years 1937 to 1941 grain collection was one of the major ways in which
administration penetrated to the local level. In this as in other duties, government
remained officially responsible for all facets of administration. However, effectiveness at the local level depended not on the workings of an impersonal bureaucracy but on face-to-face relationships and on mobilizing the peasantry,
tasks for which activists in the party were eminently suited. As the party experimented with various combinations of administrative and mobilization approaches to resolve its financial problems, new approaches were also being
developed in the sphere of electoral politics.

The "Three-Thirds System" and the Politics of United Front

The genuine cooperation characteristic of the United Front in early phases of the
war degenerated during 1938 into increasingly bitter conflicts between the
Kuomintang and communists. By 1940, just as all possibility of cooperation
appeared permanently shattered by escalating military clashes, the communists
announced an ambitious political program symbolic of their commitment to the
United Front.[71]

In the "three-thirds system" (*san san chih*) the communists formally restricted
themselves to a maximum of one-third of all positions in government and councils in the base areas. By unilaterally implementing the three-thirds system in all
base areas and giving it prominence in their propaganda, the communists accomplished three principal goals: (1) They manifested to the nation unswerving
loyalty to the principle of cooperation with all classes and parties in fighting the
common enemy, Japan. (2) They allayed fears of the bourgeoisie, an increasing
number of whom were serving prominently in communist-sponsored governments. (3) In contested areas they reduced to a minimum divisive internal forces
and thus enhanced the struggle against hostile armies, both Japanese and
Kuomintang.[72]

The theoretical basis for collaboration within the three-thirds system was
worked out by Mao Tse-tung in 1939 in "The Chinese Revolution and the
Chinese Communist Party" and further elaborated in "On New Democracy."
"During the Anti-Japanese War," he wrote, "the anti-Japanese democratic regime that ought to be established is a regime of the Anti-Japanese National
United Front, which is neither a 'one-class dictatorship' of the bourgeoisie nor a
'one-class dictatorship' of the proletariat, but a 'joint dictatorship of several
parties' belonging to the Anti-Japanese National United Front. All those who
stand for resistance to Japan and for democracy are qualified to share this political power, regardless of their party affiliations."[73]

It was not, however, until the Central Committee internal directive of March

6, 1940, attributed to Mao, that three-thirds principles were explicitly formulated and proclaimed as one of the bulwarks of communist wartime politics. The directive stated:

> According to the principles of the political power of the Anti-Japanese National United Front, we must observe the following proportion of personnel: Communists, non-party leftist progressives and the middle-of-the-roaders should each constitute one-third. . . .
>
> The progressive elements outside the Party should be permitted to constitute one-third because they are linked with the broad masses of the petty bourgeoisie. This will have a tremendous effect in winning over the petty bourgeoisie.
>
> In giving one-third of the positions to the middle-of-the-roaders our aim is to win over the middle bourgeoisie and the enlightened gentry. To win over these strata is an important step in isolating the die-hards.

The party's public pronouncements repeatedly stressed its willingness to cooperate with all patriotic elements. Intra-party discussion on the other hand frequently concentrated on the means of assuring and strengthening communist leadership within coalition governments. The same directive insisted: "We must ensure the leadership of the Communists in the organs of political power; therefore the Communists who constitute one-third must possess the best qualities. This condition alone will ensure the Party of its leadership even without greater representation . . . we should persuade and educate the people outside our Party through the Party's correct policies and our own exemplary work, so that they will willingly accept our proposals."[74]

The three-thirds system in Shen-Kan-Ning must be understood against a background of military and political developments. Its earliest experimental implementation in 1940 occurred in Sui-te and Lung-tung, areas which had but recently come under communist hegemony and where the problem of wooing the landlord elite was critical.[75] In contrast to consolidated portions of the border region, in these areas a powerful landlord and commercial elite continued to thrive, and communist party organization was weak. As the party set about creating a stable administration, it employed the three-thirds system to allay elite suspicions and incorporate many of those prepared to cooperate into the administration. In 1940, because the communists were unable as yet to carry out regular elections in the new areas, a provisional assembly was appointed. It included prominent members of the local elite in accordance with three-thirds criteria, in an effort to provide the new government with an aura of legitimacy.

Other bids were made for support of the powerful local elite. The most formidable task was assuring them that their property was safe from confiscation. During May and June 1941, *Chieh-fang jih-pao* (Liberation daily) was filled with reports of local notables from Sui-te who were transported by car to Yenan to survey the accomplishments of the border government.[76]

In 1941, the three-thirds system was expanded and directed toward other ends in the first region-wide elections since the establishment of the border region in 1937. The 1941 elections, conducted by a regional government with greater resources and sophistication, offer an interesting perspective on the evolution of New Democracy and the role of electoral politics. Among their most striking features was the use of students and women in organizing at the highest levels and in mobilizing the peasantry in each village. A regional election with a staff of 108 organized the nine-month campaign and dispatched teams to each district to direct the elections and train lower-level election cadres.[77]

If the three-thirds system was designed primarily to woo the elite, the massive educational effort which highlighted the election campaign served to mobilize the entire population for a broad range of programs. In township elections in one district, 115 propaganda teams and 881 worker and peasant groups carried the word directly to the people. Everywhere young people were instrumental in bringing the election movement to the countryside. Probably the most striking and effective work was done by *yang-ko* performing groups; these consisted of singers and actors drawn from youth and children's organizations and from elementary schools. With colorful songs and dances to attract a crowd, these groups fanned interest in the election movement and were instrumental in securing a turnout estimated at over 80 percent of the electorate.[78]

One important feature of the 1941 election movement was its coordination with a campaign for women's rights. A front-page editorial in the June 20, 1941, *Chieh-fang jih-pao* urged women to play an active role in the election movement as candidates and voters. It cited exemplary women serving in the bureaucracy and as elected officials. The case of Kuo Ching-hua, who was recently appointed the first woman district magistrate, exemplified the heights to which women could aspire. In 1941 women were elected to fill 8 percent of the seats in township councils, including over 20 percent in two districts.[79]

The sensitive problem of women's rights periodically became a major issue in succeeding years. Liberated women intellectuals in Yenan frequently chafed at the slow progress being made toward equality of the sexes. Perhaps the sharpest of these critics was the communist writer Ting Ling whose essay "Thoughts on March 8" (Women's Day) reflected her personal frustration: "If women did not marry, they were ridiculed; if they did and had children, they were chastised for holding political posts rather than being at home with their families; if they remained at home for a number of years, they were slandered as backward. Whereas in the old society they were pitied, in the new one they were condemned for a predicament not of their own making."[80] Like most feminists, Ting Ling wrote from the perspective of an intellectually emancipated elite. Their genuine frustrations notwithstanding, it was precisely this group which had made the greatest strides toward independence and integration. The far more formidable problem of the liberation of women in the remote villages of the border region remained intractable so long as their social and economic positions were virtually unchanged. Although the 1941 elections marked a stride forward in the political liberation of women, it was not until the party again focused attention on social revolution that substantial progress in women's rights could occur at the village level.[81]

Efforts to achieve three-thirds goals increased the complexity of the election campaign. Just as the transition to a united front policy had earlier aroused opposition and distrust among poor peasant beneficiaries of the land revolution and former partisans, in 1941 similar protests were voiced. These protests were not without substance. The struggle to overcome landlord domination and lay a firm foundation for a new generation of leadership committed to the gains of the agrarian revolution required continued vigilance. The united front policy now bolstered by the three-thirds system raised anew the specter of fifth columnists taking advantage of the open atmosphere to undermine previous gains. Did the three-thirds system mark a retreat that would facilitate a resurgence of the old landlord order? This was the crucial question for peasant activists jealous of newly won prerogatives.

Commitment to the Second United Front led toward the realization of potentially conflicting goals. On the one hand the communists sought the political participation of the traditional elite and the achievement of moderate socioeconomic and political reforms; on the other, they simultaneously attempted to strengthen the grip of the party over the entire region and to build a firm base among those it considered its most faithful allies, the poor peasants and other beneficiaries of the land revolution. The three-thirds system formalized and extended the united front thrust of the communist program by encouraging the increased participation of "progressives and middle-of-the-roaders" in the political process, particularly in the councils. In Sui-te and Lung-tung this hastened stabilization of volatile areas, but in politically consolidated portions of the border region it created friction with "leftists," primarily peasant revolutionaries, who were reluctant to cooperate with former class enemies. Everywhere, particularly in elected councils but also in the bureaucracy, participation of noncommunists of all classes increased.

In councils at every level, noncommunists achieved notable gains in those areas where the party's hegemony previously went unchallenged.[82] Moreover, in many other areas where communist organization was still rudimentary, the party failed to secure even one-third of the seats. It was in fact in the new areas, where party interest in the three-thirds system was strongest, that the goals of the system were most fully realized. Thus, Hsieh Chüeh-tsai observed, "In general, in new regions, the three-thirds system has been well done; even to the point that not merely do CCP members constitute only one-third, but sometimes KMT electees outnumber those of the CCP. . . . If people want to elect many Party members, there is nothing to be done. In older border regions, the number of Party members is high; in the past those who worked in the government were mostly Party members."[83]

At the regional level, in 1941 the communists retained a majority of seats, with 123 of 216 representatives. Fourteen others were identified as Kuomintang members, sixty-two had no party affiliation, and ten represented national minorities.[84]

The most comprehensive data available on the 1941 elections provide information on the class and party of more than 10,000 representatives of township assemblies in fourteen of the border region's twenty-nine districts. At this basic level, communists numbered 2,801 of 10,926 representatives, just over 25 percent of the total. Wide differences occurred in the results for different districts, with communists holding less than one-third of the seats in eight districts and exceeding one-third in six. In no instance did they hold more than 55 percent or less than 15 percent of the seats. Class data on assembly members show the overwhelming dominance of poor and middle peasants, with the former accounting for 60 percent and the latter 20 percent of the total.[85] The pattern which emerges is that of a successful effort to broaden the base of support by increasing noncommunist participation, including that by landlords, merchants, and rich peasants, in the council system. If wide variation occurred within districts, sometimes in violation of three-thirds quotas, the party could claim substantial success in its effort to demonstrate willingness to work with others. It was not content, however, merely to accept the benefits which had already accrued from this electoral experiment with coalition politics. In a move aimed at underlining its insistence that the nation and the people as a whole took precedence over sectarian interests, in April 1942 more than 100 communists recently elected to councils, standing committees, and governing committees resigned their posts in favor of noncommunists. In some instances the government achieved the desired balance by directly appointing "men of ability" to the councils. In late 1942, special re-elections for district and township councils were held in eight districts where communist representation exceeded three-thirds quotas.[86]

The three-thirds system operated not only in the election of council members but in the selection of council leadership. Particularly at the regional level, scrupulous attention was paid to the three-thirds formula, and beginning in 1941 spokesmen for landlord and commercial interests assumed prominent positions in the regional government. The vice-chairman of the regional government, Li Ting-ming, and An Wen-ch'in, vice-president of the regional council, were leading gentry figures in the Sui-te area. Li, as well as Ho Lien-ch'eng, who subsequently served as vice-chairman of the regional education department, was nominated for the regional council by the Kuomintang party branch of Mi-chih district. However, they were also included among the ten communist nominees from Mi-chih, of whom only four were communist party members. Another landlord who served conspicuously in government at this time was Ma K'o-ch'en, a leading member of the Ma clan of Mi-chih. He was a member of both the district council and governing committee and represented Mi-chih in the regional council. In 1941 he was one of ten candidates for president and vice-president of the regional council, but was defeated.[87]

Scrupulous attention was paid to incorporating noncommunist notables in the regional standing and governing committees in the precise proportions outlined in the three-thirds system. In such a bastion of gentry and commercial power as Sui-te City, the composition of the new municipal council reflected the desire for the support of the local elite to ensure economic and political stability. The Sui-te municipal council had only twelve communists, compared to fifteen Kuomintang and sixty-two nonparty members. Among the councillors were thirty-two merchants and five from the landlord-gentry class and only fifteen who were described as worker-peasant elements.[88] At the same time the communists acted to ensure maximum responsiveness of government at every level to the party's policy by strengthening discipline and leadership among party members serving in the government.

The scope of the three-thirds system in Shen-Kan-Ning was frequently more restricted than the flamboyant rhetoric of united front suggested. Although official statements reiterated that it was to apply not only to councils but to all levels of government, in practice noncommunists rarely held such authoritative posts as district magistrate, particularly in those areas of the border region where communist power had already been consolidated.[89] Occasional references suggest that the three-thirds system was to be applied throughout the bureaucracy. In March 1942 for instance, it was reportedly implemented in all departments of the Yenan district government. However, this approach was never systematically pursued.[90] In any event, the bureaucracy had never been limited exclusively to communists, although they dominated the leading posts.

The three-thirds system in Shen-Kan-Ning represented neither an abdication of communist leadership nor a sharp break with the past. It was, however, the ultimate step in broadening the spectrum of support and in utilizing administrative and leadership skills. In striking contrast to the Kuomintang, the communists demonstrated through the three-thirds system their ability to share power and work effectively with nonparty individuals. The three-thirds system in Shen-Kan-Ning and other base areas helped unify and strengthen administration and legitimized the party's claim to represent the entire Chinese nation.

The significance of the three-thirds system and other forms of cooperation was far greater in the rear-area bases than in Shen-Kan-Ning. In the rear areas, decision-making powers frequently were genuinely shared by all groups, communist and others, who rallied against the Japanese to create a resistance base area. In the face of continued attack by a superior power, political as well as military cooperation was an essential feature of the guerrilla struggle. By contrast, in Shen-Kan-Ning the three-thirds system was introduced into an already functioning administrative network in which the communist party had no direct political or military challenge. In Shen-Kan-Ning the effects of the three-thirds system were greatest in the new areas of Sui-te and Lung-tung, where communist party organization was weakest. There it helped create stable government through a broad appeal to all classes, including the most prosperous.[91] The three-thirds system represented the high-water mark of communist attempts to woo the landlord elite and the bourgeoisie at a time when united front harmony had already yielded to bitter Kuomintang-communist hostilities.

The Collapse of the Kuomintang-Communist United Front

Among the earliest manifestations of the Second United Front was the designation of Shen-Kan-Ning as a special region of the National government. Nevertheless, after 1937 the border area continued to be plagued by plundering bands, some of them politically motivated and many of them long a part of the area's bandit subculture. Reports of the summer and fall of 1938 describe the campaign to crush bandit forces, which ranged in size from a handful of men to bands of 200. Some appear to have had secret society links, others interestingly were defecting communist units. And some, it is implied in the polite phrasing of the early years of the Second United Front, had assistance from "friendly armies" (i.e., Kuomintang). Major bandit forces were decisively repelled in late 1937. In the spring of 1938 for the first time Japanese attacks were directed briefly against the border area. In November 1938 the final direct Japanese attack on the base area came with a two-day aerial bombardment of Yenan. Thereafter, the Japanese were astutely content to withdraw and permit the Kuomintang-communist rivalry to take over in this remote area that was devoid of strategic and economic value.[92]

The basic reason for the mounting antagonism was the spectacular growth of communist-sponsored governments behind Japanese lines from late 1937, coincident with the massive military setback to Kuomintang interests. Following the fall of Hankow to the Japanese in the fall of 1938, the Nationalists were driven back from the coastal areas, which had long constituted their base of power, to Szechuan in the remote southwest. While Kuomintang armies were in full retreat, communist forces spearheaded guerrilla resistance throughout North China. By 1939 the worst fears of Kuomintang critics of the United Front were confirmed. The communist-led resistance had taken advantage of foreign invasion to vastly expand its territory, despite a rapidly growing Japanese military establishment in North China.

Japanese forces, according to a communist estimate, increased from 300,000 in late 1937 to 440,000 in 1939. The following year these were supplemented by 140,000 puppet troops—Chinese soldiers armed by and fighting for the Japanese.[93] Moreover, by 1939 the Japanese had shifted the brunt of their attack from Kuomintang and warlord armies to communist forces operating behind their lines in North China. However, the communist ability to harass the Japanese and to administer large guerrilla areas was already formidable. During 1937 and 1938, four major base areas were created; these were located on the Shansi-Chahar-Hopeh border, on the Shansi-Hopeh-Shantung-Honan border, on the Shansi-Suiyuan border, and in the Shantung peninsula. By August 1939 Japanese intelligence estimated the number of communist-controlled districts at

130. By the following year regular communist forces numbered approximately 400,000, and more than 50,000,000 people lived in rear-area bases in North China. Moreover, communist strength was growing in Central China, where the most violent wartime clash with the Kuomintang would shortly occur. In 1940 orders went out to expand the New Fourth Army, the main communist force in Central China, to 100,000 men.[94]

Increasing friction between the Kuomintang and communist camps after 1938 rapidly led to fighting between the "allies," while both sides issued fervent public appeals for unity. At this time Kuomintang leaders pondered the possibility of a separate peace with Japan and formation of an anticommunist alliance. Long before the New Fourth Army incident of January 1941, the most spectacular of the military clashes, which for all practical purposes terminated the United Front, hostilities had broken out in numerous areas.

In Shen-Kan-Ning, friction was centered in those areas contested by Kuomintang and communist forces. At the time of the creation of the border region government in September 1937, the communists had achieved undisputed military and administrative control of approximately fifteen of the twenty-three districts formally included in the Shen-Kan-Ning base. For the most part, these constituted the poorest and least populated regions in the vicinity of Yenan. On the other hand, in the Sui-te and Lung-tung subregions, forming respectively the northeast and southwest portions of the border region, an uneasy balance prevailed between Kuomintang and communist forces and administrations, which were locked in "nonantagonistic" or nonmilitary competition.[95] When frictions increased, these areas, particularly Sui-te, the richest and most populous portion of the border region, become the points at which violence erupted.

Minor incidents in the first half of 1938 were smoothly arbitrated. Both sides seemed intent on preserving amity. By early 1939, however, the stage was set for more serious clashes. The Sixth Plenum of the communist party, the first since the Long March, was held in Yenan in October and November 1938. The current official interpretation of the plenum is that it "laid down the line of persisting in the anti-Japanese united front and pointed out that there should be both unity and struggle within the united front and that the proposition 'everything through the united front' did not suit Chinese conditions. Thus it criticized the mistake of accommodationism in the question of the united front."[96] The error of "accommodation" or excessive capitulation to Kuomintang demands was subsequently attributed above all to Wang Ming, Mao Tse-tung's major rival, whose eclipse began with the Sixth Plenum. Although Wang continued as a leading symbol of and spokesman for the United Front until 1940, when the immense outpouring of articles under his name came to an abrupt halt, his influence within party councils was sharply reduced after the Sixth Plenum. From this time the official attitude toward the United Front stiffened, particularly as the communist position was strengthened in North China and as military confrontation with the Kuomintang escalated.[97]

At its Fifth Plenum in January 1939, the Kuomintang's Fifth Central Executive Committee adopted "Measures to Restrict the Activities of Alien Parties," which signaled the onset of what the communists have called the "First Anti-Communist Upsurge." Steps were taken, in accordance with these "measures," to tighten control over all political activity in Kuomintang areas, and repeated military clashes with the communists culminated in December 1939 in the blockade of the Shen-Kan-Ning border region.[98] Serious fighting in Shen-Kan-Ning broke out in the Lung-tung area in May 1939 and in Sui-te in the spring of 1940 as both sides sought to mobilize and organize the population in the disputed areas.[99]

On paper, but apparently on paper only, the Kuomintang adopted policies strikingly similar to those of the communist mobilization program. These included the formation of mass political and military organizations extending to the village, stress on education and the inculcation of new ideals among the peasantry, and the linking of military and political activity. In practice, the *pao-chia* system of mutual surveillance symbolized the Kuomintang's overwhelming preoccupation with discipline and control. In Sui-te, in an effort to win over dissident peasants, the Kuomintang proclaimed a rent ceiling of one-third of the crop, but there is no indication that it was ever enforced. Moreover, in areas recovered from the communists they quickly restored redistributed land and property to former owners. In spite of Kuomintang efforts, by 1940 the communists had secured control of Sui-te and Lung-tung, but the continuing Kuomintang blockade of Shen-Kan-Ning exacted a heavy price on the region's economy.[100]

In the border region in the years 1937 to 1941 the communists shouldered the problems and responsibilities of creating institutions for governing not a class but an entire people. Its program in Shen-Kan-Ning and throughout the rear-area bases was the New Democracy, a United Front conception that combined administrative and limited mobilization techniques to create stable, responsive institutions and initiate reform. By 1941 the party could point with pride to its achievements in providing leadership to a growing network of North China base areas in which popularly based governments rose out of the ruins of war-induced anarchy, and in which socioeconomic and educational reforms had begun to take shape. Yet many of the foundations upon which the New Democracy was built had already begun to erode. In particular, a working alliance with the Kuomintang was superseded by bitter acrimony, military conflict, and blockade. Moreover, fundamental problems in the administration of the border region and other bases had become increasingly vexing. In Shen-Kan-Ning these were the result of contradictions between a distant bureaucracy that penetrated effectively only to the district level and the "feudal" conditions that prevailed in remote villages (including those in which land distribution had occurred); between the goal of stability and a commitment to press forward with the tasks of social revolution; and between cadres with a United Front orientation, many of whom were outsiders with higher education and administrative experience, and local cadres who had risen during and were committed to agrarian revolution.

Since 1937 the proliferation of bureaucracy to bring stable rule to the base area had made increasing inroads into the mobilization style of revolutionary politics. Between the two elections of 1937 and 1941 no major mobilization campaigns punctuated the process of administrative stabilization. The premium on formal administrative skills and the united front orientation reduced the role of peasant activists in the emerging order. The question confronting party leaders in Shen-Kan-Ning was whether a united front and bureaucratic administration was compatible with the fundamental resolution of problems of poverty and oppression. In the rear areas this dilemma was linked to one still more critical: In the face of intense Japanese repression, could New Democratic politics effectively sustain and reinforce the resistance? The party's answer from 1942 led to radical departures in governing the base areas, departures which profoundly shaped the subsequent course of the communist movement in China.

Notes

1. Mao, "Struggle to Mobilize All Forces for Winning in the Armed Resistance," *SW*, II, 71. Cf. Mao's slogans in the land law of February 7, 1930: "Take from those who have much to help those who have little," and "Take from those who have fertile land to help those who have poor land." Rue, 300–304.

2. Biography of Lin Po-ch'ü, in Howard Boorman, ed., *Biographical Dictionary of Republican China* (New York, 1968), II, 377–79.

3. Lin Po-ch'ü, "Yu su-wei-ai tao min-chu kung-ho-kuo chih-tu" (From soviet to democratic republic), *Chieh-fang*, 5:11–14 (May 24, 1937).

4. For additional examples of communist praise for the Three People's Principles, see *SW*, I, 256–67, and *SW*, II, 83–85. The administrative principles adopted by the first regional council of the border region in January 1939 were divided according to Sun's three categories of nationalism, democracy, and the people's livelihood. *WHHC*, 39–41.

5. Lin Po-ch'ü, *Shen-kan-ning pien-ch'ü hsüan-chü* (Necessary knowledge for the Shensi-Kansu-Ninghsia border region election; Yenan [?], 1937), 47.

6. The term, "New Democracy" became symbolic of the entire wartime program following the January 1940 publication of Mao's pamphlet "On New Democracy," his most important and comprehensive statement of the party's united front and reform policies. However, the term was in common use from the spring of 1937. On May 3, 1937, Mao had designated a "new democratic republic" (*hsin ti min-chu kung-ho-kuo*) as the appropriate form for the wartime government. See *SW*, I, 267. Shortly thereafter Lin Po-ch'ü outlined a "new democratic system" for the border region in his article, "Yu su-wei-ai tao min-chu kung-ho-kuo chih-tu," 11.

The communists occasionally equated New Democracy with "capitalist democracy" as in the explanatory sections accompanying the election laws of the Shen-Kan-Ning Border Region in Lin, *Shen-kan-ning pien-ch'ü hsüan-chü*, 26. There capitalist democracy referred to the fact that, as in Western democracies, all classes enjoyed equal political rights in contrast to a worker, peasant, and soldier soviet regime. Moreover, the communists encouraged development of certain "capitalist" economic tendencies in the "feudal" base areas in order to achieve an appropriate socioeconomic base for the subsequent transition from bourgeois-democratic revolution to socialism. On the other hand, the New Democracy was usually compared favorably to Western democracy in which elections were said to provide a façade for capitalist exploitation. Cf. Yü Ming, "Shen-kan-ning pien-ch'ü tse-yang shih le min-chu" (How was democracy achieved in the Shen-Kan-Ning border region?), *Ch'ün-chung* (The masses), 4.1:29 (Jan. 10, 1940).

7. For a brilliant discussion of democracy in a Chinese setting, particularly the vagaries of Chinese electoral politics at the time of the 1911 revolution, see Edward Friedman, "The Center Cannot Hold: The Failure of Parliamentary Democracy in China from the Chinese Revolution of 1911 to the World War in 1914," Harvard University, Ph.D. dissertation, 1968.

8. Edgar Snow, *The Battle for Asia* (New York, 1941), 317. Some American missionaries with a bent for social reform had earlier identified with the communist program of rural egalitarianism in North China. See Fox Butterfield, "A Missionary View of the Chinese Communists, 1936–1939," in Kwang-ching Liu, ed., *American Missionaries in China* (Cambridge, 1966), 249–301.

9. "The Election Laws of the Shen-Kan-Ning Border Region," May 12, 1937, 19. Originally the township governing body was called a "congress" (*tai-piao-hui*); those at all higher levels were called "councils" (*i-hui*). The term for all levels was shortly changed to *ts'an-i-hui* (also translated "council"), and the voting age was raised to 18 to synchronize with National government practice.

10. The basic source for study of the election movement is the regional government publication, *Shen-kan-ning pien-ch'ü hsüan-chü.*

11. *CFPK,* 1.

12. In an interview with Nym Wales (*My Yenan Notebooks,* 158) on August 18, 1937, Tung Pi-wu, chairman pro tem of the Shen-Kan-Ning government, gave voice to the problems the leadership faced in securing acquiescence:

> The people all liked the soviet better because it was simple and easy for them. The landlords will perhaps like the new democracy better but few are left here to enjoy it. It is very difficult only to explain the meaning of elections. . . . We find difficulty in letting the landlords have the right to vote—people do not understand why. The farmers said the land might be redistributed back to the landlords. There are two districts in Kan Lo Hsien in Shenpei, where this problem has not yet been solved. The people here will not let the landlords vote.
>
> In general the people give up the soviet easily. They trust the Communist Party to do right, only they do not see the necessity for the complex change. Some do not see how it benefits themselves.

13. Ts'ai Shu-fan, head of the department of the interior in charge of the 1937 election, told Nym Wales that the first elections in the northwest were held in February 1935 when soviet representatives of a population of 150,000 were chosen. If indeed earlier elections occurred, they may well have been in connection with the First North Shensi Soviet Congress held in January 1935. In the midst of continuous heavy fighting at that time, elections were undoubtedly restricted to a small number of relatively secure communities and to the selection of representatives from military units. Wales, *My Yenan Notebooks,* 89. Cf. Li Fu, "Pien-ch'ü ko hsiang ko ch'ü min cheng-fu hsüan-chü yün-tung ti tsung-chieh" (Summary of the people's government election movement in all townships and subdistricts of the border region), in Yang Shih, ed., *Shen-pei ti ch'ün-chung tung-yüan* (Mass mobilization in north Shensi; n.p., 1938), 25.

14. Lu Mang, *Shen-kan-ning pien-ch'ü ti min-chung yün-tung* (The mass movement in the Shen-Kan-Ning border region; Hankow, 1938), 49–51; Ch'u Yün, *Shen-hsing chi-shih* (True record of a Shensi journey; n.p., 1938), 24–25; Hsü Yung-ying's description of

township elections in Pao-an, based on Ch'u's account, is in *A Survey of the Shen-Kan-Ning Border Region* (New York, 1945), I, 60–61; Yü Ming, 30.

15. Lu Mang, 53–54.

16. BI, Yang Tsung-chou, ed., *Tiao-ch'a ts'ung-shu: Shen-kan-ning pien-ch'ü hsien-ch'uang* (Collected investigations: the present situation in the Shen-Kan-Ning border region), 43; *Hsin chung-hua pao* (Oct. 24, Nov. 19, 1937).

17. Lu Mang, 52.

18. Hsü Yung-ying, I, 5, 63; BI, *Shen-kan-ning pien-ch'ü ch'üan mao* (Complete portrait of the Shen-Kan-Ning border region; 1940), 16.

19. The further development of elections as an element of the political process is discussed below.

20. One year later the Eighth Route Army was renamed the Eighteenth Group Army. Ch'en, *Mao and the Chinese Revolution,* 223–34; Schram, *Mao Tse-tung,* 204.

21. Johnson, *Peasant Nationalism and Communist Power,* 95; Gillin, *Warlord: Yen Hsi-shan,* 257–71.

22. In Yenan district the self-defense army (*tzu-wei chün*), a part-time local militia, reportedly recruited 7,125 men in addition to 2,638 who received special training and 6,000 in the militarized Youth Corps. "Resistance Mobilization Work in the Special Area: An Introduction to Work Experience," *Chieh-fang,* 26:21–30 (December 1937); Yang Shih, 30; Ch'u Yün, 120; Ch'i Li, *Shen-kan-ning pien-ch'ü shih-chi* (A true account of the Shen-Kan-Ning border region; n.p., 1939), 14; Lu Mang, 29–34.

23. Hsü Ti-hsin, *Shen-kan-ning pien-ch'ü yü ti-hou k'ang-jih ken-chü-ti ts'ai-cheng ching-chi* (The finances and economy of the Shen-Kan-Ning border region and the anti-Japanese rear-area bases; n.p., 1941), 8; Ch'u Yün, 86–88; Hsü Yung-ying, II, 33, based on a report in *Hsin-hua jih-pao* (Oct. 6, 1942).

24. *CFPK,* 57, puts the 1937 grain collection at 13,859 piculs. "Laws for the Collection of Public Grain for National Salvation," October 1937, *CTTL,* 474–84, exempted families with an income of less than 400 piculs of grain per person. Unless otherwise noted, dollars throughout the book are Chinese *yuan.*

25. The text of the July 15 proposals is translated in Brandt, *Documentary History,* 245–47; cf. Ho Kan-chih, *A History of the Modern Chinese Revolution,* 320–21; Tso Chien-chih, "Shen-kan-ning pien-ch'ü min-chu cheng-chih ti t'e-tien chi ch'i tsai hsiang ti chü-t'i shih-shih" (The characteristics and concrete practice of democratic government at the village level in the Shen-Kan-Ning border region), *Chieh-fang,* 104:6 (Apr. 20, 1940). Tso dates the official change from Soviet to Border Region Government on September 6, 1937, as does Lin Po-ch'ü in *WHHC,* 6. On that date the border region came under the jurisdiction of the Executive Yuan of the Central Government.

26. In the absence of communist accounts, the following is based on Kuomintang intelligence sources. The twenty-three districts included in the border region were Fu-she (Yenan), Kan-ch'uan, Fu-hsien, Yen-ch'ang, Yen-ch'uan, An-sai, An-ting, Pao-an (Chih-tan), Ching-pien, Ch'un-hua, Hsün-i, Lo-ch'uan, Ch'ing-chien, Sui-te, Mi-chih, Cheng-ning, Ning-hsien, Ch'ing-yang, Ho-shui, Huan-hsien, Yen-ch'ih, Chen-yüan, and parts of Shen-mu and Fu-ku (Shen-fu). Ch'u Yün, 134; BI, *Shen-kan-ning pien-ch'ü ch'uan mao,* 27–30.

27. Ch'u Yün, 134.

28. Lin Po-ch'ü, *Shen-kan-ning pien-ch'ü hsüan-chü,* 5; Hsü Yung-ying, I, 5.

29. The size of the subsidy remains in doubt. I have accepted the figure of 100,000 dollars per month given in BI, *Complete Investigation Report,* V, 28. This sum was in addition to financial support for the Eighth Route Army in the amount of 500,000 dollars from 1937 and later 600,000 dollars per month. Hsü Yung-ying, I, 19. Another intelligence report indicates that the Central government was providing 150,000 dollars per

month for the Eighth Route Army, including funds that the communists were to use for the government and party apparatus in Shen-Kan-Ning. BI, Yang Tsung-chou, 21. This last and lower figure may have represented sums earmarked only for Shen-Kan-Ning, not including subsidy for the army in other parts of China.

30. Li Fu-ch'un, "Shen-kan-ning pien-ch'ü tang ti kung-tso" (Party work in the Shen-Kan-Ning border region), *Chieh-fang*, 90:9–12 (Nov. 20, 1939).

31. Biography of Kao Kang in Boorman, ed., *Biographical Dictionary of Republican China*, II, 233–35.

32. BI, "Shen-kan-ning pien-ch'ü kuan-chung fen-ch'ü ch'ü cheng-fu i-shang hsing-cheng tsu-chih chi ko chi chu-kuan hsing-ming piao" (Table of names of officials in administrative organs of sub-district and higher levels of the Kuan-chung sub-region of the Shen-Kan-Ning border region; circa 1941); "Kuan-yü hsiang-ts'un ko chung tsu-chih ti kuei-ting" (Resolution on various township and village organizations), printed in BI, *Kung-fei tang-wu chüeh-ting* (Communist resolutions on party affairs).

33. Pai Hsiang-yin, "Tsai chuan-pien chung ti an-sai kung-tso" (On the change in work in An-sai), *T'uan-chieh* (Unity), 1.9:9–11 (Sept. 20, 1938).

34. "Resolution on Investigation of Party Elements of the Second Congress of the Border Region Communist Party," *Chieh-fang*, 95:42–43 (Dec. 30, 1939); Li Fu-ch'un, "Kuan-yü hsin lao kan-pu ti wen-t'i" (On the question of new and old cadres), Oct. 20, 1939, reprinted in Kuo-fang pu hsin-wen-chü, ed., *Kung-fei fan-tung wen-chien hui-p'ien* (Collected documents of communist bandit reactionaries; Taipei, n.d.), I, 238.

35. BI, "Chung-kung hsien chuang tsung pao-kao" (A summary report of the Chinese communists' present situation; 1938 [?]).

36. Lin Po-ch'ü, "K'ang-chan i-lai ti shen-kan-ning pien-ch'ü" (The Shensi-Kansu-Ninghsia border region since the resistance war), *Chieh-fang* (Oct. 31, 1938), 6–8.

37. *CFPK*, 33–36; BI, *Tang-p'ai tiao-ch'a chou-pao*, 41 (Nov. 7–13, 1941).

38. BI, "Shen-kan-ning pien-ch'ü chung-kung chün-shih kai-k'uang tiao-ch'a" (Investigation of the Chinese communists' military situation in the Shen-Kan-Ning border region), 2–3.

39. *CFPK*, 27–38; Tso Chien-chih, 9; BI, "Shen-kan-ning pien-ch'ü kuan-chung fen-ch'ü ch'ü cheng-fu i-shang hsing-cheng tsu-chih chi ko chi chu-kuan hsing-ming piao."

40. Schram, *Mao Tse-tung*, 207.

41. *Shen-kan-ning pien-ch'ü chien-cheng shih-shih kang-yao* (A summary of the policy of simplified administration for the Shensi-Kansu-Ninghsia border region; Yenan [?], 1943), 16–17. This analysis suggests that the problem of "red and expert" that has preoccupied party leaders since 1949 was already being felt in Yenan. Cf. Franz Schurmann, *Ideology and Organization in Communist China*, 8, 163–67, 170–72.

42. Lin Po-ch'ü's writing and speeches best represent the effort to give substance to regular administrative practices and sound fiscal planning. The principles that he stipulated at the formation of the regional government in 1937 were the following: (1) Collective administration (*chi-t'i pan-kung*); (2) Collective leadership and individual responsibility; (3) Examination and work reports; (4) Budgeting according to work plans. Lin Po-ch'ü, "Yu su-wei-ai tao min-chu kung-ho-kuo chih-tu," 11–14.

43. The original provisions incorporated in the election laws of May 1937 stated that the regional council would meet annually. Lin Po-ch'ü, *Shen-kan-ning pien-ch'ü hsüan-chü*, 22. The first council in January 1939 revised this provision so that the regional council would theoretically convene twice a year. *WHHC*, 57, 119. The 1939 regional council also increased the frequency of meetings of lower-level councils. District councils were to meet every three months and township councils each month, compared to two and six times a year respectively according to the previous laws. The 1941 council returned to the original arrangements stipulated in 1937, reducing the frequency of the council meet-

ings, although the councils apparently continued to meet much less frequently than the law indicated.

44. Kao Tzu-li, "Wan-ch'eng Shen-kan-ning pien-ch'ü ti-fang min-chu cheng-chih ti chien-she" (Complete reconstruction of the Shen-Kan-Ning border region democratic government), *Chieh-fang,* 52:6 (Sept. 18, 1938). In 1941 Lin Po-ch'ü likewise bemoaned the failure to regularize the work of councils in holding meetings and elections as stipulated by law. *CFPK,* 25. Cf. the case of the district government in Ch'ih-shui, censured for failure to hold regular council meetings, *CFJP* (Sept. 7, 1941).

45. In 1942, when bureaucracy came under bitter attack, the prerogatives of such interorganizational committees were further expanded. These and other changes in government are discussed in Chapter 6.

46. *WHHC,* 49–66. The first six departments listed formed the basis of the provincial bureaucracy of the Central government. Cf. *CFJP* (Dec. 12, 1941).

47. *CFJP* (Feb. 8, 1944).

48. This list of department heads is based on all available data from intelligence sources and published communist records. *WHHC,* 74; BI, Yang Tsung-chou, ed. *Tiao-ch'a ts'ung-shu: Shen-kan-ning pien-ch'ü hsien-chuang,* 25; *CFJP* (Dec. 10, 1941); BI, *Shen-kan-ning shih-kuang,* 25.

49. "Cadre Regulation in the Shen-Kan-Ning Border Region Government," Apr. 25, 1943, *CTHP,* 102; *WHHC,* 50; BI, *Chung-kung chih chien-cheng yü hsiang-hsüan* (Chinese communist simplification of government and township elections; 1942), 12–15.

50. The political problems created by centralized bureaucracy and the tensions between outside and local cadres were recognized and confronted after 1942. They are discussed in Chapter 5.

51. These twenty-nine districts were virtually identical with the territory originally allotted to the border region in the agreements of September 1937. However, the communists had redefined the boundaries of several of the original twenty-three districts and created a number of new ones to give a total of twenty-nine. Blockading Kuomintang forces still held portions of a few of these districts. *CFJP* (Dec. 15, 1941); *CFPK,* 7–11.

52. *CFJP* (Dec. 13, 1941); Hsü Yung-ying, I, 69–70. Statistics are not available on the staff of all departments of the bureaucracy, but the figure of "over 1,000" for regional-level personnel seems reasonable in light of available information concerning the size of several leading departments: secretariat (105), civil affairs (91), reconstruction (335), finance (96). The department with by far the largest cadre quota and greatest responsibilities was the reconstruction department, which was charged with transforming the regional economy.

Major Governmental Departments (circa 1940)

Secretariat	Civil Affairs Department
1. General Affairs Section	1. Secretarial Office
2. Documents Section	2. Administrative Section
3. Issuing and Receiving	3. Social Welfare Section
4. Commission in Charge of Guests	4. Health Section

Finance Department	Education Department
1. Secretarial Office	1. Secretarial Office
2. Tax Collection Section	2. Administrative Section

3. Accounting Section
4. Treasury Section
5. Statistics Section
6. Border Region Bank

3. School Education Section
4. Social Education Section
5. Editorial Section

Reconstruction Department

1. Secretarial Office
2. Agricultural, Forestry,
   and Irrigation Section
3. Cooperative Section

4. Industry and Mining Section
5. Communications Section
6. Highway Management Bureau

BI, *Shen-kan-ning pien-ch'ü ch'üan mao,* 19–20; Yang Tsung-chou, 15–18; *CFJP* (Dec. 16, 20, 24, 25, 1941).

53. Lin Po-ch'ü, *Shen-kan-ning pien-ch'ü hsüan-chü,* 17.

54. A government edict of September 1941 provides comparative information concerning the salaries of workers, presumably those employed in government-run enterprises. The basic monthly grain allowance was 60 pounds of millet, identical with the quota for combat soldiers. In addition, workers received 1.3 pounds of salt, an identical amount of meat, three-fourths of a catty of oil, 80 catties of wood, and a cash allowance of 9 dollars for vegetables. Three suits of clothing were provided annually. Payment was either in border region currency or in goods, depending on local conditions. Special increments were made for skilled labor. Unskilled workers, in addition to the allowances mentioned above, received a monthly salary of 15 to 30 dollars, and skilled workers earned 30 to 100 dollars. "Resolution Concerning Workers' Salaries in Publicly Managed Factories in the Shen-Kan-Ning Border Region," *CTTL,* 653. The resolution is dated September 1941.

Several sources provide generally consistent supplementary information concerning cadre grain allowances for the years 1937 to 1941. BI, *Shen-kan-ning pien-ch'ü ch'uan mao,* 61; Yang Tsung-chou, 21–22; Hsü Ti-hsin, 18; Shen-Kan-Ning Border Region Department of Finance, "Pien-ch'ü ts'ai-cheng shih-hsing t'ung-ch'ou t'ung-chih pan-fa" (Method for carrying out unified accounting in the finances of the border region), manuscript, 1941, 2–6 (BI).

55. Hsü Ti-hsin, 18; *WHHC,* 19; BI, *Shen-kan-ning pien-ch'ü ch'uan mao,* 61; Yang Tsung-chou, 22.

56. Lo Ch'iung, *Shen-kan-ning pien-ch'ü min-chien fang-chih yeh* (The popular weaving industry in the Shensi-Kansu-Ninghsia border region; n.p., 1946), 1. These salaries were roughly equivalent to the inflated 1941 salaries mentioned above for workers in government factories. By late 1941 purchasing power of the dollar had decreased more than tenfold.

57. Jack Belden, *China Shakes the World* (New York, 1949), 83–84.

58. Theodore White and Annalee Jacoby, *Thunder Out of China* (New York, 1946), 174–75.

59. Inequalities in salary were attacked at the height of the 1942 rectification campaign. See, for example, Wang Shih-wei's biting sarcasm concerning clothing in "three different colors" and "five different grades" of grain subsidy. Wang was himself shortly attacked on charges of Trotskyism. *CFJP* (March 23, 1942), cited in Merle Goldman, *Literary Dissent in Communist China* (Cambridge, 1967), 25–27.

60. Shen-kan-ning pien-ch'ü cheng fu, min-cheng t'ing (Shen-Kan-Ning Border Region Civil Affairs Department), ed., *Shen-kan-ning pien-ch'ü hsiang-hsüan tsung-chieh* (A

summary of the township elections of the Shen-Kan-Ning border region; Yenan[?], 1941), final unpaginated chart on municipal councillors in the Shen-Kan-Ning border region.

61. Hsi Chung-hsün, for instance, united the top party, government, and military posts in Kuan-chung subregion, 1938–1941. Wang Chen and Wang Wei-chou both served concurrently as government commissioner and military commander in other subregions. BI, "Kuan-chung hsing-ming piao."

62. Ibid.

63. *CFJP* (Dec. 13, 1941). The three classifications of districts were based on populations ranging from 10,000 to 140,000 with most falling between 20,000 and 50,000. The twenty-nine districts and one municipality (Yenan) which comprised the region in 1941 included eight first-class districts with quotas of 35 to 37 cadres, fifteen second-class districts whose quotas were 29 to 33, and seven third-class districts staffed by 25 or 26 cadres. Here again quotas were not rigidly adhered to. Thus in 1941 Yen-ch'uan had 40 cadres compared to its quota of 37. *CFJP* (June 20, 1942).

64. In 1940 in Yenan district, where administration was most fully articulated, there were eight to eleven subdistrict cadres including those of the party and mass organizations as well as government. Wen-hua chiao-yü yen-chiu hui, ed., *Hsüeh-hsi sheng-huo* (Study life; Yenan [?], 1941), 48.

65. *CFJP* (June 18, Oct. 14, 1941).

66. Cf. Tso Chien-chih's description of the workings of township government, especially 9–10. An elaborate system of township committees was envisioned to supplement the work of the township head, but, as Lin Po-ch'ü later admitted, it never functioned. The township committees, exemplifying ambitious early efforts to construct stratified organization at lower levels, were officially abolished in 1943. Lin Po-ch'ü, *Shen-kan-ning pien-ch'ü san-san-chih ti ching-yen chi ch'i ying-kai chiu-cheng ti p'ien-hsiang* (Experience with the three-thirds system in the Shen-Kan-Ning border region and tendencies which should be corrected; Yenan [?], 1944), 17.

67. Tso Chien-chih, 13; *CFJP* (Sept. 11, 12, 1941, June 20, 1942).

68. Tso Chien-chih, 14. "Laws for the Collection of Public Grain for National Salvation," October 1937, *CTTL,* 474–84. Cf. Hsü Yung-ying, II, 22.

69. Hsieh Chüeh-tsai, "Cheng-shou chiu kuo kung liang ti yen-chiu yü shang-ch'üeh" (Investigation of the collection of public grain for national salvation), *T'uan-chieh,* 1.26:7–12 (Aug. 1, 1940). I P'ing, "Ardently Develop Grain Collection Work," in Shen-Kan-Ning Border Region Politburo, ed., *K'ai-chan pien-ch'ü ching-chi* (Develop the border region economy; n.p. n.d.), 22. For a general discussion of abuses in the tax system, including the lack of regularized procedures, milking of former landlords and class enemies, and so forth, see *WHHC,* 102–3, the "Resolution on Problems of Tax Collection," passed December 1941.

70. I P'ing, "Chin nien cheng-shou chiu kuo kung liang yün-tung ti ch'u-pu tsung-chieh" (Summary of the first steps in this year's movement for collection of public grain for national salvation), *T'uan-chieh,* 1.11:9–16 (Dec. 25, 1938); cf. Hsü Yung-ying, II, 23, based on an editorial in *Hsin-hua jih-pao* (Oct. 30, 1938).

71. Van Slyke, *Enemies and Friends,* 92–96.

72. The best discussion of the three-thirds system in English is in Van Slyke, *Enemies and Friends,* 142–53. Cf. Chalmers Johnson, *Peasant Nationalism and Communist Power,* 13–14; Hsü Yung-ying, I, 74–78. The fullest analysis of the three-thirds system in Shen-Kan-Ning is Lin Po-ch'ü's *Shen-kan-ning san-san-chih.* Cf. Hsieh Chüeh-tsai, "The Theory and Practice of the Three-Thirds System," 198–205, in *WHHC;* Mao Tse-tung, "Problems of Political Power in Anti-Japanese Base Area," *SW,* III, 189–92; Mao, "Questions of Tactics in the Present Anti-Japanese United Front," *SW,* III, 193–203. The term "three-thirds system" evoked the image of Sun Yat-sen by its resemblance

to his Three People's Principles and Three Cardinal Policies. Cf. Chiang Kai-shek's decision of 1926, when the First United Front was disintegrating, to limit the number of communists in any important Kuomintang organ to one-third of the total. This forced the resignation of several prominent communists including Lin Po-ch'ü, head of the Kuomintang peasant department, and Mao Tse-tung, deputy head of the propaganda department. Schram, *The Political Thought of Mao Tse-tung,* 89.

73. Schram, *The Political Thought of Mao Tse-tung,* 162. Cf. the heavily revised version in *SW,* III, 97.

74. Mao, "Problems of Political Power in the Anti-Japanese Base Areas," *SW,* III, 190. The directive, available only in the *Selected Works,* may have been subject to substantial revision.

75. Lin Po-ch'ü, *Shen-kan-ning san-san-chih,* 1–3. The three-thirds system was also implemented in 1940 in the Shansi-Chahar-Hopeh base area. Hsü Yung-ying, I, 74.

76. *CFJP* (May 25, June 2, 6, 21, 1941). Their visit, lasting a full month, was the occasion for serious political bargaining as well as blue-ribbon treatment. Among those who feted them were Mao Tse-tung, Chu Te, Lin Po-ch'ü, Kao Kang, and Wang Ming, the ranking party and government officials in the border region.

77. At the regional level, a professional core comprised of the heads of civil affairs sections from twenty-seven districts was supplemented by eighty-one students from the Chinese Women's College, the Administrative School, and the North Shensi Public School. Preparation varied considerably depending on the local conditions. In Ch'ing-chien, 217 cadres including party, army, and mass organization leaders received a week's training for the election movement. No such extensive training was possible under more unsettled conditions in the six districts of Lung-tung; nevertheless 216 committees with 1,512 members were formed there to direct township elections. Shen-kan-ning pien-chü cheng fu, min-cheng t'ing, ed., *Shen-kan-ning pien-chü hsiang-hsüan tsung-chieh,* 7–19.

78. Ibid., 24–35.

79. *CFJP* (June 21, 1941). It should be noted that Kuo Ching-hua was appointed by the regional government to replace the district magistrate of An-sai, who was transferred elsewhere. Neither she nor any other woman was elected as a district magistrate by the voters in Shen-Kan-Ning. *Shen-kan-ning hsiang-hsüan tsung-chieh,* final unpaginated statistical table on township councils in the border regions.

80. Summary of Ting Ling's essay in Goldman, 23.

81. The progress in women's liberation was more striking in combat areas where women quickly assumed vital military, political, and economic responsibilities than it was in rear areas like Shen-Kan-Ning. The tenacity of the problem of women's liberation is borne out vividly by Jan Myrdal's informants in Liu Ling, where twenty years later impressive gains could not obscure the continued difficulties, 203–39.

82. Evaluation of the three-thirds program is complicated both by official inconsistency in defining the "three-thirds" and by incomplete election results. In their analyses of the three-thirds system, Mao Tse-tung and Lin Po-ch'ü insisted that the division was to be between communists, progressives, and "middle-of-the-roaders." However, their injunctions to the contrary, available election results were invariably couched in terms of achieving a balance between communist, Kuomintang, and nonparty persons, categories which were of course easier to ascertain. Lin also chastised unnamed cadres who incorrectly divided the political pie into equal thirds for the communists, Kuomintang, and Ko-lao-hui. Lin Po-ch'ü, *Shen-kan-ning san-san-chih,* 4, 9.

83. Quoted in Van Slyke, *Enemies and Friends,* 149, from Hsieh Chüeh-tsai, "The Theory and Practice of the Three-Thirds System."

84. Hsü Yung-ying, I, 77, quoting from *Hsin-hua jih-pao* (Nov. 14, 1942).

85. Worker representatives (394), outnumbered landlords (134) and merchants (177)

but were fewer in number than rich peasants (686). Lin Po-ch'ü, *Shen-kan-ning san-san-chih*, 6. The complete data, by district, are given in Van Slyke, *Enemies and Friends*, 148. These results are confirmed by an independent report on township elections in eight districts including six in the new areas. Communist strength there was 20 percent, compared to 5 percent for the Kuomintang and 75 percent for nonparty members. Shen-kan-ning pien-ch'ü cheng fu, min-cheng t'ing, ed., *Shen-kan-ning pien-ch'ü hsiang-hsüan tsung-chieh*, 65.

86. *CFJP* (Mar. 9, Apr. 12, 1943).

87. *CFJP* (Aug. 24, Nov. 8, 1941).

88. *CFJP* (July 12, 1941).

89. Lin Po-ch'ü, *Shen-kan-ning san-san-chih*, 7. Speaking at an intra-party discussion, Lin stated that the communists should retain the majority of township head positions, with the rest to be held by a number of nonparty progressives and a few middle-of-the-roaders willing to follow the party's lead.

90. *CFJP* (Mar. 31, 1942).

91. For a comparison between Shen-Kan-Ning and the rear areas, see Michael Lindsay, "Changes in Chinese Communist Thought, 1937–1960," in Edward Szcepanik, ed., *Symposium on Economic and Social Problems of the Far East* (Hong Kong, 1962), 221–23. The implementation of the three-thirds system in other bases is discussed in Van Slyke, *Enemies and Friends* 150–51.

92. Yang Feng, "Pien-ch'ü i-nien lai ti chiao-fei kung-tso" (The past year's bandit suppression work in the border region), *T'uan-chieh*, 1.9:5–11 (Sept. 20, 1938); "A Letter to the Masses from the Shen-Kan-Ning Border Region Government of the Republic of China on the Subject of Japanese Invasion and Attack on the Border Region," *Chieh-fang*, 34:26 (Apr. 5, 1938).

93. *K'ang-jih chan-cheng shih-ch'i ti chung-kuo jen-min chieh-fang chün* (The Chinese people's liberation army in the period of the resistance war; Peking, 1953), 9, 60, 61.

94. Chalmers Johnson provides a detailed record of the communists' rapid growth in these years. *Peasant Nationalism and Communist Power*, 92–122, 193–94. Japanese intelligence sources estimated communist forces in North China in 1940 at 140,000 regulars and 160,000 guerrillas. French intelligence estimates placed the size of regular communist forces at 500,000 in 1940, including 100,000 troops in Central China. Johnson, 74, 215. One communist source estimates the size of communist forces at 400,000 and the population in the base areas at 100 million in 1940. Ho Kan-chih, 345, 375.

95. Kuomintang intelligence reports of late 1939 credit the communists with controlling only a few subdistricts in all of Lung-tung and Sui-te. BI, "Shen-pei ko hsien ti-fang t'e-shu ch'ing-hsing tiao-ch'a piao" (Record of an investigation of local conditions in all districts of north Shensi; 1939).

96. Official introduction to Mao Tse-tung's "The Role of the Chinese Communist Party in the National War," *SW*, II, 244.

97. The fullest elaboration of the Wang-Mao clash at the Sixth Plenum is given in Hu Hua, ed., *Chung-kuo ko-ming shih chiang-i* (Lectures on the history of the Chinese revolution; Peking, 1962), 378–89. Cf. McLane, *Soviet Policy and the Chinese Communists*, 118–23; Van Slyke, *Enemies and Friends*, 106–7.

98. *SW*, II, 244. Cf. Van Slyke, *Enemies and Friends* 95–97; Hu Hua, 394–95. Communist clashes with the Kuomintang in other parts of China are summarized in Hu's account. The blockade of the border region is discussed fully and with unusual frankness in a comprehensive 1941 Kuomintang intelligence report, BI, *Chien-tang tui lung-tung chih yin-mou chi wo fang tui-ts'e chih kai-shu* (The conspiracy of the bandit party in Lung-tung and our attitude; 1941), 149–51.

99. The magnitude of these clashes is suggested by Kuomintang intelligence reports that in Lung-tung alone 15,378 casualties, 4,639 of them fatal, were sustained on the

Kuomintang side. Approximately half of these were said to have been public officials. BI, *Chien-tang tui lung-tung yin-mou,* 80–81, 164; BI, *Tiao-ch'a chuan-pao* (Special investigation report), 21: 138–48 (January 1940); BI, *Tang-p'ai tiao-ch'a chou-pao* (March and April 1940), 4–6, and 10.

100. The fullest account of the Kuomintang program and its efforts to compete with the communists is given in BI, *Chien-tang tui lung-tung yin-mou,* particularly 2–45. *CFJP* (May 15, 1942) discusses Kuomintang rural policy in Sui-te.

5

Crisis and the Search for a New Order

Thrice during its rise the Chinese communist movement absorbed crippling defeats verging on annihilation. Each of these disasters led to radical innovations in its approach to war and revolution. In all three instances Mao Tse-tung eventually emerged from fierce intra-party struggle as the leading architect of the new line. The Kuomintang's anticommunist coup of 1927 destroyed the First United Front and paved the way for the development of a strategy of land revolution and guerrilla resistance. The annihilation of the Kiangsi Soviet and other bases in 1934 led to the abandonment of agrarian revolution and armed insurrection in favor of the formation of the Anti-Japanese United Front and the reform program of the New Democracy. Finally, out of the devastation and hardship wrought by Japanese offensives, coupled with the Kuomintang blockade of 1941–1942, emerged a constellation of policies associated with the "mass line" and a new attack on the problems of rural society. The Yenan Way developed out of the movement's wartime experience and crystallized in the rectification movement of 1942. The Yenan Way synthesizes the most significant and distinctive features of the Chinese contribution to the practice of people's war, revolution, and the transformation of peasant societies. We will explore its development in Shen-Kan-Ning as emblematic of larger changes taking place throughout the base areas.

The most important stimulus to change was the military crisis which confronted base areas throughout North China. On August 20, 1940, the Eighth Route Army launched its most ambitious campaign of the war, attacking Japanese forces in five northern provinces. The surprise Hundred Regiments Offensive inflicted heavy losses on Japanese troops, cut vital rail and road links, and expanded the base areas. In 1941 and 1942 the mounting communist threat, combined with the necessity for a swift victory in China if Japan were to defeat the United States in the Pacific, led to massive Japanese retaliation against North China bases. The *sankō-seisaku* (three-all policy) of "burn all, kill all, destroy all" was the heart of a Japanese counter-insurgency strategy that featured a full panoply of sophisticated "pacification" techniques, including resettlement of up-rooted peoples under concentration-camp conditions in "model peace zones." However, in the face of persistent resistance, the Japanese repeatedly resorted to the indiscriminate use of fire power, ruthlessly annihilating entire villages. In such campaigns inevitably women, children, and the elderly, rather than armed guerrillas, were the primary victims.[1] Chalmers Johnson provides a chilling de-scription of the implementation of Japan's three-all policy:

> The essence of the *sankō-seisaku* was to surround a given area, to kill every-one in it, and to destroy everything possible so that the area would be uninhab-itable in the future. Instances of the policy's implementation were common: 1,280 persons were executed and all houses burned at Panchiatai, Luan hsien, east Hopei, in 1942; the largest-scale destruction occurred in the Peiyüeh dis-trict (21 hsien) of the Chin-Ch'a-Chi border region, where more than 10,000 Japanese soldiers carried out a mopping-up campaign between August and October of 1941. The results in that area were some 4,500 killed, 150,000 houses burned and about 17,000 persons transported to Manchuria.[2]

By the end of 1942 the communists, reeling under the brunt of Japan's three-all offensive, had suffered their most serious setbacks of the war. In North China Japanese intelligence sources estimated that the population of the base areas had shrunk by almost half from 44,000,000 to 25,000,000 and the Eighth Route Army from 400,000 to 300,000 men.[3] As the Japanese attack shifted into high gear, the communists also found themselves under renewed pressure from their United Front "allies." Following the New Fourth Army incident of January 1941, in which Kuomintang troops attacked and virtually annihilated the major com-munist force in Central China, Shen-Kan-Ning was subjected to an increasingly tight Nationalist blockade.[4] Although the Kuomintang blockade had been initi-ated as early as 1939, in 1941 heavy reinforcements greatly enhanced its effec-tiveness. Moreover, just as the communists were feeling the pinch of the blockade and experiencing military defeat, the Central government at Chungking cut off its subsidy for the Eighth Route Army and the border region govern-ment.[5] Military defeat and blockade brought to light glaring weaknesses long obscured by the speed with which the movement had expanded.

Inflation

The immediate effect of the 1941 blockade intensification was to touch off rampant inflation in the border area. Although prices had risen steadily in Yenan

Table 5.1

Inflation in the Shen-Kan-Ning Border Region, 1937–1943

Year	Cost of one peck of millet (40 pounds) in Yenan (in *fa pi* dollars)	Index
1937	2.5	100
1938	2.5–3.8	132
1939	3–4.2	143
1940	4.2–7	214
1941	8.5–15.7	290
1942	63–145	4,038.3
1943	150–2,200	30,683.1

Source: Lo Ch'iung, *Shen-kan-ning pien-ch'ü min-chien fang-chih yeh* (The Popular Weaving Industry in the Shen-Kan-Ning Border Region), 1.

since 1937, the rate of inflation was substantially lower than that in nearby Sian and other areas under Central government control. But in 1941 for the first time, symbolizing the rupture of relations, the communists issued their own border region currency (*pien-pi*) and banned the use of national currency (*fa-pi*). A Nationalist source indicates that, contrary to the original plan to issue 100,000 dollars in border region currency, 2,000,000 dollars were actually circulated during 1941.[6] As a result of the disruption of trade owing to the blockade and the large issue of paper currency, prices within the base area soared. In the course of a year, the value of border currency fell twice as rapidly as that of national currency. The rising cost of millet, the staple crop in the border area, indicates the severity of inflation (see Table 5.1). During 1942, at the height of the crisis, grain prices in Yenan increased fourteen-fold over 1941 levels. Under intense blockade, it was extremely difficult to obtain cloth and cotton, the major imports, or to export the salt which accounted for over 90 percent of the region's previous exchange earnings. In the years 1940 to 1943 the price of cloth rose twice as fast as that of grain.[7] Moreover, the border region was completely cut off from "outside revenues"—primarily National government subsidies, which amounted to 10,400,000 dollars in 1940.[8]

Even as the economy felt the pinch of Kuomintang blockade, the government announced an all-time high tax of 200,000 piculs of millet for 1941; this figure was more than twice the previous levy and made life even more difficult for the beleaguered peasant.[9] The sharp tax rise reflected the crisis confronting the North China base areas and specifically Shen-Kan-Ning. For the first time since their arrival in the northwest, the communists were left with no recourse but to increase taxes, including for the first time imposing a severe tax burden on the poor peasants.

Taxation Policy

The financial policies of the regional government suggest the range of approaches with which the party experimented in moving toward the synthesis of the late Yenan period. The three major phases in taxation policy parallel the most important shifts in government approaches to the economy and society of the border region. During 1937 and 1938, taxation was extremely light inasmuch as the government relied heavily on Central government subsidies and on income from grain and property confiscated earlier during the land revolution. Following the administrative stabilization of the base area, and with the addition of the rich Sui-te region as a taxable area, levies rose sharply during the second phase, 1939 to 1941. Spiraling tax rates reflected not only the mounting costs of maintaining an expanded cadre network and new government programs, but also a response to financial difficulties created by the Kuomintang blockade. In addition, Central government subsidies were eliminated, while military setbacks in North China required further mobilization of resources to press the war effort. Finally, as the crisis atmosphere began to ease after 1942, tax levels became stable and even declined as new methods were applied to finance the war and regional administration.

The basic tax, accounting by 1940 for approximately 80 percent of regional government revenues, was the "Public Grain for National Salvation." Table 5.2 indicates its growth from an almost token levy of 10,000 piculs in 1937 to 200,000 piculs in 1941, as well as its decline in the late years of the war. Whatever the problems of equitably distributing and administering taxation in the border region, prior to 1941 the burden on poor peasant families was minimal. This situation changed dramatically as the regional government, in response to the Kuomintang's intensified blockade and cutoff of subsidies, embarked on a desperate quest for funds.[10]

As we have seen, the 1941 quota for the National Salvation Public Grain was fixed at 200,000 piculs of hulled millet, approximately 13 percent of total grain production. To achieve this ambitious goal, the government relied heavily on work teams sent to each district to assist local government, party, and army cadres in increasing both the number of families on the tax rolls and the levy on each. This method not only brought experienced administrators to the lower levels of government, it also introduced outsiders who were free from local ties and pressures which might interfere with collection. The 1941 goal was to increase the number of taxpaying families from under 20 percent in many areas to over 80 percent, with only the desperately poor and recent immigrants to the border region being exempt.[11]

The tax-exemption point which had been raised from 400 to 533 pounds of grain per person in 1940 was drastically cut in 1941. Now for the first time, individuals harvesting a mere 200 pounds of grain annually became subject to taxation. Moreover, the sliding scale which once began at 1 percent now started

Table 5.2

Grain Production and "Public Grain for National Salvation" in Shen-Kan-Ning, 1937–1945

Year	Hulled millet (*piculs*)	Grain tax (*piculs*)	Tax as a percent of production
1937	1,260,000	10,000	0.79
1938	1,270,000	10,000	0.78
1939	1,370,000	50,000	3.63
1940	1,430,000	90,000	6.29
1941	1,470,000	200,000	13.33
1942	1,500,000	160,000	10.69
1943	1,600,000	180,000	11.25
1944	1,750,000	160,000	9.00
1945	1,600,000	125,000	7.80

Source: Li Ch'eng-jui, "K'ang-jih chan-cheng shih-ch'i chi-ko jen-min ko-ming ken-chü-ti nung-yeh shui-shou chih-tu yü nung-min fu-tan" (The system of agricultural taxation and the peasants' burden in several people's revolutionary base areas during the period of the anti-Japanese war), *Ching-chi yen-chiu* (Economic research), 2:108 (1956).

Note: Comparison with contemporary data reveals that Li's figures actually represent *planned* collection quotas. During 1937 and 1938 actual collection exceeded the quota by 30 to 50 percent, and by 4 to 8 percent in 1939 and 1940 as more regular procedures developed. Li's figures on grain tax thus substantially underestimate the amount of grain collected in the early years of the border region (since the total collection was small, however, his estimates of tax as a percent of production are only slightly lower than contemporary government estimates). Particularly after 1941, which most directly concerns us in this chapter, his estimates closely approximate available contemporary data. Contemporary tax data are given in Lin Po-ch'ü's report, *CFPK,* 44, and by Hsieh Chüeh-tsai, "Cheng-shou chiu kuo kung liang ti yen-chiu yü shang-ch'üeh," *T'uan-chieh,* 1.26:8 (Aug. 1, 1940); *CFJP* (Dec. 12, 1941); *Hsin-hua jih-pao* (Oct. 27, 1942).

at 10 percent, a substantial payment for families at the subsistence level. Tax rates rose by 1 percent for each additional forty pounds to a maximum rate of 30 percent on 1,200 pounds of grain; these tax rates contrasted with previous rates of 1 to 5 percent. The 30 percent rate was levied on those whose crop exceeded 1,200 pounds per person, that is, on families who had previously been taxed at just 3 percent according to the official rate.[12]

In addition, for the first time the government initiated a tax on fodder as a supplement to the grain levy. In 1941 this amounted to 26,000,000 catties of hay. Nor was this all. Desperate to improve its financial situation, the government hastily introduced a variety of other taxes and fund-raising devices. Although the tax burden never approached that of the "harsh miscellaneous taxes" which had proliferated during the warlord era, and although most levies were eliminated after 1942, the financial pinch on all classes at this time was considerable.

A number of these new levies may be described briefly. A highly publicized campaign initiated during 1941 to sell 5,000,000 dollars in government bonds was oversubscribed by more than one million dollars.[13] New taxes on wool and cattle as well as a goods tax (*huo-wu shui*) were instituted with a goal of raising over 350,000 dollars. More important, a commercial sales tax was levied with a target of 1,280,000 dollars.[14] As the administration sought new revenue sources, it even sponsored a lottery, and in January 1942, with considerable fanfare, it awarded 400 prizes including a 10,000 dollar first prize.[15] Despite these emergency measures, the regional government was obliged to print large amounts of paper currency and to borrow 66,000 pounds of grain in 1941.[16]

The burden of taxation was exacerbated by the fact that peasants were subjected to a variety of other regular and irregular levies. Reporting on tax abuses and their correction after 1941, the press pointed to excessive irregular tax levies as pressures on lower-level cadres reversed the trend toward reliance on regular administrative procedures. In a single township, the people were called on thirty-one times to provide labor or grain in one year! Labor services included tilling the fields for soldiers' dependents and transport of grain. Special levies provided food and expenses for the local school teacher and funds for convening the township council.[17]

A captured 1942 working document of the government of Lung-tung subregion adds further dimensions to the tax picture. At that time less than 10 percent of all families in this relatively poor area were exempt from taxation, and these were mainly recent immigrants. Table 5.3 presents detailed tax data on a township in the Hsin-chi subdistrict of Chen-yüan, a district in which land revolution had not occurred. In 1942, 13 percent of the grain crop in Fifth Township was taken in taxes, an amount consistent with region-wide levies. The basic levy ranged from 10 or 11 percent in the case of tenant farmers and poor peasants to a high of 21 percent in the case of rich peasants and landlords. By virtually any other standards than those prevailing in northern Shensi these landlords and rich peasant families were far from affluent, but their harvests on a per capita basis were, on the average, three to five times greater than those of tenant farmers. From this perspective, their tax load of 21 percent, imposed by a communist government that was forced to place an extremely onerous burden on even the poorest members of the community, appears extraordinarily lenient. These were not among the richest families in the border region or even in the Lung-tung area. The record reveals that one landlord family in Ho-shui district of Lung-tung was taxed 62.9 piculs of grain, fifteen times the average landlord assessment in Third Township.[18] The highest single tax assessment with which I am familiar was a 1940 level of 121.79 piculs of grain (57 percent of income) on Ma Wei-hsin, a leading member of the Ma clan of Mi-chih. By contrast, prior to communist rule, records dating from 1912 reveal that it was a rare year in which a Ma landlord paid more than 10 percent of income.[19] The day had passed when interlocking military and political power shielded the great families from the exactions of the tax collector.

Table 5.3

Taxation in Fifth Township, Hsin-chi Subdistrict of Chen-yüan

Class	Households	Population	Harvest[a]	Harvest per family	Harvest[a] per person	Tax[a]	Tax per family	Tax per person	Percent of tax per family
Landlord	2	18	42.44	21.22	2.36	8.93	4.27	0.50	21
Rich peasant	6	96	176.39	29.40	1.84	37.81	6.30	.39	21
Middle peasant	16	187	225.22	14.07	1.21	27.11	1.69	.15	12
Poor peasant	68	491	482.03	7.09	0.98	53.58	0.79	.11	11
Tenant	90	540	286.85	3.19	.53	31.08	.32	.06	10
Migrant	9	46	17.73	1.97	.38	0	0.00	0.0	0
Total	191	1,378	1,230.66			158.51			

Source: Lung-tung pien-ch'ü cheng-fu, "Cheng-liang cheng-ts'ao kung-tso tsung-chieh pao-kao" (Summary report of grain and fodder collection work), manuscript, 1942(?), 9.

Note: [a]Statistics on grain and tax are given in piculs of millet equal to 400 pounds.

Table 5.4

1943 Taxes as a Percent of Income in Four Districts

Class	Yenan[a]	Ching-pien[a]	Ch'ing-yang[b]	Sui-te[b]
Landlord			41.5	36.5
Rich peasant	22.17	14.69	30.8	18.94
Prosperous middle peasant	21.38	11.67	25.3	13.59
Middle peasant	16.01	8.71	19.09	9.25
Poor peasant	7.78	3.89	8.05	4.85

Source: Li Ch'eng-jui, "K'ang-jih chan-cheng shih-ch'i chi-ko jen-min ko-ming ken-chü-ti ti nung-yeh shui-shou chih-tu yü nung-min fu-tan" (The system of agricultural taxation and the peasants' burden in several people's revolutionary base areas during the period of the anti-Japanese war), *Ching-chi yen-chiu* (Economic research) 2:112 (1956).

Notes:
[a]District in which land revolution had occurred.
[b]District in which no land revolution had occurred.

After 1941 the major burden of taxation rested on formerly exempt or lightly taxed poor and middle peasants. In Fifth Township, as well as in Second Township of Chen-yüan for which records also exist, poor and middle peasants accounted for approximately 75 percent of the total 1942 collection. Landlords and rich peasants contributed only one-fourth of the total.[20] In most of the border region, wherever land revolution had occurred, the percentage of the total tax contributed by poor and middle peasants was substantially higher inasmuch as all or most landlord and rich peasant resources had been redistributed.

By 1943 the tax burden on the poor was eased. The average payment among taxpaying families was 14 percent of income, but the minimum assessment had been cut from 10 to 5 percent and the exemption point had been raised slightly. The maximum rate of this time was fixed at 35 percent, but since landlords were subject to additional levies, 48.75 percent could legally be collected.[21] Li Ch'eng-jui has presented class data on tax as a percent of income for 1943; this information is set forth here in Table 5.4. Li's data, based on statistics for one subdistrict in each of the four districts, confirm other indications that the major beneficiaries of the 1943 tax reduction were the poor peasants; this was at a time when party policy emphasized enhancing the interests of the poor. In 1943 poor peasants in these districts paid only 3 to 7 percent of their grain crop in taxes, compared to more than 10 percent prior to the reduction. Moreover, many of the new and irregular taxes assessed in 1941 had been eliminated. The total tax burden leveled off and even declined as the government's financial crisis receded and vigorous efforts to increase production and to pare army and government expenses met with success.

Our immediate concern, however, is with the years 1941 and 1942, when spiraling taxation placed a severe burden on poor and middle peasants, who constituted the bulwark of communist support. At this time, as the base areas suffered massive reverses throughout North and Central China, fundamental assumptions upon which New Democratic government and united front politics had been predicated were sharply criticized within the party. The border region's second revolution was about to begin.

The Rectification Movement of 1942–1944

In the spring of 1942 the communist party launched a cadre training and rectification campaign (*cheng-feng*) of unprecedented proportions.[22] Cheng-feng marked a major turning point in the Chinese communist movement. Its importance has been emphasized by Western students of Chinese communism; indeed, for many students of Chinese communism the *cheng-feng* movement for all practical purposes *was* the Yenan period.[23] However, new perspectives on the rectification emerge when it is viewed in the context of the evolving guerrilla struggle in the base areas and the tensions implicit in New Democratic politics.

The rectification was born of the crisis precipitated by the Japanese offensive and the intensified Kuomintang blockade. In Shen-Kan-Ning tax increases and inflation reflected severe economic hardship and intensified tensions inherent in the approach to leadership and administration. As we have observed, since 1937 two political impulses and leadership styles were joined in uneasy coexistence in the border region. One, revolutionary, emphasized struggle and broad political participation. The other, bureaucratic, stressed stable administration and the reform politics of the Second United Front. The proponents of the latter approach, the administrators, were primarily intellectuals and students drawn to Yenan from throughout the country on the one hand and local landlords and former officials on the other. Although differing sharply in perspective and political style, both were members of the educated elite. The students had been exposed to new and alien ideas; they were deeply imbued with the united front spirit which initially motivated their participation in communist-sponsored governments. The local elite, skilled in the politics and administration of the warlord era, cooperated on the basis of adherence to united front principles and the desire to preserve the remnants of their economic and political power. In Shen-Kan-Ning these groups formed the bulwark of the regional and county bureaucracy, whose powers steadily increased from 1937 to 1941. On the other hand, most county magistrates and virtually all district and township cadres were local revolutionaries; for the most part they were illiterate peasant youths who had risen in the course of the armed struggle and land upheaval. Their primary commitment was to a social revolution which would eliminate oppression and bring equality and hope to the poor in the desolate villages of the border region.

There was little common ideological ground uniting cadres of varying background and experience beyond anti-Japanese nationalist ideals and a vision of a strong and free China. With the exception of the highest-level party cadres and intellectuals, there had been virtually no exposure to Marxist-Leninist thought or any other systematic educational training. Modern and reformist ideas prevalent among outside cadre administrators and intellectuals, most of them new to the party, were conceptions developed in China's coastal cities during and after the May Fourth movement. Many local cadres on the other hand, with a commitment to land revolution rooted in their familiarity with peasant misery in the border area, remained bound by complex social relationships and village loyalties. By 1941, at a time of nationwide military setbacks and blockade, increased tensions between the peasantry and the government and between cadres of varying persuasions posed fundamental challenges to the party's program in the border region. Had the traditional elite merely been replaced by a new cadre elite which left the basic problems of rural poverty and oppression unresolved? Were local cadres capable of carrying out rural reforms and permanently superseding the traditional landlord elite as the dominant power in village life? Could the border region's isolated villages be effectively linked with overall policy emanating from higher levels of party and government? Was a costly and remote bureaucracy with a monopoly on educated and experienced administrators the most effective means for governing and transforming the border region? These problems were not new. They had been brewing since 1937 with the adoption of the Second United Front and the influx of new members, many of whom were not committed to the party's vision of rural revolution. But, beginning in 1941–1942, these issues became the focus of intense intra-party debate in the *cheng-feng* movement.

Cheng-feng was directed toward building a unified party committed to common ideas, methods, and goals. It was Marxist to be sure, but the emphasis was on creative adaptation to the unique problems of people's war. The heterodox composition of the party, government, and army, whose ranks had swelled since 1937, required education and training to instill primary loyalty to the party in the face of powerful enemy forces and conflicting personal bonds. The magnitude of the problem is suggested by the twenty-fold increase in party membership from 40,000 to 800,000 in the three years after the outbreak of war in 1937. Guerrilla conditions required a maximum of flexibility and autonomy, a minimum of central direction and control. This made it imperative that local military and administrative units, particularly their leaders, share the goals and outlook of the movement. As Stuart Schram has aptly observed, the rectification campaign sought to "harmonize the two conflicting imperatives of 'conscious action' by individuals and impeccable social discipline."[24] Toward this end the party launched a cadre education campaign of unprecedented proportions. In the 1942 *cheng-feng* movement, Marxist-Leninist theory, and particularly examples of its creative application in China, provided the basis for a sweeping reassessment of the past and present problems confronting the party and individual cadres.

Before turning to the campaign itself, we must briefly consider two important precedents in the party's history. As John Rue has correctly suggested, one of Mao Tse-tung's major contributions to the development of a unified communist movement was his insistence on organizational and educational methods to resolve intra-party conflict. These alternatives to expulsion from the party, arrest, or physical violence which had characterized earlier struggles were formulated no later than 1929 and tested in December of that year at the Ninth Conference of party delegates from the Fourth Red Army, the Ku-t'ien Conference.[25]

As he prepared to launch the 1942 rectification campaign, Mao's thoughts reverted to the Ku-t'ien Conference and his own struggle for survival and supremacy within the movement. On January 23, 1942, he ordered the first printing and distribution of the Ku-t'ien resolutions for study by all army cadres down to the level of company commander.[26] Mao's 1929 resolutions reveal a preoccupation with certain problems which the *cheng-feng* movement would stress, in particular discipline, organization, and overcoming errors of "extreme democratization." But it was only in 1942 that a basic rectification methodology of intensive education, small-group study, criticism and self-criticism, and thought reform (*ssu-hsiang kai-tsao*) was developed and implemented on a sweeping scale.

Cheng-feng was preceded by and modeled upon the study movement initiated in Yenan in early 1939 immediately following Mao Tse-tung's triumph at the party's Sixth Plenum. Mao's lengthy report at the Sixth Plenum, with its emphasis upon the Sinification of Marxism, anticipated one major dimension of subsequent study and rectification movements: the nationalistic emphasis on *Chinese* experience and the insistence that ideology be studied in the context of concrete problems. "A Communist is a Marxist internationalist," Mao observed,

> ... but Marxism must take on a national form before it can be applied. There is no such thing as abstract Marxism, but only concrete Marxism. What we call concrete Marxism is Marxism that has taken on a national form, that is, Marxism applied to the concrete struggle in the concrete conditions prevailing in China, and not Marxism abstractly used. If a Chinese Communist who is a part of the great Chinese people, bound to his people by his very flesh and blood, talks of Marxism apart from Chinese peculiarities, this Marxism is merely an empty abstraction. The Sinification of Marxism—that is to say, making certain that in all of its manifestations it is imbued with Chinese peculiarities, using it according to these peculiarities—becomes a problem that must be understood and solved by the whole Party without delay.... We must put an end to writing eight-legged essays on foreign models.[27]

The little-known study movement of 1939 and 1940 involved 4,000 cadres and students within a thirty-mile radius of Yenan. Its basic aim was familiarization with Marxist approaches and their application to Chinese problems. Basic texts for study and discussion included writings of Marx, Lenin, and Stalin and the *History of the Communist Party of the Soviet Union* (Short Course), as well as Chinese works of Mao and Liu Shao-ch'i. Many cadres not only were exposed, often for the first time, to Marxist-Leninist and Chinese revolutionary theory but were also trained in such basic skills as reading, writing, and accounting, which were essential for effective fulfillment of their leadership roles.[28]

The study campaign was concluded in 1940. But in the spring and summer of 1941, at the height of the wartime crisis, the earliest rumblings of the subsequent rectification movement were heard in Yenan. On May 5, 1941, Mao fired the first salvo in his speech, "Reconstruction of Our Studies." This was followed in July and August by two Central Committee resolutions, "On Strengthening the Party Spirit" and "On Investigation and Research," both of which may have been written by Mao and certainly reflected his views. In addition, Liu Shao-ch'i's important speech, "On Intra-Party Struggles," was delivered to the Central Party School in Yenan in July 1941. All four of these documents became basic items for study in the rectification campaign.[29]

In two speeches of February 1, 1942, officially launching *cheng-feng,* Mao set forth guidelines that were followed during the next two years. His major theme was the role of ideology in the Chinese revolution, specifically in "the study of current affairs . . . historical research, and . . . the application of Marxism-Leninism."[30] Although a variety of errors including "subjectivism," "sectarianism," and "commandism" came under scathing attack, Mao reserved his sharpest barbs for theoreticians who study "Marx, Engels, Lenin, and Stalin abstractly and aimlessly, and do not inquire about their connection with the Chinese revolution . . . it's merely theory for the sake of theory."[31] With that biting sarcasm of which he was a master, Mao insisted:

> We do not study Marxism-Leninism because it is pleasing to the eye, or because it has some mystical value, like the doctrines of the Taoist priests who ascend Mao Shan to learn how to subdue devils and evil spirits. Marxism-Leninism has no beauty, nor has it any mystical value. It is only extremely useful. It seems that right up to the present quite a few have regarded Marxism-Leninism as a ready-made panacea: once you have it, you can cure all your ills with little effort. This is a type of childish blindness and we must start a movement to enlighten these people. Those who regard Marxism-Leninism as religious dogma show this type of blind ignorance. We must tell them openly, "Your dogma is of no use," or to use an impolite phrase, "Your dogma is less useful than excrement." We see that dog excrement can fertilize the fields, and man's can feed the dog. And dogmas? They can't fertilize the fields, nor can they feed a dog. Of what use are they?[32]

The *cheng-feng* campaign defined and disseminated a basic corpus of Marxist texts, particularly the interpretations of Mao Tse-tung. Its unifying principles could be directly and readily applied by party and government cadres in resolving problems in their own work.

Cheng-feng was not a purge, although it did provide an arena in which to contest the intellectual and political leadership of the movement.[33] All cadres, particularly those accused of serious errors, were subjected to "struggle" under conditions of psychological stress. However, the goal clearly was to reconstruct and reincorporate them within the movement rather than to eliminate them as enemies through exile, concentration camps, or even expulsion from the party or public office. Mao's own metaphor for this process was that of curing a sick man.

> Our object in exposing errors and criticizing shortcomings is like that of a doctor in curing a disease. The whole purpose is to save people, not to cure them to death. . . . If a person who commits an error, no matter how great, does not bring his disease to an incurable state by concealing it and persisting in his error, and if in addition he is genuinely and honestly willing to be cured, willing to make corrections, we will welcome him so that his disease may be cured and he may become a good comrade. . . . We cannot adopt a brash attitude toward diseases in thought and politics, but an attitude of "saving men by curing their ills."[34]

On February 8, 1942, directing himself specifically to foreign formalism and dogmatism in the party, Mao elaborated on this theme, suggesting that the cure of sick men involved psychological techniques which transcended ordinary education: "It is necessary to destroy these conditions and sweep them away, but it is not easy. The task must be performed properly, which means that a reasonable explanation must be given. If the explanation is very reasonable, if it is to the point, it can be effective. The first step in reasoning is to give the patient a powerful stimulus: yell at him, 'You're sick!' so the patient will have a fright and break out in an overall sweat; then he can actually be started on the road to recovery."[35] Truth and reason, Mao believed, would ultimately triumph, but when the acceptance of reason required the individual to relinquish deeply held attitudes, to remake in effect his vision of the world, a sharp stimulus was required.

Recent studies of group dynamics underline the immense psychological power groups can wield over their members. In particular, one is impressed by the awesome pressures to conform to group norms experienced by individuals who are unanimously declared "sick" or insane. The "patient" is able to save himself, in the sense of restoring his own self-esteem as well as being reincorporated in the group, only by demonstrating complete acceptance of group values and norms. These pressures were heightened in the rectification movement through small-group study and discussions that included the criticism of every cadre by his peers and searching self-criticism.[36] Communist party branches, government offices, and schools provided a group environment for self-examination in the light of concrete problems of war and revolution. In the course of *cheng-feng,* study groups examined not only individual beliefs but the full range of the tasks at hand and charted new courses in accordance with the changing needs and priorities of the movement. The result was to move toward a working consensus both on ultimate values and immediate action within cadre units, to increase communication between leadership and lower-ranking cadres as well as between cadres and the people, and to heighten cadre awareness of the integral part their own work played in a unified revolutionary movement.

A fundamental postulate of Mao Tse-tung's revolutionary world view was that people could transcend the limitations of class. In the process of making revolution, individuals of all classes could become revolutionaries. The united front politics of the Yenan period provided a rigorous test for this view by incorporating large numbers of students and intellectuals in the party. *Cheng-feng* initiated an ambitious effort to create an institutional context for individual education and transformation. As the pressures from attacking forces in the base areas increased tendencies to waver and capitulate, *cheng-feng* provided a means to strengthen commitment to the party and the revolution. Moreover, the campaign sought to broaden the commitment of cadres beyond anti-Japanese fervor to the revolutionary transformation of Chinese society. This was essential if cadre unity was to be preserved as the party, in the years after 1942, set about initiating radical changes in rural life. The success of the *cheng-feng* movement is attested by the fact that, in shifting its course to the intensification of rural revolution, the party retained the support of large numbers of cadres from elite backgrounds who had initially rallied to affirm its anti-Japanese stance. *Cheng-feng* strengthened commitment to the party and particularly to its revolutionary ideals, which had been subordinated to united front considerations during the early years of the resistance.

The basic changes in party policy accompanying the *cheng-feng* campaign were accomplished in the absence of a broad purge, although not without changes in leadership. So prominent a "sick man" as Wang Ming, Mao's former rival, apparently in Moscow at this time, retained his Central Committee membership, although he never recovered his position in the front ranks of party leadership. The writer Wang Shih-wei, the object of the most virulent public campaign of denunciation and a man adamant in his refusal to admit his "errors" and reform at the party's behest, eventually renounced his party membership rather than accept the legitimacy of the criticism against him.[37] But such cases were rare. Public criticism in the press of a few individuals provided negative examples for cadres in eliminating shortcomings in their own work. For tens of thousands of cadres and students who actively participated in *cheng-feng,* the emphasis was on preparation for new challenges and improving their own work rather than on criticism of individuals per se.

The rectification provided a means for dealing with intense friction, contradictions, policy disputes, and heterodoxy within the party and government.

Fifteen years later at the height of the Hundred Flowers campaign, Mao reflected on the *cheng-feng* movement as a successful struggle to resolve problems which arose again at a later stage in the party's history: "In 1942 we worked out the formula 'unity-criticism-unity' to describe this democratic method of resolving contradictions among the people. To elaborate, this means to start off with a desire for unity and resolve contradictions through criticism or struggle so as to achieve a new unity on a new basis. . . . In 1942 we used this method to resolve contradictions inside the Communist Party, namely contradictions between the doctrinaires and the rank-and-file membership, between doctrinairism and Marxism."[38] In applying the principle of unity-criticism-unity, the 1942 rectification was a step toward replacing expulsion, imprisonment, or death, which had commonly occurred in intra-party struggle, and established norms of group criticism. Significantly, both Mao Tse-tung and Kao Kang, who took the lead in this movement at the national and regional levels respectively, had themselves been participants in and victims of the old method of arrest and purge.

The rectification must be evaluated from the perspective of traditional Chinese leadership values and methods, which were grounded in face-to-face relationships, unquestioning obedience to personal authority, and subtle face-saving techniques to shield leadership from criticism or embarrassment. These values clashed with the effort to forge strong loyalties to the party and a movement which would override personal ties. The problem was particularly significant inasmuch as the communists were about to embark on radical new approaches to rural politics. *Cheng-feng* reduced the risk that this shift might undermine unity both within and outside the party, and create disaffection among cadres with a strong united front orientation.

Intense criticism and self-criticism was designed to break down traditional leadership conceptions and to overcome differences in values between outside and local, educated and uneducated cadres. In the process of group study and criticism, cadres were educated in and committed to ideological and policy norms while leadership dedicated to the party and its principles was identified and encouraged. Leadership which emerged in the course of *cheng-feng* had demonstrated ability to persuade and motivate peers in intense group sessions where status and face were scorned. To set oneself above the group, to rely on rank or office, implied rejection of the power of the group to evaluate each individual. Leaders were forced continually to renew their "mandate" by explaining and defending policy and its implementation.[39]

At the same time, a related leadership phenomenon of a very different kind developed. By 1942, seven years after the Tsunyi Conference, Mao Tse-tung had firmly consolidated his grasp on party leadership. In the *cheng-feng* campaign Mao increased his authority as a party and national leader. For the first time his writings and the example of his leadership were widely projected as the embodiment of party policy and spirit. In part this represented Mao's growing stature within the movement as architect first of a successful guerrilla strategy and subsequently of the Second United Front. In part, in the tradition of Chinese rebel movements, it was a deliberate effort to present a leader and personality as a rallying point for the nation. This was particularly significant at a time of mounting friction with the ruling government of the Kuomintang and when both sides were looking beyond the defeat of Japan. In 1943, following the publication of Chiang Kai-shek's *China's Destiny,* as communists and Nationalists vied openly for popular support, Mao's image was further projected as the personification of the heroic struggle in the anti-Japanese national resistance. As particular bases of leadership came under attack in the *cheng-feng* campaign, cohesion of the movement was enhanced by the presence of a personalized leader to whom all owed allegiance.[40]

With the Central Committee directive of April 3, 1942, cadres throughout the border region began an elaborate program of study and a thorough examination and revaluation of the work of every organ and individual. Special committees at all echelons of the party, government, and army directed the study campaign.[41] Throughout the border region cadres were to devote two hours per day to study, which included group discussion and criticism, preparation of study notes, and examination on designated texts. Extended study of the rectification documents over a three-month period preceded a critical investigation of each organization's work; this investigation applied newly assimilated principles to each cadre's concrete duties and to an evaluation of his performance.[42]

As the campaign proceeded, the original three-month program, found insufficient, was repeatedly extended. A directive of the party's Northwest Bureau on May 30, 1942, called for an additional six months of study of the rectification documents by all subregional and district-level cadres beginning July 1. In the course of *cheng-feng* many organizations increased study time to three or four hours daily. Schools frequently suspended their regular curriculum entirely to concentrate on the documents. In Shen-Kan-Ning the rectification campaign remained the focus of party and government work throughout much of 1942, and in parts of the region as well as in all other base areas it continued through 1944.[43]

The eighteen documents originally selected for study (their number was shortly increased to twenty-two with the addition of four more Soviet documents) reflected Mao Tse-tung's dominance within the party. Mao was identified as the author of seven, and he may personally have written as many as six of the remaining items, the latter being mainly Central Committee resolutions consonant with his views. With one selection each, Liu Shao-ch'i, K'ang Sheng, and Ch'en Yün were the other Chinese authors represented in the original collection. While Chinese leaders retained a lively interest in intellectual and other developments in the Soviet Union, the rectification movement did not attempt to establish Soviet ideological supremacy. By including only two Soviet documents among the original eighteen (one from Stalin's pen), the Chinese Communist Party asserted its independence in the area of ideological training. Henceforth party education would stress the realities of the Chinese revolution, particularly the problems of leadership, organization, cadre training, and concrete investigation of past and present work.[44]

Between 1942 and 1944 hundreds of thousands of party recruits and regulars throughout China received their baptism in Marxist ideology and above all in the writings of Mao Tse-tung in an intense environment of learning and critical self-examination. Emphasis was placed on the integration of ideology with concrete problems of war and revolution. Disparate elements within the party were welded into a more unified and effective organization. Finally, *cheng-feng* provided the occasion for a major reexamination of the party's history and its present crisis, which led to new policy departures and the articulation of a new leadership conception, the mass line.

The Senior Cadres Conference

The Conference of Senior Cadres convened by the Northwest Bureau in Yenan from October 19, 1942, to January 14, 1943, illustrates *cheng-feng* procedures at the highest levels of party, government, and army. That conference ranks among the most important in the party's history. Out of it emerged the basic program of a mass line politics which provided the focus of communist policy nationally after 1942 and was tested first in the Shen-Kan-Ning border region. For three full months 267 leading cadres from all organizations devoted themselves to study, criticism, and reexamination of the party's program in the border region. Mao Tse-tung presented two lengthy reports. The first, an analysis of Stalin's "On the Bolshevization of the Party," has never been published; the second is his important examination of "Economic and Financial Problems," which will be discussed below. Liu Shao-ch'i and Jen Pi-shih each addressed the conference for three days, and Lin Po-ch'ü, Ho Lung, Chu Te, K'ang Sheng, Ch'en Yün, and Yeh Chien-ying all delivered major speeches. The list in fact included virtually every top party leader, with the notable exception of members of the Russian Returned Student group. However, the dominant figure at the conference, after Mao, was Kao Kang, whose past and present policies in the development of the border region were vindicated and praised and whose prestige in party councils increased greatly at this time.[45]

The major task of the conference was to analyze the history and contemporary problems of the border region preparatory to defining new policy directions. Typical of the rectification movement's emphasis on concrete investigation and the practical application of ideas, during 1942 the Northwest Bureau had directed numerous field studies of rural conditions throughout the border region. It distributed its reports on socioeconomic and political problems for analysis at this time.[46] The conference focused on the problems of the rectification of the party, government, army, and people, relations among organizations, finances, and education. Following plenary addresses, the participants divided into small groups to consider facets of these problems relevant to their own work and to engage in criticism and self-criticism. Criticism was also a feature of the large meetings; at least seventy cadres engaged in self-criticism before the entire assembly. All participants kept notes or diaries containing personal reflections on the rectification documents and conference speeches. These likewise were discussed and criticized in small-group sessions.

On January 31, 1943, *Chieh-fang jih-pao* devoted its entire front page to describing the methods and accomplishments of the recently concluded Senior Cadres Conference. The conference was credited with having resolved three major problems: the party history of the border region; the quest for unified leadership; and the definition of the present tasks of the border region.

The fierce debate over the early history of the party in the border region provides a focus for examining key issues which the conference attempted to resolve, and reveals the intensity of the struggle over policy and personalities—for the two were often intertwined. When Kao Kang rose on November 17 and 18, 1942, to present his "Examination of Questions Concerning the History of the Party in the Border Region," the issue of party loyalty and the correct line had already been joined several weeks earlier following Ch'en Cheng-jen's report on party rectification. The conference record states that in the discussion on party rectification, the border region party's "oldest and most loyal cadres" had insisted that the guilty confess and mend their ways. The "loyalists" included the leadership core that had centered around Liu Chih-tan during the years of guerrilla struggle prior to 1935, including Kao Kang, Hsi Chung-hsün, Ma Wen-jui, Chang Pang-ying, Wang Shih-t'ai, and Liu Ching-fan.[47]

It was these same local partisans, and above all Kao Kang, whose strategy and leadership were affirmed in the official report on the early history of the border region and throughout the conference. But what individuals and what policy were being attacked, and what was the significance of these attacks on the evolution of policy and power in the border region? It will be recalled that Kao's report on the early partisan movement bitterly lashed out at Central Committee representatives Kuo Hung-t'ao and Chu Li-chih for leftist deviations. In 1942 they were officially censured for the arrest of local partisans, which had occurred in the summer of 1935. Although Mao Tse-tung and the Central Committee, upon their arrival in the northwest, had speedily rehabilitated the local cadres, Kuo and Chu, far from being punished, had retained important party positions. It was thus only seven years later in the *cheng-feng* campaign that Kao and his fellow partisans secured complete vindication of their strategy and official condemnation of their powerful adversaries. Despite official censure, however, neither man was forced to resign from the party or to give up responsible positions held at the time.[48]

Kao Kang's charges against Chu and Kuo are nearly identical to the charges leveled at this time by Mao Tse-tung against Russian Returned Student leadership during and after the Kiangsi period. In his summary of the Senior Cadres

Conference, Kao quotes Mao to the effect that after the outbreak of the Sino-Japanese War in 1937, the principal deviation in the party shifted from left opportunism to right opportunism, that is, to capitulation in the Second United Front. Kuo Hung-t'ao, Kao charges, was guilty of left deviations prior to 1935 and of right opportunism after the United Front went into effect. Kuo, as party secretary of the border region until May 1938, was charged with responsibility for the loss of border region territory without resistance to Kuomintang attackers. In addition, he was accused of allowing returning landlords to recover their former property and dominate the peasantry as in prerevolutionary days. For example, Kao told of a landlord who returned to An-sai district in 1937 and recovered more than 2,000 acres of previously confiscated land.[49]

In addition to his own vigorous defense, others at the conference profusely praised Kao Kang's leadership. Indeed, one result of the rectification movement in Shen-Kan-Ning was to elevate Kao to a position as the recognized authority on local problems. Kao's preeminence rested neither on his mastery of the theoretical foundations of Marxism-Leninism (among party writings available from this period, his stand out as virtually free from Marxist categories except in the most rudimentary sense) nor on his value as a united front symbol for the nation (as in the case of Lin Po-ch'ü). Rather, Kao's position rested on his close association with Liu Chih-tan in leading the land revolution and creating a soviet base as well as on his intimate knowledge of the people and problems of the border region. As the focus of party policy shifted from united front preoccupations to struggle at the village level and reassertion of the revolutionary role of poor peasants, these qualities eminently suited Kao for an expanded leadership role.

Chieh-fang jih-pao in its report on the conference blandly but decisively noted, "The Border Region, from May 1938 under the leadership of Kao Kang, after overcoming rightist tendencies in the united front policy, which existed for a time after the start of the War of Resistance against Japan, and a cadre policy of sectarianism, [followed] a political and organizational line which was entirely correct."[50] Mao himself had singled out Kao and local partisan leaders for praise in his February 1 speech initiating the rectification movement: "I came to northern Shensi five or six years ago, yet I cannot compare with comrades like Kao Kang in my knowledge of conditions here or of the people of this region. No matter what progress I make in investigation I shall always be somewhat inferior to the northern Shensi cadres."[51]

If Mao stood squarely behind Kao Kang, the latter, with considerable prestige among local cadres and peasants, numbered among Mao's staunchest supporters in his victory over challenges from the Russian Returned Students. The bond between the two men was based on a background of common struggle to forge independent guerrilla movements in the face of strictures from the party center, on a common feel for the explosive revolutionary potential of an aroused peasantry, on a personal style which combined the heroic and earthy manner of the semifictional characters of Chinese folklore, and on an impatience with abstract ideology.

In the course of the rectification campaign, both Mao Tse-tung and Kao Kang dramatically strengthened their positions within the party; each with the assistance of the other achieved wide public recognition as the preeminent party figure at the national and regional levels respectively.[52] The rectification movement provided official vindication of earlier policies in the Kiangsi and Shensi-Kansu Soviet areas, for which each had been censured, deprived of authority, and even, at least in the case of Kao, imprisoned by the party leadership. Finally, I would suggest that Mao and Kao were the staunchest proponents of the new mass line politics, which included a more radical class line, strong populist impulses coupled with suspicion of entrenched and remote bureaucracy, and emphasis on struggle within the Second United Front.

The conference reports contain numerous personal endorsements of Kao and injunctions that every cadre in the party, government, and army must obey the directives of the Northwest Bureau he headed. There were in fact two interrelated issues here. One was the personal leadership of Kao Kang. More significant, however, was the increased emphasis on peasant participation and a reduction in the power and independence of bureaucratic organs of government.

Emphasis on the primacy of the party and particularly of the Northwest Bureau in the affairs of the border region had important policy implications. We have suggested that in the years after 1937 the bureaucracy had built up considerable independent power in the administration of the border region. The renewed emphasis on the party in late 1942 was an integral part of a campaign to curb "bureaucratism" (the formulation and implementation of policy divorced from the people) and bureaucratic autonomy. The village-level programs conceived at this time were beyond the capacity of a government bureaucracy whose effectiveness ceased at the district level. At the grass-roots level, it was the party whose influence and potential effectiveness were preeminent. The attack on the bureaucracy and the effort to define a new locus of power are discussed at length below. Suffice it to say here that the "top-heavy" administrative structure, which had led to a concentration of talent in the district and higher-level offices, was revamped. Outside cadres, students, and administrators were reassigned to the villages. There, in conjunction with peasant activists, they would shortly attempt to implement a new conception of leadership and new approaches to rural problems.

The bureaucracy was the stronghold of the "intellectual cadres," primarily students from outside the border region and other elite elements who rallied to the party after 1937 primarily because of its anti-Japanese stance. On the other hand, the Northwest Bureau and lower echelons of the party (and public security forces) were bastions of strength of local partisans, many of whom had fought in the land revolution, had little education, and were attracted to the movement by its promise of revolution and social justice. So long as a premium was placed on united front and stable administration, the administrative skills of outside and elite cadres were indispensable. But the rectification movement and the mobilization emphasis of post-1942 mass line politics required different modes of leadership. Once again, as in the land revolution, leadership implied the ability to rouse latent peasant energies, this time not with the familiar cry to seize the land, but primarily to reorganize and increase production and to redefine power and community at the village level.

As the party turned to these tasks, its attention again focused on the leadership potential of local cadres and peasant activists. But like outside cadres and intellectuals, they too were subjected to criticism preparatory to meeting the challenges of new community leadership tasks. Peasant cadres were, for instance, frequently faulted for "old-style" (*lao-i-t'ao*) leadership deemed appropriate to the land revolution but not the United Front. Their primary error lay in "commandism" and overemphasizing "mobilization" work, that is, mobilization of grain for taxation and recruits for the army. In short, rather than aiding the people, they had actually increased the burden on the poor. In part this criticism veiled the major policy shifts of this period. In 1941 and 1942 the attention of party and government leaders had centered on resolution of pressing financial and military problems; this had required a maximum effort to increase taxes and recruit soldiers, and these preoccupations were passed down to local cadres. But it was also true that hard-pressed local cadres had frequently ruled by fiat, neglecting the painstaking process of popular education requisite for soliciting maximum participation and support in these bitter years. In any event, it was precisely these local cadres upon whose initiative and skill the burden of leadership would rest in the bold experiments shortly to be unveiled.[53]

Since 1937 Lin Po-ch'ü had been the primary spokesman in Shen-Kan-Ning for the values of New Democracy—primarily the Second United Front, rationalized administration, universal elections, and the three-thirds system. With the rectification movement, one hears echoes of a more down-to-earth and elemental tone, increasingly attuned to the peasantry and emphasizing the independence of the communist party within the United Front. In the border region the new tone was articulated above all by Kao Kang. "What is democracy?" Kao asked. "The first condition is that the peasants have plenty of millet, that is, the people must eat well and be well clothed."[54] The communists in the late Yenan period retained New Democratic features of the bureaucracy and electoral politics, but increasingly their preoccupation was with more fundamental problems—the elimination of exploitation, the reorganization of the rural economy, and the generation of community action at the village level.

The Senior Cadres Conference provided a high-level forum for debate and analysis of wide-ranging issues and the education of key cadres preparatory to the radical policies unveiled in 1943. The new approach placed a premium on struggle rather than unity and stability and on broad popular participation rather than the official endeavors of a rationalized elite. The result was a distinctive politics in which the style and many of the techniques developed earlier in the land revolution were utilized in the attack on nature, in overcoming the social and economic obstacles posed by a harsh terrain and remnants of landlord power, and in the attempt to create new forms of rural community. The rectification movement of 1942 prepared party, army, and government cadres to carry these tasks to the village.

Notes

1. The Japanese have not received sufficient recognition for the design and implementation of counterinsurgency. Perhaps this is a product of their defeat in China. American counterinsurgency strategy in Indochina was based explicitly on British practice in Malaya, yet the basic techniques of strategic hamlets were widely implemented in China and Manchuria decades earlier. Some critics, citing the use in Vietnam of poison gas, napalm and pellet bombs, insist that the Americans in Indochina were uniquely barbarous. Yet there is evidence that the Japanese did not blanch at the use of the most advanced technology of death in an earlier era. Johnson cites the Japanese use of poison gas in an attack on one village. Eight hundred people were killed while hiding in underground tunnels to shelter them from attack. *Peasant Nationalism,* 73. A Russian War Crimes Tribunal presents compelling evidence of massive Japanese bacteriological warfare experimentation and examples of its combat use in China. See *Materials of Former Servicemen of the Japanese Army Charged with Manufacturing Bacteriological Weapons* (Moscow, 1950), particularly 23–25, on their deployment against Chinese forces and civilians. On Japanese and American counterinsurgency, see Johnson, *Peasant Nationalism,* 54–70; Chong-sik Lee, *Counterinsurgency in Manchuria,* passim; *K'ang-jih chieh-fang chün,* 120–22; Jonathan Schell, *The Military Half* (New York, 1968); *Asian Survey* (August 1967), special issue on counterinsurgency; Noam Chomsky, "Objectivity and Liberal Scholarship," in *American Power and the New Mandarins* (New York, 1969).

2. Johnson, *Peasant Nationalism,* 56.

3. Ibid., 56–60. Ho Kan-chih, 373–74, states that during 1941 the population in base areas throughout the country was reduced from 100,000,000 to 50,000,000, and the Eighth Route Army was reduced from 400,000 to 303,000.

4. For a full assessment of the controversy which continues to cloud events surrounding the New Fourth Army incident and its political implications, see Johnson, *Peasant Nationalism,* 136–40.

5. Chu Li-chih, "Basic Problems Concerning Border Region Currency," *CFJP* (May 28, 1942). Chu, who was president of the Border Region Bank at that time, indicates that the subsidy was ended following the New Fourth Army incident. Cf. "CCWT," 94 where Mao Tse-tung states that the subsidy for administration of the border region was stopped in 1939. Chu Li-chih is apparently correct in stating that all funds from Kuomintang sources were not cut off until 1941.

6. BI, *Chung-kung ti ching-chi cheng-t'se* (Chinese communist economic policy; 1941), 107.

7. Lo Ch'iung, *Shen-kan-ning pien-ch'ü min-chien fang-chih yeh,* 1–3.

8. *CFJP* (May 28, 1942).

9. *CFJP* (Nov. 16, 1941). The precise quota as given in *CFJP* (Nov. 20, 1941) was 203,400 piculs of grain plus 25,948,200 catties of fodder.

10. The financial crisis and the emergency fiscal measures of 1941 and 1942 are frankly discussed by Mao Tse-tung in "CCWT," 190.

11. The organizational and mobilizational methods employed in the 1941 tax program are analyzed in a lengthy series of articles in *CFJP* (Oct. 23–25, 1942). Cf. "A Summary of the Work of Grain Tax Collection Work Teams," *CTTL,* 458–60. Concerning the use

of soldiers to assist in the work of tax collection, see *CFJP* (Dec. 30, 1941). *CFJP* (Dec. 20, 22, 1941) provides information on expanding the tax base.

12. Hsü Yung-ying, II, 26–27, citing *CFJP* (Dec. 12, 1941), *Hsin-hua jih-pao* (Aug. 30, 1942), and *Hsin chung-hua pao* (Dec. 10, 1942). An additional levy of 50 percent beyond these levels was imposed on landlord families.

13. *CFJP* (May 27 and July 2, 1941); *Chung-kuo chin-tai chiang-i,* 479. 6,180,000 dollars' worth of bonds were reportedly subscribed.

14. *CFJP* (Aug. 23 and Sept. 24, 1941).

15. *CFJP* (Jan. 2, 1942). *CFJP* (Feb. 12, 1942) noted that another drawing would be held on May 12 with prizes totaling one million dollars and a top prize of 30,000 dollars. The increased size of prizes in part reflected inflation.

16. Hsü Yung-ying, II, 26; *CFJP* (Dec. 21, 1941); BI, *Chung-kung ti ching-chi cheng-ts'e,* 107.

17. *CFJP* (Aug. 24, 1942). Such negative examples in the press, as in the case of positive models, often exaggerate for instructional purposes the extent of the abuse being criticized. Labor mobilization is discussed in Hsü Yung-ying, II, 32–33.

18. Lung-tung pien-ch'ü cheng-fu, "Cheng-liang cheng-ts'ao kung-tso tsung-chieh pao-kao" (Summary report of grain and fodder collection work), manuscript, 1942(?), 9.

19. *MCTC,* 140.

20. Lung-tung pien-ch'ü cheng-fu, "Cheng-liang pao-kao," 9.

21. Hsü Yung-ying, II, 28, 32.

22. The term *cheng-tun san-feng,* abbreviated *cheng-feng,* meaning "rectification," seems to have been coined by Mao Tse-tung in his speech of Feb. 1, 1942, inaugurating the campaign. See Boyd Compton, *Mao's China: Party Reform Documents, 1942–1944* (Seattle, 1966).

23. For many years after its initial publication in 1950, Compton's slim volume was virtually the only documented study of the Yenan period. Important points in Compton's pioneering appraisal, particularly his insistence that *cheng-feng* was not a purge and his emphasis on the Sinification of Marxism, tended frequently to be ignored or overlooked by many who brought models of Soviet totalitarianism to the study of China in the early 1950s.

24. Schram, *Mao Tse-tung,* 269. For a detailed official statement of these twin goals, see the September 1, 1942, "Central Committee Resolution on the Unification of Leadership in the Anti-Japanese War Bases," in Compton, 161–75, especially 162. Kao Kang discussed this balance in *Cheng-tun tang cheng chün min ko tsu-chih chien kuan-hsi wen-t'i* (On the problem of rectifying relations among all party, army, government, and mass organizations; Yenan, 1943), 7.

25. Rue, 171–88. Compton, 239–51, translates portions of Mao's Ku-t'ien resolutions as published in 1942 under the title "On the Rectification of Incorrect Ideas in the Party."

26. Schram, *Mao Tse-tung,* 233.

27. Mao, *On the New Stage,* translated in Schram, *The Political Thought of Mao Tse-tung,* 113–14. Mao's barbs against party formalism were directed primarily against his Moscow-trained rivals in the Russian Returned Student group whose power was curbed by the Sixth Plenum.

28. The study campaign is discussed at length in Wen-hua chiao-yü yen-chiu hui (The Culture and Education Research Society), ed., *Hsüeh-hsi sheng-huo* (Study life; Yenan[?], 1941), and in the pages of *Chieh-fang* for 1939 and 1940.

29. These and other *cheng-feng* documents, as well as a useful introduction to the movement, are included in Compton. Niijima Junryō relates it to the military crisis of the early 1940s and explores the development of the campaign in the context of evolving

communist policy in the base areas. *Gendai chūgoku no kakumei ninshiki: Chūso ronsō e no sekkin* (Modern China's revolutionary perception: an approach to the Sino-Soviet dispute; Tokyo, 1964). Goldman, 18–50, discusses the impact of rectification on intellectuals.

30. Mao, "Reconstruction of Our Studies," in Compton, 62.

31. Ibid., 64. Major battles to stress concrete practice appear to have been fought at the Central Party School where Mao was himself a member of the philosophy faculty. *CFJP* (Jan. 28, Feb. 5, and Apr. 1, 1942) reports successive curriculum changes providing greater stress on contemporary problems.

32. Mao, "Reform in Learning, the Party and Literature," in Compton, 21–22.

33. The debate about *cheng-feng* is addressed at length in the epilogue.

34. Mao, "Reform in Learning," in Compton, 31–32.

35. Mao, "In Opposition to Party Formalism," in Compton, 37.

36. On group pressures and the possibilities for changing individual roles and behavior patterns, see William Hinton, *Fanshen,* especially Part IV, and Robert J. Lifton, *Thought Reform and the Psychology of Totalism: A Study of "Brainwashing" in China* (New York, 1961).

37. See Goldman, 18–50, for a full discussion of the case of Wang Shih-wei and other communist writers during the rectification campaign.

38. Mao Tse-tung, "On the Correct Handling of Contradictions among the People," in *Communist China 1955–1959: Policy Documents with Analysis* (Cambridge, Mass., 1965), 278.

39. Richard Solomon's study on "Conflict, Authority and Mao's Effort to Reintegrate the Chinese Polity," in A. Doak Barnett, ed., *Chinese Communist Politics in Action* (Seattle, 1969), illuminates such characteristics of the traditional leadership style as rigid hierarchical relationships, dependency on personalized authority, fear of conflict, and the resultant problems of communication and interaction between superiors and inferiors. The *cheng-feng* movement was the first of a continuing series of assaults on these patterns of leadership.

40. See, for example, *CFJP* (July 17, Aug. 7, 1943). For one of the earliest and most elaborate exhortations to study Mao's writings, see the lengthy articles by Chang Ju-hsin in *CFJP* (Feb. 18, 19, 1942).

41. *CFJP* (Apr. 16, 19, 1942). Lin Po-ch'ü was chairman of the study committee of the regional government. K'ang Sheng and Li Fu-ch'un headed the "Central Systems Study Committee," which included the highest party officials and students at central party schools.

42. "Report of the Propaganda Bureau of the Central Committee on the Reform Movement," in Compton, 3–8. The report was printed as an editorial in *CFJP* (Apr. 7, 1942). The decision to have government cadres devote two hours per day to study was announced in *CFJP* (Feb. 4, 1942).

43. *CFJP* (May 16, June 16, Aug. 5, 1942).

44. The original list of eighteen documents and the four Soviet items added in April 1942 are given in Compton, 6–7.

45. The significance of this conference is stressed in Mao, *SW,* IV, 148; cf. *HTHSL,* 152, 211; *CFJP* (Jan. 31, 1943). Many of the speeches were published in 1943 for limited circulation at high levels of the party. Important developments were summarized in a report issued by the Northwest Bureau: *Kuan-yü shen-kan-ning pien-ch'ü tang kao-kan hui ching-kuo chi ching-yen ti tsung-chieh* (Summary of the proceedings and experience of the Senior Cadres Conference of the Shen-Kan-Ning border region; Yenan, 1943).

46. *Kuan-yü shen-kan-ning kao-kan hui tsung-chieh,* 5–6; *CFJP* (Mar. 23, 1942). The material on the Ma clan of Mi-chih was collected at this time.

47. *CFJP* (Jan. 31, 1943). Ch'en Cheng-jen's report of October 21 is not available. Cf. *Kuan-yü shen-kan-ning kao-kan hui tsung-chieh,* 4.

48. They were in fact censured in absentia. Both had already been transferred to other base areas where they continued to serve in important posts. Kao, *Kao Kang t'ung-chih tsai hsi-pei-chü kao-kan hui shang ti chieh-lun* (Comrade Kao Kang's summary at the Senior Cadres Conference of the Northwest Bureau; Yenan, 1943), 8–17.

49. Ibid., 12–14. For Mao Tse-tung's analysis of the left and right deviations of Wang Ming and the Russian Returned Student leadership, see the Central Committee's "Resolution on Some Questions in the History of Our Party," in Mao, *SW,* IV, 171–218; "The Question of Independence and Autonomy Within the United Front," *SW,* II, 262–66.

50. *CFJP* (Jan. 31, 1943). Cf. *CFJP* (Dec. 6, 1943).

51. Mao, "Reform in Learning," in Compton, 25.

52. Kao's praise for Mao during a 1943 conference for labor heroes suggests something of the mutual reinforcement each provided the other in staking out a claim to leadership. "Who is the leader of the Chinese Communist Party?" Kao asked. "Its leader is Chairman Mao. . . . Chairman Mao is the savior of the Chinese people, the shining light of the workers and peasants, the banner of the broad laboring masses." *Tsu-chih-ch'i-lai* (Let's organize), Shansi-Suiyuan Bureau of the Central Committee, ed. (n.p., 1944), 8.

53. Jen Pi-shih, "Kuan-yü chi-ko wen-t'i i-chien" (Opinions about a few problems), in *Cheng-tun san-feng ts'an-k'ao ts'ai-liao* (Rectification reference materials; n.p., 1943[?]), 84. In a strong critique of *"lao-i-t'ao"* leadership, Jen warned that the party was in danger of becoming completely divorced from the masses. Mao Tse-tung also had harsh words for cadres and policies that "exploit" rather than aid the masses. See "CCWT," 3, 8; "Let Us Get Organized," *SW,* IV, 150, 154.

54. *CFJP* (Jan. 31, 1943).

6

The Yenan Way

The *cheng-feng* movement marks a major watershed in the development of Chinese communism. In 1936, six years earlier, the party had deliberately curbed agrarian revolution in favor of nationwide anti-Japanese resistance and a vigorous but moderate program of reform in the base areas. If the revolutionary component of antilandlord class struggle had been muted in the interests of unity, the impact of the party's program on the war-shattered fabric of Chinese rural society was nevertheless profound. In guerrilla areas the political monopoly of the landlord class was broken. Under conditions of constant Japanese attack, the effectiveness of the movement and the new institutions it sponsored rested on broad peasant participation and active support. Base-area governments effectively responded to the elemental needs of an impoverished peasantry by providing military security, reducing landlord-usurer exactions of rent and interest, and establishing an equitable tax scale. New political institutions enabled many peasants to speak for the first time with pride of "our government" rather than with fear of a remote and threatening state. At the same time, elite participation in base-area governments was secured through appeals to anti-Japanese nationalism and through economic and political accommodation.

In the years 1937 to 1940 these policies proved spectacularly successful nationally. In the late 1930s guerrilla bases spread throughout North China and posed the major threat to Japanese aspirations in East Asia. But the very success of this program undermined its united front basis: rapid expansion precipitated sharp clashes with the Kuomintang which effectively ended cooperation between the two parties. Moreover, by 1941 the brunt of the Japanese attack had shifted from the Nationalists to the communists at the very moment when the Kuomintang blockade of Shen-Kan-Ning was tightened. The border region as well as the guerrilla areas thus faced mounting military, economic, and financial threats.

As the movement confronted the strains of the early forties, limitations of the New Democracy were sharply revealed. If the most blatant forms of elite exploitation in the old society had been eliminated, it became evident that in critical respects life in the isolated villages of the border region went on as before. In Shen-Kan-Ning, the land revolution prior to 1937 had improved the lot of the poor. However, the movement faced the challenge of creating institutions that would permanently break the cycle of rural oppression and stagnation. Also, in many districts, land revolution had not taken place.

In the *cheng-feng* campaign new policies were designed to meet these challenges, and cadres everywhere were prepared for their implementation. The essence of these policies was mobilization in the service of the reconstruction and transformation of the economy. The development of the stagnant agrarian economy was the key to the success of all other programs and ultimately to wartime victory. From 1942, in Shen-Kan-Ning the movement's primary task lay in transforming the fabric of social and particularly economic life at the village level. Shortly the drive spread to every base area in North and Central China.

The scope and intent of the policies implemented throughout the base areas at this time are suggested by the major campaigns launched by the party and government. Viewed as an integrated program, the Yenan Way represents a distinctive approach to economic development, social transformation, and people's war. Its characteristic features included popular participation, decentralization, and community power. Underlying this approach was a conception of human nature which held that people could transcend the limitations of class, experience, and ideology to act creatively in building a new China. Here we may briefly suggest the dimensions of the major campaigns before analyzing their significance in detail:

1. The campaign for crack troops and simple administration (*ching-ping chien-cheng*) reduced organs and personnel in the army and particularly in the government bureaucracy. The independent power of administrative organs of government was curbed. District magistrates as well as the party assumed broad new coordinating powers. The focus of government work shifted downward from regional and district offices to the township and village levels. Simplification was designed to reduce administrative costs, to transfer power from a remote bureaucracy to local communities, and to encourage a style of popular leadership appropriate to people's war.

2. The "to-the-village" campaign (*hsia-hsiang*) brought many outside or "intellectual" cadres to the countryside, resulting in an influx of leadership to hundreds of isolated communities and for the first time the direct involvement of large numbers of cadres in labor in the fields and factories. The campaign was designed to destroy barriers between an educated elite and the most deprived elements in the countryside as well as between mental and manual labor.

3. The campaign for the reduction of rent and interest aroused the peasantry

in areas where there had been little or no land revolution. In the struggle against landlord power and oppression, activist peasant leadership emerged to spearhead the restructuring of village social and political relationships and to redefine the possibilities for community action.

4. The cooperative movement, based on traditional forms of mutual aid, was the party's first major effort to reorganize the village economy. Cooperative principles embedded in the economic life of the village had broad implications not only for agricultural development but for the reorientation of social and political relations, the very essence of community life.

5. The production movement introduced a variety of new approaches to the economy of the border region. One of these was an "organizational economy" in which every organization and every cadre participated in tasks ranging from management of new industries to collecting manure for the cooperative vegetable garden of the local party branch. Cadre labor was designed to increase production, reduce the tax burden, and provide management experience with labor. It was also hoped that stimulating positive attitudes toward physical labor would overcome barriers between mental and manual labor. Another approach focused on "labor-hero campaigns," which sought to overcome traditional disdain for manual labor and to encourage and reward the forgotten men and women in the fields and factories, stimulating them to renewed creative efforts. Labor heroes not only served as models in their local communities, they also received special training to lead the transition to a cooperative agricultural economy and other community action programs.

6. The popular education movement expanded the scope and modified the form and content of education, spreading literacy and introducing new ideas to remote villages. The new education played an integral role in the social, economic, and cultural transformation of rural society.

These programs, many of them new, others pioneered in Kiangsi or developed earlier in anti-Japanese base areas, culminated in a conception of leadership in which popular participation was enshrined as the party's fundamental approach to war, revolution, politics, and economics. Out of the struggle for survival in the resistance base areas came the clear perception that a rationalized bureaucracy staffed by even the most dedicated party and technical elite was insufficient to crack the cycle of rural poverty and oppression. Revolution from above could never lead the peasantry into the modern world. The impetus for rural transformation had to come from and be sustained by revolutionary forces within the village.

Two impulses, one (elitist) toward rationalized hierarchy and centralized organization, the other (populist) stressing reliance on the force generated by an aroused peasantry, had always been present in communist revolutionary approaches. We have observed how mobilization provided the dominant motif in land revolution and guerrilla warfare. In 1942 mobilization approaches became the key for generating economic development and social change in the base areas. "To organize the forces of the masses is one kind of policy," Mao told a 1943 meeting of labor heroes,

> but is there a policy contrary to this? Yes, there is. It consists in rejecting the standpoint of the masses and refusing to rely on them or to organize them; in paying attention only to organizing a handful of persons in the financial, supply or trading organizations, and neglecting the broad masses in the villages, the armed forces, offices, schools and factories; and in thinking that economic work is not a broad movement or a struggle on a broad front, but merely an expedient for meeting fiscal deficits. This is the other kind of policy, and a wrong policy. The Shensi-Kansu-Ninghsia border region pursued this policy in the past, but after it had been repeatedly criticized throughout all these years, especially after the senior cadres' meeting last year and the mass movement this year, the number of people entertaining this wrong notion has probably dwindled.[1]

In Shen-Kan-Ning and the rear areas the policies of the *cheng-feng* period paved the way for distinctive Chinese approaches to development. In 1943 a mobilization style of leadership in war and revolution was raised to the level of theory as the mass line. To trace its development and assess its significance in Shen-Kan-Ning, we begin with the policy innovations of 1942.

The Movement for Crack Troops and Simple Administration

The 1941 economic and financial crisis following the tightening of Kuomintang blockade and the cutoff of Central government subsidies precipitated the movement for crack troops and simple administration. Material difficulties—the shortage of supplies and funds to maintain the border region's large administrative establishment—necessitated sweeping economy moves in all organs and particularly government. These problems were even more acute in the rear-area bases facing crippling Japanese offensives at this time.[2]

The campaign began modestly enough with a suggestion by Li Ting-ming, the noncommunist vice-chairman of the border government, to investigate administrative efficiency. The committee appointed for that purpose became the leadership organ for a sweeping government reorganization carried out over the next two years.[3] In its early stages, this administrative reorganization had two basic goals. The first was to cut the size and cost and increase the efficiency of administration, particularly by streamlining the organizational structure and reducing cadres in the district and regional bureaucracy. Second, it sought to strengthen lower echelons of government, particularly the township and subdistrict, by transferring cadres (mainly outside intellectuals) from higher bureaucratic organs in connection with the "to-the-village" movement. As the campaign proceeded, the second goal became predominant and an additional aim was delineated: to curb independent bureaucratic power by increasing the coordinating functions of the party, district magistrates, and interdepartmental committees over individual branch-type (*pu-men*) bureaucratic organs. In short, simplification of government was part of a broad-gauged attack on entrenched bureaucracy which sought to strengthen lower-level leadership and to increase popular participation.

As conceived in December 1941, the goal was a 20 percent reduction of cadres in government, party, self-defense forces, and mass organizations from 7,900 to 6,300.[4] The regional bureaucracy bore the brunt of the cuts. Its "more than 1,000 cadres" were to be decreased by one-third. The 4,021 cadres serving at the subregional, district, and subdistrict levels were to be reduced by 625 (about 15 percent) to 3,396. Limited reductions were planned in the military. Five hundred regular army men (*ching-wei-tui*) were to be demobilized and sent to work in factories. One thousand militia (*tzu-wei-chün*) leaders, formerly full-time cadres, retained their posts, but without salary. To support themselves they became farmers once again. Finally, 1,100 cadres in mass organizations were to be cut by almost half to 600. Those whose positions were eliminated were transferred directly to other posts, sent to school prior to reassignment, or went to work in factories or farming.

The initial reduction of cadres was designed to increase efficiency and eliminate the "top-heaviness" of government, whose trained personnel was overwhelmingly concentrated at higher levels. Administration was consolidated by amalgamating regional and district departments. This freed many cadres who were dispatched to expand and fortify subdistrict and township governments. The result was to inject new leadership and administrative skills at lower levels and to familiarize cadres with the concrete problems of rural life. A full-time secretary, usually a student but occasionally an administrator, was dispatched to assist the township head in governing at this basic administrative level. In many instances secretaries were assigned to subdistrict governments and in some cases district governments where the level of literacy and administrative efficiency was low.[5]

Local cadres such as township and subdistrict heads typically were semi-literate or illiterate peasant revolutionaries whose allegiance to the party dated back to the land upheaval. Consequently secretaries performed such important tasks as maintaining communications with higher echelons and training local administrators who would shortly replace them. Outside cadres brought new ideas to the isolated rural communities, particularly those ideas emphasized in the recent *cheng-feng* movement. Moreover, they were committed in their careers to furthering the party's program and were unfettered by local personal relations. Former administrators were now called on to become leaders in the rural communities to which they were assigned.[6]

These were the goals of the first campaign for crack troops and simple administration carried out in the border region in early 1942. In April a second campaign was launched to deepen the movement. Throughout 1942 many more cadres went to work at lower echelons. In May, for instance, 200 cadres were transferred from the regional bureaucracy to the subdistrict and township levels; of these, 80 percent served in the subdistricts and 20 percent served in the townships. In the course of the campaign, many highly trained cadres were reassigned to strengthen lower levels of administration. As the tasks of revolutionizing rural life received top priority, their new jobs offered the greatest challenge in the administration of the border region. At the same time, many local cadres returned from district and township posts to assume informal leadership roles in their villages. In eight subdistricts of Yen-ch'uan, for instance, the number of cadres was reduced by seventeen to a total of thirty-eight. Of these seventeen cadres, eleven were returned to the private sector of the economy, four became township heads, and two were sent to Yenan for further training.[7] Meanwhile by the summer of 1942, the effort to provide a secretary in each township had been completed in many districts and was continuing elsewhere.[8] These changes frequently engendered serious tensions. Not only were these new men "outsiders" to the local population and to the prevailing network of ties and loyalties, but they found themselves in roles for which their education and administrative experience had ill prepared them. Moreover, their arrival often cost a local cadre his official position. The party addressed the resultant tensions in the "to-the-village" movement discussed below.

By the conclusion of the second campaign in December 1942, many cadres and students had been transferred downward. However, the goal of substantially reducing the government payroll remained elusive. When a third campaign was launched in early 1943, Lin Po ch'ü" reported that 8,200 cadres were serving in all levels of government and its subsidiary organs. This actually exceeded the estimated 7,900 who were serving at the outset of the movement in December 1941! In addition, the government was supporting 3,300 students at middle-level schools, exclusive of military schools. Including all dependents (but exclusive of Eighth Route Army forces), 22,500 persons were supported at public expense. Lin reiterated the call for a reduction in cadre and middle school enrollment from 11,500 to 7,500 students, a slash of about one-third. At the same time he stressed raising the quality of leadership, particularly by sending intellectual cadres to the lower levels. By the completion of the campaign for crack troops and simple administration in January 1944, the number of organs directly subsidiary to the regional government was reduced from thirty-five to twenty-two; one-fourth of all departments at the regional level were eliminated by amalgamation, and those at the subregional and district levels were reduced from eight or nine to four or five.[9]

The importance of the administrative reform lay neither in dramatic budget cuts nor in substantial reductions of "surplus" bureaucrats. Efforts to reduce the number of cadres on the public payroll, a chronic problem in Republican China, apparently proved inconclusive. At any rate no final statistics were issued. The significance of the campaigns lay rather in the changes inaugurated in the structure, composition, and conception of government. Lower-level administration, particularly that of the township, was strengthened, and its responsiveness to directives from above was increased by the presence of outside cadres, either experienced administrators or students, who were unfettered by local ties and committed to carrying forward the transformation of rural society. Some former local officials who had manifested leadership ability during the land revolution but lacked administrative skills and experience returned to their villages. Many of them shortly assumed informal leadership roles during the production drive of 1943. These changes paved the way for an expanded assault on the problems of village life, initiated frequently by the party and government but relying heavily on the active participation of the local population.

Vertical and Dual Rule

In the course of the administrative simplification, lines of power were redrawn to reduce the independence of departments of government. These changes strengthened controls over individual departments by county magistrates and governing committees exercising broad coordinating powers. They also increased the leverage of the party with respect to government. The goal was to bring government closer to the people and to heighten its responsiveness to local needs.

From the early years of the Second United Front and during the relative peace after 1937, government decision-making was centralized in the regional bureaucracy, and administration was concentrated in its district sections. Staffed predominantly by outside intellectual cadres, these organs established powerful branch or vertical networks penetrating downward from the regional level. In short, major structural elements drawn from China's bureaucratic tradition were incorporated into the administration of the base areas. Prior to 1942, departments such as finance, education, reconstruction, and civil affairs, with a virtual monopoly of the expertise for stable and efficient administration, enjoyed broad autonomy in fulfilling their specialized functions. This was vertical rule. For example, educational policy was drafted in the department of education of the regional government. Orders for its implementation were channeled directly to the education section in each district and eventually to lower-level education offices or schools. In this vertical organization, there were few checks on departmental autonomy by party or government cadres outside the department. In particular, neither the magistrate nor the party could bring significant influence to bear on district administration since cadres within bureaucratic sections were responsible to departmental superiors at the regional level. The system established a clear-cut chain of responsibility and command within each department and concentrated power in Yenan.

This centralization of authority at the regional level made it extremely difficult to coordinate the work of departments at the district and lower levels or to respond creatively to local variations and emergencies. The price of uniform and stable administration was a tendency toward administrative rigidity, which was the very antithesis of the egalitarian and participatory thrust of mobilization politics. The tasks of government were to be left to the experts in a manner more reminiscent of the imperial bureaucracy than of the political style of agrarian revolution and people's war. One significant corollary of this system was the concentration of state resources such as schools and industry in the regional centers, the regional and district capitals where administrative efficiency and controls were maximized. As a result, most townships and villages remained without and remote from schools and publicly financed industry.

These practices were attacked and substantially modified in the campaign for crack troops and simple administration. Dual rule superseded vertical rule as the dominant administrative pattern, and the leadership of the party and of government officials with broad coordinating functions increased in importance.[10] The classic statement for the implementation of dual rule is contained in Mao Tse-tung's "On Methods of Leadership," a 1943 resolution written for the Central Committee.

> In assigning a task (such as prosecution of the revolutionary war, production, education, the rectification campaign, checking up work, examining cadres, propaganda, organizational or anti-espionage work, etc.) to a subordinate unit, the higher leading organization and its departments should act through the leader who has overall responsibility for the lower organization concerned, so that he can undertake the assignment with a full sense of responsibility, thereby achieving a division of duties under unified leadership (centralized authority). It is inadvisable for one department of a higher organization to have contacts only with its counterpart in lower organizations (for example, the organizational, propaganda or anti-espionage departments of a higher organization to have contacts only with the corresponding departments of lower organizations), leaving the responsible head of a lower organization (for example, the secretary, chairman, director or school principal, etc.) uninformed and unable to answer for the work assigned. It is essential that the leader of a lower organization concerned as well as the heads of its particular departments should be informed of the assigned task and held answerable for its fulfillment. Such a centralized authority, i.e., division of duties under unified leadership, permits the leader at the top to mobilize a large number of people—on occasion even the entire personnel of an organization—to carry out a particular task; in this way, shortage of workers in particular units can be remedied and a large number of people can be drawn in as active participants in a given task. This is also a form of linking up the leadership with the masses.[11]

The dynamic and flexible conception of mobilization politics outlined here directly challenged administrative tendencies toward stabilization and bureaucratization. It pointed to a campaign style of politics and broad popular participation. In this approach popular and cadre energies would combine to concentrate on immediate and pressing problems. Narrow specialization and monopolization of power by an administrative elite were deliberated rejected. In those base areas whose villages and towns comprised the front lines of an incessant struggle against Japanese forces, this approach was basic to the guerrilla strategy of rapid military and political mobilization. In Shen-Kan-Ning, which was secure from attack although subjected to blockade, the same principles were applied to revolutionizing the social and economic fabric of rural life.

In the border region the immediate repercussions of the new politics are clearly reflected at the district level in the interaction between administrative sections linked to the regional bureaucracy and local governments with roots in the villages. Beginning in 1942, under dual rule a section head was no longer solely or even primarily responsible to his superiors within the department at the regional level. He had to account regularly to a coordinating committee of the district government and to the magistrate. Moreover, the chain of command was altered, and directives to district sections of the bureaucracy were rerouted. For example, the district section of the education department no longer received orders directly from its departmental superiors. These orders were transmitted to the district affairs committee headed by the magistrate, before being passed on to the educational section. Likewise, most directives from the district section of the education department down to lower offices or schools as well as up to the regional department were once again channeled through the governing committee. The formal differences between vertical and dual patterns of government are illustrated by the two diagrams on the following page.

The magistrate had always attempted to coordinate and control bureaucratic sections operating within his district, but his power was circumscribed by the fact that bureaucrats were appointed by and responsible to their superiors in Yenan. Dual rule shifted the locus of power from regional offices, which framed broad policy lines, to lower levels, which implemented them. The advent of dual rule placed the district affairs committee and magistrate in a pivotal role. Directives and communications to and from higher-level departments of the bureaucracy had to secure the approval of local officials; this was true also of information flowing from departments to subordinate organizations. This was the first step toward making the magistrate master of government work within his district. The result was increased flexibility and responsiveness to local priorities and initiatives. Dual rule increased the power of local cadres, many of whom had been active in the land revolution and whose power had been eclipsed by outside administrators after 1937.

Other measures taken simultaneously reinforced these tendencies. The district magistrate increased his power over personnel matters. The appointment of the district political affairs secretary, bureaucratic section chiefs, and the commander of the district self-defense army remained the prerogative of the regional government, but all their subordinates were henceforth to be hired and transferred at the discretion of the magistrate.[12] The magistrate's position was further strengthened by the addition of two or more intellectual cadres to his staff, who served as

Vertical and Dual Rule: Channels of Communication and Responsibility*

Vertical Rule

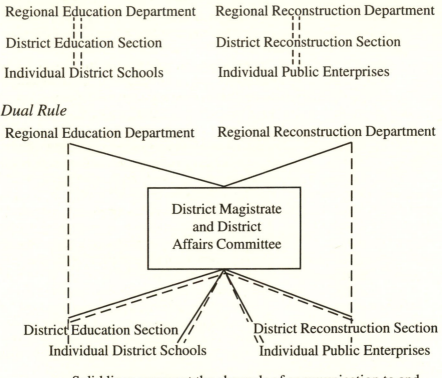

Regional Education Department   Regional Reconstruction Department

District Education Section   District Reconstruction Section

Individual District Schools   Individual Public Enterprises

Dual Rule

Regional Education Department   Regional Reconstruction Department

District Magistrate
and District
Affairs Committee

District Education Section   District Reconstruction Section
Individual District Schools   Individual Public Enterprises

———— Solid lines represent the channels of communication to and from bureaucratic departments.

— — — Dotted lines represent the pattern of responsibility of bureaucratic departments.

*Compare Franz Schurmann's conceptualization of dual rule during the Great Leap Forward, *Ideology and Organization in Communist China,* 194.

general affairs secretary and political affairs secretary. As many magistrates were illiterate or only semiliterate, this increased their ability to deal effectively with bureaucratic organs operating in their districts, at least to the extent that they were able to control the activities of their new secretaries. In short, local officials obtained increased authority at the same time that efforts were made to securely link local government with higher echelons.[13]

One additional step in consolidating dual rule was the development of a system of regional and district committees with extensive powers to coordinate policy at each level of administration. District affairs committees (*hsien-wu wei-yüan hui*) ideally met each week under the chairmanship of the magistrate to plan the full range of government policy. Their membership included the heads of each section, the judge, the security chief, and in some cases party and military representatives. These committees, familiar with local conditions and priorities, coordinated the activities of individual departments with the work of various mobilization task forces.[14]

The increased power of the magistrate and the formalization of political affairs conferences substantially reduced departmental autonomy. Moreover, within departments, power which had been highly centralized at the regional level now shifted downward to the district. As coordination at the district level increased, it became impossible to monopolize intra-departmental decision-making powers in Yenan. Increasingly key decisions were made on the spot in sections and interdepartmental meetings. Sections thus won greater autonomy vis-à-vis departmental superiors, but they were subject to greater integration and control locally.

The tasks of the official in a district section of the bureaucracy under dual rule involved more than routine enactment of policies handed down from above; he was required to modify and adapt policy, and above all to articulate and defend it in the district affairs conference. It was precisely these qualities of open discussion and group cohesion which the party simultaneously sought to foster through small-group criticism in the *cheng-feng* movement. The cadre with a broad grasp of local conditions and the ability to coordinate and unify diverse policies was at a premium. These qualities were critically important for the effective functioning of the magistrate. In his expanded role he mobilized cadres from all departments as well as the people to participate in campaigns designed to achieve breakthroughs in critical areas. This, of course, was the antithesis of earlier procedures that emphasized centralization and specialized expertise. The rising power of the magistrate was a direct result of the increased emphasis on mobilization politics.

The shift from vertical to dual rule was accompanied by increased power of the party, particularly at the district level and below. It will be recalled that one of the major demands which emerged from the Senior Cadres Conference of 1942 was the strengthening of the "unified leadership," that is, the coordinating powers, of the party. Accompanying the reduction in departmental autonomy was an increased stress on party leadership of government.[15]

In 1942 the party, whose members held positions among the leadership and rank-and-file in all government agencies as well as the army and mass organizations, was given the power to coordinate diverse activities and provide overall leadership of the government and army:

> The unity and centralization of leadership in the War Bases should be expressed in each War Base in the existence of a united Party committee with

over-all leadership (Central Committee bureaus, district committees, and local committees). Consequently it has been decided that organs representing Central Committee (Central Committee bureaus and subbureaus) and Party committees at each level (district and local committees) are to be the highest leading organs in the districts, that they are to unify the leadership in all Party, governmental, military and mass work within a district. . . .

The character and composition of Party committees at all levels must be changed; Party committees at all levels should not merely be committees which guide local work, but should also be unified organs for Party, governmental, military and mass leadership in that district (they should not, however, be joint conferences). For that reason, they must include the principal responsible Party members and cadres in Party affairs, the government and the army.[16]

In politics and administration at the district level, the emphasis under dual rule was policy coordination. In concert with the district affairs committee, the party provided coordination and leadership of all cadres and of the people in the series of campaigns launched during and after 1942. Before turning to those campaigns and the leadership conception they embodied, we must consider the changes that occurred in the village politics of the border region as the result of the infusion of new leadership.

The "To-the-Village" Movement

As regional and district government was restructured in accordance with principles of dual rule, basic changes occurred in the townships and villages. To understand the altered dimensions of village life after 1941, we must recapitulate briefly the relevant consequences of the land revolution carried out in much of the border region in 1935 and 1936. That revolution had undermined or destroyed the landlord elite and created new leadership primarily among poor peasant youths. Many of these peasant cadres continued to dominate local government and party organization after the termination of the land revolution and the formulation of a united front government. But the Second United Front also permitted and indeed encouraged the return of former elite elements who had fled during the revolution. After 1937 many landlords and former landlords served prominently in the government, and some even became party members. Particularly in villages where party organization was weak and in areas where land redistribution had not occurred, the landlord elite often retained or restored its grip on the economic and political life of the community.

By 1941, both in districts which had experienced the land revolution and in newer areas which had not, local power frequently was shared by peasant revolutionaries and the traditional elite. Despite periodic political mobilization of the peasantry, the official emphasis on unity and stability after 1937 allowed social life in many isolated villages to revert increasingly to prerevolutionary patterns. Work teams from the outside occasionally came to the villages. However, their temporary presence had a minimal effect, particularly since their major functions were to collect taxes and recruit soldiers. No method had been devised to maintain the organized strength of the peasantry, manifested in land revolution, once peace was restored and attention shifted to routine farming, local administration, and war preparations. However, under the crisis conditions of 1941, party leaders became increasingly aware of the failure to break the isolation and economic stagnation of village life. This failure was attributed principally to the fact that the postrevolutionary village economy remained virtually untouched. If tenancy had been largely eliminated by the land revolution in many districts, primitive agricultural technology and productive methods still prevailed, and patterns of landlord oppression (particularly where land revolution had not occurred) continued. The pattern of individual family farms remained unchanged in the years after 1937. Despite an elaborate organizational structure of locally elected township and village governments and a variety of mass political and military organizations and local party units, many fundamental aspects of peasant life were unaltered. What was missing was the dynamic impetus to fundamental change which would go beyond the egalitarian impulses of land revolution to generate and sustain economic and community development.[17]

The reorganization of village politics was aimed at developing more effective local leadership which would pursue new production-oriented and community action goals. One of the earliest and most significant signs of renewed interest in transforming local politics, and a symbol of the populist spirit of the Yenan era, was the "to-the-village" movement. "To the village" began quietly in July 1941 with reports of cadres and students proceeding to the countryside to assist in the grain harvest. This aspect of the movement, cadre assistance during peak production periods, continued in subsequent years. But more significant departures soon developed. The pragmatic and short-run goals of using "nonproductive labor" to overcome temporary labor shortages gave way to a new conception of the relationship between leaders and the people that grew out of the interaction of outside cadres and intellectuals with peasants and local cadres.[18]

This second and critical phase of *hsia-hsiang* was inaugurated in the spring of 1942 in connection with the rectification movement. Students and intellectuals, after study in Yenan, were assigned to villages. They primarily assisted in the tasks of the local party and government while also assisting in peak-season agricultural labor. A typical example is that of 178 middle school students who left Yenan to establish and teach winter schools in remote villages.[19] The aim was to bridge the gap between town and back country, and to overcome barriers separating mental and manual labor. Intellectuals participating in physical labor under primitive village conditions would experience at firsthand the hardship and problems but also the possibilities of peasant life. They also would bring new skills and ideas to villages cut off from the outside world. The "to-the-village" movement was one facet of the response to the critical problems that all developing nations face: how to create an environment in which the most educated youths will be willing to commit their talents and their lives to the development of backward rural areas? And, how to effectively utilize those talents outside of the advanced urban areas in which they were nurtured?

In addition, it was hoped that insights gathered by painters, writers, and musicians in the countryside or at the front would subsequently appear in their art, an art to be devoted to the resistance and to improving the quality of rural life.[20] As K'ai Feng, head of the propaganda department of the Central Committee, remarked in a speech to party intellectuals, the purpose of *hsia-hsiang* was for "intellectuals [to] truly serve the workers, peasants and soldiers, [to] reflect their livelihood and work."[21]

The skills of intellectuals were to be utilized in new ways in the villages rather than in the regional or district capitals where their offices and schools were concentrated. Two decades earlier, in the May Fourth era, the populist impulses of Chinese revolutionary youth were manifested in the drive to carry their revolutionary message to the people. Now a new program brought cadres and intellectuals in direct contact with the problems of rural life not only to teach but simultaneously to learn from the peasantry.[22]

"To the village" was an integral part of the contemporary movement for administrative reform. Not only artists, writers, and students but also cadres from the regional and district bureaucracy were dispatched to strengthen local politics and administration. The downward transfer of trained cadres reduced the isolation of the villages, linked local governments more effectively with higher levels, and introduced new conceptions of leadership, particularly those developed during the *cheng-feng* movement. In addition, "to the village" worked to improve literacy and develop rudimentary administrative skills among local cadres and students, preparing them for independent leadership roles.[23]

What did *hsia-hsiang* mean to the cadres, intellectuals, and students sent down to spearhead the production movement, overcome the "feudal remnants" of village life, and, in the process, educate themselves? There can be no question that for some, particularly older and more experienced cadres secure in bureauc-ratic routines, the new tasks represented onerous punishment or demotion in status as well as a blow to effective administration. But for many youths, it was apparently an exhilarating and moving experience which must be perceived in terms of war-induced patriotism and a faith in the compelling ideology of national salvation and public service. The spirit of wartime Chinese youth was directed in *hsia-hsiang* not only to bringing an urgent revolutionary message of development and social transformation to the countryside but to sharing in and learning from the experience of the people as well.

Frictions quickly arose as students and cadres attempted simultaneously to reform and share in village life. The position of outsiders could be a tenuous one. In many cases there was intense resistance to change. Often *hsia-hsiang* precipitated power struggles in villages whose leaders felt threatened by the new cadres. Party leaders found it necessary to reiterate that outsiders came to aid, not usurp, the position of local cadres, that the secretary to the township head was an assistant, not the boss of local government.[24] Finally, a clash of ideas was inevitable inasmuch as these cadres, many of them trained and educated outside the border region or in Yenan, brought a vision of revolution and society which challenged many deep-rooted village values. Despite all of these difficulties, *hsia-hsiang* contributed to the attack on the problems of rural life in the base areas.

The Campaign for the Reduction of Rent

The united front policy of the war years included termination of land redistribution as the communist party's fundamental approach to the peasantry. Among "The Ten Great Policies," comprising its wartime program was its goal to "reduce rent and interest rates."[25] Nevertheless, from 1937 to 1940 in Shen-Kan-Ning and the newly created base areas, no official effort was made to implement rent reduction. Beyond the commitment to preserve the gains of land redistribution and to guarantee private ownership of land, it might almost be said that at this time there was no land policy. Landlordism and related problems of exploitation were assumed to have been basically eliminated in most of the border region, and problems of land tenure were rarely mentioned. Neither in the laws and documents of the first regional council (1939) nor in the extensive party and government publications of the period 1937 to 1939 is rent reduction discussed. In Shen-Kan-Ning as in other base areas, during the heyday of the Second United Front little attention was paid to the peasant economy or to social and political relations in the villages.

In late 1938, with the decline of the United Front, this situation began to change. During 1939 and 1940 fighting between the communists and Kuomintang brought substantial territories of Sui-te and parts of Lung-tung, where landlord power remained entrenched, under the effective control of the regional government. The incorporation of these districts occurred at a time when blockade and military friction with the Kuomintang as well as the party's increasing power nationally reinforced communist advocates of a more aggressive united front and class policy. Nevertheless it was not until the party faced the crisis situation precipitated by the New Fourth Army incident and the Japanese offensive of 1940 and 1941 that reduction of rent was vigorously pursued in the context of new approaches to the peasant and the village.[26]

On January 28, 1942, three days prior to the start of the *cheng-feng* campaign, the Politburo issued the party's first major statement on land policy since the outbreak of the war of resistance. Written by Mao Tse-tung, "The Decision of the Central Committee on Land Policy in the Anti-Japanese Base Areas" established basic guidelines which remained in effect until 1946.[27] Reappraising the relationship between United Front and rural revolution, it established guidelines for rent and for the new political economy which developed shortly in the base areas. Three basic tenets were emphasized:

> (1) Recognize that peasants (including hired farm hands) constitute the basic strength of the anti-Japanese war as well as of the battle of production. Accordingly it is the policy of the Party to assist the peasant, reduce feudal exploitation by the landlords, carry out civil liberties, political rights, land rights, and economic rights of the peasants in order to improve their living conditions and enhance their enthusiasm for the anti-Japanese war and for production.
>
> (2) Recognize that most of the landlords are anti-Japanese, that some of the enlightened gentry also favour democratic reforms. Accordingly, the policy of the Party is only to help the peasants in reducing feudal exploitation but not to liquidate feudal exploitation entirely, much less to attack the enlightened gentry who support democratic reforms. Therefore, after rent and interest rates are reduced, the collection of rent and interest are to be assured; and in addition to protecting the civil liberties, political, land, and economic rights of the peasants, we must guarantee the landlords their civil liberties, political, land, and economic rights. . . .
>
> (3) Recognize that the capitalist mode of production is the more progressive method in present-day China and that the bourgeoisie, particularly the petty bourgeoisie and national bourgeoisie, represent the comparatively more progressive social elements and political forces in China today . . . the policy of the Party is not to weaken capitalism and the bourgeoisie, nor to weaken the rich peasant class and their productive force, but to encourage production by rich peasants and ally with the rich peasants, on the condition that proper improvements are made in the living conditions of the workers.[28]

The land resolution of January 1942 did not explicitly contravene earlier wartime formulations concerning the United Front or the land question. However, it departed from previous official statements in two respects. First, it introduced the theme of the "production battle," placing it virtually on a par with the anti-Japanese war itself. The battle for production would shortly preoccupy party and government in blockaded Shen-Kan-Ning and other bases; from 1942 their major task was defined as increasing productivity, particularly in agriculture, a task which led to a focus on the problems of village life. The production battle became the central motif for unifying the national resistance and rural reform. Second, the party after five years of consistent homage to the idea of *national* unity, tentatively reintroduced the *class* rhetoric of landlord "feudal exploitation" and emphasized its primary commitment to the poor and oppressed. Official guidelines stressed that the party "should not take a one-sided stand either for the landlord or for the peasant." However, as peasant activists again carried forward the struggle against landlord exploitation, the party's stricture "only to help the peasants in reducing feudal exploitation but not to liquidate feudal exploitation entirely" was frequently ignored. Rent-reduction campaigns, often coupled with tax and other fiscal measures, sometimes liquidated large landlord holdings entirely.[29] The resolution on land thus initiated a more militant effort to break the social and economic grip of the landlords through organized peasant power.

The January 1942 "Decision on Land Policy" is frequently cited to illustrate the party's moderate wartime land policy in contrast with its greater militancy after the total collapse of the United Front in 1946.[30] However, in the context of evolving policy, its significance lies in its initiation of mass campaigns to reduce rent and challenge landlord supremacy, tasks which were resumed after five years of emphasis on the politics of united front. In this sense it was a step toward a more radical class position which reached its culmination in 1946 in full-scale agrarian revolution.

The effort to link land revolution in its limited form as rent reduction with the drive to increase and transform production suggests new concerns and growing sophistication in the party's approach to the peasantry and the economy. Land revolution during the Kiangsi period was based on a vision of prosperity and equality which roused the peasantry to radical action. However, a frequent by-product of land upheaval was severe economic disruption resulting from war devastation, expropriation of commercial enterprises, fear of further confiscations, and uncertainty on the part of both peasants and merchants concerning the new economic ground rules. In any event, the creation of an economy of roughly equal small peasant proprietors mitigated the immediate hardships of poverty without significantly stimulating economic development. One striking achievement of the 1942 policy synthesis was the joining of the dynamism of agrarian revolution (in the guise of rent reduction) with the commitment to rural development and the transformation of village society.

Rural surveys of land tenure conducted throughout the border area in early 1942 led to a drive to register or reregister all lands to ascertain ownership, area, productivity, and tenant relationships.[31] This was no routine bookkeeping operation. The emphasis was on discovering evasions and violations of the new land laws. For instance, investigators found that many landlords who returned to the border region in 1937 illegally recovered property which had earlier been confiscated and redistributed, or took possession of public land. Since the land revolution had been carried out under conditions of confusion and stress, land was often improperly registered by its new owners.[32]

Following pilot programs in Sui-te in 1940 and 1941, in 1942 the party led a drive for the reduction of rent in approximately ten districts, most of them in the new areas of Sui-te and Lung-tung where landlord power was still formidable. The explicit goals of the campaign were the reduction of rent by 25 percent and the establishment of a rent ceiling set at 37.5 percent of the crop. As in a number of their wartime programs, the communists deliberately adopted legislation which had long been on the books of the National government but had not been implemented.[33] The 1942 rent-reduction campaign was launched on a note of moderation and class cooperation. However, by the time it attained peak intensity in the latter part of 1942 and again after the 1943 harvest, there were echoes of violent class struggle. A considerable effort was made in the early stages to obtain the voluntary support of landlords on the basis of aiding the war effort. Statements urging cooperation in the reduction of rent by such prominent gentry as An Wen-ch'in, a wealthy Sui-te landlord and vice-president of the regional council, were widely publicized. Landlords from the Ma clan of Mi-chih served on committees established to carry out rent reduction.[34] However, as the campaign progressed, pressures on the landlords increased, and reports of landlord cooperation were replaced by those of antilandlord struggle. Recalcitrant landlords, including two who headed subdistrict governments in Mi-chih, were prosecuted, punished, and publicly denounced for violations of the rent-reduction laws.[35]

In late 1942, as the campaign was intensified, its focus became the mobilization of peasant associations and other organizations to demand and enforce rent reduction. After four years of restraint in the interests of stability and unity, peasant activists were encouraged to rouse the masses. If their goals and means were limited (there was, for instance, virtually no physical violence reported), the promise of a new order based on equality was reminiscent of the earlier land revolution.

The basic problem in rent reduction as in land revolution was to overcome peasant fears of landlord reprisal. In areas targeted for rent reduction, peasants lived in the shadow of landlord power, bound by a relationship which had remained basically unchanged under communist rule. How could they defy the all-powerful landlord at whose sufferance they tilled the soil? The answer lay in the creation of peasant associations to provide leadership and the power to confront recalcitrant landlords. Group meetings allayed peasant fears and stirred a militant spirit. A crucial step was taken when peasant associations and local governments firmly guaranteed tenant rights and enjoined landlords from arbitrarily repossessing land.

Peasant fears were well grounded. Landlords of the Ma clan, for instance, had previously evicted tenants who pressed claims for reduction of rent. In 1940 Ma Jui-t'ang's tenants demanded that rent be lowered to 30 percent, but threats of eviction eventually forced them to continue paying 50 percent. In campaigns conducted during 1942, and again in 1943 and 1944, however, more militant and effective peasant organizations scored significant victories. In 1943 Ma Wei-hsin was confronted by his tenants vociferously demanding reduction in rent, and an agreement was reached. Nonetheless, the fact that the campaign against the Ma landlords and others had to be repeated suggests the difficulty of fully resolving the problem without eliminating landlordism entirely.[36] Many tenants who vigorously and outspokenly supported the peasant associations also made covert supplementary payments of rent. Peasant fears and insecurities died slowly under these circumstances.

The psychological impact of an agreement to reduce rent, while significant, was obviously not comparable to the complete humiliation, flight, or killing of landlords and the total destruction of the system which had occurred during full-scale land revolution. As the studies of William Hinton and Frantz Fanon graphically reveal, the sense of liberation from a repressive order may be intimately linked with active participation in the violent destruction of the oppressor.[37] This was rarely the case in Shen-Kan-Ning in the early 1940s when peasant antagonisms were channeled into more moderate demands for reduction of rent, demands which restricted but did not destroy landlord power. Indeed, many landlords maintained their incomes despite campaigns for reduction of rent through manipulation of the complex rental options common in the border region.[38] Nevertheless, the lessons of organized resistance and cooperation among peasant households were forcefully brought home to many for the first time in the heat of the rent reduction campaign.

Rent reduction was an integral part of the drive to simultaneously liberate the peasantry and stimulate the economy. It was believed that involvement in rent reduction would heighten "productive enthusiasm." The peasant who received a greater share of the harvest would be prone to work more diligently to increase crop yields. Moreover, a larger income would enable him to purchase better tools, seeds, fertilizer, and perhaps even a draught animal, thereby further increasing production. Finally and most important, the peasant, aroused in the course of a dynamic mass movement, would respond more enthusiastically to the cooperative programs soon to be introduced.[39]

The difficulties in enforcing reduced rentals continued to plague peasant organizers as long as landlords and fear of them remained. Nonetheless, successive annual campaigns after 1942 gradually eroded landlord power, and this was accomplished without the disruptive side effects which had previously accompanied violent revolution. In addition, rent reduction eased the economic and psychological burdens of tenancy and provided an effective vehicle for developing community organizations. The peasant associations which spearheaded rent reduction subsequently played an important role in reorganizing rural economic life through the production drive and cooperative movement.

The Cooperative Movement

The 1942 Senior Cadres Conference initiated a restructuring of the social, economic, political, and military dimensions of village life. The core of the program was a new approach to the most important problem of rural life: agricultural production. Previous attempts to radically alter agrarian patterns through violent land upheaval had left unaffected the system of small-scale family farms. Indeed, one of the ironic consequences of the land revolution in Shen-Kan-Ning was to reinforce the pattern of autonomous family farming and to reduce the traditional practice of cooperative labor. For example, it was not until 1940 that the number of people engaged in mutual aid in the districts of Yenan and An-sai reached prerevolutionary levels.[40]

In 1942 the campaigns for administrative reform and rent reduction paved the way for participation in mutual-aid groups. Mutual aid was to transform productive processes, stimulate the rural economy, and provide a focus for community development. As Mao Tse-tung pointed out in an address of October 1943:

> In the past, feudal exploitative relations restricted the border region's productive power and prevented its development. Half of the region, through land revolution, has destroyed these feudal bonds, and half, through reduction of rent and interest, has weakened the feudal bonds. Taken together, the great majority of feudal relations in the border region have been destroyed. This is the first revolution.
>
> However, if we cannot change the methods of production from individual to collective labor, then productive power still cannot develop. For this reason, it is essential to create labor mutual-aid organizations on the basis of the individual economy (do not destroy the individual private base), that is, the peasants' agricultural production cooperatives. Only thus can productive power be greatly raised.[41]

Communist concern with the economy and efforts to organize it long antedated the cooperative movement of 1943. Various types of cooperative organizations, particularly consumer and transportation cooperatives, had been introduced more than a decade earlier in the Kiangsi Soviet. Within weeks of the arrival of the first wave of troops from the Long March, cooperatives of a similar kind were launched in northern Shensi.[42] However, the cooperatives developed prior to 1943 were organized almost exclusively from above and were dominated by party and government officials. Peasant initiative and power had little place in these developments. Hence the peasants viewed the cooperatives not as their own but merely as agencies of government. The methods used to initiate early cooperatives were described by Mao in late 1942 as follows:

> Before 1939, everywhere cooperatives were based on government share-capital, in addition to assessing the masses for shares. At this time they came increasingly under the management of the district and subdistrict government. Cooperative enterprise was not concerned with the masses but primarily with government, acting for government to solve problems of finance. All decisions were made by government. This was the first stage. After 1939, the slogan "Popularize (ch'ün-chung hua) the cooperatives" was proposed; but everywhere the old method of going among the masses and exacting shares was increased in carrying out so-called "popularization." For this reason the masses still viewed the cooperatives as burdensome, and did not recognize them as their own. Cooperative personnel still seemed like officials who wanted the masses to do substitute cultivation. The masses saw the cooperatives not as serving their own interests but on the contrary as increasing their labor burden.[43]

With a few exceptions, these earliest cooperatives had only a peripheral impact on the economic life of the region. In no way did they affect agricultural production, being concerned primarily with commercial transactions. By 1940, recognizing the failure of the movement, the communists abolished virtually all existing cooperative organizations, with the exception of a small number of successful transport and consumer cooperatives.[44] One which survived and flourished, however, was the model Nan-ch'ü (southern subdistrict) Cooperative of Yenan, which was repeatedly cited as a guide for the development of the movement after 1943.

The origins and tortuous development of the Nan-ch'ü Cooperative illustrate important facets of the cooperative movement. Although constantly held up as a model for emulation, its history was marked by striking failures as well as successes. Nan-ch'ü was a "combined cooperative"; that is, it performed comprehensive functions in the fields of transportation, consumption, and agricultural and industrial production. Its spectacular growth was owing to progressive expansion into new sectors of the economy. By 1943 the Nan-ch'ü Cooperative, with over 4,000 shareholder households, was capitalized at more than 6,000,000 dollars; in addition, it had "18,000,000 dollars invested in transport," a reference presumably to its official monopoly on salt and government-supply transport. It had become the dominant force in the economy of the entire Yenan district, assuming a pivotal role in the ambitious district-wide program to develop agricultural and industrial production. Its far-flung activities included consumer buying, grain storage, restaurants, weaving factories, and credit extension.[45]

A number of special characteristics help to explain why Nan-ch'ü became a model for and the showpiece of the cooperative movement. Its center at Liu-lin was on the highway connecting Sui-te, Yenan, and Sian, that is, on the border region's major trade artery and its only motor road. Situated near Yenan, Liu-lin was politically advanced and convenient for official observation. The area early became a major center for the resettlement of immigrants from densely populated Sui-te and refugees from outside the border region. The cooperative assisted these settlers who in turn provided an important labor supply for its expanding enterprises.[46]

The sprawling growth of the Nan-ch'ü Cooperative, the branching out into new and often totally unrelated enterprises as need and opportunity arose, and the combination and recombination of branches and organizations within the cooperative are all characteristic of modern Chinese business practices. Franz Schurmann has aptly described this configuration as the General Motors model of a diversified business according considerable autonomy to its component operations, in contrast to the Ford (and the Soviet Union's) model of technically integrated, centrally controlled industry.[47] However, unlike General Motors, the Nan-ch'ü Cooperative did not grow primarily by amalgamating already existing firms; in most cases it began new enterprises from scratch to fill a service gap in the community or administration.

Although the Nan-ch'ü Cooperative was eventually hailed as an exemplary "popularly managed" (*min-pan*) enterprise, its origins exemplify "official management" (*kuan-pan*) practices. Its aims were frequently inseparable from those of the state. District, subdistrict, and township government provided most of the initial resources and management.

The history of the "Thirty-Mile Shop" of the Nan-ch'ü Cooperative is illustrative of the early history of cooperative development. Established by the subdistrict government with a 2,000 dollar investment in the winter of 1938, its purpose was to compete with rapacious local merchants in the trade between the first and seventh townships. Within nine months, however, it was forced to close. The official explanation for its failure was the inability of the responsible cadre to establish close relations with the masses whose dissatisfaction led to its demise. In November 1939 the head of the subdistrict government reestablished the cooperative branch, this time on a new basis, urging the people to invest. The laconic description of his method is of some interest: "First, using personal relations, he called on a local merchant, Wen Piao-liu, to take responsibility for organizing private capital." The result was an enterprise incorporating both official and merchant capital: 100 dollars invested by the subdistrict government, 200 dollars by the subdistrict cooperative, and 700 dollars by seven individuals, each of whom invested 100 dollars. If the first efforts to form a cooperative had directly challenged the merchants, the second attempt was predicated on their active support. One hundred dollars was of course a substantial sum, which few could afford. Thus private investors were drawn exclusively from the prosperous, inasmuch as the cooperative's by-laws explicitly restricted membership to investors of 100 dollars or more. Eventually, at the urging of the district government and the reconstruction department, this rule was changed. In succeeding years, the "Thirty-Mile Shop" flourished. Its capital reportedly grew to 140,000 dollars, and it had more than 300 members.[48]

The history of this branch illustrates a central dilemma for cooperative organizers: whether to work with or attempt to destroy private merchants. Should they rely on the peasant masses who initially showed little interest, had less capital or experience, and were unfamiliar with mercantile and cooperative concepts, or should they attempt to induce merchant investment and participation, risking subversion of the service aims of the cooperative? If both groups were encouraged to join, should the size of individual investments be limited and safeguards instituted against merchant domination? Was the balance of decision-making power to lie among large shareholders (merchants and landlords) or small shareholders (peasants)? Related to these questions were the fundamental aims of the cooperative: Was it primarily or exclusively to serve and profit its members through share dividends and reduced prices? Or was it to serve the interests of the entire community by making loans generally available to the needy or by passing on lower prices to everyone? Finally, to what extent should it serve as the handmaiden of the government? On the basis of seven years of trial and error in Nan-ch'ü and other areas, the communists were prepared to relinquish official control in favor of a more dynamic community role. The ideal of popular management continued to be tempered by a tendency to revert to official supervision and by efforts to align the cooperatives with such government goals as aiding the poor and tax collection. But experience had shown that cooperatives had to be anchored in the villages and serve the economic needs of their members if they were to become self-sustaining and financially independent community organizations.[49]

By 1943 many basic problems which had plagued the Nan-ch'ü Cooperative throughout its development were successfully resolved. With a guaranteed monopoly on the salt trade and government purchases for the entire Yenan district, the cooperative was instrumental in the border region's internal trade expansion during the latter years of the war. Increasingly it assumed an intermediate position between state and society as government controls and investment were reduced and the cooperative penetrated more fully into the economic life of the participating communities. However, the synthetic or combined cooperative of the Nan-ch'ü type did not provide a direct model for the 1943 cooperative campaign. Its scope and conception were too advanced for universal application throughout the border region. Most important, it was not primarily concerned with the basic problem of the regional economy, agricultural production. In addition, its experience suggested the necessity for large government investment at least in the initial stages, clearly an impossibility on a regional scale given the strained financial situation of the government after 1941. However, culling important lessons from the successes as well as the failures of the Nan-ch'ü Cooperative, the party initiated a drive to transform the border region's agrarian economy by means of mutual aid.

Mutual Aid and Agricultural Development

Despite the long history of cooperative experiments dating back to Kiangsi, the available party literature of the early Yenan period contains virtually no discussion of cooperative agriculture. However, in 1942 experimentation began with both new and traditional forms of agricultural mutual aid. In his report "Economic and Financial Problems" delivered in December 1942 at the Senior Cadres Conference, Mao Tse-tung astutely assessed the results of numerous pilot projects. This report represents a milestone in the development of Mao's analysis of the problems of the transformation of rural society and his fullest statement on economic development. Containing a perceptive assessment of the relevance and limitations of traditional methods of mutual aid vis-à-vis regional socioeconomic problems, it provided the analytical basis for the cooperative movement, the heart of the party's new approach to the peasantry. Immediately following the conference, organization of agricultural mutual-aid teams became the most important element of the strategy to transform agricultural production.

Two basic types of mutual aid (and dozens of variations) had long been practiced by the peasants of northern Shensi. These were *pien-kung,* a form of cooperative labor among landowning farmers, and *cha-kung,* the hiring-out of organized labor teams. In *pien-kung* a small number of families, usually two or three, exchanged labor during such periods of peak agricultural activity as the planting and harvesting seasons. Sometimes *pien-kung* included the exchange of draught animals and tools. Because trust was essential, *pien-kung* was traditionally based on long-standing personal relationships and in many cases was limited to kinship groups. Moreover, particularly when draught animals were involved, it tended to be restricted to rich peasant families. In fact, examples of successful *pien-kung* among poor peasants were rare.

In the *cha-kung* form of collective labor, a group of workers, often ten or more, hired out as a team. These were actually work gangs, usually operating locally in the service of a patron (*kung-chu*) who was invariably a rich peasant or landlord. *Cha-kung* teams were organized and led by a boss (*kung-t'ou*) who acted as intermediary between the workers and the patron or other landlords who employed the team. *Cha-kung* was not based on cooperative principles. It was much more highly organized and disciplined, and it lacked the spirit of mutual cooperation characteristic of *pien-kung.* Moreover, *cha-kung* contained obvious elements of exploitation in the roles of the boss and patron.[50]

Early party statements, notably Mao's report "Economic and Financial Problems" and a *Chieh-fang jih-pao* editorial of January 25, 1943, which officially launched the mutual-aid movement, suggest a sound grasp of the region's economic problems as well as the possibilities of mutual aid and community action for resolving them. They also reflect the excitement of men who have grasped a bold new vision of society and who are confident in their ability to succeed in its implementation. Mao's report frankly details the pitfalls of previous experiences with cooperative labor movements organized from above, that is, created by the state. There was, in addition, clear recognition of the exploitive characteristics and the pivotal role played by personal relations in the *pien-kung* and *cha-kung* forms of mutual aid. Undesirable features of traditional cooperative efforts were to be eliminated, and labor efficiency and output were to be increased through the formation of new types of small-scale mutual-aid teams. The vision of a cooperative economy rested on the spirited participation of the entire population, with each man, woman, and child contributing to the limit of his ability and resources. The goal was national salvation through strengthening the economy, but now there was an important element of self-interest involved for every peasant participant. For if cooperative efforts proved successful, members could anticipate improvement in their meager livelihoods. Here again was Mao's principle: "Those who have labor give labor; those who have much give much; those who have little give little; human and animal power are put together. Thus one can avoid violating the seasons, and is able to plow in time, sow in time, hoe in time, and harvest in time."[51]

In launching the cooperative movement in the border region, the party committed itself to the most formidable organizational task it had yet undertaken. To be sure, in the land revolution the personal risks had been far greater, but the rewards of victory were obvious. The party's millennial appeal struck an immediate response among a poverty-stricken peasantry with a long tradition of rebellion. In 1943 party attention focused once again on the villages of the border region, but this time the task was to lead the peasantry in transforming the rural economy. The communists were keenly aware that the initial stimulus for mutual aid would have to come from outside the village, from cadres sent down to educate and organize. But the long-range success of the cooperative movement was predicated on peasant support and the development of committed local leadership. In the final analysis, unless mutual aid shortly produced visible returns in terms of increased productivity and effective community action, no amount of adept leadership could overcome peasant skepticism and resistance. As the cooperative movement developed in 1943, official literature revealed a keen awareness of these problems.

> But there we must take heed: labor mutual-aid organization must be grounded on a basis of voluntarism of the masses, in order to prevent formalisms, in whatever way they may arise, such as forcibly issuing orders or "compiling name lists." If we take people who have no clear understanding of mutual aid and forcibly organize them into *pien-kung* or *cha-kung* brigades, make up name lists thinking that thus "all will turn out well," then not only will production efficiency and work morale not rise, but on the contrary will be lowered.
>
> Moreover, in organizing labor mutual aid we must remember that it is something active and concrete; we must absolutely give heed to concrete conditions in the areas concerned and not regard them as uniform. Thus if we today strive to expand one kind of mutual-aid labor organization among the people, the *pien-kung* brigades organized must not be too large. Neither the township nor the administrative village must be taken as production units. Because if organization is too large, it can waste a great deal of labor power and a lot of time. It is best to take the natural village as a unit. . . .
>
> In regard to the leadership of mutual aid in labor, one must proceed through the masses and select and promote as leaders individuals who are respected by the masses, positive in production and capable.[52]

The basic principles—flexibility in adapting to local conditions, limiting the size of cooperative units, and selection of the village or a subdivision of it rather than any artificial administrative unit as the organizational basis for mutual aid—indicate a sensitivity to the problem of broad participation and support. Large mutual-aid units, particularly multivillage units, would have compounded problems of communications and coordination, greatly increased administrative burdens, and above all involved the peasant in relationships far beyond the scope of his experience. The long-range goals of transforming the village involved a vision of expanding awareness and social relationships beyond the confines of the village, but these efforts to build a Chinese nation in which the peasant was an integral part could not be implemented overnight without risking alienation and resistance. The formation of mutual-aid teams, the creation of a functioning socioeconomic network beyond the family unit, was a crucial step in bringing the peasant into a national state and a new society. This perception was refined and inculcated in cadres at all levels during the *cheng-feng* movement. With the groundwork laid through interrelated campaigns for administrative reform, "to the village," and reduction of rent, the communists proceeded to modify traditional forms and develop new forms of agricultural mutual aid.

The drive to make mutual aid the basis of the rural economy was launched prior to spring planting in 1943. Official reports estimate that 15 percent of the border region's full-time labor force of 300,000 people formed mutual-aid teams at that time. During the summer months, anywhere from 25 to 40 percent of the labor force, or more than 75,000 people, participated in mutual-aid teams. Such summer tasks as weeding had traditionally been common mutual-aid endeavors. They proved particularly conducive to organization since they did not entail the complexity of exchanging draught animals. Reports for 1944 claimed the participation of 50 to 75 percent of the border area's peasant population in mutual-aid activity, compared to 28 to 45 percent the following year when the campaign entered a period of retrenchment and consolidation. In the early stages, many mutual-aid teams existed in name only inasmuch as overzealous cadres reported the formation of teams which never actually functioned. One investigation revealed that of 6,794 persons officially enrolled in *pien-kung* labor-exchange teams for spring planting in Ch'ü-tzu district in 1943, only 2,700 actually participated.[53] Although statistics remain problematic, during the years 1943 to 1945, tens of thousands of peasants throughout the border region restructured their economic life along cooperative lines.

We cannot explore fully the complex economic and social reorganization that was involved in experimentation with various forms of cooperative and collective labor, leadership techniques, and economic and ideological incentives. We shall instead focus on two central problems, analyzing conflicting tendencies within the movement and attempts to resolve them. The first is the issue of voluntarism and independence from government control, of pressures from above as opposed to leadership generated within the village; the second is the conflicting goals of the cooperatives, which were designed to ensure member profits, increase overall production, and provide services to the community or government.

When the cooperative movement was launched, the communists decided to build on traditional forms of mutual aid, despite an awareness of their dangers and limitations. As Franz Schurmann has observed:

> The task of setting up cooperatives on the basis of existing village social organization was not simple. Traditional forms of labor cooperation were so

bound up with complex social relationships, such as kinship and friendship, that it was difficult for outsiders (Party cadres) to penetrate them. Moreover, rich and middle peasants usually had the greatest power over labor cooperation. . . .

The Communists would face this dilemma again and again. Making use of traditional forms of labor cooperation seemed a wise move. Yet the kinship-oriented work groups were particularistic in the extreme. Once Party cadres infiltrated these groups, the latter lost their particularism and much of the strength which gave them cohesion. . . . A delicate balance had to be maintained between imposed and self-generated organization.[54]

The issue of discipline and organization versus spontaneous enthusiasm was embedded in the very virtues and limitations of the traditional forms of mutual aid: thus *cha-kung* was valued for the former and *pien-kung* for the latter. The modified forms of *pien-kung* and *cha-kung* ultimately favored suggest a compromise between predilections for maximum cooperation and the practical realization that individual landownership and initiative formed the basis for increasing production. Although *pien-kung* groups involving seventy-five or more persons or even whole villages were tried, optimum results were obtained with up to ten workers. An effort was made to overcome the lack of structure characteristic of former *pien-kung* groups by insisting on obedience to an elected leader, and by expanding membership beyond the narrow limits of friends and relatives, particularly to include poor peasants. *Pien-kung* groups increasingly operated throughout the production cycle rather than disbanding after the planting or harvesting season.

A modified form of *cha-kung* frequently assisted immigrants who had no land or capital in claiming uncultivated lands. Many oppressive features inherent in the system of bosses and patrons were eliminated. Rather than working in the employ of a rich peasant, the government helped new *cha-kung* teams to labor on their own behalf, dividing among themselves the land they collectively opened. In addition, loans from cooperatives or the government sometimes enabled the poor to hire *cha-kung* teams, a prerogative that was formerly limited to the wealthy.[55]

A crucial problem for the cooperative movement lay in establishing criteria for income distribution, particularly in the assessment of labor versus material contributions such as land and animals. The issue centered on ambivalent communist attitudes toward the rich peasants. On the one hand rich peasants with plentiful lands and draught animals were valued for their contributions in material resources and skills, but there remained the fear of rich peasant domination at the expense of the poor and the belief that labor should be the primary determinant of income. By 1943, rich peasants were encouraged to participate in mutual-aid teams, and it was realized that the success of the movement required the preservation of private ownership rights. The best production results were achieved when income was calculated on the dual basis of labor and investment in land, draught animals, and tools, a system that provided maximum incentives both for the prosperous and for the poor. Labor payment was usually calculated on a per diem basis rather than according to skill or productivity. Leadership as well as community pressures were directed toward increasing cooperative membership and spurring production within the cooperatives. However, since family farming had not been eliminated, and, indeed, since members of mutual-aid teams also maintained acreage which they cultivated privately, cooperatives had to be economically competitive or face the inevitable withdrawal of members and resources.[56]

In Mao's vision, the cooperatives served as an intermediary between the state and the family. Rather than the government directly taxing the peasantry, cooperatives would eventually contribute assessments for their members; when funds were required locally for schools or the militia, the government would avoid direct imposition on the people inasmuch as funds could be channeled from the cooperatives' surplus. The potential of the mutual-aid teams and cooperatives lay in providing effective popular channels for directing the economic, social, political, and military life of the community. The locus of power and the key to rural development lay neither in the individual family farm nor in state management but in the cooperative community.[57]

Mutual-aid teams represented a familiar approach to the peasant, involving the creation of an indigenous organization embedded in the economic life of the village. They were not organs of the state, although they received official encouragement and were sometimes initiated by outside cadres sent down explicitly for that purpose. Mutual aid not only led to a basic restructuring of economic patterns and increased possibilities for sustained development, it also created opportunities for social and political change within villages long isolated from reform currents. Cooperative principles were essential to the 1943 drive to overcome peasant particularism and, in the process, to generate rural transformation and sustained development.

The 1943 Production Movement

In the year 1943 the party turned its attention from political and military concerns to economic matters in an all-out effort to strengthen the base areas. The new goal was the creation of a self-sufficient and more prosperous economy organized on cooperative, mobilizational and participatory principles. This was the production war. Begun in Shen-Kan-Ning, it quickly spread to all other base areas. The mutual-aid movement was reinforced by a number of innovations introduced on a large scale for the first time in 1943. The most important of these were "organizational production" and new material and ideological incentives based on the emulation of labor heroes.

Organizational production called for a basic economic contribution on the part of party, government, schools, and particularly the army. Beginning in 1943, all organizations became deeply immersed in agriculture and in the primitive industrial and commercial sectors of the economy. The use of troops and civilian cadres was not new. In 1936 Edgar Snow reported on a system of "Saturday Brigades" in which "every Soviet official, Red partisan, Red guard, women's organization, and any Red Army detachment that happened to be nearby, were mobilized to work at least one day at farming tasks."[58] However, "Saturday Brigades" soon disappeared; at least no more is heard of them. Before long, though, selected army units were actively engaged in farming.

Mao Tse-tung's description of initial experiments with organizational production vividly reveals how an ad hoc emergency measure eventually led to a fundamental departure in the party's conception of leadership. In Kiangsi, Mao relates, the military played no part in production because grain had been plentiful. In 1938 in northern Shensi, army units began to experiment with sowing grain, raising livestock, and making their own shoes. The aim was to improve the livelihood (and presumably morale) of underpaid and underfed soldiers guarding remote areas of the border region. In 1939 the first region-wide production campaign was launched to counter the Kuomintang blockade.[59] At this time, the party became aware of the immense but as yet "unproductive" reservoir of labor in the army and other organizations. Why should these able-bodied men not support themselves in addition to performing their duties as soldiers, party and government cadres, or students? Thus began the effort initiated by the military to engage in and direct productive enterprises.[60] To the goal of improving the livelihood of the troops was added a realization that the burden of the military on the strained financial resources of the people could be correspondingly lightened. However, it was only in the aftermath of the economic and financial crisis of 1941 and the *cheng-feng* movement that organizational production developed throughout the border region. As of 1943 a commitment to achieve economic self-sufficiency for the border region was coupled with a drive for self-sufficiency among military units and all other organizations.

The 1943 production drive was geared to realizing the full potential of the organizational sector of the economy. Henceforth *all* cadres were to participate extensively in labor and management. In the party everyone, including Mao Tse-tung and other Central Committee members, engaged in some aspect of production, usually of a cooperative nature; the same was true of army generals and government leaders. These were not isolated acts. They formed an integral part of the new conception of the cadre in political *and* economic activity: he was to function as leader *and* participant. Just as small-group criticism introduced during the *cheng-feng* movement had brought leadership down from its pedestal and into the arena of competing ideas and action, the production movement sought to foster solidarity between leaders and those whom they led, between cadres and the people, through the unification of mental and manual labor.

We may briefly examine the role of the military in the organizational economy. Although the military played a leading role in the production movement, its activities are representative of those of other groups. By 1943 all military units were engaged in production; they concentrated primarily on agriculture, but units were operating and managing commercial and small-scale industrial enterprises as well. Indeed, from 1943, military budgets were predicated upon reduced government subsidy and assumed partial self-sufficiency. The outstanding unit was Wang Chen's model 359th Brigade, which since 1938 had been the leader in military production at Nan-ni-wan.

The initial experiments at Nan-ni-wan were explicitly modeled on the *t'un-t'ien* or "camp-field" system of frontier military colonies developed two millennia earlier during the Han and Six Dynasties periods. Sent to a wretchedly poor wasteland which had been devastated in the Moslem Rebellion almost a century earlier, the 359th Brigade received title to a barren, mountainous tract of land. The land was owned collectively by the brigade, and the fruits of production on it, as well as those of the animal husbandry, small industry, and commerce which soon developed, went exclusively to supply the brigade.[61]

Here is Wang Chen's description of the initial endeavors of his troops to achieve self-sufficiency:

> When I led my troops here to start our first army-production project four years ago, there were no caves or houses for us to live in, there was no food to buy, there were no tools, and no farmers whom we could ask to work for us.
>
> The Border Region as a whole was so poor at that time that we could not bring enough food and scarcely any implements. We received little money from the government in Yenan. Right from the beginning we had to provide for ourselves almost everything we needed. We cut down wood for primitive shelters and dug a few caves. We reclaimed a bit of land each to get some vegetables. We didn't have enough to eat in the meantime.
>
> To have something to exchange for the goods we needed most urgently we cut hard pines, which the people in the adjoining areas like for coffins, and sold them to the villagers. The magistrates in the areas through which you rode helped us borrow some old tools from the peasants who were ready to assist as much as they could.
>
> Our tool problem was solved at last when one of my soldiers, young Company Commander Liu, discovered a big, old iron bell on the top of a hill in a long-abandoned temple. It was too heavy to bring down and I don't know how it ever got up there. Liu dug a big hole underneath and smelted it on the spot, and we found some blacksmiths who were willing to teach our men how to make tools from the two thousand pounds of iron we got from the bell and from scrap we collected in the distant villages.[62]

Such feats were the stuff of which the Yenan legend was made. The exploits of the men of Nan-ni-wan and others were embellished, and then told and retold in the form of stories, songs, dances, and above all plays, which dramatized the fact that soldiers throughout the border region were deeply immersed in the production struggle.[63]

Wang Chen's description highlights two central themes of the production campaign in the military. The first is the theme of self-reliance and self-sufficiency, of man conquering nature by the toil of his hands. The 359th Brigade was sent out with no tools, with virtually no funds, and certainly with no "experts" on economic development. It had to rely on its own manpower resources and available local help. Its success was related to a second theme: that of ingenuity, of devising new techniques which required little or no capital to meet the needs of production. Melting down the iron bell was such a feat. Nan-ni-wan soon became a showpiece for visitors to the border region and the nationwide model for military production, which by 1943 had become an integral feature of army life in all base areas. The spirit of Nan-ni-wan became a byword for the virtues of spartan dedication and serving the people.[64]

In 1943 the 359th Brigade submitted a budget in which its own labor accounted for 82 percent of revenues. Mao's 1943 injunction to all troop units to achieve 80 percent self-sufficiency was never fulfilled, but the military did meet an increasing share of its own needs (perhaps one-third to one-half by 1944) and reduced pressure on the beleaguered economy of the entire region.[65]

The economic role of the military typifies an important difference between communist armies and those of the Kuomintang and warlords. In contrast to other armed forces riding roughshod over the peasantry, communist armies sought to create a symbiotic relationship with the rural population through mutual resistance to Japanese invasion and the perpetual struggle to eke out a livelihood on the land. In Shen-Kan-Ning the burden of supporting a large standing army was substantially reduced by attempts to achieve military self-sufficiency. Moreover, the army as a major repository of skilled labor and organizational experience provided a stimulus to the growth of small and medium industry in the border region.

Industrial Development

In agriculture, organizational production played a significant but distinctly subordinate role, being overshadowed by the private sector. However, in industry and to a lesser extent in commerce, organizational and government-sponsored enterprise was a dominant factor in efforts to achieve development and self-sufficiency. Prior to the creation of a base area in the border region, there had been virtually no industry or handicraft. Commerce was limited for the most part to the import of yarn and cloth and the export of salt. After the Long March, such items as printing presses, paper, military supplies, and agricultural implements were required. At the height of the Second United Front, nearly all such items were imported and paid for in part by the National government subsidy. However, beginning in 1939, the blockade forced the leadership to turn to their own resources and improvise the production of these necessities. Lacking an indigenous industrial tradition and with local technical and entrepreneurial skills in

Table 6.1

Industrial Production in the Shen-Kan-Ning Border Region, December 1942

Kind of factory	Number of factories	Number of workers	Capital
Cloth	18	1,427	$26,900,000
Blankets and shoes	8	405	11,001,100
Paper	12	437	4,100,000
Printing	3	379	5,200,000
Chemicals (oil, soaps, etc.)	12	674	17,030,000
Tools	9	237	3,662,792
Lime	12	432	1,777,070
Total	84	3,991	$69,670,962

Source: "CCWT," 104. These statistics apparently exclude production of weapons and ammunition. The totals given for the number of factories and the amount of capital differ from those I have arrived at above by addition. Those totals were reported as 62 factories and 59,670,963 dollars. The discrepancies may reflect typographical errors or the fact that some factories produced several categories of goods.

short supply, the communists relied on officially sponsored and financed industry. Deep-seated suspicion of the bourgeoisie, despite an official policy of encouraging capitalist development, and the necessity to control strategic resources in wartime naturally reinforced this decision.

The limited scope of industry in both the public and private sector is suggested by the official statistics set forth in Table 6.1. Compiled in late 1942, these figures also point up the strenuous effort to develop industry. Almost all of the factories mentioned in Table 6.1 were started after 1939, most of them in 1941 when the intensification of blockade forced renewed efforts to achieve self-sufficiency.[66] At the same time they suggest the rudimentary level of development in this region of 1,400,000 people; by the end of 1941, there were fewer than 4,000 "industrial workers" employed in factories which averaged fewer than fifty workers each.

The textile industry, the most important in the border region as well as in most other base areas, offers a typical example of the rapid but tortuous pattern of industrial development (see Table 6.2). In 1938, less than 5 percent of the region's cloth supply was internally produced, and most of that small amount of cloth was the product of home industry. In 1939 government and cooperative enterprises were started on a small scale. The Kuomintang blockade, however, strengthened determination not only to raise the cloth output but, for the first time, to grow cotton and develop a native yarn industry as well. Three years later Mao Tse-tung was able to announce that almost one-half of the cotton required

Table 6.2

Cotton Cloth Production in Shen-Kan-Ning, 1938–1943

Production category	Year	Number of shops	Number of workers	Number of bolts[a]
Public factories	1938	1	96	125
	1939	1	210	1,426
	1940	11	850	14,740
	1941	29	1,845	18,750
	1942	16	1,083	14,565
	1943	23	1,357	32,968
Cooperative factories	1938	—	—	—
	1939	2	25	400
	1940	4	82	850
	1941	22	352	4,600
	1942	27	385	4,500
	1943	38	374	6,000
Private factories	1938	5	34	1,620
	1939	16	154	5,690
	1940	20	185	4,500
	1941	40	205	8,460
	1942	50	310	12,000
	1943	—	702	19,634
Home production	1938		5,000	5,625
	1939		8,000	8,750
	1940		10,000	12,500
	1941		13,000	14,500
	1942		13,500	14,158
	1943		41,540	45,700
All categories	1938		5,130	7,370
	1939		8,369	16,266
	1940		11,117	32,590
	1941		15,402	46,310
	1942		15,278	45,223
	1943		43,973	104,302

Source: Compiled from information in Hsü Yung-ying, *A Survey of Shensi-Kansu-Ninghsia Border Region,* II, 93. The original data appeared in *Hsin-hua jih-pao* (May 29, 1944).

Note: [a]A bolt of cloth measured 120 by 3 English feet.

to supply the border region, nearly 1,800,000 English pounds, was being produced internally.[67]

The tightening of the blockade led to a sharp increase in total government investment in the industrial sector. In 1941, this was reflected in the expansion of the textile industry just as efforts to raise cotton domestically began to bear results. By the end of 1941, twenty-nine public factories with over 1,800 workers were producing cloth. However, in 1942 the pattern of swift expansion was reversed. Textiles, as well as other industries, entered a period of forced retrenchment in an effort to raise efficiency, reduce costs, and improve quality through centralization and more rigorous controls. This was in fact the industrial counterpart of the campaign for crack troops and simple administration, which was then in the process of consolidating administrative organization. By the end of 1942 the number of public textile factories had been reduced to sixteen, and the number of workers had dropped to 1,083. As industry became concentrated in fewer and more efficient units, marginal operations and expendable managerial personnel were eliminated. In 1942, cotton cloth production, which since 1938 had increased by 30 to 60 percent annually, was slightly less than it had been in 1941. The consolidation of textile factories was part of a larger retrenchment in which the number of government factories of all kinds was reduced from ninety-seven to sixty-two while overall industrial output remained stable. This cutback in the number of public factories merely set the stage for another wave of expansion in 1943, but this expansion was carried out in accordance with a new perspective on industrial growth. Once again the number of public factories in the textile industry increased sharply (as it did in other industries), and production more than doubled. However, at this time the most phenomenal growth occurred neither in public nor private factories but in home weaving.

In 1938, prior to the government-sponsored expansion of the textile industry, an estimated 5,000 women engaged in household production had accounted for 76 percent of all cloth woven in the border region. The household sector had, however, been largely eclipsed by the subsequent emphasis on factory production. In the 1943 production movement the communists made the first serious attempt to mobilize, train, and organize men and particularly women of the border region in home industry. By the end of 1943 the number of women weaving at home had climbed from 13,500 to 41,540 and their output reached 45,000 bolts, far outstripping factory production.

The pattern of textile development in the border region is illustrative of the basic innovations of 1943. In that year the communists applied basic principles characteristic then and subsequently of their distinctive approach to industrial development. "Centralized leadership and dispersed management" meant unified planning and the establishment of broad economic goals in Yenan, coupled with decentralized production and the dispersal of economic power throughout the border region. In practice, the government proclaimed and encouraged the fulfillment of economic priorities for the border region, but the responsibility for fulfilling these goals was vested not in a centralized bureaucracy but in cooperatives, public and private factories, and homes dispersed throughout the region. In part this represented an effort to "resolve the contradiction between production and distribution." In an area of primitive communications and with a widely scattered population, the concentration of industry in a few centers meant heavy transportation costs both for raw materials and for the distribution of the finished product. After 1941, cotton, for example, was grown in widely scattered parts of the border area. Decentralization meant that yarn was spun and cloth was woven and sold locally. In the process, peasants throughout the border region gained familiarity with the basic technology of spinning and weaving; moreover, the most backward areas, hitherto remote from cloth-production centers, now had the opportunity to share equally in its consumption. In 1943 the communists abandoned a policy of industrial centralization and tight official control to take advantage of local initiative and reduced transportation costs; this policy placed increased reliance on household and popularly managed industries scattered throughout the region.[68]

The development of household production was an integral part of the drive for decentralization. In 1942, economic planners, their resources strained to the limit, became acutely aware that a shortage of labor was hindering the development of the border region. Their solution was to mobilize all available nonproducers. We have already noted the involvement of the army as well as party and government cadres and students in economic activity. In the case of the textile industry, the communists built on a tradition of home weaving. As with mutual-aid teams, they expanded from this traditional base, utilizing available local expertise to develop the textile industry. During 1943 and the following years, thousands of peasant women were successfully mobilized for part-time weaving on simple home looms.

Measured in terms of output per loom, home textile production was extremely inefficient compared to factory production. Looms in public factories averaged seventy-three bolts of cloth annually compared to eighty bolts in private factories and thirty-three in cooperatives. Home looms produced an average of only one bolt per year. But home looms utilized former "nonproducers" and others during the slack agricultural season. They also eliminated transportation and factory costs. By 1943 the drive toward self-sufficiency enabled the local textile industry, essentially begun just four years earlier, to produce 104,000 bolts or 32 percent of the total cloth needs of the border area. A considerable and increasing proportion of textiles were woven on home looms.[69]

Two additional factors figured prominently in the decision to decentralize industry. One of these was the tactical consideration that dispersed industry was less vulnerable to enemy attack. The other, which will be discussed below, was the desire to spread new ideas, both economic and political, universally throughout the border region in an effort to break down stubborn traditional values impeding development and community action. Bringing industry to isolated villages in the form of household production was an important step in this direction. This was the industrial corollary of "to the village" and the movement to strengthen local government. In conjunction with the spread of cooperative agriculture, the introduction of cottage industry led the peasantry further along the road to the transformation of village life.

The textile industry exemplifies the basic patterns of industrial development during the war of resistance. Because of the scarcity of capital and technical expertise the industrial drive was initially channeled through organs with the most advanced administrative skills—the government and army. Early approaches reflected the tension between the desire for rapid development and the reality of limited resources and skills, producing a pattern of overexpansion and retrenchment, but one also of overall significant growth. Eventually, in 1943 and after, rapid expansion was coupled with decentralization, and the economic role of women was greatly expanded as they participated on a large scale in home industry.

Through the cooperative and textile movements and, in the rear-area bases, above all as a result of their valuable contributions to the guerrilla struggle, Chinese women contributed significantly to the economic, political, and military life of the base areas. The resistance period was thus crucial in bringing Chinese women out of the home toward the mainstream of Chinese society. It marked a period of advance in the achievement of women's political, educational, and economic rights, commensurate with their positive new social contributions.

Other significant facets of the border region's industrial development are best revealed in the primitive efforts to produce iron and fashion arms and munitions. Iron had of course never before been produced in this area, the small quantities required by the military and industry being imported. However, in 1941, using iron ore and coal mined in the border region, the first crude pig iron was smelted. In the absence of experienced technicians and modern equipment, "backyard furnaces" produced some of the iron that was desperately needed for weapons and tools. By 1943 they reportedly succeeded in processing one-third of the required supply of iron. Gunther Stein has provided a vivid description of one of the border region's primitive arsenals:

> "We cannot make steel in our regions," the director of an arsenal said as he took us through his plant. "Wherever possible, we are using steel rails which our troops tear up from Japanese-occupied railroads. But transportation across the enemy lines to Yenan is difficult and we must as a rule be satisfied with local-made iron, which is plentiful. We even make good trench mortars from iron."
>
> The little arsenal where 330 men are working has about a dozen low buildings with the strangest assortment of machinery I ever saw in use: ancient lathes, planing, drilling, rolling and stamping machines made in China, the United States, England and Germany which were bought second-, third-, or probably tenth-hand in Sian before the Kuomintang blockade; and simple new machines of various kinds made in the arsenal itself or in one of the Border Region's new engineering workshops. All the machines are well kept. And

they run—driven by an old truck engine with a home-produced charcoal-burning attachment.

The various departments of the arsenal make cast iron, neat looking mortars, cartridges, bayonets, Very pistols, and—since the farmer enjoys a high priority everywhere—copper syringes for veterinary use in the campaign against cattle epidemics.[70]

Such plants were the pride of the border region. Beginning in 1943, there was frenetic experimentation on the basis of the primitive human and natural resources available. Crude iron produced in these plants was important not only because it yielded the best available raw material for certain weapons and implements, and because it was frequently more economic in human and dollar terms to produce it than it was to run the blockade, but because it symbolized man's conquest of nature and led to the development of a new sense of the possible. In the war against overwhelming Japanese weaponry and in the attack on the harsh natural environment of the border region, the expansion of human capacities, immeasurable in quantifiable terms, had profound significance.

We have seen that from 1943 the communists concentrated their financial and manpower resources on economic and social problems. One major goal was to maximize the economic contribution of all individuals, particularly former "nonproducers," including cadres in the party and government, students, women, immigrants, and idlers. In the organizational economy, in the "to-the-village" and cooperative movements, and in industrial decentralization, new institutional forms were devised which involved all of these types of people in the economy and provided a basis for sustained economic development and social transformation.

Labor Heroes

If long-term development was to rely on community action and peasant initiative, effective incentives and stimulation had to be provided. One approach to this problem was the use of the labor hero as a leader and model. Building on a Chinese tradition of emulating models of filial piety as well as on the experience of the Russian Stakhanovite movement, the communists added their own innovative flair. The border region's first labor-hero campaign was launched in the summer of 1943 with a vigorous promotion drive linked to the production movement. In every village, township, and district, outstanding workers were selected, honored, and rewarded with gifts of symbolic and material worth. The climax of the campaign, which was repeated each year after the autumn harvest, was a two-week conference that brought to Yenan 180 labor heroes from throughout the border region. The accomplishments of these men and women, who represented all facets of agriculture and industry and who included outstanding party, government, and army cadres, were widely publicized.

Mao Tse-tung's welcoming talk of November 29 to the labor heroes suggests both the contemporary mood and the direction of the production drive. After dwelling on the accomplishments of the past year and the importance of the organizational economy, Mao turned to the many types of cooperative labor which had begun to revolutionize production in the border region.

> With these four types of cooperatives of the masses of the people and the collective labor cooperatives in the armed forces, offices and schools, we can organize all the forces of the masses into a huge army of working people. This is the only road to lead the masses of the people to liberation, to lead them from poverty to prosperity and to the victory of the War of Resistance. . . . Among the Chinese people there are in fact thousands upon thousands of "Chukeh Liangs," every village, every town having its own. We should go into the midst of the masses, learn from them, sum up their experiences so that these experiences will become well-defined principles and methods, and then explain them to the masses (through agitation work), and call upon the masses to put them into practice in order to solve their problems and lead them into liberation and happiness.[71]

In 1943 the communist party developed and applied a variety of techniques for effectively grounding its leadership in the economic life of the people. Campaigns emphasized the creative development of local forms and traditions, as in the case of mutual aid and home weaving. Labor heroes were natural leaders whose creativity and intimate knowledge of village life enabled them to develop indigenous means for resolving intractable economic and social problems. Mao's invocation of the name of the legendary military hero Chu-ko Liang symbolized the importance accorded production and the peasantry. This perspective was developed in the course of the labor-hero movement. As a *Chieh-fang jih-pao* editorial pointed out, "Hitherto, the only heroes were warriors or political figures, but now laborers also can become heroes."[72]

The labor-hero movement provided opportunities to identify, train, and motivate leaders committed to revolutionary change within their villages. Township and district labor heroes, as well as the select few who journeyed to Yenan as the most honored workers in the border region, were prepared to return to their villages or factories with new ideas, new incentives, and the prestige to carry forward the production movement. Labor heroes also spearheaded the competitions waged between individuals, factories, army units, cooperatives, and whole districts which became a distinctive feature of the economy in 1943.[73]

Along with leadership which emerged in the land revolution and later in the campaign for reduction of rent, labor heroes presented another challenge to the control of the traditional village elite. In concert with other local activists and cadres sent down in the *hsia-hsiang* movement of 1942, they provided a leadership core within the villages that could carry forward the reorganization and development of the economy and rural society.

The Yenan Model for Economic Development

The production war launched by the party in 1943 represented more than a reaction to critical circumstances: viewed as a whole, it marked a major synthesis in the approach to the social and economic development of rural China. At the 1942 Senior Cadres Conference, Mao underlined the historic significance of the party's new policies by contrasting them with major models of economic development: "The publicly managed economic enterprises begun in the past five years are an extremely great accomplishment. This accomplishment is precious both for us and for our nation. That is, we have created a new model for the national economy. This new form is neither the old Bismarckian national economy nor the Soviet Union's newest national economy; rather it is a New Democratic or Three People's Principles' national economy. . . . The people's needs can as yet only be met through the impetus to organize provided by the party and government and by the action of the masses themselves."[74]

In the virtual absence of capital, he proposed a labor-intensive development program involving popular mobilization at the village level. All available material and human resources, including former nonproducers—army, government and party cadres, students, women, and vagrants—were utilized. Their labor was channeled into rationalized and cooperative ventures. Much of the initial impetus and direction in the production movement were provided by the party and government, but the financing, adaptation to diverse conditions, and subsequent development depended heavily upon local resources, above all on the active participation of the entire population. The leadership in Yenan could offer broad guidelines for the social and economic transformation of the village, but, as in a guerrilla campaign, success rested on the initiative, dedication, and skill of autonomous groups. This was the production war, a guerrilla model for economic development which grew out of the struggle for survival in Shen-Kan-Ning and the rear-area bases during the anti-Japanese war. This was the Yenan Way.

In defending this program, Mao lashed out at defeatists who scoffed at the possibility of economic development in the backward border area or who considered such development irrelevant to the party's immediate task of winning the war. He was equally critical of development approaches derived exclusively from foreign experience, particularly the view that economic resources should be channeled immediately into heavy industry. Once again Mao aligned himself with Sun Yat-sen, the seminal figure of Chinese nationalism, in describing the path to development as the Three People's Principles or New Democracy. But in fact, neither Sun's economic pronouncements nor Mao's own "On New Democracy," written in late 1939, provided the inspiration or the direction for the departures of 1943. The brief and rather abstract section on the economy in "On New Democracy" offers no hint of the broad reforms introduced just three years later.[75] The Yenan model for economic development emerged gradually from the bitter experience of war-induced crisis and was crystallized during the 1942 *cheng-feng* movement.

We must at this point assess the contribution of these approaches to economic development in Shen-Kan-Ning. The task is a formidable one, compounded by the fact that the period in which the experience may be judged was brief (the communists were driven from Shen-Kan-Ning in 1947) and by the dearth of empirical data. If earlier production statistics for the agrarian sector had been little more than gross estimates or educated projections, post-1942 statistics are still more problematical. Decentralization of government and the economy, a key feature of the 1943 program for rural development, inevitably compounded the statistical difficulties. Nonetheless, despite the shortage of reliable region-wide statistics, certain broad conclusions clearly emerge. It is significant to note first that the ambitious attempts to restructure the rural economy on a cooperative basis and to mobilize tens of thousands of nonproducers did not precipitate large-scale economic and social disruption. The early phase of creating a cooperative economy seems to have been smooth. This success is attributable in large measure to the communists' skill in building upon traditional cooperative practices within the familiar village context. The nuclear family was preserved as the primary economic and landowning unit while the peasant was gradually introduced to mutual aid.

Grain production, the basic economic indicator of the regional economy, apparently continued to increase steadily throughout the period of transition, but the increases were not spectacular.[76] Significant production gains were reported in 1943 for textiles, the border region's major industry; however, statistics for subsequent years are unavailable. Organizational production, particularly the contribution of the 50,000 regular army men, seems to me to have been successful under conditions of economic crisis. Soldiers and some government cadres not only provided a valuable manpower supply, but, more important, many possessed industrial, commercial, and managerial skills otherwise lacking in the border area. Particularly from 1943 they were widely and effectively used to bolster the economy. The use of mobilization techniques, coupled with the revival of traditional cooperative forms and home weaving, represented an astute appraisal of the possibilities for developing production at the village level. Moreover, these changes in the economy had profound social and political effects on village life. Most important, from the perspective of the subsequent course of the Chinese revolution, the production war launched in 1943 came to be viewed by the party as a resounding success.

Education and Social Change

The political and economic innovations of 1942 and 1943 were essential features of a broad vision of rural development. The basic concept, as we have seen in the case of the cooperative movement, was the creation of local institutions run by and for the people (*min-pan*). The *min-pan* concept, embodying popular participation in and community control of activities formerly monopolized by bureaucrats, technical experts, or a landlord elite, soon embraced the full range of village life. Significant educational developments—indeed a radical new approach to education—were central to the transformation of rural life.

During 1944 *min-pan* schools were opened throughout the border region to meet the growing demand for education appropriate to changing rural needs. In thousands of hamlets which had never had and never dreamed of having a school, local cadres, labor heroes, and village leaders assumed the responsibility to create appropriate forms for local education. At the same time, the principles of expanded community responsibility were applied to propagate fundamentals of health and hygiene in remote villages. Finally, a new dimension was added to the culture movement. From 1942 the symbol of popular culture in the border region became the *yang-ko,* native folk songs and dances which were redesigned and combined with dramatic programs to expose social evils and to propagate the virtues of the new society. They provided vivid illustrations of contemporary problems and policies in a medium which could be appreciated by an illiterate peasantry. Beginning in 1942 *yang-ko* teams toured remote areas of the border region, bringing the new culture directly to thousands of peasants. The goal was to link culture more closely with rural life by drawing on traditional popular themes, developing them, and then carrying them to the countryside to entertain and educate the people.[77]

By conventional standards, the contributions of the regional administration in health, education, and popular culture were already impressive. Against the background of desolation, poverty, and neglect particularly characteristic of northern Shensi, and in a period in which the urgency of the war effort reduced all other expenditures to a bare minimum, the administration had made significant progress. It did so in part through an impressive expansion of educational opportunity; through a drive to reduce the toll of disease by the introduction of basic health and hygiene; and through introducing popular culture whose message was revolution and hope. However, by 1942 the limitations of earlier efforts had become clear. Many living in remote areas remained untouched by these developments. Moreover, problems arose from the application of approaches which frequently were transplanted from advanced coastal areas or borrowed from the West rather than those which grew out of the concrete needs of the border region.

We cannot here elaborate on each of the contemporary social and cultural movements. The evolution of the theory and practice of education, however, adds such significant dimensions to the evolving conception of rural transformation that we must briefly examine its most salient features. The critique of education developed during the *cheng-feng* movement paralleled criticisms of bureaucratic administration. By 1942, the education system, despite five years of rapid development, had barely scratched the surface of the overwhelming illiteracy of the border region. The party had actively encouraged peasant attendance in the expanding school system. But education remained centered in district capitals, catered largely to families who could afford to send children there for study, and left most villages without schools or convenient access to them. The number of primary school students had soared impressively from 5,600 in early 1937 to 22,000 by late 1939 and to 29,500 in early 1944. Yet this meant that out of a school-age population estimated at 165,000, only one child in six was receiving even the most rudimentary formal education.[78] Despite adaption of the curriculum, by early 1944 critics asserted that it remained largely irrelevant to peasant life. Students, rather than being prepared to spearhead the rural revolution in their villages, acquired a disdain for productive labor; consequently they frequently had a divisive influence on the family when they returned home.

From 1943, as attention focused on production and other village problems, the results of the educational system posed dilemmas of the first magnitude. If education was to reinforce Yenan-style economic development and community reform, it had to be physically and intellectually integrated with rural life, that is, located within the villages and responsive to local problems. But with government resources already strained to the limit, where were the teachers and funds to be found for an ambitious expansion of educational opportunities? And would not reactionary village mores triumph in a contest on their home ground against experimental and reformist perspectives? Would the net result simply be a decline in the quality of education, which was already woefully inadequate? These issues of mass versus elite education, of community versus professional control of the schools, and of the political and technical context of education in a changing society lay at the heart of the educational debate of 1944.

The stress of the popular education movement was on spreading rudimentary literacy and practical economic skills which would yield quick and visible returns within the village. The 1944 slogan "develop production, expand the schools" made this goal explicit. Education was closely linked with the cooperative and production drives. Primary schools located in the district capitals and administered by the district government and education department frequently were divided and placed under the jurisdiction of subdistricts, townships, or even villages. While some of these schools continued to be staffed by their former teachers, many new teachers, frequently young men and women with no formal teaching qualifications or experience, became instructors in the expanding network of local schools.

New schools were designed for the part-time education of peasants and workers. They included night schools, half-day schools, winter schools, and literacy groups often directly linked to production units. These schools operated on principles of "management by the people with the assistance of government" (*min-pan kung-chu*). This meant that education officials continued to offer advice on broad principles of curriculum and some help in providing teachers. But basic responsibility for financing, staffing, and defining a course of study shifted from the education ministry and professional teachers to localities. Often the school principal or teacher was a prominent labor hero or local cadre, perhaps himself illiterate. These teachers were frequently joined by cadres or students sent to the village to teach and train local teachers. Such teachers frequently rotated from village to village leaving behind a "little teacher," usually an outstanding student, to continue the lessons until their return. Just as the party had attempted to bridge the gap between a cadre elite and the people in the *cheng-feng* and "to-the-village" movements, in the popular education movement it sought to redefine the role of teacher. Young and old, literate and illiterate, farmers and cadres could all be found among the ranks of both teachers and students. The new schools thus played a prominent role in the contemporary effort to overcome barriers between mental and manual labor, to unite thought and action, to bring together those who worked with their hands and those who worked with their minds.

The *min-pan* school was inseparable from social movements and community needs. Its students lived at home, and both students and teachers engaged regularly in labor and other tasks to assist the family and village. Even in the towns, the curriculum in regular and cadre schools was modified to stress participation in and education for production. The new popular education brought together learning and doing with educational responsibility shared by students, teachers, and the community. The curriculum outlined for the new middle schools, for instance, was to "begin with the *concept* of how to serve the people of the border region (principles of reconstruction) and end with the *skills* to serve (production and medical knowledge)."[79] Education emphasized practical knowledge, analysis of contemporary and historical conditions, and above all service.

In 1944 education in the border region assumed many of the characteristics of other popular movements: transfer of authority from professionals at higher levels to cadres and labor heroes working and living in the villages; decentralization; stress on popular rather than elite education; and integration of education with the social and economic life of the community. The party did not entirely abandon regular forms or deliberately sacrifice quality, although educational resources were strained to the limit, priorities were reordered, and the teaching in some advanced centers was diluted in the interests of mass education. The movement brought the first taste of education to hundreds of isolated villages at a time when new skills and ideas could be effectively utilized in carrying forward the transformation of rural society.

The education movement of 1944, following on the heels of the cooperative movement, instilled the consciousness that community action could produce a better future. To accomplish this task in the face of deep-seated peasant fatalism and values which frequently ran counter to the dynamic and cooperative thrust of the movement required innovation. Yet it is significant that the leadership did not wantonly strike out against *all* traditional values and institutions but sought to build selectively on peasant strengths. The most explicit statement of these principles is found in Mao's speech of October 30, 1944:

Among the 1,500,000 population of the Shensi-Kansu-Ninghsia border region, there are more than one million illiterates and two thousand practitioners of witchcraft, and the broad masses are still under the influence of superstitions. . . . We must tell the masses that they should wage a struggle against their own illiteracy, superstitions and unhygienic habits. To carry out such a struggle there must be a broad united front. And such a united front has to be a particularly extensive one in a place like the Shensi-Kansu-Ninghsia border region, which is thinly populated, poorly provided with communication facilities, culturally backward and, in addition, embroiled in war. Thus in our education there must be not only large, regular primary and middle schools, but also small, irregular village schools, together with newspaper-reading groups and literacy classes. We must not only have schools of the modern style but also utilize and remould the old-style schools in the villages. In the arts, we must have not only modern drama, but also the Ch'in operas and *yang-ko*. In medicine this principle is even more important. . . .

Unless the masses are awakened and willing, any kind of work that needs their participation will turn out to be an empty formality and end in failure.[80]

Mao sought a synthesis of opposites or dual development in which the old and new were joined in a "united front." The party and administration might provide leadership and inspiration as well as general guidelines for development and change, but success or failure ultimately depended upon popular creativity. During 1944 and 1945 application of these principles in a region-wide educational movement spread rudimentary literacy, new ideas of cooperative labor, health, and hygiene, and new art forms throughout the border region.

The Mass Line

The radical departures in party policy developed during the *cheng-feng* movement led beyond economic development to a broad vision of man and society in revolution. At this time the principles of the mass line were fully articulated to define the relationship between leaders and the people in the new society which was taking shape in the base areas. Mao Tse-tung's Politburo resolution of June 1, 1943, "The Methods of Leadership," represents the earliest as well as the classic statement of mass line principles: "The two methods which we Communists should employ in carrying out any tasks are, first, the linking of the general with the specific, and, second, the linking of the leadership with the masses. . . . In all practical work of our Party, correct leadership can only be developed on the principle of 'from the masses, to the masses.' . . . The basic method of leadership is to sum up the views of the masses, take the results back to the masses so that the masses can give them their firm support and so work out sound ideas for leading the work on hand."[81] The mass line emphasis on forging close links between leadership and the people represents a synthesis of major insights drawn from guerrilla experience. In the final years of the resistance war these principles were applied to the development and transformation of China's peasant society.

Jack Gray has sensitively analyzed the present day relevance of mass line approaches to developing societies:

> . . . it is the process by which the politically conscious leadership puts itself in direct contact with the inarticulate, largely illiterate and politically undeveloped mass of the local community, learns from the members of that community what are their aspirations, their sense of possibilities, their doubts and problems; sums up these ideas in terms of the wider experience and responsibilities and of the theory of the leadership; returns them to the masses in an articulate form, and poses new questions; then with the agreement of the majority, puts the consequent decisions into practice, and studies the results in the same terms. The advantages of this political method are that it prevents rule by *fiat* and elitist pretensions, it involves the whole population in active discussion and explicit commitment to policies, and it forms a process of education by which the mass of the people gradually overcome their inarticulateness, their suspicion of change, their ignorance of modern technical and organizational possibilities, their narrow family and clan outlook, the extreme shortness of their economic perspectives, their ignorance of comparable situations elsewhere, and their ingrained fear of governments.[82]

The mass line was geared to the problems and limitations of a peasant society. But it was also attuned to a realization of the creative potential of peasant activists and community action at the grass-roots level—a potential abundantly realized during the resistance struggle and in the economic and social movements of 1943.

During the rectification and production movements of 1942 and 1943, a new conception of the communist ideal man emerged. This ideal transcended barriers of specialization and status to combine in a single individual the values and accomplishments of the laborer, the leader, the soldier, and the student. These qualities were exemplified by the local activist who not only introduced and propagated new values and methods in his own village or factory but played a key role in the guerrilla resistance and struggled to educate himself and others in his "spare time." The gulf which separated leaders from those whom they led as well as mental from manual labor was thus appreciably narrowed. In war and in production tight bonds of common struggle were formed at the community level. The labor hero or outstanding local activist was an informal intermediary between higher levels of leadership and the village, at once actively committed to the creation of community ties and action leading to the transformation of rural life.

The great contribution of the Yenan period was the discovery of concrete methods for linking popular participation in the guerrilla struggle with a wide-ranging community attack on rural problems. In people's war community action penetrated to every village and every family, and involved every individual. This required new approaches to leadership which were eventually raised to the level of theory as the mass line. In the final triumphant years of the war of resistance against Japan, the mass line took root in base areas and on battlefields throughout China.

Notes

1. "Let Us Get Organized," *SW*, IV, 150.

2. The financial and other difficulties responsible for the movement are discussed in an editorial in *CFJP* (Oct. 7, 1942). The editorial, written by Mao Tse-tung, is translated in *SW*, IV, 94–97, under the title "An Extremely Important Policy." As indicated in the following discussion, the campaign, despite its name, was confined largely to government with few actual cuts in the military establishment.

3. Li Ting-ming's role was widely cited in party statements as exemplifying the importance of nonparty persons in the administration of communist base areas. See *CFJP* (Dec. 7, 1941); Mao Tse-tung, "Serve the People," *SW*, IV, 219. On the work of the committee on government headed by Liu Ching-fan, see *CFJP* (Dec. 13, 1941).

4. The original program is described in detail in *CFJP* (Dec. 13, 1941). Cf. Lin Po-ch'ü, *Chien-cheng wen-t'i* (Problems in the rectification of government; Yenan, 1943). These and other sources are frequently ambiguous concerning personnel figures on party, local military, or mass organization cadres. The figure 7,900 full-time cadres apparently included all of these but did not include public security or Eighth Route Army forces in the border region.

5. The goals of placing intellectual cadres in township and subdistrict governments are described in Lin Po-ch'ü, *Chien-cheng wen-t'i*, 17–19.

6. *CFJP* (May 20, 25, June 4, 9, 1942).

7. *CFJP* (June 20, 1942).

8. *CFJP* (July 11, 12, 15, 1942) reported the completion of this task in Yenan, Sui-te, and An-sai districts.

9. Lin Po-ch'ü, *Chien-cheng wen-t'i*, 13, 18–19; *CFJP* (Dec. 13, 1941). *CFJP* (Feb. 8, 1944) contains the official summary of the results of the campaign in a report by Li Ting-ming.

10. The terms "vertical rule" and "dual rule" are defined and discussed by Franz Schurmann in *Ideology and Organization in Communist China*, 88–89, 102, 188–210. Schurmann brilliantly analyzes the political implications of the shift from vertical to dual rule in 1958 during the Great Leap Forward. As we shall observe, certain striking features of the 1943 movement anticipated both the Great Leap Forward and the Great Proletarian Cultural Revolution. For one Cultural Revolution example of the effort to resolve problems of bureaucratic administration by means of administrative simplification, see "A County Revolutionary Committee Takes the Road of Having 'Better Troops and Simpler Administration,'" *Peking Review*, 38 (Aug. 9, 1968). Cf. Hsü Yung-ying, I, 52–53.

11. *SW*, IV, 115. Cf. Boyd Compton's translation in *Mao's China*, 181.

12. *CFJP* (June 13, 14, July 9, 1942); Lin Po-ch'ü, *Chien-cheng wen-t'i*, 2, 3, 14–16; "Draft of the Revised Shen-Kan-Ning Border Region District Government Provisional Organizational Laws," proclaimed Apr. 25, 1943, *CTHP*, 85–88.

13. "A Summary of the Implementation of Policies of Simple Government in the Shen-Kan-Ning Border Region," *CTHP*, 9.

14. At the regional level these were called political affairs conferences (*cheng-wu hui-i*). District affairs committees are discussed in the "Provisional Organization Laws for District Affairs Committees in the Shen-Kan-Ning Border Region," passed June 30, 1942, by the Border Region Political Affairs Conference, *CTTL*, 59–62. The powers of political affairs conferences at all levels of government are defined and their importance stressed in the "Draft Summary of Political Regulations in the Shen-Kan-Ning Border Region," *CTHP*, 72–76. Cf. Hsü Yung-ying, I, 52.

15. One device for increasing party leverage within government was the use of party

fractions, organized groups of party members within the administration. References to party fractions in Shen-Kan-Ning are rare even in available intra-party directives. One of the most explicit is a secret document distributed by the Lung-tung subregion party propaganda department, "Cheng-ch'uan chung ti 'tang-t'uan' chiang-shou ta-kang" (Teaching outline of "party fractions" in government; 1942[?]), BI.

16. "Central Committee Resolution on the Unification of Leadership in the Anti-Japanese War Bases," passed by the Political Bureau of the Central Committee, Sept. 1, 1942, in Compton, 162–63. These changes were essential for the preeminent role the party was to play under dual rule.

17. The merits and defects of village organization were publicly debated in critical letters and articles in *Chieh-fang jih-pao* at the height of the *cheng-feng* movement in the summer of 1942. Hung Yen-lin, for instance, cited a survey conducted in Yen-ch'ang which found that of every eight persons, one served in some cadre capacity, that is nearly one person per family. In Ch'ing-chien at the township level a typical government consisted of seven committees of five men each, plus the township head and his assistant, for a total of thirty-seven persons. When the commander of self-defense forces, a secretary, the head of the substitute-tilling brigade, and leaders of each of the mass organizations were included, the total reached fifty-seven. Moreover, since the five administrative villages averaged twelve cadres, the number of cadres in the entire township was 321 in a population of only 819. A report published the following day indicated that the number of cadres had been reduced from 321 to 198 by the end of the second campaign for administrative simplification. Huan Nan, in a letter published Sept. 25, cited the example of a township of 1,200 persons with seventy-seven cadres, only twelve of whom served full time. Most townships probably fell somewhere between in the degree of organized life and the number of regular cadres. In contrast to full-time professional cadres at district and higher levels, the overwhelming majority of township cadres served without salary and were privately engaged in full- or part-time production. Further discussion of township government is in *CFJP* (Apr. 29, May 15, 1942).

18. *CFJP* (July 3, 15, 1941, June 24, 1944, Mar. 31, 1945).

19. *CFJP* (Apr. 15, Oct. 7, 25, 1942) provides examples of *hsia-hsiang.*

20. See Mao Tse-tung, "Talks at the Yenan Forum on Art and Literature," *SW,* IV, 63–93.

21. *CFJP* (Mar. 28, 1943).

22. Niijima Junryō, 124–43, provides a perceptive account of the goals and achievements of the intellectuals' *hsia-hsiang* experience in Shen-Kan-Ning. An excellent discussion of "to the village" emphasizing its rationality in the light of economic development in the years after 1949 is Rensselaer W. Lee, "The Hsia Fang System: Marxism and Modernization," *The China Quarterly,* 40–62 (October–December 1966). A. Doak Barnett presents a critical view of *hsia-fang* as practiced since 1957, *Cadres, Bureaucracy and Political Power in Communist China* (New York, 1967), 51, 60–61, 174–76.

23. Lin Po-ch'ü, *Chien-cheng wen-t'i,* 17; *CFJP* (Apr. 23, May 20, June 9, June 20, 1942).

24. See, for example, the editorial in *CFJP* (July 9, 1942).

25. "The Ten Great Policies of the Chinese Communist Party for Anti-Japanese Resistance and National Salvation" was issued on Aug. 15, 1937. It is translated in Brandt, *Documentary History,* 242–45. The following section concentrates exclusively on the problem of rent reduction. Although usury and indebtedness had been chronic problems, there was little discussion of them after 1937. Official regulations stipulated a maximum interest rate of 1.5 percent per month, but no campaign was launched around the problem. "Principles for Handling Confusion in Land Mortgages and Old Debts," *CTHP,* 134–36.

26. An excellent analysis of the rent-reduction campaigns in the Shansi-Hopeh-Shantung-Honan border area is found in Ch'i Wu, ed., *I-ko ko-ming ken-chü-ti ti ch'eng-ch'ang*

(The growth of a revolutionary base; Peking, 1958), 116–31. Chalmers Johnson summarizes Ch'i Wu's data in "Chinese Communist Leadership and Mass Response: The Yenan Period and the Socialist Education Campaign Period," in Ho Ping-ti and Tang Tsou, eds., *China in Crisis: China's Heritage and the Communist Political System* (Chicago, 1968), 418–21.

27. The document is attributed to Mao in *Chung-kuo chin-tai chiang-i,* 460. It is translated in Brandt, *Documentary History,* 276–85.

28. Brandt, *Documentary History,* 278–79.

29. A vivid example of this is given in Ch'i Wu, 127.

30. See Chao Kuo-chun, *Agrarian Policy of the Chinese Communist Party* (New York, 1960), 38–44; Brandt, *Documentary History,* 275–76.

31. The Northwest Bureau took the lead in conducting surveys to determine patterns of land tenure and farming methods as well as political relationships at the village level. In early February it established a special committee on land relations, and Kao Kang himself headed a delegation of party leaders to Sui-te. After two months of investigation, reports were issued on land tenure and tenancy, the three-thirds system in government, and economic reconstruction. *CFJP* (Feb. 19, Mar. 23, 24, 26, 1942). Investigations in other parts of the border region were also reported in *CFJP* (Apr. 15, July 25, Oct. 15, 21, 1942).

32. Abuses in land tenure relationships and attempts to rectify them are treated in detail in reports of investigations conducted for the reregistration of land, *CFJP* (Mar. 18, Apr. 15, May 12, 15, June 6, July 25, 1942).

33. "I want to remind you," Mao Tse-tung told a visiting correspondent in 1944, "that in 1930 the Kuomintang government in Nanking issued an agrarian law restricting land rents to 37.5 percent of the tenant's main crops while no rent was to be paid from secondary crops. But the Kuomintang has proved unable and unwilling to carry it out in practice." Gunther Stein, *The Challenge of Red China* (New York, 1945), 113. A 1942 communist law to protect tenant rights to the land was reportedly based on a National government edict of 1932.

34. *CFJP* (Nov. 9, 25, Dec. 6, 1942).

35. *CFJP* (Nov. 28, Dec. 18, 23, 27, 1942).

36. *CFJP* (Oct. 30, 1943, Dec. 20, 1944). An uneasy political accommodation with landlords of the Ma clan appears to have been reached by 1940 prior to the rent-reduction campaign. Several served prominently in government and retained large holdings, although steps were taken to curb their power through heavy taxation. Ma Wei-hsin, the most prosperous of these landlords, still had 121 tenant families in 1942. *MCTC,* 86.

37. Hinton; Frantz Fanon, *The Wretched of the Earth* (New York, 1965).

38. The 1942 laws of the regional government stipulated both the percentage of reduction and the maximum rent to apply in the case of each form of land tenure. Under these laws, rent ceilings ranged from 30 percent to a maximum of 45 percent in cases where the landlord provided food, lodging, and tools. It should be noted that the 30 percent maximum applied to standard tenancy situations, perhaps reflecting the poverty of the border region, and represented a more radical stance than the 37.5 percent guideline established in the Central Committee land law. "Supplementary Explanation of the Shen-Kan-Ning Border Region Land Rent Laws," Dec. 9, 1942, in *CTHP,* 120–28. *CFJP* (Jan. 23, 1943).

The basic forms of tenure prevalent in the border area were fixed rent (*ting-tsu*) and flexible rent (*huo-tsu*). Fixed rent, providing that the peasant pay an absolute annual fee calculated in grain, was prevalent among absentee landlords. In Sui-te, where land was scarcest but more fertile and rent highest, the fixed rent was usually set at about 35 to 40 percent of an average year's crop. Elsewhere the landlord's share ranged downward to 20 percent and was even less in extremely mountainous low-yield areas. Flexible rent obligated the peasant to pay a fixed percentage of the annual crop, usually 40 to 50 percent prior to rent reduction. Several variants on flexible rent involved higher percentages of the crop in return for tools, housing, and food provided by the landlord. These were particularly common among immigrants to the border region. *HTHSL*, 263.

39. See Mao, *SW*, I, 142, *SW*, IV, 129; *HTHSL*, 263; *CFJP* (Dec. 23, 1942, Oct. 1, 30, Nov. 14, 1943).

40. *CFJP* (Feb. 10, 1944).

41. Mao Tse-tung, "Lun ho-tso-she" (On cooperatives), *HC* (1944), 207. Mao viewed the cooperatives as a transitional stage toward more advanced forms of collectivization. See *HTHSL*, 241–42; Mao, "Let Us Get Organized," *SW*, IV, 151.

42. Early experiments with cooperative labor are discussed in Chapter 3.

43. "CCWT," 56.

44. *CFJP* (Feb. 10, 1944).

45. *I-chiu-ssu-san ti ching-yen*, 1–64; Ho Chün, "The Establishment and Development of Yenan's Nan-ch'ü Cooperative," and Pai Sen, "How the Branches of the Nan-ch'ü Cooperative Were Organized," 249–53 and 254–58 respectively in *Tsu-chih ch'i-lai*. Cf. "CCWT," 56–81.

46. Certain of the features which made this a model area in the 1930s were perpetuated in the 1960s. The "Willow Grove" described in Jan Myrdal's *Report from a Chinese Village* is at Liu Lin, where the Nan-ch'ü Cooperative began.

47. Schurmann, 298–308.

48. Pai Sen, 256–57.

49. Some basic contradictions in cooperative policy are intelligently discussed by Liu Chien-chang, director of the Nan-ch'ü Cooperative, in "Some Experiences of Cooperative Management," in *Tsu-chih ch'i-lai*, 264–69.

50. A full description of traditional forms of *pien-kung* and *cha-kung* is given in the report of the Northwest Bureau "Various Old Forms of Agricultural Mutual-Aid in the Villages of the Shen-Kan-Ning Border Region," in *HTHSL*, 3–14. Cf. Ajiya keizai kenkyujo, *Chūgoku kyōsantō no nōgyō shūdanka seisaku* (Chinese communist agricultural collectivization policy; Tokyo, 1961), 5–25.

51. "Let's Organize the Labor Force," *CFJP* (Jan. 25, 1943). The editorial is reprinted in *HTHSL*, 145–49. It is translated in full and perceptively assessed in Schurmann, 418–25. The style and force of the editorial strongly suggest that it was written by Mao Tse-tung.

52. "Let's Organize the Labor Force," Schurmann, 421–22. Minor changes have been made in orthography and terminology.

53. *HTHSL*, 244. Statistics on participation in mutual aid are given in *CFJP* (Apr. 24, 1944, and Dec. 21, 1945) and *HTHSL*, 211, 216.

54. Schurmann, *Ideology and Organization*, 423–25.

55. *HTHSL*, 25, 84, 217–60.

56. Efforts to implement more ambitious cooperative principles frequently ended in failure. In one experiment in Yenan district, newly opened land remained the property of the team, and the harvest was distributed to each family on the basis of its contribution in men and animals rather than on the number of days actually worked. This approach was quickly discarded when it was discovered that peasants preferred to work on their private lands since their share in the crop of the cooperative was already assured. *HTHSL*, 237–38.

57. "CCWT," 59.

58. Snow, *Red Star,* 241.

59. See Li Fu-ch'un, "Chia-chin sheng-ch'an chien-ch'ih k'ang-chan" (Intensify production, support the resistance war), *Chieh-fang,* 65:8–13 (Dec. 28, 1938); I P'ing, "Shen-kan-ning pien-ch'ü ko hsien ti sheng-ch'an yün-tung" (The production movement in all districts of the Shen-Kan-Ning border region), *Chieh-fang,* 81:24 (Aug. 20, 1939); Li Fu-ch'un, "Shen-kan-ning pien-ch'ü sheng-ch'an yün-tung ch'u-pu tsung-chieh" (Summary of the first steps in the Shen-Kan-Ning border region production movement), *Chieh-fang,* 85:7–9 (Sept. 30, 1939).

60. "CCWT," 93–98.

61. Mao Tse-tung identifies the *t'un-t'ien* system as the historical model for the production efforts of the 359th Brigade in "CCWT," 144–45, 156. Cf. Feng Yu-hsiang's dream of colonizing and developing the northwest, Sheridan, 151–56. Nan-ni-wan is located at the intersecting district borders of Yenan, Yen-ch'ang, and I-ch'uan.

62. Stein, 67–68. A full report on the early productive efforts of the 359th Brigade is in "CCWT," 123–44.

63. For one example of the semifictional literary celebrations of such exploits as the production work at Nan-ni-wan, see Hsieh Kuang-chih, "Nan-ni-wan Reclamation," in *Saga of Resistance to Japanese Invasion* (Peking, 1959), 157–67. Several important campaigns to improve military-civil relations and to protect the army as a model were organized around the theme of military contributions to the regional economy and military assistance to the people.

64. The "Nan-ni-wan spirit" in the Yenan period and in the 1960s is discussed in Chalmers Johnson, "Chinese Communist Leadership and Mass Response," 423–25, 435–37. The reintroduction of the production war during the Great Leap and the projection of the army as the highest embodiment of revolutionary practice during the Cultural Revolution have important historical antecedents in the Yenan period.

65. In 1943 the border region's 50,000-man army reportedly produced 31,000 piculs of grain and, *excluding grain,* achieved 79.5 percent self-sufficiency in all other supplies. In January 1945, Mao Tse-tung told a conference of labor heroes that the 1944 budget for troops and all public agencies was equivalent to 260,000 piculs of millet. Of this total, 160,000 was supplied by the people in taxes, and the remainder, approximately 40 percent, was produced by the units and agencies themselves. "CCWT," 123, 155–56; Harrison Forman, *Report from Red China* (New York, 1945), 74; Mao Tse-tung, "We Must Learn to Do Economic Work," *SW,* IV, 231–32.

66. Official sources list only 270 industrial workers in the border region in 1938 and 700 by the end of 1939, compared to 3,991 in late 1942. Shen-kan-ning pien-ch'ü cheng-fu, pan-kung t'ing, ed., *Wei kung-yeh-p'in ti ch'üan-mien tzu-chi erh fen-tou* (Struggle for complete industrial self-sufficiency; Yenan[?], 1944), 42.

67. "CCWT," 11. Approximately 4,000,000 pounds of raw cotton were needed to clothe the entire population.

68. "CCWT," 107–8, analyzes and defends the theory of "centralized leadership and dispersed management." Note the similarities to principles underlying the mutual-aid teams initiated at this time.

69. The preceding data on cotton and cloth production have been gathered from Kao Tzu-li's report of May 24, 1944 in Shen-kan-ning pien-ch'ü cheng-fu, pan-kung t'ing, ed., *Wei kung-yeh-p'in ti tzu-chi,* 42–52; Hsü Yung-ying, II, 87–109; "CCWT," 48–54, 93–108.

70. Gunther Stein, 174–75. The development of iron production is discussed in Shen-kan-ning pien-ch'ü cheng-fu, pan-kung t'ing, ed., *Wei kung-yeh-p'in ti tzu-chi,* 55, and Forman, 78. These wartime experiments in making iron locally were of course the origin of the backyard furnaces revived during the "production war" of the Great Leap Forward.

71. Mao Tse-tung, "Let Us Get Organized," *SW,* IV, 152–53. Chukeh Liang (Chu-ko Liang) was a military strategist of the Three Kingdoms Period, subsequently immortalized as a popular hero in the novel *The Romance of the Three Kingdoms Period.* His ingenuity was legendary. For a sensitive analysis of his appeal as a popular hero, see Robert Ruhlmann, "Traditional Heroes in Chinese Popular Fiction," in Arthur F. Wright, ed., *The Confucian Persuasion* (Stanford, 1960), 158–66.

72. *CFJP* (Apr. 8, 1943).

73. A vast body of contemporary literature is devoted to the labor-hero campaigns. See, for example, Chao Yüan-ming, *Shen-kan-ning pien-ch'ü ti lao-tung ying hsiung* (Labor heroes of the Shen-Kan-Ning border region; n.p., 1946). Numerous volumes, each describing the activities of an individual labor hero, are collected at the Hoover Institution, Stanford University. Also see *CFJP* (Feb. 18, Apr. 30, Sept. 13, 1942, Feb. 3, July 5, Nov. 25, 1943, July 12, 1944) for several of the most important articles.

74. "CCWT," 99. While emphasizing the historic importance of the Yenan model, Mao did not suggest its superiority in any ultimate sense to patterns of development in the Soviet Union. His concern lay with its value in the context of people's war.

75. Mao, "On New Democracy," *SW,* III, 122–23.

76. Grain production statistics are given in Chapter 5.

77. Concerning the application of *min-pan* principles to health and hygiene, see for example *CFJP* (Nov. 20, 1944); on culture and the *yang-ko,* see *CFJP* (Apr. 11, May 27, 1944). See also Stein, 219–21.

78. *CFPK,* 63; Shen-kan-ning pien-ch'ü cheng-fu, pan-kung t'ing, ed., *Shen-kan-ning pien-ch'ü ts'an-i hui ch'ang-chü hui ti shih-i tz'u cheng-fu wei-yüan hui ti wu t'zu lien-hsi hui-i ti chüeh-ting chi yu-kuan ching-chi wen-hua chien-she ti chung-yao t'i-an* (The decisions and the important proposals of the joint session of the 11th meeting of the Standing Committee of the Assembly and the 5th meeting of the Government Committee of the Shensi-Kansu-Ninghsia border region concerning economics, culture, reconstruction, and other matters; Yenan[?], 1944), 41–43. Statistics on prerevolutionary (1918) education in northern Shensi highlight the important gains registered under communist administration after 1937. Students enrolled in primary schools numbered approximately 0.5 percent of the population. In Sui-te, where primary school education had its peak development, there were 1,400 students out of a population of 103,000. Fewer than 3 percent were girls. Stauffer, 304.

79. *CFJP* (May 27, 1944). Among the most important items in the voluminous literature on education and the 1944 reform are the following: Chiao-yü chen-ti-she, ed., *Ken-chü-ti p'u-t'ung chiao-yü ti kai-ko wen-t'i* (Problems in the reform of ordinary education in the base area; Kalgan, 1946); Shen-kan-ning pien-ch'ü cheng-fu, pan-kung t'ing, ed., *Ssu-ko min-pan hsiao-hsüeh* (Four people's elementary schools; Yenan[?], 1944); Shen-kan-ning pien-ch'ü cheng-fu, pan-kung t'ing, ed., *Shen-kan-ning pien-ch'ü chiao-yü fang-chen* (The educational policy of the Shensi-Kansu-Ninghsia border region; Yenan[?], 1944). Cf. *CFJP* (Mar. 11, 22, Apr. 17, May 27, Aug. 10, 1944).

80. Mao Tse-tung, "The United Front in Cultural Work," *SW,* IV, 225–26.

81. "On Methods of Leadership," *SW,* IV, 111–14. Cf. the translation in Compton, 176–80. For a discussion of the mass line in Chinese communist ideology and practice, see John W. Lewis, *Leadership in Communist China* (Ithaca, New York, 1963), 70–100; Townsend, 57, 72–74, 94–95, 101–2.

82. Jack Gray and Patrick Cavendish, *Chinese Communism in Crisis: Maoism and the Cultural Revolution* (New York, 1968), 49–50. Gray also notes the utility of this approach for forging national unity and labor discipline and minimizing official corruption and rigidity.

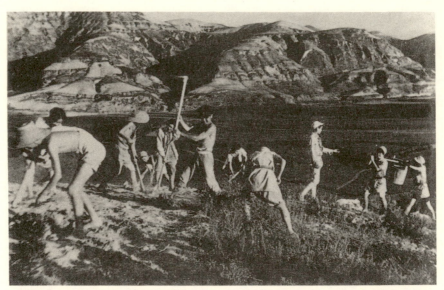

Students and teachers at the Yenan Cadre School open wasteland for cultivation.

Growing rice at Nan-ni-wan, the production base of the 359th brigade. Growing rice in the inhospitable climate of Northern Shensi was symbolic of the promethean spirit of self-reliance.

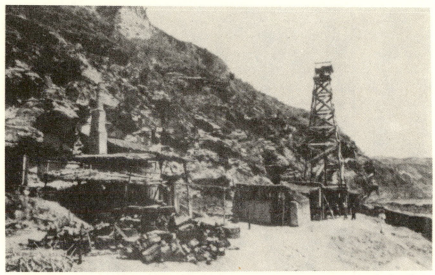

Oil wells at Yench'ang in 1945. This early oil well was the single foreign investment in the Border Region. The kerosene and gasoline provided an important source of exchange for the region.

Cotton spinning in a Yenan courtyard. Cotton spinning was an important component of the 1943 production drive symbolic both of the effort to draw more women into production and to strengthen self-reliance.

Immigrants find new homes in the border region. The print highlights the welcome accorded immigrants who were encouraged to open wasteland, and shows the diversity of sideline occupations from spinning to forestry, pigraising, and carpentry that the party encouraged. *(Print by artists affiliated with the Yenan University Arts Academy)*

Yenan grade schoolers in a gunless rifle drill.

Yenan Central Hospital and a view of a ward in a cave.

Delegates to the 1941 Shen-Kan-Ning Border Region Council. Front row, second to left is Lin Po-ch'ü, chairman of the government and third left Li Ting-ming, vice-chairman and a "democratic personage" central to the communist claim to united front government. Li was regularly credited with proposing the 1942 campaign for "crack troops and efficient government" which (for a time) reduced government personnel and sent numerous cadres and intellectuals to work at the grass roots.

A woodblock print showing a village election held in a local temple with women and men, old and young, peasants and merchants queuing to cast their ballots. The slogans praise the New Democracy and call for carrying out democracy. *(Print by artists affiliated with the Yenan University Arts Academy)*

A wall in Yenan in 1937 with posters and proclamations including one to support the rebel cause in the Spanish Civil War.

"Brother and Sister Clear Wasteland" a *yang-ko* performance before thousands by the Lu Hsün Academy of Art Propaganda Troupe. Younger sister carries a porridge pot and (not shown) steamed buns on a pole while Elder Brother shoulders his mattock. Portraits in the background include Lenin.

Performance by the Public Security Office troupe features Stalin and the hammer and sickle. The troupe received large numbers of writers, composers, and performers who were sent down for "study" in 1944.

Hitler begs Tojo for help in a 1945 comedy as the Axis power were on the verge of defeat. Portraits of Mao, Chiang Kai-shek, Churchill, Roosevelt and Stalin form the backdrop.

Support Our People's Own Army, woodblock by Ku Yuan. The theme highlights the unity and mutual support of army and people. In an unusual counterpoint to the upbeat mood of the poster and the medium, a veteran who has lost a leg is shown as is a wounded soldier borne on a stretcher.

A crowd watches a puppet drama in Shih Lu's woodcut.

Wall newspapers played an important part in education and information dissemination. *(Photograph by Edgar Snow)*

Conclusion

The wartime resistance, with the Chinese communist movement at its center, was a landmark event in the anticolonial struggles that erupted in the decades following World War II. The resistance centered in the base areas helped thwart Japanese designs to subjugate China in a series of lightning blows both by frustrating the invaders' efforts to pacify the area behind their own lines and by pressuring the Kuomintang not to surrender. The network of wartime base areas became the building blocks for a reunified China. If U.S. air, naval, and atomic power and the Soviet declaration of war were decisive in forcing Japan's surrender, the Chinese resistance, which tied down some two million Japanese troops for fifteen years in an unwinnable war, exacted a heavy toll and contributed to Japan's ultimate defeat in the Pacific War.[1] For the first time in a century of triumphant colonialism, the might of an industrial power was curbed, its dreams of empire thwarted, by a people in arms. Moreover, out of the rubble and destruction of war emerged a distinctive social vision and a concrete approach to the development of an agrarian society. The spirit and socioeconomic institutions that characterize the Yenan Way constitute distinctive contributions to the theory and practice of war and revolution, contributions whose importance transcends the wartime epoch.

This study has shown that the ability of communist revolutionaries to respond creatively and effectively to war-aggravated problems of rural society lies at the heart of their popular success during the resistance. Their ability to mobilize villagers and to sustain the resistance in the face of Japanese offensives was rooted in an effective combination of administration, reform, and social programs. The new patriotism harnessed in the rural base areas was linked to the revitalization of the social and economic life of the village and the rise of new social classes, particularly the growing strength of the owner-cultivator majority. Both in areas where local power-holders fled and those in which they cooperated with communist-sponsored governments, the landlords' political monopoly was broken, their economic position weakened, and owner-cultivators gained in numbers, wealth, and strength.

Popular mobilization, the fundamental postulate of the resistance, was at the center of new approaches to addressing wartime political, economic, and security needs. The party's wartime mobilization nevertheless contained multiple contradictory possibilities. This study has emphasized mobilizational, egalitarian, and participatory elements inherent in the program. The party worked to educate and enfranchise politically powerless rural people and to expand the ranks and the position of independent cultivators as well as to mobilize the poorest strata. In significant ways it initiated processes that benefited and empowered the destitute through redistributive political, economic, and educational programs.

The wartime synthesis featured tax reform, rent reduction, and promotion of mutual aid. These reforms cumulatively ushered in a silent revolution, strengthened the position of independent cultivators, and curbed the power of the wealthy while assuring the primacy of the family farm and the market within a mixed economy. Political reforms, including the united front and multicandidate elections, broadened representation beyond the ranks of the party (though never challenging its dominance) and, where successful, strengthened the popular basis for the resistance. At times these multiple processes simultaneously empowered the poor and deepened and tightened the reach of the party down into the village. In the Epilogue I reconsider the implications of the mass line and of mobilizational approaches in party praxis in light of the subsequent history of the revolution, my more recent research, and alternative interpretations of revolutionary change.

Unlike the postindependence leaders of much of the Third World—who streamed back to national capitals from London, Paris, and New York and from jail or rose from subordinate positions in the colonial civil service—the Chinese leaders, from village cadres to members of the Central Committee, assumed power with a mandate based on victory in a common rural-based armed struggle, first against Japan and then in civil war. The communists would thus assume national power following two decades of experience in grappling with problems of the countryside under wartime conditions, an experience that profoundly shaped their subsequent approaches to state building, international relations, and development.

Note

1. Western histories of the Pacific War rarely note the critical Chinese contribution to Japan's defeat. Studies that appreciate this contribution include H.P. Wilmot, *The Great Crusade*, and Steven Levine's introduction to Hsiung and Levine, *China's Bitter Victory: The War with Japan, 1937–1945*.

Epilogue

The essential facts are clear. Twice defeated, routed from the revolutionary base areas they had constructed in nearly a decade of guerrilla war and land revolution, on the eve of the Sino-Japanese War the Chinese Communist Party and its besieged army were essentially confined to a poor and peripheral area of the northwest, having narrowly escaped extermination during the Long March.[1] Less than a decade later, the Japanese armies in China had been fought to a standstill. By the time of Japan's 1945 surrender, Mao's party-army held sway over 100 million people mainly in North, Northeast, and North Central China. In the course of the anti-Japanese resistance, the communists forged a broad coalition of forces that built, administered, and coordinated activities in widely dispersed rural base areas in China's interior. The bases provided the springboard for nationwide victory in the subsequent civil war that ended in Kuomintang defeat and the establishment of the People's Republic. These facts are clear, yet explanations for the communist victory and assessments of the character of the resistance, its global significance, and the relationship between Yenan communism and the subsequent course of revolutionary change and development in the People's Republic and elsewhere remain controversial. In this chapter I examine major interpretations of the wartime resistance since the 1940s and conclude with a critical reassessment of the Yenan Way as a framework for analyzing the revolutionary praxis both of the Shen-Kan-Ning border region and of the wider wartime resistance.

I conducted research for *The Yenan Way* in the 1960s, before international scholars had access to mainland archives, before the spate of publication of Chinese documentary sources, and before opportunities existed for doing research in the base areas and interviewing participants. This was nevertheless a rewarding time for researchers. It was the beginning of the era of archival and documentary study of the wartime period that produced a succession of base area and thematic studies of the resistance that tapped archival, documentary, and press sources in Taiwan, Hong Kong, Japan, and the United States. The present discussion draws on the scholarship of subsequent decades, including my own, involving archival, documentary, and interview research in rural China.

The Yenan Way was written at the height of the period of U.S.-Chinese antagonism that was intensified by deepening U.S. involvement in the Indochina War, a war that was widely and correctly understood as a proxy U.S.-China war. It was also the beginning of a period of critical reaction in the United States against Cold War ideology and scholarship that coincided with the growth of the antiwar movement. Analysis of cycles in international historiography of Chinese resistance and revolution underlines the sensitivity of interpretive trends to global conflict and particularly to contemporary patterns of U.S.-Chinese relations, whose dramatic shifts since the 1940s are mirrored in the works assessed here.

The Yenan Way in Revolutionary China offered a close documentary study of the origins and political economy of a single important base area as a foundation for advancing certain propositions concerning the national movement and its global significance. The basis for this extrapolation is not that Shen-Kan-Ning was representative of conditions in all the base areas. Shen-Kan-Ning was unique among the wartime bases in four important ways:

— it was the poorest base area;
— it alone had completed land redistribution in significant areas prior to the shift to united front strategies;
— it was largely spared Japanese invasion (though subject to Japanese bombing and blockade and to military conflict with Kuomintang forces) so that guerrilla warfare assumed a less central role than in the rear-area bases;
— finally, it was the home of the central party and military leadership and a mecca for thousands of intellectuals drawn to the resistance.

While recognizing distinctiveness, I argue (and research on other bases confirms) that essential institutional and mobilizational features of the wartime political economy in Shen-Kan-Ning emerged in the most developed base areas, notably the Chin-Ch'a-Chi, Chin-Chi-Lu-Yu, and Chin-Sui base areas, and shaped not only the outcomes of the war but the subsequent course of the Chinese revolution. From this perspective, Shen-Kan-Ning was both a microcosm and a critical node in the development of the theory and praxis of revolution. To fully assess the resistance, we must investigate the experience of each of the base areas, including their self-reliant features and their position within the larger movement headquartered in Yenan, as well as their relationship to and conditions in Kuomintang-dominated, warlord-dominated, and especially Japanese-occupied zones.

The Yenan Way proposed an understanding of the national movement and the dominant forces of the epoch within a framework of people's war and social revolution. Where many studies of the Sino-Japanese War sought to explain the *reasons* for communist victory, *The Yenan Way* also attempted to chart the consequences of revolutionary processes for the people of the base areas. That is, it assessed revolutionary processes as *developmental* processes from the perspective of the transformation of the political economy and society of the base areas.[2] I understood the Yenan Way as a fluid conception, a spirit and praxis of revolutionary change that initiated a redefinition of relationships among the party, the peasantry, and the local elite. It encompassed approaches pertinent to waging a war of national independence, but it also embodied dimensions of political, economic, and social change whose implications extended beyond the temporal and spatial boundaries of the wartime base areas to the full range of problems associated with peripheral development and agrarian transformation.

I begin this reassessment by evaluating the understanding and insights of contemporary observers, the journalists, writers, and scholars who directly experienced and recorded the events of war and revolution and whose writings anticipated much subsequent analysis and interpretation of the Chinese revolution. In the following sections, I reconsider the Yenan Way in light of major interpretations of the Chinese revolution and portions of the comparative literature on revolutionary change and agrarian societies as well as of specific criticisms of the original work.[3] Finally, I conclude with a critical reassessment of *The Yenan Way.*

First-Generation Interpretations: Contemporary Observers

Foreign journalists, writers, and government analysts of the 1930s and 1940s foreshadowed the most important theories explaining peasant support for the Chinese communists that subsequently received political and scholarly elaboration.[4] In 1936 the American journalist Edgar Snow became the first to slip through the Kuomintang blockade and pay an extended visit to the communist base area in the northwest. His observations and interviews with communist leaders, published the following year in *Red Star Over China,* made him the most influential author-chronicler of the wartime communist movement, significantly shaping not only international perceptions but also Chinese public opinion.

Snow was the first of many observers to hold that the party's socioeconomic program was the sine qua non for forging bonds between a revolutionary party and an impoverished peasantry whose deepest concerns were land, food, and security. In *Red Star* and subsequent books and articles, he stressed the critical role of the party's *redistributive programs.* Both in his own words ("in the rural areas their activity centered chiefly on the solution of the immediate problems of the peasants—land and taxes")[5] and in presenting the words and views of communist leaders, Snow hammered home the point. For example, quoting General P'eng Teh-huai, he offered a rare contemporary public statement that posed issues of peasant mobilization in terms of class struggle. After detailing problems of "economic bankruptcy" as a result of imperialism, landlordism and militaristic wars, enormous taxes, and unemployment, P'eng observed: "Because the masses are interested in the practical solution of their problems of livelihood, it is possible to develop partisan warfare only by the *immediate* satisfaction of their most urgent demands. This means that the exploiting class must be promptly disarmed."[6]

As party programs and priorities in 1936–1937 shifted from confiscatory land reform and full-scale attack on the landlords to the united front and gradual reform characteristic of the anti-Japanese resistance, confrontational class struggle disappeared from the public record though not entirely from internal party documents and praxis. Throughout, the claim to protect the material interests of the peasantry remained central to communist assertions of legitimacy.[7]

Perhaps more than any other writer of the period, Snow captured for both Chinese and Western readers a sense of the distinctiveness of the revolutionary movement and of the response it evoked among significant numbers of villagers and intellectuals. Yet like other journalists, Snow was far more familiar with politics and society in the White areas, and his report on the communist movement perforce relied heavily on transcriptions of the words of revolutionary leaders and activists, supplemented by his own on-the-spot observations.[8] Reading Snow and other contemporaries is particularly helpful for grasping the patriotic and idealistic response that the movement evoked, notably among intellectuals and youth as well as among other sectors of the rural population.

As early as 1940, George Taylor drew on personal observations of North China guerrilla bases to argue that the key to communist success lay in the ability to exploit *nationalist reaction to Japan's invasion* by providing party leadership for the rural resistance. In contrast to Snow's insistence on the primacy of the land program, Taylor held that Japanese "brutality was, of course, an excellent argument for the guerrillas," provided "that they had been in a district long enough to organize and infuse a new morale and political outlook into the peasantry."[9] In short, Taylor held that the Japanese invasion offered communist organizers a golden opportunity to launch a nationalist movement in the countryside. Taylor was thus among the first to suggest that war-induced nationalism, not the social and economic program, held the key to the party-peasant relationship.

Authors such as Snow, Harrison Forman, Gunther Stein, Jack Belden, Theodore White and Annalee Jacoby, and many others, writing in the late years of the anti-Japanese resistance and the civil war viewed the communist movement against a background of their growing antipathy and disillusionment with Kuomintang corruption, brutality, and malfeasance. They argued that communist success in mobilizing the peasantry lay in the introduction of *democracy* to a peasantry that had been politically marginalized, indeed excluded from politics under Kuomintang and warlord rule.

The entire Communist political thesis could be reduced to a single paragraph: If you take a peasant who has been swindled, beaten, and kicked about for all his waking days and whose father has transmitted to him an emotion of bitterness reaching back for generations—if you take such a peasant, treat him like a man, ask his opinion, let him vote for a local government, let him organize his own police and gendarmes, decide on his own taxes, and vote himself a reduction in rent and interest—if you do all that, the peasant becomes a man who has something to fight for, and he will fight to preserve it against any enemy, Japanese or Chinese.[10]

Theodore White and Annalee Jacoby, reflecting the widely shared populism of the wartime movement and responding to efforts to implement electoral processes in the communist-led base areas, captured one aspect of the excitement generated by wartime mobilization politics. At the same time they exaggerated the role of intellectuals and local elites and the power of the peasantry to shape political processes, and they underestimated the party's power to set a range of policies that directly affected rural life. In my view they rightly grasped the responsiveness of the party to popular needs and aspirations in a period of protracted social disintegration and its ability to mobilize through elections and mass organizations in ways that conveyed a populist, even proto-democratic flavor. Their analysis is most compelling in its critique of the manifestly authoritarian and pro-landlord behavior they found in Kuomintang, warlord, and Japanese forces.

White and Jacoby, among others, saw the issues of democracy as closely related to the communist socioeconomic program, as suggested by their reference in the above passage to rent and interest reduction. This poses critical questions to which I return below: Did many contemporary Western and Chinese observers exaggerate the democratic elements of the movement? Were they misled in their view that the participatory and mobilizational politics of the base areas could be a harbinger of a democratic future? And if they were not, how are we to explain the subsequent course of Chinese politics from the era of Mao Tse-tung and the Cultural Revolution to that of Teng Hsiao-p'ing and the repression of the democratic movement in 1978–1979 and 1989 and after? The same question must also be posed to *The Yenan Way*.

American foreign service officer John Service, who paid a lengthy visit to Yenan with the Dixie Mission and spoke at length with Mao, Chou En-lai, and other leaders, also called attention to the democratic character of the political process in the base areas. In a dispatch of September 4, 1944, Service explained that the rapid growth of Chinese communist armies "would not have been possible without the support of the people of the areas in which they have operated. This widespread popular support must, under the circumstances in which it has occurred, be considered a practical indication that *the policies and method of the Chinese Communists have a democratic character*."[11] Service spelled out the basis for peasant support in terms that linked the party's socioeconomic program with democracy:

The peasants support, join and fight with the Communist armies because they have been convinced that the Communists are fighting for their interests, and because the Communists have created this conviction by producing some tangible benefits for the peasants.

These benefits must be improvement of the social, political or economic condition of the peasants. Whatever the exact nature of this improvement, it must be—in the broader sense of the term as the serving of the interests of the majority of the people—toward democracy.[12]

This view of democracy does not rest on multiparty elections, parliamentary systems, checks and balances, or other features of liberal democracy. Indeed, it highlights a party-peasant bond secured through improvement of the material conditions of impoverished villagers as a precondition for a democratic polity.

This perspective on party-peasant relations downplays such explicitly political issues as the party's efforts to expand the scope of electoral processes and, under certain circumstances, to share political power with its united front allies. It is worth noting, however, that it was *exclusively* in the communist-led base areas that China experienced gains in institutionalizing electoral processes and expanding the political power and participation of the rural population.

Passages like the above, though framed in terms of democracy, bring Service close to those who emphasize the contribution of the party's socioeconomic program to improving conditions for broad strata of the peasantry. Service and others implied (but never, to my knowledge, fully articulated) a position that socioeconomic issues and not electoral politics were crucial to the possibilities of achieving democracy in rural China, where landlord and rich peasant elites dominated society and politics. Arguably, the party's rent reduction and tax reforms, in strengthening the owner-cultivator ranks while reducing the power of the richest and most powerful families, created socioeconomic foundations that could support a democratic polity far better than could a society with vast imbalances of wealth and power.[13] Service's recognition of the high levels of popular support that communist forces enjoyed in the countryside was widely shared by many American observers in the mid- to late 1940s and was one reason for attributing a democratic character to the movement.[14]

A fourth perspective viewed skeptically the claims of democracy and nationalism and held that *organizational superiority* was the key to the communist ability to fill the gap created by war, Kuomintang retreat, and rural anarchy. The U.S. War Department report of June 1945 stated the point succinctly:

The Chinese Communists *are* Communists. They are the most effectively organized group in China.

The "democracy" which the Chinese Communists sponsor represents "Soviet democracy" on the pattern of the Soviet Union rather than democracy in the Anglo-American sense. It is a "democracy" more rigidly controlled by the Chinese Communist Party (CCP) than is the so-called "one-party dictatorship" of the Chungking Government controlled by the Kuomintang.[15]

Such a "realist" view, a harbinger of Cold War perspectives that would dominate American scholarship in the 1950s and enjoy a resurgence in the 1990s, assessed communist strength from the perspective of organization and manipulation and stressed close adherence to the Soviet Russian "party line" while tending to ignore or denigrate populist and nationalist elements of the party-peasant bond and the socioeconomic program.

Each of the four interpretations cited above contains elements that were woven into subsequent analyses of the period, including my own. Each was resurrected in diverse ways as the course of the revolution, from land reform to collectivization, the Great Leap Forward, the Cultural Revolution, the 1980s economic reforms, and the rise and demise of the democratic movement brought to the fore alternative strains and tendencies within Chinese communism.

The preceding discussion has highlighted four competing but also potentially complementary theses explaining the strengths of the wartime communist movement and of the communist-peasant bond that were elaborated in the 1940s by the first generation of Western observers, ranging from journalists and writers to foreign service officers and military personnel. Their analyses emphasized, respectively, a socioeconomic program, nationalism, democracy, and organization/manipulation.

Many of these authors did not insist on a single thesis but saw communist achievement as multifaceted. Snow, for example, stressed the importance of material appeals, including land, taxes, and cooperatives. But he also recognized the ability of the communists to tap the burgeoning patriotism of rural youth, some of whom they introduced to the world beyond their villages for the first time.[16] White and Jacoby complemented their discussion of democracy with the observation that "the Communists won their real popularity by the war they waged against Japan. The black nature of Japanese conquest was common foe to every man, rich or poor, learned or ignorant."[17] And Service pointed to the intertwined character of democratic appeals and the communist socioeconomic program.

Many of these first-generation authors rightly shared with numerous other contemporary observers an appreciation for the dedication, patriotism, and accomplishments of the communists that was reinforced by their critical stance toward an aggressive Japan bent on subjugating China and their growing perceptions of the Kuomintang as corrupt, faction-ridden, and incapable of dealing with the social, economic, political, and security problems that overwhelmed the Chinese nation. Their works contain deeply felt, often perceptive firsthand observations on Chinese society, and the authors drew extensively on interviews with a range of leaders, peasants, and intellectuals in the base areas and beyond. Most relied on interpreters and guides for their predominantly oral information, but there were important exceptions like John Service, John Davies, George Taylor, and a few other foreign service and military officers who had grown up in China in missionary families and spoke and read Chinese. As a group they had years of experience in observing and reporting from China and at learning firsthand about Chinese economy and society at the grass-roots level.

In contrast to the next generation of writers, who were predominantly university- or government-trained China specialists or students of communist affairs and who enjoyed access to a wide range of primary source materials (including party and government documents and intelligence reports collected in the United States, Taiwan, Hong Kong, and Japan) but were unable to conduct research in or even visit China, the first generation relied predominantly on their eyes and ears as trained reporters and on-the-spot observers. And in contrast to a generation of reporters who returned to China in the 1970s and 1980s only to find their activities circumscribed and their contacts limited by tight government controls, the wartime generation enjoyed remarkable access to people of all ranks and walks of life and in diverse regions of China with the important exception of Japanese-occupied zones. This is one reason why, half a century later, life in Japanese-controlled areas remains underresearched and virtually unknown.

Most Western accounts of the communist movement in the mid- to late 1940s, such as those of Joseph Stilwell and other American military advisers, criticized Chiang Kai-shek and the Kuomintang for their recalcitrance and ineptitude in fighting Japan, or for their callousness to the plight of the poor, the rampant corruption and profiteering that virtually all independent and foreign observers recorded at a time when Washington continued to support the Kuomintang as a key ally and the exclusive conduit for U.S. aid to China. Jack Belden, for example, set off his positive assessment of economy and society in the communist-led Chin-Chi-Lu-Yu border region against a description of the "desolate land, fallow fields and empty houses, tumbling with decay" that he encountered in Honan in 1941. "Then peasants told me they had left their ancestral plots because Kuomintang tax collectors and requisition agents for Chiang Kai-shek's armies were demanding more grain from them than the land could possibly produce."[18] Belden, as well as White and Jacoby, analyzed the problem in terms of a nexus of power of landlords and the Kuomintang, who took advantage of war-exacerbated famine to buy up land from farmers forced to sell their land or starve. Like many contemporary observers, they compared Kuomintang, warlord, and landlord rapacity to a communist movement notable for its commitment to social justice and its aura of incorruptibility.

The first-generation American works examined here were written during or shortly after the end of the Pacific War, at a time when the spectre of fascism placed a premium on democratic values and when American populist and egalitarian impulses were reinforced by experiences in China, where the United States was allied with forces resisting a rapacious Japanese imperialism. This conjuncture produced a telling critique of Japanese imperialism and, particularly for the years 1945–1949, of Kuomintang ineptitude and corruption.[19] It also facilitated appreciation of the broad popular support that the communist-led resistance enjoyed in the base areas and among many intellectuals. Likewise, with U.S.-Soviet alliance as the pivot of the Allied war effort in Europe, and with Ford and Chrysler touting their contributions to keeping the Soviet Red Army rolling, it was not until some time after the Allied victory in World War II that hostility toward the Soviet Union structured popular American thinking about communist conspiracy. Above all, it was the outbreak of the Korean War in 1950 and subsequent Sino-American military confrontation that froze public discussion on many of the issues concerning the Chinese revolution that had been so vigorously debated over the preceding decade.

The Chinese Revolution in the Era of Sino-American Confrontation: From the Totalitarian Model to Peasant Nationalism

With the Cold War, American preoccupations shifted from the national and social revolution and party-peasant-elite relations to the search for conspirators in high places. The key political question became *who* lost China. In the McCarthy era in the early 1950s, the answers frequently took the form of denunciations of foreign service officers, including Service and Davies, and culminated in the purge of virtually the entire corps of American diplomatic personnel with China expertise. Also targeted for scapegoating were academics such as John Fairbank and Owen Lattimore, who had played government or advisory roles in wartime China and subsequently took up leading university posts. The chilling impact of McCarthyism on the fledgling field of China studies and on perceptions of China was profound. Scholarly and political analysis and debate were stunted by an enforced intellectual-political consensus that precluded critical discussion of the issues shaping revolution and imperialism in China and Asia and the exercise of U.S. power in Asia.

In the 1950s and early 1960s, at the height of U.S.-Soviet and U.S.-Chinese antagonism, American scholarly interest in the party-peasant relationship, imperialism, and the anti-Japanese resistance declined. Two issues drove public discussion of China and defined the contemporary literature. One was Soviet and Comintern machinations in China.[20] Simultaneously, research shifted from the period of anti-Japanese resistance to 1920–1935 and from an emphasis on distinctive indigenous features of revolution to the Soviet role in shaping—that is, manipulating—the Chinese communist movement. Much of this literature focused on Comintern conspiracy, ignoring the social and economic roots of revolution, and highlighted a perceived slavish adherence of the Chinese communist movement to Soviet theory and praxis.[21] Consistent with U.S. government denunciations of a monolithic, Moscow-dominated communist movement, a view reinforced by the Sino-Soviet alliance and by Chinese statements of support for Soviet foreign policy in the early 1950s, scholarship of the period concentrated on Soviet manipulation of the Chinese revolution.[22]

In the 1960s and 1970s, scholars returned to the issues of the anti-Japanese resistance. Denied access to archival sources or participant interviews in China, researchers for the first time began to draw on Japanese military and diplomatic archives, on the Chinese documentary sources of the Bureau of Investigation in Taiwan, and on Stanford University's Hoover collection of wartime materials.

Chalmers Johnson's *Peasant Nationalism and Communist Power* ignited debate with a forceful presentation of the view that peasant nationalism, inspired by Japan's invasion, occupation, and pacification, was the key to communist victory in China. Breaking with conspiracy theories and with versions of the "organizational weapon" and totalitarian models transplanted from Soviet studies, Johnson drew attention to the importance of the war as a factor in redefining the parameters of Chinese politics, particularly the party-peasant relationship. From the observation that earlier attempts to build rural base areas through guerrilla warfare and land revolution had ended in defeat, he concluded that the party's wartime socioeconomic program was irrelevant and, as George Taylor had argued earlier,[23] that war-induced nationalism was the decisive ingredient of communist victory.

Peasant Nationalism not only became the dominant interpretation of the period among China specialists but was also influential in the fields of comparative communism and social movements.[24] Because of its continuing influence in comparative studies, because it provided an important stimulus that led to my own interpretation in *The Yenan Way,* and because it offers a springboard for addressing issues of nationalism, I take up Johnson's analysis in some detail. This first monograph to draw extensively on Japanese intelligence sources offers a useful military history of the Sino-Japanese War and drew attention to the importance of war-induced peasant nationalism as a unifying factor contributing to its outcome. By securing the major cities, the railroads, and the coastal areas, Japan forced a vastly weakened Kuomintang to retreat from its coastal urban and industrial base to Southwest China. This not only prevented the Kuomintang from taking advantage of the historic defeat of the Central Soviet to consolidate its rule, it also opened new terrain behind Japanese lines where the communists would eventually build a powerful guerrilla movement and establish the rural base areas that sustained the resistance.

In focusing on Japanese invasion and subsequent military campaigns, however, *Peasant Nationalism* virtually ignored Chinese social and economic reality, above all slighting endemic sources of rural unrest rooted in landlord-peasant and state-peasant conflict, including the roles of the landlord-usurer, tax gouger, warlord, and others shaping the rural milieu in an epoch of disintegration and social conflict. In short, it ignored the nature of the contending political and social forces with their profoundly different approaches to the countryside. Even the specific outcomes of Japanese military campaigns as they affected the Chinese countryside fade into insignificance as Johnson assumes that the Japanese presence in all situations fueled wartime nationalism. It is difficult, however, to accept Johnson's premise of a universally thriving wartime nationalism, particularly as he defined it (following Karl Deutsch), in terms of social mobilization. In 1942–1943, notably in the base areas that bore the brunt of Japanese attack, the resistance bases contracted from forty-four million to twenty-five million people. In these years the Eighth Route Army declined from 400,000 to 300,000 soldiers, and 90 percent of the plains areas fell to Japan.[25] Far from constituting social mobilization, the result was a far-reaching demobilization that brought the resistance to the brink of collapse. There was no inevitability to survival of the resistance forces and base areas, still less to victory, whether explanations are framed in terms of nationalism or a mix of other factors.

A number of scholars have perceptively challenged central propositions of the peasant nationalism thesis. Examining diverse areas across North China following the Japanese invasion, Kathleen Hartford observed that "the local resistance forces were not formed spontaneously and ... the spontaneously organized forces were not formed for the purpose of resistance."[26] Hartford and Van Slyke have documented that much of the resistance sprang up in areas outside the specific localities of Japan's advance, and by 1939, when most villagers began to feel the bite of Japanese military might, the major base areas had already been established.

In studies of areas under nationalist and warlord rule, Lloyd Eastman found a lack of nationalist concern "everywhere apparent," noting that "many Chinese— especially the peasantry—were by no means hostile" to the Japanese. Indeed, from half a million to one million troops served in Japanese-sponsored forces, many of them defectors from Nationalist armies.[27]

Hartford has shown that Japanese repression, far from strengthening the base areas and the resistance by provoking a powerful nationalist response, frequently stifled mass activism, drove guerrilla forces from even consolidated regions, and reduced or eliminated entire base areas.[28] The central point Van Slyke, Eastman, and Hartford demonstrated is that there was no automatic or reflexive peasant nationalist response to Japanese conquest and brutality. Where the Japanese military succeeded in ruthlessly crushing opposition forces, nationalist reaction or any other form of resistance was at best weak and ineffectual. To understand not only popular responses to war and revolution but also the volatile interaction among villagers, local elite, and competing party-armies, we need to explore both the complex world of rural society and the nature of competing programs implemented by Japanese, Kuomintang, warlord, and communist administrations, as well as the balance of forces in particular times and places.

If a reflexive peasant nationalism was decisive, why was a renegade communist party and not the national government the principal beneficiary of this windfall of "war-induced anarchy" provided by an imperialist invader? After all, in 1937, at the outbreak of the war, the national government had consolidated power. It was and continued to be internationally recognized as the government of China. By 1935 it had curbed its major warlord and communist challengers, and, it, too, sought to organize rural resistance. The Kuomintang was, in short, well positioned to reap the political benefits of war-induced patriotism, as did ruling groups in the United States, Britain, Germany, the Soviet Union, and Japan. China's communist party, by contrast, barely surviving in a poor and peripheral region of the northwest at the start of the war, enjoyed no such advantage. In the end, a discussion of peasant nationalism divorced from the analysis of the party's agrarian program and praxis offers little insight into why the communists were more successful than their rivals in building rear-area bases and strengthening their forces in a period of Kuomintang decline.

Neither *Peasant Nationalism* nor *The Yenan Way* paid sufficient attention to the Kuomintang's as well as communist forces' contest for the terrain behind Japanese lines. The communist-led bases enjoyed far greater success than their Kuomintang rivals in overcoming the material and financial advantages of Japanese forces. This reinforces the view that the differences in socioeconomic and political programs that distinguished the parties were important in determining the outcomes. As David Paulson observed in explaining the striking inability of Nationalist forces to resist Japanese mop-up campaigns in Shantung, "Neither extensive mass organization nor reform was part of the Nationalist approach."[29] To understand why, half a century later and despite pressing economic problems, regime support remains particularly strong in China's old communist base areas, we need to understand the ways in which nationalism was grounded in wartime socioeconomic and political programs that proved highly effective in linking villagers to the movement.

The outcome of the war, particularly the dynamic growth of the communist movement and the waning of Kuomintang power, hinged on the outcomes of political, social, economic, and military programs of contending political forces in widely differing localities. Yet *Peasant Nationalism* touched on communist wartime land policy only to discount its significance. Noting correctly that the party had abandoned the radical redistributive program of the Kiangsi era in favor of economic reforms, it concluded summarily that "the communists' success in winning peasant support cannot be attributed to their carrying out an 'agrarian revolution.'" The issue is not, however, whether the wartime socioeconomic program constituted an "agrarian revolution." It is whether agrarian policies such as rent reduction, tax reform, and mutual aid helped to forge strong party-peasant bonds essential to the survival and growth of the movement.[30] As Yung-fa Chen rightly observed, "It was primarily redistribution that enabled the Communist Party to involve peasants in the anti-Japanese resistance."[31]

War-induced nationalism is not the inevitable response to invasion, combat, and terror. Other widely noted responses in China and elsewhere include fear, flight, fatalism, even fury directed against resistance forces for provoking Japanese repression. Studies of a range of war zones confronting Japanese attack reveal diverse popular responses in the face of challenges to survival. Only by understanding the multiplicity of state-society relations, ranging from defense to social and economic policy and political restructuring, can we begin to comprehend the various outcomes resulting from efforts by competing forces to dominate the countryside.

The outpouring of literature on nationalism since the 1980s and the explosion of virulent nationalist conflicts from the Sino-Vietnamese-Cambodian wars of the 1970s and 1980s to the breakup of the Soviet Union and Yugoslavia in the 1990s have produced analytical and historical bases for reconceptualizing issues of Chinese nationalism. Benedict Anderson has astutely observed that nationalism "is imagined as a *community,* because, regardless of the actual inequality and exploitation that may prevail in each, the nation is always conceived as a deep, horizontal comradeship. Ultimately, it is this fraternity that makes it possible, over the past two centuries, for so many millions of people, not so much to kill, as willingly to die for such limited imaginings."[32] In *The Yenan Way* I have suggested that the Chinese resistance offers an historical example of an imagined community with strikingly different implications from the typical pattern Anderson has described. The resistance created intellectual and institutional foundations for a national community in two important senses: first, it provided a defensive community against foreign invasion and domination; and second, this community was defined in part by a reform agenda that addressed certain important forms of "actual inequality and exploitation" in Chinese society. This dynamic synthesis was at the heart of the Yenan Way.

The term "community" in this context does not, of course, imply a face-to-face relationship involving all members of a national movement. I use it in an effort to capture important elements of common purpose that meet Anderson's criteria. At the same time, wartime nationalism raises other difficult questions of community—for example, its assumptions about shared interests of Han and minority peoples, assumptions whose problematic character would become clearer in the decades following the founding of the People's Republic. That is, wartime (and postwar) Chinese nationalism *assumed* an identity of interests between Han and minorities without addressing deeply rooted patterns of inequality and oppression. Nationalism, which seems to me to have had significant emancipatory elements as a focus for the wartime resistance, would become a vehicle after 1949 for reifying the mythos of the infallibility of the party, the state, its leader, and its cadres, thus reinforcing numerous forms of inequality and subordination.

The contribution of the *Peasant Nationalism* thesis was its break with Cold War shibboleths by countering conspiracy theories, recognizing the patriotic role of the communist-led resistance, and even in a sense initiating a process of bringing the peasant back into history. *Peasant Nationalism* showed that peasant purposes mattered. At the same time, Johnson's denial of the salience of redistributive social and economic programs (a perspective shared by proponents of the "organizational weapon" thesis that Philip Selznick pioneered in Soviet studies and Tetsuya Kataoka and Roy Hofheinz applied to China) constituted a slighting of central elements defining the wartime rural experience and the crucible of the party-peasant relationship.[33]

Organizational issues, placed within larger frameworks of state building and social change, constitute important dimensions for assessing the movement. Both Kuomintang and communist parties figured in the expansion and deepening of state power that is among the salient features of twentieth-century Chinese politics. Yet the processes differed fundamentally. The growing reach of Kuomintang state power was centered in the Nanjing decade (1927–1937), and its most notable feature was the expanded extractive power of the state, which gave rise to powerful popular opposition movements.[34] The enlarged scope of party, government, and mass organizations throughout the resistance base areas—above all the extension of a continuous party and governmental organizational presence in the township and in some localities down to the natural village—was a distinctive feature of communist state building. In establishing mutual-aid teams and other forms of cooperation in Shen-Kan-Ning, Chin-Ch'a-Chi, and a number of other bases in the 1940s, moreover, the state began to extend its reach down to productive and marketing processes in local communities. In myriad ways this extension was bound up with new forms of social and economic networks that contributed to survival and strengthened the resistance.

It is useful to contrast the deepening of Kuomintang power in rural areas in the 1930s and 1940s, particularly its preoccupation with extraction and control, to the broader reform agenda that was at the heart of the emerging political economy of the resistance bases. Both efforts were driven in part by fiscal and power concerns in the midst of intense competition for control of the countryside. It is a central thesis of *The Yenan Way* that the revolution brought with it a restructuring process that was critical to wartime mobilization. Organizational networks contributed to survival in the face of Japanese and Kuomintang attack. The central point here is not organizational skills per se, but the close association between organization and the party's broad program addressing rural issues. We cannot ultimately assess communist gains and the decline of the Kuomintang without grasping the differences in their respective approaches to the socioeconomic problems of the countryside.

The issues can also be approached from the perspective of the multidimensional debate over dynamism versus disintegration/stagnation in the twentieth-century Chinese countryside. There are conflicting assessments of long-term patterns of growth, rural income, and distribution and the relationship between commercialization and development in the era of protracted war and foreign penetration that spanned the final decades of the Ch'ing and the Republic. One view, advanced most forcefully in recent years in the writings of Ramon Myers, Thomas Rawski, and Loren Brandt and resting heavily on the pioneering research of John Buck, holds that "foreign and interregional trade in North China speeded up commercialization and enabled farms to maintain their same per capita income over time, even as population steadily rose."[35] This modernization perspective, which locates the primary obstacle to rural development in the lack of modern inputs, denies the salience of the fundamental socioeconomic or institutional crisis in the twentieth-century countryside and views global incorporation generally as having provided a positive (if insufficient) economic stimulus for rural development.

By contrast, a number of Chinese and Western studies have stressed long-term rural stagnation, immiseration, class exploitation, the heavy burdens of state extraction, and/or involutionary patterns of growth without income gains, that is, social structural factors that impeded rural development in the late Ch'ing and Republican periods.[36] Among the important works pursuing this line of analysis have been those by Philip Huang, Kang Chao, Carl Riskin, Victor Lippit, Linda Arrigo, and Kathryn Bernhardt. Their approaches build on and broadly reinforce the conclusions of numerous Chinese studies ranging from those of Mao Tse-t'ung to Fei Hsiao-t'ung. The studies in this second group differ in their assessments of the nature, extent, and sources of rural exploitation, oppression, and immiseration and in their understanding of the link between commercialization and China's rural development as measured, for example, by changing patterns with respect to per capita income and social class. They share, however, a sense of crisis manifested in rural immiseration and exacerbated in the twentieth century by protracted civil war and foreign invasion. This distributionist perspective emphasizes the primacy of structural and class obstacles to rural development.

The Yenan Way is distributionist in stressing immiseration, social disintegration, and structural/class barriers to development. It also suggests the importance of spatial approaches to gauging diverse outcomes in China's countryside. Whatever the energizing or modernizing impact experienced by core areas of China, in the rural backwaters that included virtually all the base areas, most mountain zones, and the inland North China periphery, disintegration, polarization, and economic stagnation were the norm.[37] What is particularly germane is that peripheral poverty regions like Shen-Kan-Ning and the base areas generally, as mountainous terrain remote from major cities and modern transport and communications and as the traditional home of bandits, warlords, and *éléments déclassés,* remained beyond the pale of any energizing impact associated with China's incorporation, commercial development, and production for international markets. The base areas manifested in extreme form woes that were the product jointly of warlordism, foreign invasion, economic stagnation, and landlord domination. The Yenan Way constituted a creative response, under conditions of extreme resource constraint, to war-exacerbated immiseration, exploitation, and stagnation in a number of such peripheral rural regions.[38]

Recent Scholarly Perspectives: Base Area Studies and the Reassessment of the Chinese Revolution

Since the 1970s numerous studies have probed the relationship between the impact of war and the socioeconomic and political programs of contending

forces in an effort to better grasp changing party-peasant and state-society relationships. Significant new research has focused on individual base areas and
regions and has extended the microsocietal approach to explore localities down
to the county and village level. At their best, local and regional studies illuminate
the complex interaction of a specific ecology, political economy, war situation,
and competing socioeconomic programs so as to place the locality within regional, national, and global frameworks. The experiences of other areas provide
perspectives from which to reassess *The Yenan Way* both as a study of Shen-
Kan-Ning and as an interpretation of the national movement.

Analysis of the wartime economic, political, and social programs in the base
areas provides the most important vehicle for judging the impact of the party on
the outcome of the war, on popular mobilization, on new forms of state building,
and on the character of social change. The best-known component of the wartime social and economic program was the reduction of rent and interest, which
replaced the party's earlier confiscatory land distribution. In most contested
areas, however, including those parts of Shen-Kan-Ning that had not earlier
experienced land reform, tax reform was more widely implemented and deeply
felt than rent and interest reduction. There were several reasons for this. First,
low tenancy rates in most of North and Central China, including the largest and
most important of the base areas, meant that most households paid no rent and
many who did were taxpaying owner-tenants. Tax issues were far more pressing
for the overwhelming majority. Second, as Lucien Bianco, Prasenjit Duara, and
Ralph Thaxton have well documented, twentieth-century peasant protest and
insurrection had long been directed predominantly against taxes and an aggran-
dizing state rather than against the landlord class.[39] The party's wartime united
front program, embracing even landlord and rich peasant families, made it possible to build on this antistate animus and create coalitions that could be directed
against Japanese puppet administrations that enforced onerous taxation and
corvée policies.

Third, particularly in contested areas, resistance forces lacked the strength and
security to carry out rent reduction, which required sustained mobilization of
poorer strata and had the potential to weaken the united front by inflaming class
divisions. Tax reform, by contrast, which shifted a larger share of the fiscal
burden to richer families, could be implemented administratively and without
overt class struggle that threatened to divide and weaken resistance forces. It was
far more widely implemented.[40] One result was that income differentials in the
base areas were reduced more sharply than were differentials in property ownership.[41] In exempting the destitute entirely from taxes and in reducing the fiscal
burden on a significant group of poorer households, tax reform helped consolidate a broad party-peasant bond. Together with rent reduction, it contributed to a
general process of expanding and strengthening the owner-cultivator majority
and reducing income and wealth differentials. This was frequently accomplished
without significantly reducing the overall tax burden, a necessity for sustaining

the costly war effort. As Yung-fa Chen sums it up with respect to Eastern and Central China, "There is no evidence that the CCP's rate of extraction was lighter than the KMT's in terms of the tax burden on the entire community. We can only be sure that the poor fared better than the rich."[42]

Rent and interest reduction and particularly tax reform exemplify the party's approach to curbing the power of the rural elite and equalizing income and landownership through a "silent revolution" that gradually shifted the fiscal burden from poorer strata to the more prosperous and strengthened the position of a growing majority of owner-cultivators.[43] Chen has shown for East and Central China that both programs encountered fierce landlord resistance, particularly in contested areas or where the party was weak.[44] Where it effectively implemented, however, as in a number of the older North China base areas, including Chin-Ch'a-Chi, Shen-Kan-Ning, and parts of Chin-Chi-Lu-Yu, progressive taxation and rent reduction had redistributive effects that consolidated the party's base both among the poorest strata and broadly among the self-cultivating majority.[45] In many instances, moreover, tax reform and rent-reduction programs did not rupture the united front by driving the local elite into the arms of the Japanese or out of the area. In short, limited reforms that neither eliminated nor thoroughly alienated the local elite and that were predicated on the continued economic and social predominance of family farm and market underpinned a broadly based united front. In subsequent sections I return to the range of measures that base area administrators deployed in seeking to strengthen the resistance.

The wartime program, embracing tax reform, rent and interest reduction, and, in more secure base areas, mutual aid and elementary forms of cooperation, initiated limited but significant social change, including gradual transformation of state-society and inter-class relations. The rich frequently declined in wealth and power while the poor, as well as sections of the independent cultivator majority, achieved palpable if fragile (in that shifting fortunes in the guerrilla war could quickly erase them) economic, social, and political gains. The relative decline in the power of the rich was reinforced by the general wartime decline of commercial agriculture and the expansion of food crops at the expense of commercial crops as cultivators sought to assure subsistence and base area governments to promote trade in an epoch of insecurity.[46] The result was an increasingly homogeneous social basis for the consolidation of power by the party-army leading the resistance in the rear areas of North and Central China.

Several issues remain contested in assessing the wartime program, in part because of varying evidence derived from different regions. One concerns the relationship between resistance forces and the local elite. In Central Hopeh and throughout Chin-Ch'a-Chi, the resistance worked to win over patriotic members of the local elite as well as the poor. In united communities it often succeeded in bringing some of the rich and their scions into local government. The party on occasion bridged the gap between the prosperous and the poor through a shared commitment to the resistance and implementation of an economic and fiscal program that proved minimally acceptable to significant parts of the elite.[47] More than a shared patriotism was involved. Where resistance forces enjoyed sustained dominance, army enlistment by the sons of elite families could secure tax exemptions and strengthen the family's political position. In short, a range of factors came into play in party efforts to mobilize patriotic elite rural youth and the scions of independent cultivators, many of whom subsequently rose within the party, army, and government.

Yung-fa Chen found in contrast that "no matter how willing the rich might be to serve, the party had to rely on the poor for military manpower. Its ideological commitment, as a matter of fact, discriminated against the rich. Perhaps for this reason the party advocated a volunteer army, which enabled it to recruit exclusively from the poor with the slogan 'Those with money contribute money and those with strength contribute strength.'"[48] The poor, including tenants and hired laborers as well as the dispossessed, certainly constituted the backbone of the Eighth Route Army, as they had historically in all Chinese armies. However, in Shen-Kan-Ning and Chin-Ch'a-Chi, the two base areas that I have studied most closely, and in others, too, communist political and military recruiters effectively used appeals to patriotism and threat of confiscation to woo the rural elite. The party, whose own top leaders were drawn from the ranks of educated youth from elite families, well understood the importance of their contributions as military officers and political organizers. Patriotic youth rose rapidly within the movement and in the army, helping their elite families secure their position with the locally dominant political and military force. Of course, where class struggle was intense, military mobilization frequently was integral to processes of isolating and controlling the rich, as Chen reported for East China. The critical point, however, is that one strength of the resistance was its ability to employ a gamut of strategies to win support from diverse social classes, including the rural elite.

The issues intersect with broader debates over dynamics of revolutionary change. It is now possible to transcend both the middle peasant thesis emphasizing the centrality of owner-cultivators, as advanced by Hamza Alavi and Eric Wolf, and the uprooted peasant thesis emphasizing the revolutionary role of dispossessed peasants, as put forward by James Petras and Edward Friedman. If the resistance at first recruited heavily among poor and marginal villagers, it was by no means restricted to the utterly destitute, whether defined as those whose ties to land and village had been severed or more broadly to include poor tenants and hired laborers within the village. As shown above, some independent cultivators and the scions of more prosperous families rallied to the communist-led resistance and assumed leadership roles in party, government, and mass organizations as well as in militia and army. Moreover, the party's own rent-reduction and progressive tax policies enlarged and strengthened the ranks of independent cultivators (Wolf's middle peasants).[49] I consider below the implications of the strengthening of an owner-cultivator majority for democratization in rural China.

The moral-economy–rational-peasant debate, framed in the writings of James Scott and Samuel Popkin, offers another approach for explaining why substantial numbers of villagers of diverse social classes supported the resistance.[50] With reference to the moral-economy argument, which highlights the primacy of subsistence and security considerations, we note both party efforts and villager responses to policies that sought to secure subsistence. But our research also suggests that the juxtaposition of subsistence versus markets may misconstrue a situation in which communist forces simultaneously sought to assure subsistence *and* promote market activity. Positive peasant responses to the expansion of market opportunities were by no means restricted to independent cultivators and the more prosperous but extended to the poor and landless. In rural China widely shared understanding of the essentials of a good life, a moral life, meant a proper marriage and burial and the wherewithal to celebrate the new year and other important festivals in appropriate ways. This required cash, which could only be obtained in the market.

After coming to power, and particularly after 1957, the communist party would brand such customs as feudal superstition and seek to eliminate not only central motifs of popular culture but the markets that sustained them. But in building the resistance, the party-army generally protected both custom and the market, rightly seeing in them powerful weapons essential for the survival and growth of the base areas. David Holm has shown how the party in Shen-Kan-Ning and other areas drew on and adapted popular cultural themes. For example, *yang-ko* performing troupes fanned out across the countryside, visiting each courtyard in turn on New Year's Day, improvising congratulatory songs and verses considered auspicious for the new year, exploding firecrackers, paying respects to the small shrine to T'u-ti at the main gate, and even exchanging *hung feng-tse*, gifts of money in red envelopes. Holm shows, too, the ways in which culture became a battleground, as some intellectuals resisted popularization policies and as the party moved to replace such enshrined and popular cultural motifs as sexually explicit or lewd male-female bantering and to introduce contemporary mobilization priorities such as the production movement and rent reduction.[51]

Consistent with the rational peasant perspective's emphasis on market-derived cash income, research shows that in Shen-Kan-Ning and Chin-Ch'a-Chi diverse social classes looked to the market. But the quest for cash was never the exclusive preoccupation suggested by some rational choice theorists, whose conception of rationality begins and ends with profit maximization and who rule out cultural factors entirely. Indeed, in the desperate times of blockade, pillage, and famine that consumed much of wartime rural China and above all the besieged border areas, both party and villagers rationally prioritized subsistence guarantees over cash incomes. Moreover, the rural crisis placed a premium on familial, lineage, and village groupings and networks rather than on the striving of autonomous individuals. It is most fruitful in thinking about rural China to understand that "moral" and "rational" values were wedded in popular consciousness and that their relative weight changed in response to historical conditions. Prevailing conceptions of the good and moral life, a life that honored ritual norms from birth through marriage to burial, of course presupposed subsistence but looked beyond it.

The market made possible realization of the cash incomes essential for the fulfillment of ritual norms. It was also the locus of much culturally sanctioned activity, from the performance of local opera to worship in temples to marriage negotiations. The resistance party sought to assure both subsistence and cash incomes, and this meant encouraging, but also sometimes regulating, markets. In short, some of the polar positions that have defined much discussion of peasant values and agrarian revolution dissolve in the face of rural realities in the base areas and the chemistry of party-villager relations.

The preceding discussion has underscored the party's success in important base areas in building broad rural coalitions that included the destitute and sections of more prosperous strata around issues of tax reform, rent and interest reduction, and mutual aid. This political and economic program contributed to the unity and élan that made possible the survival of the base areas in the face of Japanese and Kuomintang blockade and attack. Important dimensions of the wartime program in Shen-Kan-Ning, notably tax reform, mutual aid and cooperation, the formation of mass organizations and mobilization for local and regional elections, spread and took root in more stable base areas.[52] These programs facilitated the broadening of a social base and a reduction in the sharpest class antagonisms that threatened to divide the resistance. On these issues the recent literature contributes to a broadening and deepening of approaches first proposed in *The Yenan Way*.

Subsequent research has confirmed that essential elements of *The Yenan Way* model can, with appropriate attention to variations, be applied to other base areas and the wartime movement overall. The periodization of the epoch proposed in *The Yenan Way*, pivoting on the institutional-political-ideological watershed of 1942–1943 and stressing the multifaceted response to the Japanese offensive that jeopardized the survival of several bases, remains generally valid not only for Shen-Kan-Ning but for the national movement. Similarly, the focus on the socioeconomic foundations of the relationship between party and villagers in peripheral regions under wartime conditions offers a basis for the comparative study of the base areas leading to a deeper understanding of the dynamism of the resistance. Finally, the wartime resistance constitutes not only the most innovative period of the Chinese communist movement but a seminal experience foreshadowing and influencing subsequent anticolonial movements throughout Asia, Africa, and Latin America. In these dimensions *The Yenan Way* has stood the test of time.

Is so positive an appraisal of the wartime resistance tenable in the 1990s, in light of what we now know of the communist party that presided over the Great

Leap Famine, that led China on the devastating course of the Cultural Revolution, that presided over the Tiananmen massacre, and much more? In the discussion that follows, I consider anew some of the core judgments of my earlier *Yenan Way* in light of these issues and particularly in light of important new evidence on the period of the resistance. I insist, however, as in the earlier work, that judgments include but not be limited to such comparative frameworks as those of Ch'ing and Republican China, other Asian colonial and semicolonial societies, and poor and divided agrarian nations then and subsequently. *The Yenan Way* must also be assessed in light of the subsequent course of the Chinese revolution, not by any simple extrapolation from present to past or vice versa, but by rigorous assessment of historical processes. The following reassessment of *The Yenan Way* addresses the book's most important challenges.

Toward an Autocritique of *The Yenan Way*

The central issues pivot on democracy and authoritarianism, including questions of fundamentalism, the cult of Mao, and the nature of political mobilization, all of which have been at the heart of debate over the nature of Yenan communism.[53]

I begin by considering an example of a kind rarely encountered in the published documentary, and even in the intelligence record, that provided the research base for *The Yenan Way*. Examples of commandism from a Hopeh plains region that could be multiplied many times include a 1944 instance in which outsiders forced a small and struggling cooperative to accept norms of income distribution based predominantly on labor at the expense of return on land. To do less, the cadres claimed, would constitute "exploitation."[54] The new policy drove half the households, particularly those that were slightly better endowed with land, out of the struggling cooperative (membership at that time was genuinely voluntary). Responding to the virtual collapse of cooperation, the leadership quickly restored former distributive norms. But it was too late to bring back those who had bolted.

Where unchecked, commandism, fundamentalism, and insensitivity to local values sometimes produced deadly consequences. In an instance of heavy-handed politics in the service of an exemplary cause, outside cadres promoted night school for young married women. They neglected, however, to undertake the preparatory work required to make such activity socially acceptable in a community in which women were expected to remain within courtyard walls and in which many viewed their education as irrelevant or worse. Irate family members beat to death several married women who persisted in seeking education. In extreme cases such insensitivity jeopardized the lives of individuals and the survival of the resistance. The issue is the distinction between mobilizational approaches responsive to local perceptions and needs, approaches that could expand the horizons of social justice, and the imposition of externally derived and rigidly imposed formulae. Frequently, a fine line separated effective popular mobilization from repressive commandism. Where the party imposed policies that lacked a popular basis, repression or violence could contribute to passivity, disunity, or worse. Because judgments had to be made under conditions of guerrilla warfare in the face of military repression and at times under pressure from party officials with little knowledge of local conditions and values, the issues became all the more poignant.

These examples illustrate tensions within the mass line to which I paid too little attention in my original work. At its best, the mass line, an approach designed to mediate and resolve such antagonisms, rallied broad strata of the population in the service of shared national resistance goals and those of social and economic reform. *The Yenan Way* highlighted such instances of leadership praxis responsive to popular needs and values. Such a politics, where attuned to popular needs and desires, could contribute to social and economic equity. At its worst, however, it was capable of destructive forms of fundamentalism resting on party claims to exercise a monopoly on morality and truth.

The dark side of mobilizational politics would be amply manifested in the political scapegoating, personality cult, repression, and manipulation that crescendoed in the late Mao years, particularly during the Great Leap Forward and Cultural Revolution, and continued in the reign of Teng Hsiao-p'ing as well. Earlier, under wartime conditions, where survival of the movement depended on sustaining popular support, the party generally succeeded in curbing commandist and fundamentalist tendencies. It displayed a tactical and strategic flexibility and sensitivity in dealing with a range of social classes. For example, the party pressed electoral campaigns that brought noncommunists into local administration, though, to be sure, in ways that never challenged its predominance in the base areas it led. But successful democratic transitions almost invariably begin with some measure of elite continuity.[55] The evidence from the resistance suggests that there was a significant democratizing potential within the communist movement, if that was by no means the only potential. This was among the factors that contributed to the high levels of popular support the party enjoyed, as contemporary observers amply noted. Nevertheless, writing in the 1990s, my affirmation of the democratic promise of the movement is more guarded than it was at the time of the original work.

The movement achieved substantial success in implementing wartime reform programs responsive to popular needs, particularly those of poorer strata, in establishing socioeconomic preconditions favorable to democracy, and in broadening the scope of the political process. By what standards? Certainly by comparison with anything found in the rural areas under Kuomintang, warlord, or Japanese rule and by comparison with most other contemporary poor and peripheral nations. Both in Shen-Kan-Ning and in the base areas behind Japanese lines, the socioeconomic and political programs of this period rank among the most innovative to emerge anywhere in a century of national independence struggle and communist revolution in the colonial and semicolonial regions of the periphery. The achievements include bringing substantial numbers of marginalized people into the political process and expanding their economic, cultural, and political resources. *The Yenan Way* recognized and highlighted these seeds of a democratic transition. As we look back from the 1990s, however, it is equally important to understand why the seeds of democracy sown in the resistance failed to germinate—or rather were repeatedly crushed—in the People's Republic. Among the reasons is that the resistance movement also carried within it the seeds of party despotism, ideological fundamentalism, and the cult of the leader.

Looking beyond the resistance to the People's Republic, we see that centralist, authoritarian, and fundamentalist strains present in incipient form within the wartime movement came to the fore once the party achieved national power and encountered obstacles, both domestic and international, to attaining its ambitious developmental and restructuring goals. Many of the most hopeful elements of the Yenan Way were then suppressed. The Mao cult and the party's tight monopoly on power stifled the reformist sprouts associated with the influx of intellectuals, the united front, and social policy achievements of the resistance era. The spirit of mutual aid and cooperation that had been latent in peasant experience and had earlier been encouraged by the party within the framework of a mixed economy was undermined by the imposition of giant collectives modeled on Stalin's kolkhoz but with little or no mechanization. The possibilities of a mixed economy of household, cooperative, and market after 1955 yielded to extreme forms of antimarket collectivism.

The revolution brought gains in basic health care and sanitation that permitted China to achieve life expectancy levels far beyond those of other nations at comparable income levels and even to approach advanced world levels. However, particularly since the mid-1950s, the interests of villagers were sacrificed in the service of a vision of development and national power that took heavy industry as its goal and the countryside as the primary source of accumulation to achieve it. While the party claimed legitimacy as heir to the Yenan Way, in the late Mao years this legacy was defined ever more persistently as one of asceticism, hard work, class struggle, self-sacrifice, and boundless loyalty to the leader, themes acceptable to many in the course of the resistance but subsequently worn thin. The urban-rural gap and the gap between officials and villagers widened into chasms. Most villagers, particularly those in poorer locales, experienced a system in which cash virtually disappeared and more work brought no per capita income gains. Notably in the Great Leap Forward and the Cultural Revolution, the party embarked on a course that would lead it to break with many of the most hopeful principles and approaches of the earlier movement, sacrificing the interests of the countryside for industry and the cities and presiding over processes of interminable scapegoating and political violence.[56]

By reconsidering the 1942 party rectification movement, we may address other critical issues. This study was the first to recognize the rectification as a vehicle for building consensus within the party and preparing cadres and intellectuals for the important political and institutional changes that would emerge between 1942 and 1944 at the heart of the Yenan Way: the movements for mutual aid and tax reform, the production campaign that brought many women into the social economy, the expansion of the organizational economy, and innovations in education and health care. These and other initiatives, such as promulgating a cultural policy to face the countryside, were bound up with preparations for a transfer of cadres and intellectuals to the villages. In short, the rectification contributed to building the organizational unity required to formulate, evaluate, and implement far-reaching institutional changes in the base areas.

The rectification was also a means of mediating conflicts. In this respect I contrast it to earlier resort to assassination and execution as a means of intraparty conflict resolution. The original work supported Boyd Compton's findings that the rectification was not a purge, though it did provide a venue for sharp political-intellectual struggle.[57] The appearance of new evidence and the subsequent course of the Chinese revolution requires us to rethink the rectification from the perspective of its repression of dissenting views, its significance for intra-party political processes, and the administration of justice.

The rectification was a pivotal event not only in establishing Mao's dominant position within the party, particularly his theoretical hegemony, but in the creation of a cult of Mao and in crushing independent thought among intellectuals and party activists. These tendencies that would be carried to disastrous extremes in the People's Republic surfaced in the resistance years. Tai Ch'ing's seminal work in exhuming the case of the writer Wang Shih-wei brings into focus perhaps the single most important case for gauging repressive dimensions of the wartime movement. I take up Wang's case both as the most extreme example of its kind presently known as well as one I addressed in my original work. As the first edition of *The Yenan Way* noted, Wang's real crime—his scathing attack on elitist tendencies within what by most standards was a most egalitarian movement—was compounded in the eyes of party leaders by the presumptuousness of a little-known writer who persisted in judging the party by its own highest standards. Wang charged the party with hypocrisy in providing its own officials with privileged access to food, clothing, shelter, and sex. He derided "the three classes of clothing and five grades of food" as an unnecessary, indeed immoral, luxury at a time when all were asked to sacrifice for the survival of an independent China. When the thirty-six-year-old Wang refused to back down by accepting criticism of his views (the communist writer Ting Ling and all others under attack made at least token self-criticisms), he was incarcerated.

The work of Tai Ch'ing revealed that after five years of imprisonment on charges of Trotskyism, Wang became the victim of a grisly execution. David Apter and Timothy Cheek correctly conclude that the issues are systemic, that is, emblematic "of Yenan's dark side, as authentic a part of Yenan's inner 'symbolic capital' as the outer manifestations of frugality, self-sacrifice, and national salvation."[58]

I read the case at several levels. Most importantly, it and the rectification movement of which it was a part illuminate a stage in the formation of a thought-control apparatus within the Chinese Communist Party, a critical moment in creating mechanisms of repression and control that would intensify and expand in scope to become the norm once the party consolidated power in the People's Republic.

Other issues were also at stake. Wang had championed a position that was at odds with Mao in the cultural-intellectual debates that led up to the rectification. As Mao and his associates pressed for a new culture and art drawing on China's own folk traditions and providing a basis for bridging the gap between intellectuals and villagers, Wang emerged as a primary exponent of the "high culture" or modernist view that denied the potential contribution of folk and popular arts to a new art and literature. The issues were critical during a period when Mao and others sought "to harness the energies of the intelligentsia, both literary and technical, for a concentrated assault on illiteracy, ignorance, superstition and chronic ill health among the rural poor—in other words to obviate the main cultural barriers to forced-pace economic growth and political mobilization in the countryside."[59]

The case is revealing in terms of the space and limits of dissent that were possible within the wartime movement. Wang was not without supporters in the early phases of the campaign. He succeeded not only in publishing his two dissenting essays but in mobilizing support for his position and fighting back within the party with some initial success prior to his incarceration. Such opportunities to contest leadership decisions would subsequently disappear. Since the 1980s, as more information became available, Wang's case has rightly received attention in China and abroad both as the most extreme case of its kind in this epoch and, more importantly, for its chilling impact on the political milieu in the border region and beyond.

The treatment of Wang Shih-wei exposes the manipulative and coercive side of Yenan communism. Because of the strength of populist, reformist, and even proto-democratic tendencies within the wartime movement, it is essential to understand why the authoritarian and repressive tendencies illustrated by Wang's case triumphed in the subsequent People's Republic, from the antirightist movements of the 1950s to the Cultural Revolution to the crushing of democratic aspirations throughout the 1980s and 1990s.

In assessing the resistance period, Philip Huang observes that "the Chinese Communist movement enjoyed much greater popular support than did the Kuomintang," but he goes on to balance this judgment with another: "There can be no denying the strongly conspiratorial mentality and workstyle of the Leninist Communist Party, its protestations of a 'mass line' notwithstanding."[60] The latter judgment is one that I share when applied to the years in power, particularly if couched in terms of an authoritarian rather than a conspiratorial mentality. Moreover, in facets of the rectification movement such as the crushing of dissent in the cases of Ting Ling and Wang Shih-wei, I find the roots of the repression of intellectuals and the formation of a Mao cult that would so profoundly shape the movement subsequently.

Nevertheless, as a comprehensive judgment on the party of the resistance epoch, that is, one in the midst of a fight for national survival and incipient civil war, Huang's perspective seems to me one-sided. I wonder if it is not also teleological, reading back from the subsequent course of the revolution. Cases like Wang Shih-wei's appear to have been rare in base areas, far more rare than in the incarceration and killing of critics or foes by, for example, the Japanese or the Kuomintang. If the dark side of Yenan communism was understated in *The Yenan Way,* as it surely was, we should not lose sight of distinctive features of the movement in this, perhaps its most open and creative period. Only in this way can we begin to grasp how it succeeded in attracting the extraordinary loyalty of a broad range of patriotic Chinese of diverse classes, many of whom sacrificed their lives in the wartime struggle. And only then can we understand the democratic voices within the party, including those of villagers, workers, and intellectuals, who continued to struggle against authoritarianism after 1949.

This is not to condone manipulative, violent, or fundamentalist elements that surfaced in the party during the resistance. It is, however, to suggest that these tendencies were generally held in check not only by the imperatives of survival in the face of powerful enemies, that is, by an objective situation that required winning and retaining substantial popular support, but also by the populist character of the wartime movement, whose constituency included many of China's outstanding intellectuals as well as broad rural support.

In a second major challenge to *The Yenan Way* perspective, Yung-fa Chen has shown that from 1943 to 1945 the Shen-Kan-Ning economy and government finance became heavily dependent on the production and sales of a "special product" that, he concludes, could only have been opium. Working with budgetary, sales, and export data, as well as with published diaries, Chen demonstrates (and the as yet unpublished findings of other researchers confirm) that the party-army responded to crushing budget deficits that threatened survival by growing and selling substantial quantities of opium. He presents strong circumstantial evidence that the opium traffic was controlled by the 359th Brigade under General Wang Chen (the regional model of military self-sufficiency) and by the Nanch'ang Company (the regional model of state-supported cooperation). Chen holds that Mao personally approved the opium sales in 1943, banning them only when the crisis eased in 1945. Chen sums up his discussion in the form of a critique of the findings of *The Yenan Way:* "No one can deny the communists' achievement in developing the Shen-Kan-Ning Border Region through the mass line in the 1940s. But ignorance of the role played by the revenues from the opium trade led Selden to exaggerate the economic accomplishments and overlook the internal constraints imposed by the poverty and backwardness of the Border Region. . . . As the size of opium trade testifies, the Border Region never achieved the goal of genuine self-reliance."[61] Chen's research provides compelling testimony of the desperate struggle for survival in the rural backwater of

Shen-Kan-Ning. It also suggests dimensions of historical continuity linking modern revolutionaries and traditional rebels in a manner Elizabeth Perry pioneered earlier in her studies of the Huai-pei region.[62]

With the poverty of the border region exacerbated by blockade and war, and with the end of Kuomintang subsidies in 1940, the economic and financial options available to resistance forces were narrow. Even in the absence of war-induced resource constraints, the border region economy would have been severely strained by the substantial influx of soldiers, administrators, and students that coincided with and followed the arrival of the Red Armies. Chen underlines the distinction between the communists' desperate turn to opium and characteristic warlord behavior, noting that the party not only effectively banned opium smoking within the border region but ended opium sales as soon as the crisis eased. Chen's findings require reconsideration of the nature of the politics and economics of survival in the border area. They also draw attention in new ways to the critical role of the market in making possible the survival of the resistance in its time of trial.[63]

Surprisingly, Chen does not directly address the findings of the most exhaustive effort thus far to analyze the economic performance of the region, Peter Schran's *Guerrilla Economy*.[64] Schran provides detailed analysis of the range of state-directed efforts mounted in response to the economic and financial crisis of the early 1940s, including the institutional economy, substantial tax increases coupled with tax reforms that redistributed the burden, printing of currency, import-substituting industrialization, and the mobilization of female and other labor in production campaigns. Schran shows that the border region administration sustained large and growing budget deficits each year between 1941 and 1944, despite increased revenues provided by the institutional economy. The deficits would presumably have been substantially larger in the absence of opium revenues.[65]

Chen's new evidence is central in the calculus both of economics and politics. Yet his critique of earlier scholarship is not quite persuasive. Neither Schran's *Guerrilla Economy* nor *The Yenan Way* contended that the self-reliant efforts solved the problems of poverty, technological backwardness, or government deficits in the Shen-Kan-Ning region. Those two studies and others that probed economics and finance in other border regions in fact emphasized the heavy fiscal pressures on the regime and offered rather modest assessments of the economic and developmental results. At a time when the border region supported a large military and administrative population and faced blockade and protracted war, no economic breakthrough occurred. Nor could it have. My narrower claim in *The Yenan Way* has been rather that the combination of rent and tax reform, mutual aid, the market, and self-reliance bolstered the war effort. I further hinted at the potential value of these approaches for subsequent development efforts but made no claim of economic breakthrough.

Part of the process whereby the revolutionary armies and party adapted to the harsh conditions of border region life, it is now clear, included continuing as well as attempting to control the opium trade that had long provided an important source of revenue for both cultivators and the state in an impoverished region. The continuing significance of the opium trade helps illuminate one of the ways in which survival in the poverty-stricken periphery was possible and underlines the point made earlier that border region officials encouraged, even as they sought to direct, critical levers in the market.

Future understanding of economy and finance in the border area will incorporate analysis of the revenues derived from opium in the late war years (Chen contends that it accounted for 27 percent of Shen-Kan-Ning government spending in 1944 and 40 percent in 1945) to assess regional self-reliance. The opium factor is one of several domains in which the wartime communist movement will be seen less in terms of historic rupture and more in terms of continuity with ecologically and culturally conditioned patterns. That certainly includes the effort to take advantage of market opportunities, a key element of the wartime economy that now must be understood to include opium, at least in 1943–1945. Opium is one of many examples illustrative of realms in which differences between Shen-Kan-Ning and areas under Kuomintang and warlord jurisdiction are less pronounced than many researchers, including myself, previously assumed.

Recent research permits us to address anew several important issues in the Yenan Way. To what extent did the resistance constitute a "peasant revolution" in the sense that peasants not only provided the mass base of revolutionary armies but that their moral universe informed the trajectory of revolution? This view has been advanced by historians of a moral-economy persuasion—most forcefully by Friedman for the early Republic and by Thaxton for the resistance era.[66] Here the conventional wisdom concerning the Leninist vanguard party is essentially reversed, with the party learning from the masses and framing a socioeconomic and cultural program that springs primarily from popular values, particularly villagers' aspirations to right the wrongs of a world dominated by imperialist invaders, rapacious landlords, and warlords, and shaped by lineage and religious values. In this view the party, if it is successful at all, becomes the expression of rural values and aspirations.

The strength of this perspective applied to the resistance lies in its recognition of how a party whose membership was overwhelmingly rural and that spent two decades in the countryside en route to national power learned from and was shaped by villagers and rural values. It is suggestive for understanding how the party-army regularly adapted programs and values in the attempt to win the support of diverse rural constituencies even when it assumed it was transmitting "correct ideology" to a feudal peasantry. It recognizes that rural people not only brought their values and beliefs into the party but retained many of them. And it helps to pinpoint important ways in which the rural origins of the vast majority of party members and soldiers shaped the character of the movement. This perspective can be used to explore areas of shared values—ranging from egalitarian to patriarchal to market-oriented to religious values—linking party activists and leaders on the one hand and villagers on the other.

Critics of such a peasant-centered perspective have, however, attacked certain of its premises. Bianco convincingly observes that the communists "could not have won without the peasant armies and the support of so many villagers. Yet without the communists the peasants would quite simply never have conceived the idea of a revolution."[67] In the absence of the communists or other extra-village forces, China's peasants throughout the twentieth century had mounted numerous uprisings and rebellions directed variously against the state, local landlords and other elites, and against other communities. The very qualities that made possible the eruption of thousands of protests and uprisings made difficult their expansion from isolated locality to sustained national movement.[68] For millennia, the dynamic of large-scale and successful peasant rebellions and peasant movements was one that united a popular rural base with leadership drawn from those with wider horizons, whether cultivated by education, elite position, or extra-village experience.

The poverty, exploitation, and social disintegration shaping rural life constituted necessary preconditions for the Chinese revolution. Yet as Bianco argues, the peasantry alone could not bring the revolution to fruition.[69] In the course of protracted war, the communists, with their urban, cosmopolitan leadership and historical origins and committed to national independence and ultimately to the building of a prosperous, powerful socialist China, succeeded in knitting together disparate forces including broad rural strata and urban intellectuals. This is not to deny the peasant character of the army, most of whose recruits and some of whose leaders were of rural origin. Nor is it to overlook the shaping of party programs and priorities in ways responsive to peasant values. The strength of this perspective lies in drawing attention to the diverse elements that coalesced and the points of tension within the movement: between coastal and inland areas, between values shaped in the cities and in the countryside, between military and civilian perspectives, and between party and society. Its limit, in my view, lies in its complete dichotomization of party and peasantry and its failure to recognize ways in which a two-way socialization process occurred in which peasants were not merely molded by the party but in turn shaped the character of the party. Looking decades ahead, we must now read the entire history of the People's Republic at one important level as the persistent—and ultimately successful—effort from below to restore the role of markets that socialist party leaders had accepted during the resistance but sought to suppress once they were in power.[70]

This Epilogue has explored questions of democracy and power in the base areas from several angles. *The Yenan Way* highlighted egalitarian, participatory, and cooperative achievements of the wartime resistance. In the course of the resistance, the party challenged landlord power, strengthened the position of the poor and of independent cultivators through rent and tax reform, and initiated fruitful forms of mutual aid, all within the context of a mixed economy resting on foundations of the family farm and market access. At the same time the movement promoted literacy and education, and it introduced a mobilizational politics that embraced the rural poor and women. These were among the factors that seemed to me to constitute foundations for a socialist transition that could expand villagers' political roles and ultimately empower them.

Writing in the mid-1990s, I see this approach as inadequate. The appropriate question is why, given promising beginnings conducive to a democratic transition, particularly the strengthening of an independent cultivator majority, was subsequent development of a democratic polity so meager? Why did the reformist and democratic elements of the party's New Democracy wither and die in subsequent decades? Why were important gains reversed as the party exercised a tight monopoly on power that it retains at this writing? And why did villagers who provided the core of the wartime revolutionary force and were in many ways beneficiaries of party policies framed in the course of the resistance experience such hardship in the era of mobilizational collectivism associated with the final decades of Mao's rule? Part of the answer, but only a part, lies in more explicitly recognizing the limits of democratic progress of the resistance era. In particular, it is necessary to grasp the ways in which democratic impulses remained subordinated to party-army mobilization. In the course of the resistance, the popular gains associated with the revolutionary movement coincided with growing party hegemony. We can trace the origins of subsequent conflicts between party and people and between city and countryside to tendencies that can already be discerned in Yenan.

In *The Yenan Way* I rightly noted the significance of sprouts of democracy associated with the introduction of forms of electoral politics, the growth of an independent cultivator majority, and the emergence of a cooperative economy. But I insufficiently grasped that these were part of a package associated with a party-dominated mass line and a conception of mobilization that could pose formidable obstacles to further democratic advance and economic and political empowerment of rural producers in the years ahead.

Reflecting anew on the Yenan Way in the 1990s leads me to the following conclusions:

1. The Yenan Way, as the summation of the Chinese Communist Party's experience in the resistance, constituted an important moment in the history of anticolonial resistance and revolutionary change in the periphery. It also offered hints applicable to the political economy of development, including the contributions of policies empowering an owner-cultivator majority through rent and tax reforms that constituted a "silent revolution" and preliminary steps toward mutual aid, cooperation, and democracy. This central thesis of the original work remains intact.

2. The Yenan Way also, however, encapsulated repressive and regressive tendencies that I insufficiently appreciated in my initial study. When carried to extremes in the People's Republic, notably in the Great Leap Forward, the Cul-

tural Revolution, and the repression of democratic aspirations and movements from 1957 to 1979 to 1989 and beyond, the results were frequently tragic and certainly conflict with the revolution's finest proclivities, including those toward democracy, equality, and the uplifting of a poverty-stricken countryside.

We can trace these and other unresolved tensions in Chinese political economy back to the synthesis I have called the Yenan Way. It is worth appreciating in all its complexity so as to keep alive its most humane possibilities while identifying the repressive forces detrimental to further progress toward social and economic development and human liberation.

Notes

1. Gregor Benton's excavation of what he calls the "Three Year War" for survival has rescued from oblivion the rearguard effort of southern guerrillas who remained to fight as the Long March headed toward the northwest. Despite the existence of these and other scattered forces, some of which eventually reestablished ties with the party, the focus of resistance had clearly shifted from the southern part of Central China to the northwest, from which it would shortly move to North China. See *Mountain Fires: The Red Army's Three Year War in South China, 1934–1938* (Berkeley, 1992). The tenacity of the Chinese resistance is particularly noteworthy by comparison with Southeast Asian regions that fell to Japan in the aftermath of Pearl Harbor. Within a matter of months, Japan's war machine defeated and expelled British forces from Malaysia, Singapore, Burma, and Hong Kong; the Americans from the Philippines; and the Dutch from Indonesia. In none of these instances did a local resistance movement significantly challenge Japanese rule prior to the U.S. counterattack that began in 1944.

2. In this sense *The Yenan Way* addressed broad themes of social revolution that have been explored in such works as Barrington Moore's *The Social Origins of Dictatorship and Democracy: Lord and Peasant in the Making of the Modern World* (Boston, 1966); Theda Skocpol's *States and Social Revolutions: A Comparative Analysis of France, Russia, and China* (Cambridge, England, 1979); and Schurmann's *Ideology and Organization in Communist China* (Berkeley: 1966). But where each of these authors chose a broad canvas, and in the cases of Moore and Skocpol a grand comparative framework, my focus was on the small Shen-Kan-Ning base area.

3. I have benefited from three incisive surveys of the literature and the period of the Sino-Japanese War. See "Introduction: Perspectives on the Chinese Communist Revolution," by Kathleen Hartford and Steven Goldstein in Hartford and Goldstein, eds., *Single Sparks: China's Rural Revolutions* (Armonk, 1989), 3–33; Lyman Van Slyke, "The Chinese Communist Movement During the Sino-Japanese War, 1937–1945," in Fairbank and Feuerwerker, 609–722; and Yung-fa Chen, *Making Revolution: The Communist Movement in Eastern and Central China, 1937–1945* (Berkeley, 1986), especially "Conclusions," 499–523.

4. The leading Western chroniclers of the wartime era, many of whose works are discussed below, were Edgar Snow, Agnes Smedley, Jack Belden, John Service, George Taylor, Theodore White and Annalee Jacoby, Nym Wales, Harrison Forman, Anna Louise Strong, Evans Carlson, Gunther Stein, and Michael Lindsay. Although European and Japanese authors have written on the period, in both the first generation and subsequently, the most influential authors have been Americans, a phenomenon appropriate to the rise of the United States as the dominant power in the region in the war and its aftermath. In this light the attention paid to American works and authors is more than parochial.

5. Edgar Snow, *Red Star Over China,* rev. and enl. ed. (New York, 1968).

6. Ibid., 274. See also 445.

7. See, for example, Edgar Snow, *Scorched Earth* (London, 1941), 310–16, 320–21.

8. In this respect, and in his empathy for the underdog and the oppressed, Snow well exemplified the finest traditions of American journalism. The limits of the approach lie in the slight attention he paid to published and documentary sources such as government and party documents, the Chinese press, books, and so on. The Chinese language was one formidable obstacle to such an approach. Perhaps no Western journalist of the wartime period had a working knowledge of written Chinese. The issues run deeper, however, to the nature of American conceptions of the journalist's enterprise, which valorizes the interview, emphasizes visual impressions, and has a deadline-driven tendency to slight research in written and historical sources.

9. Taylor, 101. The argument received abbreviated discussion a year earlier in Haldore Hanson's *"Humane Endeavor": The Story of the China War* (New York, 1939), 274.

10. White and Jacoby, 201–2. The passage quoted here recalls the extent to which the literature views problems of the countryside as problems of *male* villagers. *The Yenan Way,* and in my view subsequent base area studies, including my own, have thus far failed effectively to address gender and familial issues. These issues remain elusive in part because they were rarely systematically treated in party and government documents.

11. Joseph Esherick, ed., *Lost Chance in China: The World War II Despatches of John S. Service* (New York, 1974), 217. Original italics.

12. Ibid., 219. Service and many other officers in China subsequently faced charges of disloyalty and most were driven out of the foreign service. Although Service was cleared of all charges in loyalty and security hearings in 1946, 1947, 1949, 1950, and 1951, Secretary of State Dean Acheson dismissed him from the foreign service in 1951. It is interesting to note that Service clearly reported that "the Communists have controlled all political indoctrination and propaganda and have not discouraged this tendency of the peasants to regard them as their benefactors." Despatch of September 10, 1944, ibid., 230.

13. This position, most brilliantly articulated by Barrington Moore in his *Social Origins and Democracy,* is at the heart of my understanding of the democratizing potential of socioeconomic reform as expressed in both *The Yenan Way* and in *Chinese Village, Socialist State.* My understanding of the Chinese resistance on this point led me to far more hopeful conclusions than those of Moore.

14. Some who wrote of communist wartime accomplishments and harshly criticized Kuomintang corruption and malfeasance were more cautious in assessing the degree of democracy in the base areas. An example is the prescient note in Belden, 503: "The Chinese Communists, in the process of raising a people's rebellion, freed the peasants from feudal burdens and the nation from domination by the West. But it is very doubtful if they have liberated the people from the encroachments of state power. They will be freer of arbitrary authority and brutal masters than they were under Chiang Kai-shek, but probably less independent of power itself."

15. Lyman Van Slyke, ed., *The Chinese Communist Movement: A Report of the United States War Department, July 1945* (Stanford, 1968), 1. The quoted passage from the introduction (and particularly the summary report prepared by General Paul Peabody, chief of military intelligence) exemplifies the organizational weapon perspective. The complete report drew on accounts from a range of wartime observers, including John Service and Edgar Snow.

16. Snow, *Red Star,* 244; Snow, *Scorched Earth,* 347.

17. White and Jacoby, 205.

18. Belden, 97. White, in a report on the Honan famine of 1941–1943 originally

censored by his editors at *Time,* drew similar conclusions: "The peasants as we saw them were dying. They were dying in the roads, in the mountains, by the railroad stations, in their mud huts, in the fields. And as they died, the government continued to wring from them the last possible ounce of tax. . . . No excuses were allowed; peasants who were eating elm bark and dried leaves had to haul their last sack of seed grain to the tax collector's office. . . . Small government officials, army officials and rich land owners who still had food were engaged in purchasing the peasants' ancestral areas at criminally low prices." White and Jacoby, 174.

19. In contrast to their sometimes probing critique of *Japanese* imperialism, these works offer virtually no insight into the nature of the United States as a rising Pacific power or of the nature of American, British, French, or Dutch colonial rule in Asia or elsewhere. That is, the U.S. wartime alliance with China against Japan meant that populist versions of China's struggle for autonomy were perfectly compatible with uncritical support for U.S. regional and global goals.

20. We can trace a series of cycles in American and Western China scholarship from the predominantly "external" perspectives of such pioneering figures as H.B. Morse in the late nineteenth and early twentieth centuries to the "internal" perspectives championed by the modernization school with John Fairbank as the representative figure, to the external perspectives of many Kremlinologists in the 1950s, and the rather different external perspectives advanced by those emphasizing the role of imperialism in shaping China, some of them associated with the rethinking prompted by the Vietnam War and the formation of the Committee of Concerned Asian Scholars in the 1960s and 1970s. The sharpest debate on these issues began with Jim Peck's salvo "The Roots of Rhetoric: The Professional Ideology of America's China Watchers" in *Bulletin of Concerned Asian Scholars,* 2.1:59–69 (1969), and "An Exchange" between Harvard graduate student Peck and his teacher, the doyen of American China scholars, John Fairbank in 2.3:51–70 (1970). See also Edward Friedman and Mark Selden, eds., *America's Asia: Dissenting Essays on Asian-American Relations* (New York, 1971). These debates continued in the 1970s and 1980s with countercritiques of the China field by Ramon Myers and Thomas Metzger, "Sinological Shadows: The State of Modern China Studies in the U.S.," *Australian Journal of Chinese Affairs,* 4:1–34 (1983); by Simon Leys, *Chinese Shadows* (New York, 1977); and by Stephen Mosher, *China Misperceived: American Illusions and Chinese Reality* (New York, 1990), whose charges and tone frequently evoked the spectre of 1950s McCarthyism but lacked political clout. With China's incorporation in the capitalist world economy from the nineteenth century forward, the internal-external distinction becomes more and more tenuous as a basis for gauging social formations, the economy, and much more. In a sense *The Yenan Way* attempted to break through this internal-external distinction by providing a microsocietal study that was sensitive to both internal forces, particularly Japanese imperialism, and domestic forces associated with patterns of socioeconomic and political disintegration and discontents that derived from impositions associated with state building. For an influential critique of American China scholarship, particularly of external perspectives, see Paul Cohen, *Discovering History in China: American Historical Writing on the Recent Chinese Past* (New York, 1984).

21. The first two issues of *China Quarterly* present the seminal debate on the issues involving Karl Wittfogel and Benjamin Schwartz. "Debate on Chinese Communist History," *The China Quarterly,* 1:72–86 (January–March 1960), 2:16–42 (April–June 1960). Schwartz's analysis of Maoism as a distinctive and original development of Marxism-Leninism, particularly in *Chinese Communism and the Rise of Mao,* marked an important step in advancing the study of the Chinese revolution. *The Yenan Way* extends Schwartz's recognition of the creative and indigenous (as opposed to the transplanted and Soviet) in exploring the synthesis of the wartime period. This perspective seems to me particularly

compelling for the period of resistance when the Chinese Communist Party achieved high levels of independence and the Russians were preoccupied with survival in the face of German invasion. Representative works of the 1950s, focusing on Soviet machinations in China in the Kiangsi period and deeply informed by the Cold War premises of the era, include Tso-liang Hsiao, McLane, North, and Wilbur and How.

22. We now know that John Foster Dulles and other U.S. policy makers in the 1950s quickly recognized the existence of Sino-Soviet tensions and sought to exploit them. Public discourse (and American China scholarship) through the 1960s, however, continued to highlight the monolithic force of the totalitarian enemy. See Gordon Chang, *Friends and Enemies: The United States, China, and the Soviet Union, 1948–1972* (Stanford, 1990).

23. See his 1940 *Struggle for North China.*

24. A particularly interesting example of the influence of the peasant nationalism thesis, in light of its author's contributions to social history and its attention to class conflict, is Moore's *Social Origins of Dictatorship and Democracy,* 223. "The decisive ingredient in the communist victory," Moore concluded, "was the Japanese conquest and the occupation policies of a foreign conqueror."

25. Van Slyke, "The Chinese Communist Movement," 680.

26. See Kathleen Hartford, "Step-by-Step: Reform, Resistance and Revolution in the Chin-Ch'a-Chi Border Region," Stanford University Ph.D. dissertation, 1980, quoted in Van Slyke, "The Chinese Communist Movement," 631.

27. *Seeds of Destruction: Nationalist China in War and Revolution, 1937–1945* (Stanford, 1984), 141.

28. "Repression and Communist Success: The Case of Jin-Cha-Ji, 1938–1943," in Hartford and Goldstein, 94.

29. "Nationalist Guerrillas in the Sino-Japanese War: The 'Die-Hards' of Shandong Province," in ibid., 145–46.

30. Six years after the publication of *Peasant Nationalism,* Johnson casually abandoned the monocausal thesis by recognizing the role of rent reduction in the base areas. See his "Chinese Communist Leadership and Mass Response: The Yenan Period and the Socialist Education Campaign Period," in Ho Ping-ti and Tang Tsou, eds., *China in Crisis* (Chicago, 1968) vol. 1, 397–437. See "Peasant Nationalism Revisited: The Biography of a Book," *The China Quarterly,* 72:775 (December 1977).

31. Chen, *Making Revolution,* 99. "Only after the peasants were mobilized," and the party's organization was locally implanted, Chen argued, could the communists "exploit anti-Japanese feeling." In my view the critical issue is not the temporal sequence of mobilization but the interaction between the dislocations of war and the party's socioeconomic program.

32. *Imagined Communities: Reflections on the Origin and Spread of Nationalism* (London, 1983), 16.

33. Philip Selznick, *The Organizational Weapon: A Study of Bolshevik Strategy and Tactics* (New York, 1952); Tetsuya Kataoka, *Resistance and Revolution in China: The Communists and the Second United Front* (Berkeley, 1974); Roy Hofheinz, *The Broken Wave: The Chinese Communist Peasant Movement, 1922–28* (Cambridge, 1977).

34. Prasenjit Duara, *Culture, Power and the State: Rural North China, 1900–1942* (Stanford, 1988); Friedman, Pickowicz, and Selden, *Chinese Village, Socialist State* (New Haven, 1991).

35. Ramon Myers, "How Did the Modern Chinese Economy Develop? A Review Article," *Journal of Asian Studies* 50.3: 604–28 (August 1991); Myers, *The Chinese Peasant Economy: Agricultural Development in Hopeh and Shantung, 1890–1949* (Cambridge, 1970); Thomas Rawski, *Economic Growth in Prewar China* (Berkeley, 1989); Loren Brandt, *Commercialization and Agricultural Development in East-Central China,*

1870–1937 (Cambridge, England, 1989). The quote is from Myers, "How Did the Modern Chinese Economy Develop?" 604. Cf. Philip Huang's response in the same issue.

36. Fei Hsiao-tung, *Peasant Life in China: A Field Study of Country Life in the Yangtze Valley* (New York, 1939); Kang Chao, *Man and Land in Chinese History: An Economic Analysis* (Stanford, 1986); Philip Huang, *The Peasant Economy and Social Change in North China* (Stanford, 1985) and *The Peasant Family and Rural Development in the Yangzi Delta, 1350–1988* (Stanford, 1990); Friedman, Pickowicz, and Selden; Victor Lippit, *Land Reform and Economic Development in China* (White Plains, 1974); Carl Riskin, *China's Political Economy: The Quest for Development Since 1949* (Oxford, 1987); Gail Arrigo, "Landownership Concentration in China: The Buck Survey Revisited," *Modern China,* 12.3:259–360 (1986); Kathryn Bernhardt, *Rents, Taxes, and Peasant Resistance: The Lower Yangzi Region, 1840–1950* (Stanford, 1992). The debate is most fully explored in the special issue "New Perspectives on the Chinese Rural Economy, 1885–1935: A Symposium," *Republican China,* 18.1 (November 1992) and in contributions to *Journal of Asian Studies,* 50.3 (August 1991) and 51.3 (August 1992).

37. This position differentiating state-making priorities in core and peripheral regions has been most forcefully articulated and documented by Kenneth Pomeranz, *The Making of a Hinterland: State, Society and Economy in Inland North China, 1853–1937* (Berkeley, 1993). Cf. Susan Mann, who distinguishes state-making outcomes in core and peripheral regions, *Local Merchants and the Chinese Bureaucracy, 1750–1950* (Stanford, 1987); and Friedman, Pickowicz, and Selden.

38. The evidence presented in *The Yenan Way* and by Peter Schran in *Guerrilla Economy: The Development of the Shensi-Kansu-Ninghsia Border Region, 1937–1945* (Albany, 1976) suggests that the wartime program contributed to possibilities for the survival of the resistance in a region whose slender resources were pressed to the limit by the influx of large numbers of soldiers, students, and officials. Tragically, half a century after Japan's defeat, Shen-Kan-Ning and a number of other resistance base areas remain economic backwaters and stagnant poverty zones. Indeed, the party's investment and development priorities shifted after 1949 to more dynamic rural regions and the cities, with the important exception of the security-driven Third Front industrial transfer program initiated at immense cost in the mid-1960s and continued until after Mao's death.

39. Lucien Bianco, "Peasant Movements," in Fairbank and Feuerwerker, 270–308; Duara; Ralph Thaxton, "State Violence and Peasant Revenge in Marketbound China," manuscript in preparation. Elizabeth Perry has added further important dimensions. Her study of a century of rural struggles in the central China Huai-pei region underlines the multiplicity of rebel targets, including the predatory and protective strategies of entire communities. *Rebels and Revolutionaries in North China, 1845–1945* (Stanford, 1980).

40. Friedman, Pickowicz, and Selden, 40–44. Carl Dorris, "Peasant Mobilization in North China and the Origins of Yenan Communism," *The China Quarterly,* 68:704–9 (December 1976).

41. Van Slyke, "The Chinese Communist Movement," 700.

42. Chen, *Making Revolution,* 375; see also 265–67, 365–75.

43. The concept and consequences of diverse programs including tax reform and rent reduction that together constituted the "silent revolution" are analyzed for Central Hopeh in Friedman, Pickowicz, and Selden, ch. 4.

44. Chen, *Making Revolution,* 420–21.

45. Hartford and Goldstein, 101; Tetsuya, Kataoka, *Resistance and Revolution,* 122–33, 249–51; Thaxton, *China Turned Rightside Up,* 103–9; Friedman, Pickowicz, and Selden, 40–44.

46. Ramon Myers, "The Agrarian System," in Fairbank and Feuerwerker, 267. In contrast to communist efforts from the 1950s through the 1970s to eliminate private

commerce, the wartime party worked to expand trade—both administered and private—in the face of Kuomintang and Japanese blockade. Friedman, Pickowicz, and Selden, ch. 4 and 5, and Thaxton, "State Violence and Peasant Revenge" (forthcoming), document initiatives to promote private as well as cooperative and state trade in two North China base areas during the war years.

47. Friedman, Pickowicz, and Selden, ch. 2.

48. Chen, *Making Revolution*, 405.

49. Hamza Alavi, "Peasants and Revolution," in Ralph Miliband and John Saville, eds., *The Socialist Register* (London, 1965), 241–77; Eric Wolf, *Peasant Wars of the Twentieth Century* (New York, 1969), 291–93. See also Wolf's "Peasant Rebellion and Revolution," in Norman Miller and Roderick Aya, eds., *National Liberation: Revolution in the Third World* (New York, 1971). There is little Chinese evidence to support Wolf's conclusions that the middle peasant is "the most vulnerable to economic changes wrought by commercialism" or "the most exposed to influences from the developing proletariat" (292). In any event Wolf recognizes the presence of an external army and/or a location of the peasantry in a peripheral area as a basis for the "tactical mobility" required for participation in a revolutionary movement, criteria that apply well to the wartime base areas. Cf. James Petras, "Toward a Theory of Twentieth-Century Socialist Revolutions," in James Petras, ed., *Critical Perspectives on Imperialism and Social Class in the Third World* (New York, 1978), 179–80. Edward Friedman's analysis of the White Wolf in the 1910s similarly stressed the recruitment to revolutionary armies of the uprooted and destitute. "It is these ex-tillers and ex-villagers and not the backbone tillers remaining in the village who form the backbone of the so-called peasant armies." *Backward Toward Revolution: The Chinese Revolutionary Party* (Berkeley, 1974), 124.

50. James Scott, *The Moral Economy of the Peasant: Rebellion and Subsistence in Southeast Asia* (New Haven, 1976); Samuel Popkin, *The Rational Peasant: The Political Economy of Rural Society in Vietnam* (Berkeley, 1979).

51. David Holm, *Art and Ideology in Revolutionary China* (Oxford, 1991), 160–62, provides a vivid depiction of *yang-ko* at New Year's; passim for a subtle discussion of cultural tensions within the party and between urban intellectuals and party leaders.

52. Pauline Keating's close and astute reading of contrasting patterns of mutual aid and cooperation in two subdistricts of Shen-Kan-Ning suggests the centrality of the cooperative program not only to the regional economy but to grass-roots politics as well. The relationship between cooperation and democratic transitions, implied but not explored in *The Yenan Way*, is an important underresearched area of inquiry. "The Yan'an Way of Cooperativization, 1937–1945," paper presented at the annual meeting of the Association for Asian Studies, Los Angeles, March 25–28, 1993; "The Ecological Origins of the Yan'an Way," *The Australian Journal of Chinese Affairs*, 32:123–53 (July 1994).

53. My current views on the Chinese revolution are most fully elaborated in Friedman, Pickowicz, and Selden, *Chinese Village, Socialist State*, and Selden, *The Political Economy of Chinese Development*.

54. This and the following example drawn from oral history are discussed in Friedman, Pickowicz, and Selden, ch. 3.

55. This is a central theme developed in Edward Friedman, ed., *The Politics of Democratization: Vicissitudes and Universals in the East Asian Experience* (Boulder, Colo., 1994).

56. *The Political Economy of Chinese Development* as well as Friedman, Pickowicz, and Selden and a successor volume in progress, *The Agony of Village China*, offer my fullest assessment of the political economy of the People's Republic and the relationship between the Yenan Way and the subsequent course of the movement.

57. Compton, *Mao's China: Party Reform Documents, 1942–44*.

58. "Introduction: The Trial," in Dai Qing, *Wang Shiwei and "Wild Lilies": Rectifica-

tion and Purges in the Chinese Communist Party, 1942–1944, David Apter and Timothy Cheek, eds. (Armonk, N.Y., 1993), 19. See also Peter Seybolt, "Terror and Conformity: Counterespionage Campaigns, Rectification and Mass Movements, 1942–43." *Modern China,* 12.1:39–73 (January 1986).

59. Holm, 93.

60. "The Paradigmatic Crisis in Chinese Studies," *Modern China,* 17.3:325 (July 1991). The point finds strong resonance in the writings of Tetsuya Kataoka and Chen, *Making Revolution.*

61. "The Blooming Poppy Under the Red Sun: The Yenan Way and the Opium Trade," in Tony Saich and Hans van de Ven, eds., *New Perspectives on the Chinese Coimmunist Revolution* (Armonk, N.Y., 1994).

62. *Rebels and Revolutionaries.*

63. On these issues, particularly the role of markets, see the discussion in Friedman, Pickowicz, and Selden, ch. 3–5.

64. Schran notes without comment the contemporary Kuomintang charges of opium trafficking. Like all earlier studies of the economy of the wartime bases, Schran's provides a detailed analysis of the economic performance and government finance with no reference to opium.

65. Schran, 198–99.

66. Friedman, *Backward Toward Revolution*; Thaxton, *China Turned Rightside Up.*

67. "Peasant Movements," in Fairbank and Feuerwerker, 270.

68. Ibid., 274. This point has also been well argued by Perry, *Rebels and Revolutionaries.*

69. Ibid., 327. Van Slyke draws comparable conclusions with respect to the relationship between locals and outsiders in "The Chinese Communist Movement," 648. See also Chen, *Making Revolution,* 161.

70. This is a central thesis of *The Agony of Village China* (forthcoming).

Glossary

Well-known names and terms cited in the glossary in Brandt et al., eds. *A Documentary History of Chinese Communism* and Howard Boorman, ed., *Biographical Dictionary of Republican China*, are omitted here.

cha-kung 札工
Chang Ch'ing-fu 張慶孚
Chang Chung-liang 張仲良
Chang Mu-t'ao 張慕陶
Chang Mu-yao 張慕堯
Chang Pang-ying 張邦英
Chang Wen-hua 張文華
Chao Tsung-jun 趙宗潤
Ch'en Cheng-jen 陳正人
Ch'en Kuei-chang 陳珪璋
Ch'en Shu-fan 陳樹藩
cheng-wu hui-i 政務會議
Ch'eng Fang-wu 成仿吾
Ch'eng Tzu-hua 程子華
chi-chung ling-tao, fen-san ching-ying
    集中領導分散經營
Chi Hen 季根
chi-t'i pan-kung 集體辦公
Chia Te-kung 買得功
ch'ih-wei tui 赤衛隊
chin 斤
Ching-kuo chün 靖國軍
Ching-pei ch'ü 警備區
ching-ping chien-cheng 精兵間政

ching-wei tui 警衛隊
Ching Wen-lung 井文龍
Ching Yüeh-hsiu 井岳秀
ch'ing-nien t'uan 青年團
chiu kuo kung liang 救國公粮
Chou Hsing 周興
Chou Wen 周文
Chou Yang 周揚
Chu Li-chih 朱理治
Chung-hua fan-ti i-yung chün hsi-pei
    hsien-feng tui 中華反敵義勇軍西北先
    鋒隊
ch'ü 區

fa-pi 法幣
fen-ch'ü 分區
Feng Ch'in-tsai 馮欽哉

Ho Chin-nien 賀晉年
Ho Lien-ch'eng 賀連城
Ho Ying-ch'in 何應欽
ho-tso she 合作社
Hsi-pei fan-ti t'ung-meng chün 西北反敵
    同盟軍

Hsi-pei jen-min 西北人民
hsia-fang 下放
hsia-hsiang 下鄉
hsiang 鄉
hsiang 响
hsiang-chang 鄉長
Hsieh Chüeh-tsai 謝覺哉
Hsieh Tzu-ch'ang 謝子長
hsien 縣
hsien-wu wei-yüan-hui 縣務委員會
hsin min-chu chih-tu 新民主制度
hsin ti min-chu kung-ho-kuo 新的民主
   共和國
hsin-cheng chang-kuan 新政長官
hsing-cheng hui-i 行政會議
hsing-cheng ts'un 行政村
Hsü Ch'üan-chung 許全忠
Hsü Ts'ai-sheng 許才昇
Hu Ching-i 胡景翼
Huang Tzu-wen 黃子文
Huo-chung 夥種
huo-tsu 活租
Huo Wei-te 霍維德
huo-wu-shui 貨物稅

I Ch'eng 一成
i-hui 議會

kan-shih hui 幹事會
K'ang-jih ch'ih-wei chün 抗日赤衛軍
k'ang-ti hou-yüan hui 抗敵後援會
Kao Kuei-tzu 高桂滋
Kao Lang-t'ing 高朗亭
Kao Shuang-ch'eng 高双成
Kao Tzu-li 高自立
Keng Ping-kuang 耿炳光
ko-lao-hui 哥老會
ko-ming wei-yüan-hui 革命委員會
kuan-pan 官辦
kuei-hui pei-shan 歸回北山
kung-chu 功主
Kuo Hung-t'ao 郭洪濤
Kuo-min chün 國民軍

lao-pai-hsing 老百姓
lao-tung hu-chu she 勞動互助社
Li Chieh-fu 李傑夫
Li Chün 厲君
Li Miao-chai 李妙齋
Li Ting-ming 李鼎銘
Li Tzu-ch'eng 李自成
Li Tzu-chou 李子洲
liang-t'iao lu-hsien 兩條路線
lien-hsi hui-i 聯席會議
Liu Chen-hua 劉鎮華
Liu Ching-fan 劉景範
liu-mang 流氓
Lo Chang-lung 羅章龍

Ma Ming-fang 馬明芳
Ma Ko-ch'en 馬閣臣
Ma Wei-hsin 馬維新
min-pan 民辦
min-pan kung-ch'u 民辦公處
min-t'uan 民團
mou 畝

Nan Han-ch'en 南漢宸
Nieh Hung-chün 聶洪鈞

pao 堡
pao-an tui 保安隊
pao-chia 保甲
Pei-yang chün-fa 北洋軍閥
pien-ch'ü 邊區
pien-pi 邊幣
pien-kung 變工
p'in-min hui 貧民會
p'in-min t'uan 貧民團
P'u Chien-sheng 蒲建生
pu-men 部門

Shih K'o-hsüan 史可軒
Shih Lao-yu 史老幼
Shui-hu chuan 水滸傳
ssu-hsiang kai-tsao 思想改造
Sung Che-yüan 宋哲元

ta t'ung 大同
tai-keng 代耕
Tai Chi-ying 戴季英
tai-piao hui 代表會
tai-piao t'uan 代表團
tan 擔
tang-t'uan 黨團
T'ang Shu 唐樹
t'e-ch'ü 特區
ting-tsu 定租
tou 斗
ts'ai-p'an yüan 裁判員
ts'an-i-hui 參議會
Ts'ao Li-ju 曹力如
Ts'ui T'ien-fu 崔田夫
Ts'ui T'ien-ming 崔田鳴
Tsung-te-hou 宗德厚
ts'un 村
Tu Heng 杜衡
tu-chün 督軍

t'un-t'ien 屯田
tzu-li keng-sheng 自力更生

Wang Chen 王震
Wang Fo-tsung 王佛宗
Wang Kuan-lan 王觀瀾
Wang Lin 王林
Wang Shih-t'ai 王世泰
Wang Ta-ch'eng 王達成
Wang T'ai-chi 王太吉
Wang Wei-chou 王維舟
Wei Yeh-ch'ou 魏野疇

yang-ko 秧歌
Yang Kuo-tung 楊國棟
Yen Hsiang-wen 閻相文
yu-chi-tui 游擊隊
Yü Ch'ih 愚痴
Yü Yu-jen 于右任

Bibliography

Items marked with an asterisk pertain to the Senior Cadres Conference held in Yenan from October 19, 1942, to January 14, 1943.

I. Chinese Communist Sources

Chao Yüan-ming. *Shen-kan-ning pien-ch'ü ti lao-tung ying hsiung* (Labor heroes of the Shen-Kan-Ning border region). N.p., 1946.

Che Fu. "Kuan-yü hsin-ch'ü kung-tso chung ti chi-ko wen-t'i" (Some problems concerning work in the new areas), *Tang ti kung-tso* (Party work), 12 (Sept. 14, 1936).

Chen-li. (Truth). Sian, 1931.

Cheng-feng wen-hsien (Rectification documents). Kuang-chou, 1950.

Ch'i Sheng. *Chieh-fang ch'ü ti kung-ch'an ching-ying yu kuan-li* (Factory management in the liberated areas). N.p., 1946.

Ch'i Wu, ed. *I-ko ko-ming ken-chü-ti ti ch'eng-ch'ang: k'ang-jih chan-cheng ho chieh-fang chan-cheng shih-ch'i ti chin-chi-lu-yü* (The growth of a revolutionary base: the situation in the Shansi-Hopeh-Shantung-Honan border area in the anti-Japanese and liberation wars). Peking, 1958.

Chiao-yü chen-ti-she, ed. *Ken-chü-ti p'u-t'ung chiao-yyü ti kai-ko wen-t'i* (Problems in the reform of ordinary education in the base area). Kalgan, 1946.

Chieh-fang (Liberation). Yenan, 1937–1941.

Chieh-fang jih-pao (Liberation daily). Yenan, 1941–1945.

Chieh-fang she, comp. *K'ang-jih min-tsu t'ung-i chan-hsien chih-nan* (A guide to the anti-Japanese National United Front), vols. 2–10. N.p., 1938–1940.

"Ch'ing-chu chung-kuo kung-nung hung-chün shen-kan-ning yu-chi-tui ch'ung-p'o pai-chün ti ying-yung sheng-li" (Celebrate the courageous victory of the Chinese workers' and peasants' Red Army guerrilla forces of Shen-Kan-Ning in smashing the White Army), *Tou-cheng,* 11: 8 (April 30, 1932).

Ch'ün-chung (The masses). Hankow, Chungking, 1937–1945.

Chung-kuo chin-tai kuo-min ching-chi shih chiang-i (Lectures on China's modern national economic history), Hu-pei ta-hsüeh cheng-chih ching-chi hsüeh chiao yen-chiu shih, ed. Peking, 1958.

Chung-kuo ch'ing-nien (Chinese youth). Peking, 1924–1927.

Chung-kuo k'o-hsüeh yüan, li-shih yen-chiu so, ti san so, ed. *Shen-kan-ning pien-ch'ü ts'an-i hui wen-hsien hui-chi* (Collected documents of the assembly of the Shensi-Kansu-Ninghsia border region). Peking, 1958.

Chung-kuo kung-ch'an-tang, Chung-yang shu-chi-ch'ü, ed. *K'ang-chan i-lai chung-yao wen-chien hui-chi* (Collected important documents since the outbreak of the resistance war). Yenan(?), 1942.

Chung-kuo kung-ch'an-tang ti liu-chung ch'üan-hui wen-chien (Documents on the Sixth Plenum of the Central Committee of the Chinese Communist Party). Chungking, 1939.

*Ho Lung. *Cheng-chün wen-t'i* (Army rectification problems). Yenan(?), 1943.

Hsing-cheng-yüan nung-ts'un fu-hsing wei-yüan-hui (Rural Rehabilitation Commission of the Executive Yuan). *Shen-hsi sheng nung-ts'un tiao-ch'a* (Shensi province rural investigation). Shanghai, 1934.

Hsü Hai-tung. "Shen-pei hui-shih" (Junction in north Shensi), *HCPP*, III, 181–82.

Hsü Ti-hsin. *Shen-kan-ning pien-ch'ü yü ti-hou k'ang-jih ken-chü-ti ts'ai-cheng ching-chi* (The finances and economy of the Shen-Kan-Ning border region and the anti-Japanese rear-area bases). N.p., 1941.

Hu Hua, ed. *Chung-kuo ko-ming shih chiang-i* (Lectures on the history of the Chinese revolution). Peking, 1962.

Hua Ying-shen, ed. *Chung-kuo kung-ch'an-tang lieh-shih chuan* (Biographies of Chinese communist martyrs). Peking, 1951.

Hung-ch'i (Red flag). Shanghai(?) 1929–1930.

Hung-ch'i chou-pao (Red flag weekly). Shanghai, 1931–1933.

Hung-ch'i p'iao-p'iao (Red flag flutters). 17 vols. Peking, 1957, 1966.

I-chiu-ssu-san nien sheng-ch'an yün-tung chung ti ching-yen (Experience in the production drive of 1943), ed. Chung-kuo kung-ch'an-tang, hsi-pei chung-yang chü, tiao-ch'a yen-chiu shih. Yenan(?), 1944.

*Jen Pi-shih. "Kuan-yü chi-ko wen-t'i i-chien" (Opinions about a few problems), pp. 71–108 in *Cheng-tun san-feng ts'an-k'ao ts'ai-liao* (Rectification reference materials). N.p., 1943(?).

K'ang-chan pao (Resistance war newspaper). Sui-te (Shensi), 1944.

K'ang-jih chan-cheng shih-ch'i ti chung-kuo jen-min chieh-fang chün (The Chinese people's liberation army in the period of the resistance war). Peking, 1953.

K'ang-jih ken-chü-ti cheng-ts'e t'iao-li hui-chi: shen-kan-ning chih pu (Policies and statutes of the anti-Japanese bases: Shensi-Kansu-Ninghsia). 3 vols. Yenan(?), 1942.

*Kao Kang. *Cheng-tun tang cheng chün min ko tsu-chih chien kuan-hsi wen-t'i* (On the problem of rectifying relations among all party, army, government, and mass organizations). Yenan, 1943.

*———. *Kao Kang t'ung-chih tsai hsi-pei-chü kao-kan hui shang ti chieh-lun* (Comrade Kao Kang's summary at the Senior Cadres Conference of the Northwest Bureau). Yenan, 1943.

*———. *Pien-ch'ü tang ti li-shih wen-t'i chien-t'ao* (Examination of questions concerning the history of the party in the border region). Yenan, 1943.

Kuan Feng. "Hung erh-shih-liu chün ti erh-t'uan shih-pai ti ching-yen yü chiao-hsün" (The experience and lessons of the defeat of the second regiment of the 26th Red Army), *Tou-cheng* (Struggle), 61: 41 (Jan. 12, 1934). Bureau of Investigation, Ch'ing-t'an, Taiwan.

———. *I-chiu-ssu-wu nien pien-ch'ü ti chu-yao jen-wu ho tso-feng wen-t'i* (Problems concerning the main tasks and working spirit of the border region). Yenan(?), 1945.

———. *Shih-shih k'o-k'o wei lao-pai-hsing hsing-li ch'u-pi* (Always promote that which is profitable and abolish that which is evil for the people). N.p., n.d.

*Kuan-yü shen-kan-ning pien-ch'ü tang kao-kan hui ching-kuo chi ching-yen ti tsung-

chieh (Summary of the proceedings and experience of the Senior Cadres Conference of the Shen-Kan-Ning border region). Chung-kung chung-yang hsi-pei-chü (Northwest Bureau of the Central Committee). Yenan, 1943.

Kung-ch'an-tang jen (The communist). Yenan(?), 1939–1940. Bureau of Investigation, Ch'ing-t'an, Taiwan.

Li Ch'eng-jui. "K'ang-jih chan-cheng shih-ch'i chi-ko jen-min ko-ming ken-chü-ti ti nung-yeh shui-shou chih-tu yü nung-min fu-tan" (The system of agricultural taxation and the peasants' burden in several people's revolutionary base areas during the period of the anti-Japanese war), *Ching-chi yen-chiu* (Economic research), 2 (1956).

Li Li-kuo. "Wei-pei su-wei-ai ti ch'uan-shih-jen chih i—Wen Yeh-ch'ou" (Wei Yeh-ch'ou: A founder of the north Anhui soviet), *HCPP*, V, 20–27.

Liao Hsing-hsü. "Shen-hsi kung-ch'an-tang chih chiu-fen" (Confusion in the Shensi communist party), *Chen-li* (Truth), 1 (April 12, 1931).

Lin Po-ch'ü. *Shen-kan-ning pien-ch'ü hsüan-chü* (The Shensi-Kansu-Ninghsia border region election). Yenan(?), 1937. Bureau of Investigation, Ch'ing-t'an, Taiwan.

———. Chien-cheng wen-t'i (Problems in the rectification of government). Yenan, 1943.

———. Shen-kan-ning pien-ch'ü san-san-chih ti ching-yen chi ch'i ying-kai chiu-cheng ti p'ien-hsiang (Experience with the three-thirds system in the Shensi-Kansu-Ninghsia border region, and tendencies which should be corrected). Yenan(?), 1944.

———. "Yu su-wei-ai tao min-chu kung-ho-kuo chih-tu" (From soviet to democratic republic), *Chieh-fang*, 5:11–14 (May 24, 1937).

Lo Ch'iung. *Shen-kan-ning pien-ch'ü min-chien fang-chih yeh* (The popular weaving industry in the Shensi-Kansu-Ninghsia border region). N.p., 1946.

Lung-tung pien-ch'ü cheng-fu. "Cheng-liang cheng-ts'ao kung-tso tsung-chieh pao-kao" (Summary report of grain and fodder collection work), manuscript 1942(?).

*Mao Tse-tung. "Ching-chi wen-t'i yü ts'ai-cheng wen-t'i" (Economic and financial problems), *Mao Tse-tung hsüan-chi*, V, 1–204. Shansi-Chahar-Hopeh, 1944.

Mao Tse-tung hsüan-chi (The selected works of Mao Tse-tung), ed. Chin-ch'a-chi jih-pao she (Shansi-Chahar-Hopeh daily). 5 vols. 1944.

Pei-fang hung-ch'i (Northern red flag). Peiping, 1929–1933.

Pien-ch'ü ch'ün-chung pao (Border region mass newspaper). Yenan, 1944.

Pu-erh-sai-wei-k'o (Bolshevik). Shanghai(?), 1930–1932.

Shen-kan-ning pien-ch'ü cheng-fu wei-yüan hui. *Shen-kan-ning pien-ch'ü cheng-fu kung-tso pao-kao (1939–1941)* (1939–1941 work report of the Shen-Kan-Ning border region government). Yenan(?), 1941. Bureau of Investigation, Ch'ing-t'an, Taiwan.

Shen-kan-ning pien-ch'ü cheng fu, min-cheng t'ing, ed. *Shen-kan-ning pien-ch'ü hsiang-hsüan tsung-chieh* (A summary of the township elections of the Shensi-Kansu-Ninghsia border region). Yenan(?), 1941.

Shen-kan-ning pien-ch'ü cheng-fu, pan-kung t'ing, ed. *Shen-kan-ning pien-ch'ü cheng-ts'e t'iao-li hui-chi hsü-p'ien* (Policies and statutes of the Shensi-Kansu-Ninghsia border region: a supplement). Yenan(?), 1944.

———. Shen-kan-ning pien-ch'ü chiao-yü fang-chen (The educational policy of the Shensi-Kansu-Ninghsia border region). Yenan(?), 1944.

———. Shen-kan-ning pien-ch'ü ts'an-i hui ch'ang-chu hui ti shih-i tz'u cheng-fu wei-yüan hui ti wu tz'u lien-hsi hui-i ti chüeh-ting chi yu-kuan ching-chi wen-hua chien-she ti chung-yao t'i-an (The decisions and the important proposals of the joint session of the 11th meeting of the Standing Committee of the Assembly and the 5th meeting of the Government Committee of the Shensi-Kansu-Ninghsia border region concerning economics, culture, reconstruction, and other matters). Yenan(?), 1944.

———. Ssu-ko min-pan hsiao-hsüeh (Four people's elementary schools). Yenan(?), 1944.

―――. *Wei kung-yeh-p'in ti ch'üan-mien tzu-chi erh fen-tou* (Struggle for complete industrial self-sufficiency). Yenan(?), 1944.

Shen-kan-ning pien-ch'ü chien-cheng shih-shih kang-yao (A summary of the policy of simplified administration for the Shensi-Kansu-Ninghsia border region). Yenan(?), 1943.

Shen-kan-ning pien-ch'ü wen-chiao ta-hui. *Wen-chiao kung-tso ti hsin fang-hsiang* (New tendencies in culture and education work). Yenan(?), 1944(?).

"Shen-pei kung-tang fa-chan ti kai-k'uang" (The situation in the development of the communist party in north Shensi), manuscript. N.p., 1935. Internal evidence strongly suggests that the anonymous author of this report was Kuo Hung-t'ao. Hoover Institution, Stanford University.

Shih Ching-t'ang et al., eds. *Chung-kuo nung-yeh ho-tso-hua yün-tung shih-liao* (Materials on the agricultural cooperativization movement in China). 4 vols. Peking, 1957.

Shih-shih wen-t'i yen-chiu hui, ed. *K'ang-chan chung ti chung-kuo cheng-chih* (Chinese politics during the war of resistance). Yenan(?), 1940.

―――. *K'ang-chan chung ti chung-kuo chiao-yü yü wen-hua* (Chinese education and culture during the war of resistance). Yenan(?), 1940.

―――. *K'ang-chan chung ti chung-kuo ching-chi* (Chinese economics during the war of resistance). Yenan(?), 1940.

*Su-chung-ch'ü tang-wei (Central Kiangsu Party Committee). *Cheng-tun san-feng ts'an-k'ao ts'ai-liao* (Rectification reference materials). N.p., 1943(?).

Tang ti kung-tso (Party work). Shensi, 1936. Harvard Yenching Library.

Tou-cheng (Struggle). Shanghai, 1932–1934.

Tou-cheng (Struggle). Shensi, 1936.

Tou-cheng yü hsüeh-hsi (Struggle and study). Sian(?), 1932–1933.

Tso Chien-chih. "Shen-kan-ning pien-ch'ü min-chu cheng-chih ti t'e-tien chi ch'i tsai hsiang ti chü-t'i ti shih-shih" (The characteristics and concrete practice of democratic government at the village level in the Shen-Kan-Ning border region), *Chieh-fang,* 104: 6 (Apr. 20, 1940).

Tsu-chih ch'i-lai (Let's organize). N.p., 1944.

T'uan-chieh (Unity). Yenan(?), 1938–1941.

Wen-hua chiao-yü yen-chiu hui, ed. *Hsüeh-hsi sheng-huo* (Study life). Yenan(?), 1941.

Yang Ying-chieh. "Yen-ch'uan hsien yü-chü ch'ü san hsiang ti chieh-chi kuan-hsi chi jen-min sheng-huo" (Class relations and the people's livelihood in the Third Township of Yü-chü subdistrict in Yen-ch'uan district), *Kung-ch'an-tang jen* (The communist), 3: 51–75 (circa December 1939).

Yen Sheng. *"Wei-nan ti nung-min ho ch'ing-nien i-nien lai tou-cheng ti ch'eng-chi"* (Accomplishments of the past year's struggle of peasants and students in Wei-nan), *Chung-kuo ch'ing-nien* (Chinese youth) 52:45–46 (Jan. 29, 1927).

Yenan nung-ts'un tiao-ch'a t'uan (Yenan Village Investigation Group). *Mi-chih hsien yang-chia-k'ou tiao-ch'a* (Investigation of Yang-chia-k'ou in Mi-chih district). Peking, 1957.

Yü Ch'i, comp. *Shih-lun hsüan-chi* (Collection of current documents). Shanghai, 1937.

Yü Ming. "Shen-kan-ning pien-chü tse-yang shih le min-chu" (How was democracy achieved in the Shen-Kan-Ning border region?), *Ch'ün-chung* (The masses), 4.1:29 (Jan. 10, 1940).

II. Other Chinese and Japanese Sources

Ajiya keizai kenkyūjo (Institute of Asian Economics). *Chūgoku kyōsantō no nōgyō shūdanka seisaku* (Chinese communist agricultural collectivization policy). Tokyo, 1961.

BI (Bureau of Investigation).

The following items are the most important reports on communist activity in the northwest compiled by the Bureau of Investigation (formerly the Bureau of Investigation and Statistics) [Tiao-ch'a chü] of the Nationalist government. These were prepared for the internal use of this intelligence agency and are in handwritten or mimeographed form. They are collected in Ch'ing-t'an, Taiwan.

———. *Chien-tang tui lung-tung chih yin-mou chi wo fang tui-ts'e chih kai-shu* (The conspiracy of the bandit party in Lung-tung and our attitude). Kansu sheng tiao-ch'a shih. 1941.

———. *Chung-kung chih chien-cheng yü hsiang-hsüan* (Chinese communist simplification of government and township elections). 1942.

———. *Chung-kung chung-yang cheng-chih chu* (Politburo of the Chinese Communist Party); "Mu-ch'ien cheng-chih hsing-shih yü tang ti jen-wu" (The present political situation and the party's tasks), manuscript, Dec. 25, 1936.

———. *Chung-kung kai-k'uang tiao-ch'a piao* (Investigation of the Chinese communist situation). 1940.

———. *Chung-kung ti ching-chi cheng-ts'e* (Chinese communist economic policy). 1941.

———. *Chung-kung tsai kan-su chih tsu-chih yü huo-tung* (Chinese communist organization and activity in Kansu). 1941(?).

———. *Chung-kung tsui-chin tang-nei tou-cheng nei-mu* (Behind the scenes in the Communist party's most recent intra-party struggle). 1944.

———. *Erh-shih-ssu-nien ch'üan-kuo p'o-an tsung-chi-tsai* (General record of mopping-up throughout the country in 1935).

———. *Ko pien-ch'ü ch'ih-fei liu-ts'uan chih kai-k'uang* (Red bandit disturbances in all border areas). June 1937.

———. *Kung-fei tang-wu chüeh-ting* (Communist resolutions on party affairs).

———. *Liang-nien lai chih chung-kuo kung-ch'an-tang, 1931–1933* (Two years of the Chinese Communist Party, 1931–1933).

———. Liao Hsing-hsü. *Shensi kung-ch'an-tang chih chiu-fen* (Confusion in the Shensi communist party). Circa 1931.

———. *Pan-nien-lai shen-kan-ning chi ch'uan-k'ang pien-ching ch'ih-fei ts'uan-jao kao-k'uang* (Red bandit disturbances during the past half year on the Shen-Kan-Ning and Szechuan-Sikang borders). March 1937.

———. *San-shih nien-tu wei shen-kan-ning pien-ch'ü chung-kung huo-tung shih-k'uang* (The true situation of the Chinese communists on the Shen-Kan-Ning border during 1941). 1941.

———. *Shen-kan-ning pien-ch'ü ch'üan mao* (Complete portrait of the Shen-Kan-Ning border region). January 1940.

———. *Shen-kan-ning pien-ch'ü ch'ün-chung yün-tung t'e-chi* (Special collection on the mass movement in the Shen-Kan-Ning border region). 1939.

———. *Shen-kan-ning pien-ch'ü shih-k'uang* (The true situation in the Shen-Kan-Ning border region). Circa 1939–1940.

———. *Shen-kan-ning pien-ch'ü tiao-ch'a chuan-pao* (Special investigation report on the Shen-Kan-Ning border region). N.d.

———. *Tang-p'ai tiao-ch'a chou-pao* (Weekly report on parties). 1940–1945.

———. *Tang ti chien-she* (The party's reconstruction). Taipei, 1951.

———. *Tiao-ch'a chuan-pao* (Special investigation reports). Lengthy periodic reports on communist activities, 1938–1941.

———. Yang Tsung-chou, ed. *Tiao-ch'a ts'ung-shu: Shen-kan-ning pien-ch'ü hsien-ch'uang* (Collected investigations: the present situation in the Shen-Kan-Ning border region. July 1938.

Chao Ch'ao-kou. *Yen-an i-yüeh* (A month in Yenan). Nanking, 1946.

Ch'en Yen. *Shen-kan tiao-ch'a chi* (Record of an investigation of Shensi and Kansu). 2 vols. Peiping, 1936.

Ch'i Li. *Shen-kan-ning pien-ch'ü shih-chi* (A true account of the Shensi-Kansu-Ninghsia border region). N.p., 1939.

Ch'u Yün. *Shen-hsing chi-shih* (True record of a Shensi journey). N.p., 1938.

Fukushima Masao.*Chūgoku no jinmin minshu seiken* (China's People's Democratic Government). Tokyo, 1965.

Hatano Kanichi. *Chūgoku kyōsantō shi* (History of the Chinese Communist Party). 7 vols. Tokyo, 1962.

Itagaki Teiji. "Personal Reflections," in Office of Information, Department of General Affairs, Council of State (Manchukuo), *Senbu Geppo* (Pacification monthly report), 4.4 (April 1939).

Kuo-fang pu hsin-wen-chü, ed. *Kung-fei fan-tung wen-chien hui-p'ien* (Collected documents of the communist bandit reactionaries). 5 vols. Taipei, n.d.

Kuo-fang pu shih-cheng-chü (Historical Office of the Department of Defense), ed. *Chiao-fei chan-shih* (History of bandit suppression wars). 11 vols. Taipei, 1962.

Lu Mang. *Shen-kan-ning pien-ch'ü ti min-chung yün-tung* (The mass movement in the Shensi-Kansu-Ninghsia border region). Hankow, 1938.

Meng Po-ch'ien. *Hui hsiang jen-tao* (Return to humanity). Hong Kong, 1953.

Niijima Junryō. *Gendai chūgoku no kakumei ninshiki: Chūso ronsō e no sekkin* (Modern China's revolutionary perception: an approach to the Sino-Soviet dispute). Tokyo, 1964.

Pien-ch'ü jen-min (People of the border region). N.p., 1942–1943.

Shen-pei chien-wen (Visit to north Shensi). N.p., 1944.

Shensi sheng nung-ts'un tiao-ch'a (Shensi province rural investigation). Hsing-cheng yüan nung-ts'un fu-hsing wei-yüan hui (Rural Rehabilitation Commission of the Executive Yuan), ed. Shanghai, 1934.

Wang Chien-min. *Chung-kuo kung-ch'an-tang shih-kao* (Draft history of the Chinese Communist Party). 3 vols. Taipei, 1965.

Wang Chung-ming, ed. *Shen-pei chih hsing* (Journey to north Shensi). Chungking, 1945.

Yang Shih, ed. *Shen-pei ti ch'ün-chung tung-yüan* (Mass mobilization in north Shensi). N.p., 1938.

III. Western Language Sources

Alavi, Hamza. "Peasants and Revolution," in Ralph Miliband and John Saville, eds., *The Socialist Register*. London: Merlin Press, 1965.

Anderson, Benedict. *Imagined Communities: Reflections on the Origin and Spread of Nationalism*. London: Verso, 1983.

Arrigo, Gail. "Landownership Concentration in China: The Buck Survey Revisited," *Modern China* 12.3 (1986).

Band, Claire and William. *Two Years with the Chinese Communists*. New Haven: Yale University Press, 1948.

Barnett, A. Doak. *Cadres, Bureaucracy and Political Power in Communist China*. New York: Columbia University Press, 1967.

———. ed. *Chinese Communist Politics in Action*. Seattle: University of Washington Press, 1969.

Baron Richthofen's Letters, 1870–1872. Shanghai: n. pub., n.d.

Belden, Jack. *China Shakes the World*. New York: Harper, 1949.

Benton, Gregor. *Mountain Fires: The Red Army's Three Year War in South China, 1934–1938*. Berkeley: University of California Press, 1992.

Bernhardt, Kathryn. *Rents, Taxes, and Peasant Resistance: The Lower Yangzi Region, 1840–1950.* Stanford: Stanford University Press, 1992.

Bianco, Lucien. "Les paysans et la révolution: Chine, 1919–1949," *Politique étrangère,* 13.2–3: 117–41 (1968).

Boorman, Howard, ed. *Biographical Dictionary of Republican China.* New York: Columbia University Press, 1968.

Borst-Smith, Ernest F. *Mandarin and Missionary in Cathay: The Story of Twelve Years' Strenuous Missionary Work During Stirring Times Mainly Spent in Yenanfu, a Prefectural City of Shensi, North China, with a Review of Its History from the Earliest Date.* London: Seeley, Service, 1917.

Brandt, Conrad. *Stalin's Failure in China, 1924–1927.* Cambridge: Harvard University Press, 1958.

Brandt, Conrad, et al., eds. *A Documentary History of Chinese Communism.* Cambridge: Harvard University Press, 1959.

Brandt, Loren. *Commercialization and Agricultural Development in East-Central China, 1870–1937.* Cambridge: Cambridge University Press, 1989.

Buck, John Lossing. *Land Utilization in China: A Study of 16,786 Farms in 168 Localities, and 38,256 Farm Families in Twenty-Two Provinces in China, 1929–1933.* Shanghai: Commercial Press, 1937.

Butterfield, Fox. "A Missionary View of the Chinese Communists, 1936–1939," in Kwang-ching Liu, ed., *American Missionaries in China.* Cambridge: East Asian Research Center, Harvard University, 1966.

Carlson, Evans Fordyce. *Twin Stars of China.* New York: Dodd, Mead, 1941.

Chang, Gordon. *Friends and Enemies: The United States, China, and the Soviet Union, 1948–1972.* Stanford: Stanford University Press, 1990.

Chao Kuo-chun. *Agrarian Policy of the Chinese Communist Party.* New York: Asia Publishing House, 1960.

Ch'en, Jerome. *Mao and the Chinese Revolution.* London: Oxford University Press, 1965.

———. "Defining Chinese Warlords and Their Factions," *Bulletin of the School of Oriental and African Studies,* 31.3: 563–600 (1966).

Chen, Yung-fa. "The Blooming Poppy Under the Red Sun: The Yenan Way and the Opium Trade," in Tony Saich and Hans van de Ven, eds., *New Perspectives on the Chinese Communist Revolution.* Armonk, N.Y.: M.E. Sharpe, 1994.

———. *Making Revolution: The Communist Movement in Eastern and Central China, 1937–1945.* Berkeley: University of California Press, 1986.

Chesneaux, Jean. *The Chinese Labor Movement, 1919–1927.* Stanford: Stanford University Press, 1968.

Chiang Kai-shek. *Soviet Russia in China: A Summing-up at Seventy.* New York: Farrar, Straus and Cudahy, 1957.

China International Famine Relief Commission. *Annual Reports.* Peiping, 1928–1934.

The China Quarterly. London, 1960–1994.

The China Yearbook. London: George Routledge, 1912–1939.

Chomsky, Noam. *American Power and the New Mandarins.* New York: Pantheon, 1969.

Chow Tse-tsung. *The May Fourth Movement: Intellectual Revolution in Modern China.* 2 vols. Cambridge: Harvard University Press, 1960.

Clark, Robert Sterling, and Arthur de C. Sowerby. *Through Shen-Kan.* London: Fisher Unwin, 1912.

Clubb, O. Edmund. *Twentieth Century China.* New York: Columbia University Press, 1965.

Cohen, Arthur. *The Communism of Mao Tse-tung.* Chicago: University of Chicago Press, 1964.

Cohen, Paul. *Discovering History in China: American Historical Writing on the Recent Chinese Past.* New York: Columbia University Press, 1984.

Communist China 1955–1959. *Policy Documents with Analysis,* Cambridge: Harvard University Press, 1965.

Compton, Boyd. *Mao's China: Party Reform Documents, 1942–44.* Seattle: University of Washington Press, 1952.

———. *Mao's China: Party Reform Documents, 1942–1944.* Revised and expanded edition. Seattle: University of Washington Press, 1966.

Cressey, George B. *China's Geographic Foundations: A Survey of the Land and Its People.* New York: McGraw Hill, 1934.

———. *Land of the Five Hundred Millions.* New York: McGraw Hill, 1955.

Dai Qing. *Wang Shiwei and "Wild Lilies": Rectification and Purges in the Chinese Communist Party, 1942–1944.* David Apter and Timothy Cheek, eds. Armonk, N.Y.: M.E. Sharpe, 1993.

Dorris, Carl. "Peasant Mobilization in North China and the Origins of Yenan Communism," *The China Quarterly,* 68 (December 1976).

Duara, Prasenjit. *Culture, Power and the State: Rural North China, 1900–1942.* Stanford: Stanford University Press, 1988.

Eastman, Lloyd. "Nationalist China during the Sino-Japanese War, 1937–1945," in John Fairbank and Albert Feuerwerker, eds., *Republican China 1912–1949. The Cambridge History of China,* vol. 13, part 2. Cambridge: Cambridge University Press, 1986.

———. *Seeds of Destruction: Nationalist China in War and Revolution, 1937–1945.* Stanford: Stanford University Press, 1984.

Epstein, Israel. *The Unfinished Revolution in China.* Boston: Little, Brown, 1947.

Erikson, Erik H., ed. *The Challenge of Youth.* New York: Doubleday, 1965.

Esherick, Joseph, ed. *Lost Chance in China. The World War II Despatches of John S. Service.* New York: Random House, 1974.

Eto Shinkichi. "Hai-Lu-Feng—The First Chinese Soviet Government," *The China Quarterly,* 8–9 (October–December 1961, January–March 1962).

Fairbank, John, and Albert Feuerwerker, eds. *Republican China 1912–1949 in the Cambridge History of China,* vol. 13, part 2. Cambridge: Cambridge University Press, 1986.

Fanon, Frantz. *The Wretched of the Earth.* New York: Grove Press, 1965.

Fei Hsiao-tung. *Peasant Life in China: A Field Study of Country Life in the Yangtze Valley.* New York: Dutton, 1939.

Forman, Harrison. *Report from Red China.* New York: Whittlesey House, 1945.

Friedman, Edward. *Backward Toward Revolution: The Chinese Revolutionary Party.* Berkeley: University of California Press, 1974.

———. "The Center Cannot Hold: The Failure of Parliamentary Democracy in China from the Chinese Revolution of 1911 to the World War in 1914." Harvard University, Ph.D. dissertation, 1968.

———, ed. *The Politics of Democratization: Vicissitudes and Universals in the East Asian Experience.* Boulder: Westview, 1994.

Friedman Edward, and Mark Selden, eds. *America's Asia: Dissenting Essays on Asian-American Relations.* New York: Pantheon, 1971.

Friedman, Edward; Paul Pickowicz; and Mark Selden. *Chinese Village, Socialist State.* New Haven: Yale University Press, 1991.

Gelder, Stuart, ed. *The Chinese Communists.* London: Gollancz, 1946.

Geographical Handbook Series. *China Proper.* N.p. 1944, 1945.

Gillin, Donald. "'Peasant Nationalism' in the History of Chinese Communism," *Journal of Asian Studies,* 23.2 (February 1964).

————. *Warlord: Yen Hsi-shan in Shansi Province, 1911–1949.* Princeton: Princeton University Press, 1967.

Goldman, Merle. *Literary Dissent in Communist China.* Cambridge: Harvard University Press, 1967.

Gray, Jack, and Patrick Cavendish. *Chinese Communism in Crisis: Maoism and the Cultural Revolution.* New York: Praeger, 1968.

Griffith, Samuel B. *Mao Tse-tung on Guerrilla Warfare.* New York: Praeger, 1961.

Hanson, Haldore. *"Humane Endeavor": The Story of the China War.* New York: Farrar and Rinehart, 1939.

Hartford, Kathleen. "Step-by-Step: Reform, Resistance and Revolution in the Chin-Ch'a-Chi Border Region." Stanford University Ph.D. dissertation, 1980.

Hartford, Kathleen, and Steven M. Goldstein, eds. *Single Sparks: China's Rural Revolutions.* Armonk, N.Y.: M.E. Sharpe, 1989.

Hinton, William. *Fanshen: A Documentary of Revolution in a Chinese Village.* New York: Monthly Review, 1966.

Ho Kan-chih. *A History of the Modern Chinese Revolution.* Peking: Foreign Language Press, 1960.

Ho Ping-ti. *Studies on the Population of China, 1368–1953.* Cambridge: Harvard University Press, 1959.

Ho Ping-ti and Tang Tsou, eds. *China in Crisis: China's Heritage and the Communist Political System.* Chicago: University of Chicago Press, 1968.

Hobsbawm, E.J. *Primitive Rebels: Studies in Archaic Forms of Social Movement in the 19th and 20th Centuries.* New York: W.W. Norton, 1965.

Hofheinz, Roy Mark, Jr. *The Broken Wave: The Chinese Communist Peasant Movement, 1922–28.* Cambridge: Harvard University Press, 1977.

————. "The Peasant Movement and Rural Revolution: Chinese Communists in the Countryside (1923–1927)," Harvard University, Ph.D. dissertation, 1966.

Holm, David. *Art and Ideology in Revolutionary China.* Oxford: Clarendon Press, 1991.

Hsiao Kung-chuan. *Rural China: Imperial Control in the Nineteenth Century.* Seattle: University of Washington Press, 1960.

Hsiao Tso-liang. *Power Relations within the Chinese Communist Movement, 1927–1934.* Seattle: University of Washington Press, 1961.

Hsiung, James C., and Steven I. Levine, eds. *China's Bitter Victory: The War with Japan, 1937–1945.* Armonk, N.Y.: M.E. Sharpe, 1992.

Hsü Yung-ying. *A Survey of the Shensi-Kansu-Ninghsia Border Region.* 2 vols. New York: Institute of Pacific Relations, 1945.

Huang, Philip. "The Paradigmatic Crisis in Chinese Studies," *Modern China* 17.3 (July 1991).

————. *The Peasant Economy and Social Change in North China.* Stanford: Stanford University Press, 1985.

————. *The Peasant Family and Rural Development in the Yangzi Delta, 1350–1988.* Stanford: Stanford University Press, 1990.

Isaacs, Harold Robert. *The Tragedy of the Chinese Revolution.* Second rev. ed. Stanford: Stanford University Press, 1962.

Israel, John. *Student Nationalism in China, 1927–1937.* Stanford: Stanford University Press, 1966.

Johnson, Chalmers A. "Chinese Communist Leadership and Mass Response: The Yenan Period and the Socialist Education Campaign Period," in Ping-ti Ho and Tang Tsou, eds., *China in Crisis: China's Heritage and the Chinese Political System.* Chicago: University of Chicago Press, 1968.

————. *Peasant Nationalism and Communist Power: The Emergence of Revolutionary China, 1937–1945.* Stanford: Stanford University Press, 1962.

Kang Chao. *Man and Land in Chinese History: An Economic Analysis*. Stanford: Stanford University Press, 1986.

Keating, Pauline. "The Ecological Origins of the Yan'an Way," *The Australian Journal of Chinese Affairs* 32 (July 1994).

———. "The Yan'an Way of Cooperativization, 1937–1945." Paper presented at the annual meeting of the Association for Asian Studies, Los Angeles, March 25–28, 1993.

Keyte, J.C. *The Passing of the Dragon: The Story of the Shensi Revolution and Relief Expedition*. London: Hodder and Stoughton, 1913.

Kirby, William. "The Chinese War Economy," in James C. Hsiung and Steven I. Levine, eds., *China's Bitter Victory: The War with Japan 1937–1945*. Armonk, N.Y.: M.E. Sharpe, 1992.

Lee, Chong-sik. *Counterinsurgency in Manchuria: The Japanese Experience, 1931–1940*. Rand Corporation Memorandum RM–5012–ARPA, 1967.

Lewis, John Wilson. *Leadership in Communist China*. Ithaca: Cornell University Press, 1963.

———. "The Study of Chinese Political Culture," *World Politics*, 18.3: 503–24 (April 1966).

Leys, Simon. *Chinese Shadows*. New York: Viking, 1977.

Li Chien-nung. *The Political History of China, 1840–1928*, tr. Teng Ssu-yü and Jeremy Ingalls. Princeton: Van Nostrand, 1956.

Lifton, Robert J. *Thought Reform and the Psychology of Totalism: A Study of "Brainwashing" in China*. New York: W.W. Norton, 1961.

———. "Yu su-wei-ai tao min-chu kung-ho-kuo chih-tu" (From soviet to democratic republic), *Chieh-fang*, 5:11–14 (May 24, 1937).

Lindsay, Michael. "Changes in Chinese Communist Thought, 1937–1960," in Edward Szcepanik, ed., *Symposium on Economic and Social Problems of the Far East*. Hong Kong: University of Hong Kong Press, 1962.

———. *Notes on Educational Problems in Communist China, 1941–1947*. New York: Institute of Pacific Relations, 1950.

Lippit, Victor D.. *Land Reform and Economic Development in China*. White Plains: International Arts and Sciences Press, 1974.

Liu, F.F. *A Military History of Modern China, 1924–1949*. Princeton: Princeton University Press, 1956.

Liu, Kwang-ching, ed. *American Missionaries in China*. Cambridge: East Asian Research Center, Harvard University, 1966.

MacNair, Harley Farnsworth. *China in Revolution: An Analysis of Politics and Militarism under the Republic*. Chicago: University of Chicago Press, 1931.

Mann, Susan. *Local Merchants and the Chinese Bureaucracy, 1750–1950*. Stanford: Stanford University Press, 1987.

Mao Tse-tung. "On the Correct Handling of Contradictions among the People," in *Communist China 1955–1959: Policy Documents with Analysis*. Cambridge: Harvard University Press.

———. *Selected Works of Mao Tse-tung*. 4 vols. New York: International Publishers, 1954–1956.

Marsh, Robert M. *The Mandarins: The Circulation of Elites in China, 1600–1900*. Glencoe, 1961.

Materials of Former Servicemen of the Japanese Army Charged with Manufacturing Bacteriological Weapons. Moscow: Foreign Languages Publishing House, 1950.

McColl, Robert. "The Oyüwan Soviet Area, 1927–1932," *Journal of Asian Studies*, 27.1: 41–60 (November 1967).

————. "A Political Geography of Revolution: China, Vietnam, and Thailand," *Journal of Conflict Resolution,* 11.2: 153–67 (June 1967).

McLane, Charles B. *Soviet Policy and the Chinese Communists, 1931–1946.* New York: Columbia University Press, 1958.

Meisner, Maurice. *Li Ta-chao and the Origins of Chinese Marxism.* Cambridge: Harvard University Press, 1967.

Military Intelligence Division, War Department, U.S. Government. "The Chinese Communist Movement," 1945, published in *Institute of Pacific Relations Hearings Before the Subcommittee to Investigate the Administration of the Internal Security Act and Other Internal Security Laws of the Committee on the Judiciary, U.S. Senate 82nd Congress,* pp. 2305–2474.

Moore, Barrington. *The Social Origins of Dictatorship and Democracy: Lord and Peasant in the Making of the Modern World.* Boston: Beacon Press, 1966.

Mosher, Stephen. *China Misperceived: American Illusions and Chinese Reality.* New York: Basic Books, 1990.

Muramatsu, Yuji. "A Documentary Study of Chinese Landlordism in the Late Ch'ing and Early Republican Kiangnan," *Bulletin of the School of Oriental and African Studies,* vol. 29, pt. 3 (1966).

————. "Some Themes in Chinese Rebel Ideologies," in Arthur F. Wright, ed., *The Confucian Persuasion.* Stanford: Stanford University Press, 1960.

Myers, Ramon. "The Agrarian System," in John Fairbank and Albert Feuerwerker, eds., *Republican China 1912–1949* in *The Cambridge History of China,* vol. 13, part 2. Cambridge: Cambridge University Press, 1986.

————. The Chinese Peasant Economy: Agricultural Development in Hopeh and Shantung, 1890–1949. Cambridge: Harvard University Press, 1970.

————. "How Did the Modern Chinese Economy Develop? A Review Article," *Journal of Asian Studies* 50.3 (August 1991).

Myrdal, Jan. *Report from a Chinese Village.* New York: Pantheon, 1965.

Nichols, Francis H. *Through Hidden Shensi.* New York: Scribner, 1901.

North, Robert C. *Moscow and Chinese Communists.* Stanford: Stanford University Press, 1953.

Perry, Elizabeth. *Rebels and Revolutionaries in North China, 1845–1945.* Stanford: Stanford University Press, 1980.

Petras, James. "Toward a Theory of Twentieth-Century Socialist Revolutions," in *Critical Perspectives on Imperialism and Social Class in the Third World.* New York: Monthly Review Press, 1978.

Petras, James, and Maurice Zeitlin, eds., *Latin America, Reform or Revolution: A Reader.* New York: 1968.

Pomeranz, Kenneth. *The Making of a Hinterland: State, Society and Economy in Inland North China, 1853–1937.* Berkeley: University of California Press, 1993.

Popkin, Samuel. *The Rational Peasant: The Political Economy of Rural Society in Vietnam.* Berkeley: University of California Press, 1979.

Powell, Ralph. *The Rise of Chinese Military Power, 1895–1912.* Princeton: Princeton University Press, 1955.

Ravines, Eudocio. *The Yenan Way.* New York: Scribner, 1951.

Rawski, Thomas. *Economic Growth in Prewar China.* Berkeley: University of California Press, 1989.

Riskin, Carl. *China's Political Economy: The Quest for Development Since 1949.* Oxford: Oxford University Press, 1987.

Rue, John. *Mao Tse-tung in Opposition, 1927–1935.* Stanford: Stanford University Press, 1966.

Ruhlmann, Robert. "Traditional Heroes in Chinese Popular Fiction," in Arthur F. Wright, ed., *The Confucian Persuasion*. Stanford: Stanford University Press, 1960.

Schell, Jonathan. *The Military Half*. New York: Vintage, 1968.

Schram, Stuart R. *Mao Tse-tung*. Harmondsworth, England: Penguin, 1966.

———. "Mao Tse-tung and Secret Societies," *The China Quarterly*, 27 (July–September 1966).

———. *The Political Thought of Mao Tse-tung*. New York: Praeger, 1963.

Schran, Peter. *Guerrilla Economy: The Development of the Shensi-Kansu-Ninghsia Border Region, 1937–1945*. Albany: State University of New York Press, 1976.

Schurmann, Franz. *Ideology and Organization in Communist China*. Berkeley: University of California Press, 1966.

Schwartz, Benjamin. *Chinese Communism and the Rise of Mao*. Cambridge: Harvard University Press, 1951.

Scott, James. *The Moral Economy of the Peasant: Rebellion and Subsistence in Southeast Asia*. New Haven: Yale University Press, 1976.

Selden, Mark. "People's War and the Transformation of Peasant Society: China and Vietnam," in Edward Friedman and Mark Selden, eds., *America's Asia: Dissenting Essays in Asian-American Relations*. New York: Pantheon, 1971.

———. *The Political Economy of Chinese Development*. Armonk, N.Y.: M.E. Sharpe, 1993.

———. "Revolution and Third World Development: People's War and the Transformation of Peasant Society," in Roderick Aya and Norman Miller, eds., *National Liberation: Revolution in the Third World*. New York: Free Press, 1971.

Selznick, Philip. *The Organizational Weapon: A Study of Bolshevik Strategy and Tactics*. New York: McGraw-Hill, 1952.

Seybolt, Peter. "Terror and Conformity: Counterespionage Campaigns, Rectification and Mass Movements, 1942–43," *Modern China* 12.1 (January 1986).

Sheridan, James E. *Chinese Warlord: The Career of Feng Yu-hsiang*. Stanford: Stanford University Press, 1966.

Shih Nai-an. *Water Margin* (Shui-hu-chuan), tr. J.H. Jackson. 2 vols. Hong Kong: Commercial Press, 1963.

Skinner, G. William. "Marketing and Social Structure in Rural China," *Journal of Asian Studies*, 24.1–3 (1964–1965).

Skocpol, Theda. *States and Social Revolutions: A Comparative Analysis of France, Russia, and China*. Cambridge: Cambridge University Press, 1979.

Smedley, Agnes. *The Great Road: The Life and Times of Chu Teh*. New York: Monthly Review Press, 1956.

Snow, Edgar. *The Battle for Asia*. New York: Random House, 1941.

———. *Random Notes on Red China (1936–1945)*. Cambridge: Harvard University, East Asian Research Center, 1957.

———. *Red Star Over China*. New York: Grove Press, 1961.

———. *Red Star Over China*. Revised and Enlarged Edition. New York: Random House, 1968.

———. *Scorched Earth*. London: Victor Gollancz, 1941.

Solomon, Richard. "Conflict, Authority and Mao's Effort to Reintegrate the Chinese Polity," in A. Doak Barnett, ed., *Chinese Communist Politics in Action*. Seattle: University of Washington Press, 1969.

Stauffer, Milton T., ed. *The Christian Occupation of China: A General Survey of the Numerical Strength and Geographical Distribution of the Christian Forces in China*. Shanghai: n. pub., 1922.

Stein, Gunther. *The Challenge of Red China*. New York: Whittlesey House, 1945.

Swarup, Shanti. *A Study of the Chinese Communist Movement 1927–1934*. Oxford: Clarendon, 1966.

Tawney, R.H. *Land and Labour in China*. Boston: Beacon Press, 1966.

Taylor, George E. *The Struggle for North China*. New York: Institute of Pacific Relations, 1940.

Teichman, Eric. *Travels of a Consular Officer in North-west China*. Cambridge: Cambridge University Press, 1921.

Tetsuya Kataoka. *Resistance and Revolution in China: The Communists and the Second United Front*. Berkeley: University of California, 1974.

Thaxton, Ralph. *China Turned Rightside Up: Revolutionary Legitimacy in the Peasant World*. New Haven: Yale University Press, 1983.

Thomson, James C., Jr. "Communist Policy and the United Front in China, 1935–1936," *Papers on China*, vol. 11, Harvard University, East Asian Research Center, 1957.

Todd, O.J. *Two Decades in China, Comprising Technical Papers, Magazine Articles, Newspaper Stories and Official Reports Connected with Work under His Own Observation*. Peking: The Association of Chinese and American Engineers, 1938.

Townsend, James R. *Political Participation in Communist China*. Berkeley: University of California, 1967.

Van Slyke, Lyman P., ed. *The Chinese Communist Movement: A Report of the United States War Department, July 1945*. Stanford: Stanford University Press, 1968.

———. "The Chinese Communist Movement during the Sino-Japanese War 1937–1945," in John Fairbank and Albert Feuerwerker, eds., *Republican China 1912–1949* in *The Cambridge History of China*, vol. 13, part 2. Cambridge: Cambridge University Press, 1986.

———. *Enemies and Friends: The United Front in Chinese Communist History*. Stanford: Stanford University Press, 1967.

Wales, Nym. *Inside Red China*. New York: Doubleday, Doran, 1939.

———. *My Yenan Notebooks*. Madison, Conn., mimeographed, 1961.

———. *Red Dust*. Stanford: Stanford University Press, 1952.

Watson, Andrew, ed. *Mao Zedong and the Political Economy of the Border Region. A Translation of Mao's Economic and Financial Problems*. Cambridge: Cambridge University Press, 1980.

White, Theodore H., and Annalee Jacoby. *Thunder Out of China*. New York: William Sloan, 1946.

Wilbur, C. Martin, and Julie Lien-ying How, eds. *Documents on Communism, Nationalism and Soviet Advisors in China, 1918–1927*. New York: Columbia University Press, 1956.

Wilmot, H. P. *The Great Crusade*. London: 1989.

Wolf, Eric. "Peasant Rebellion and Revolution," in Norman Miller and Roderick Aya, eds., *National Liberation: Revolution in the Third World*. New York: The Free Press, 1971.

———. *Peasant Wars of the Twentieth Century*. New York: Harper & Row, 1969.

Yakhontoff, Victor A. *The Chinese Soviets*. New York: Coward-McCann, 1934.

Wright, Arthur F., ed. *The Confucian Persuasion*. Stanford: Stanford University Press, 1960.

Index

Page numbers containing "n" denote endnote pages followed by the endnote number.

Mark Selden teaches sociology and history at the State University of New York at Binghamton. He is the author of numerous books on China including *The Political Economy of Chinese Development*, also published by M. E. Sharpe. His co-authored *Chinese Village, Socialist State* was the 1994 recipient of the Joseph Levinson Prize of the Association for Asian Studies. He is the editor of the M. E. Sharpe series "Socialism and Social Movements."

SOCIALISM AND SOCIAL MOVEMENTS

★ ★

Series Editor: Mark Selden